*T*he *A*merican *B*ilingual *T*radition

The American Bilingual Tradition

Heinz Kloss

EWBURY HOUSE PUBLISHERS, INC. / ROWLEY / MASSACHUSETTS

Library of Congress Cataloging in Publication Data

Kloss, Heinz.
    The American bilingual tradition.

    (Studies in bilingual education)
    Bibliography: p.
    Includes index.
    1. Education, Bilingual–United States. I. Title.
LC3731.K58   371.9'7   76-45393
ISBN 0-912066-06-7

Cover design by Kathe Harvey

NEWBURY HOUSE PUBLISHERS, INC.

Language Science
Language Teaching
Language Learning

68 Middle Road, Rowley, Massachusetts 01969

Printed in the U.S.A.   First printing: April 1977
                         5 4 3 2 1

CONTENTS

FOREWORD

The popular image of the United States as a nation united by one language and one culture has always been illusory. It was an ideal engendered by the now outmoded values of nineteenth century nationalism. Although the American melting pot has indeed fused millions of second- and third-generation immigrant families into unilingual English-speaking Americans, unmelted or partially melted millions have also survived whose isolation or regional dominace has permitted them to maintain their ethnic identity in their new and spacious land.

It is only fitting that it should be so. For the concepts of diversity and political pluralism are the very ones which permitted the creation of the United States some two hundred years ago. The idea of a central nation-state was foreign to the authors of the Declaration of Independence. The resolution of July 7, 1776 (adopted on July 2), introduced in the Continental Congress by Richard Henry Lee and later used as a basis for the Declaration of July 4, refers to a group of colonies ("these United Colonies") and not to a single nation; and the Declaration of Independence was made in the name of "thirteen united States"—in lowercase and in the plural.

"The colonies," as John Adams remarked, "had grown up under constitutions of government so different, there was so great a variety of religions, they were composed of so many different nations, their customs, manners and habits had so little resemblance, and their intercourse had been so rare, and their knowledge of each other so imperfect, that to unite them was certainly a very difficult enterprise." But the idea of local independence permitted the growth of an ever-widening federation. It is as though the Declaration of Independence were reenacted dozens of times as each new component achieved statehood, a process continuing into our own day with the recent admissions of the states of Alaska and Hawaii.

During the nineteenth and twentieth centuries, however, European nationalism exerted its influence on America, abetted by the cruel lessons of the Civil War and the galvanizing conformism brought about through united national efforts needed in the fighting of foreign wars. It was, ironically, at the very moment when "these united States" was trying to become "The United States" that the victims of European nationalism fled to America in search of some measure of independence, refusing to be integrated against their will into some nation-state they could not love and through a language they did not know. For the idea of a national language had developed in Europe as the touchstone of nationality and national culture. The Romantics had found in each language a soul which was the embodiment of the national spirit. Those maintaining a language other than the national tongue just did not belong. Millions fled from the uniformity of European nationalism to the diversity of American pluralism. For in diversity there was hope.

There was also hope in the possibility of betterment. The American political system based on the idea of change created a country that was consciously and continually evolving; and two hundred years after its founding, America was still in the making. After flirting with nationalism and unilingualism, America in the nineteen sixties began to regain consciousness of its bilingual tradition and its multicultural makeup. Compare, for example, the U.S. entries in volumes 1 and 2 of the *International Bibliography on Bilingualism* (Quebec: Laval University Press).

The new acceleration of awareness came about largely as a result of witnessing economic injustice made evident through the enormous increase in mobility and urbanization since the turn of the century. Beneath the gray monolith of a single united nation, one could discern the colorful mosaic of a multicultural society.

In the United States there had indeed existed, alongside a seemingly all-dominant monolingualism, a tradition of bilingualism—chiefly below the national level, a tradition long neglected by American historians. In this nation of immigrants, which has conducted one of history's most successful experiments in political pluralism, it would have been surprising if there had been no room for the flowering of different cultures in different regions.

It remained for Heinz Kloss in two major German-language publications (*Das Volksgruppenrecht in den Vereinigten Staaten, Vol. 1: 1940; Vol. 2: 1942* and *Das Nationalitätenrecht der Vereinigten Staaten, 1963*) to isolate, describe, and analyze this important characteristic of American society. In 1968, the International Center for Research on Bilingualism decided to publish an updated English version of Dr. Kloss' *Nationalitätenrecht*. This new version is the basis of the present volume which, after many delays, we now take pleasure in presenting to the public on the occasion of the United States Bicentennial.

The American bilingual tradition which Dr. Kloss so well describes has depended so much on bilingual schooling and legislation that it seemed appropriate to include this study as part of a series on bilingual education the purpose of which is to inform the public on how people have used more than one language in educating their children. For a good deal of what Dr. Kloss has to tell us bears directly on the problems of non-English or bilingual schools which have operated under the American flag. Those parts of the book dealing with self-government and public administration also have something to do with bilingual and bicultural education. Take, for example, the action of the U.S. Congress in 1852. By giving territorial status to New Mexico it launched the New Mexicans on the road to self-government and to the exercise of rights which they had never enjoyed before in their history, rights which implied the handling of two languages at all levels of government—local, county, and territorial. This constituted an important educative process.

Even though here—and in other instances—all Americans can by no means claim to have put all these ideals into practice with the unselfishness that the wording of their resolutions implied, the very creation of a new status gave the minorities some of the means necessary to survival.

This is both a very human tale of generous and less-than-generous acts and attitudes and also a story of memorable educational achievements. It is this story, as told by one of the world's leading authorities on ethnic law, that we here present as a fitting tribute for the Bicentennial.

International Center for Research on Bilingualism   William Francis Mackey
Quebec, Thanksgiving Day 1975

PREFACE

The contents of this book will seem to be strange and much will seem new even to the American reader. What is strange is not that someone succeeded in unearthing the facts presented here but that this took place so late despite the fact that nearly all the material included in this book has long been easily accessible in such printed sources as statute books and handbooks of judicial decisions, all of them as a rule well indexed and available in central state libraries or legislative reference rooms.

The explanation is not difficult to find. We all like to pride ourselves on the age in which we live, an age where man has matured sufficiently to investigate and analyze all historical events with complete objectivity. In practice, however, our minds work with remarkable selectivity, singling out subconsciously, as a rule, those facts which fit in with and reinforce some notions dear to us. One notion dear to Americans has been that the American society has wrought miracles in assimilating the numberless hordes of non-English immigrants, performing a feat that was an indispensable part of the American Dream. Making the offspring of these immigrants shed languages inherited from their forefathers meant a change for the better and accrued benefits to both the American nation and the seemingly transformed ethnic groups.

Occasionally one might stumble across such facts as the former status of Louisiana, which was a fully binational state under its 1845 constitution, somewhat like present-day New Brunswick, or that Pennsylvania at one time had a German State Printer, or that in New Mexico Spanish remained official well into the twentieth century. But these and many other facts were felt to be nothing to be proud of. Language shift was better than language loyalty.

It was thus no accident that a European, steeped in the traditions of his continent, was the first to consider the American bilingual tradition as a distinctive asset. What was important in this connection was not whether I was Danish, Finnish, German, or Rumanian, but that I was a European with the prevailing attitude that language maintenance is the normal thing and language shift an exception rather than the rule. This attitude also prevails in Asia. In Africa and the two Americas, however, the reverse was true; but for vastly divergent reasons it was, and in many regions still is, felt to be a necessary concomitant of development that most of the smaller speech communities would have to yield to the great national tongues.

North American life was thoroughly permeated by this sentiment when (in 1940 and 1942) I first published my findings concerning past American language policy. After the War, some copies found their way to American libraries, and in 1948, Professor W. J. Cahnman published in the *American Journal of Sociology* a long and positive review calling for "a commission consisting of a historian, a sociologist, and an expert in public administration . . . to devise an American version of Kloss' book." There was, however, no follow-up.

In my earlier publication I intended the work to be of use to readers unfamiliar with the German tongue. The two volumes contained no fewer than 473 excerpts from English sources, and a separate "Table of English Excerpts" was added in volume II (pp. 975-995). Volume II furthermore contained a number of maps, some of which had an original value of their own, especially the maps of the French, German, and Spanish elements in the states of Louisiana, Pennsylvania, and New Mexico, respectively, maps which were prepared on the basis of official statistics indicating denominational affiliation.

When in 1963 I published another study—the one on which the present volume is based—I had to state in a postscript that "actually the state of research is at the moment what this new book shows: exactly the same as if its forerunner had never appeared" (1963, pp. 33-334).

The new version was both less and more ambitious than its predecessor. But it had to be much shorter; consequently it contained few literal quotations in German and none in English. Nor were any maps included. On the other hand, it went much further in covering areas and polities under the American flag outside the North American mainland. While the earlier publication had chapters on Hawaii and Puerto Rico, the new book included also Guam, Samoa, the Virgin Islands, the Canal Zone, the Ryukyus, the Bonin Islands, and even the pre-1945 Philippines.

Germany at that time was not a country where scholars would eagerly take to the data displayed in this book, what with the traumatic withdrawal from ethnicity so characteristic of the first postwar decades, in a country where ethnic problems were held to be either unimportant or too touchy. Outside Germany, and especially in North America, knowledge of the German language was decreasing. But perhaps the most significant single factor was the timing. In 1963 there were—even in the United States—no "kairos," no auspicious moments to talk about American ethnic problems other than those of racial discrimination and language shift; the whole concept of language loyalty and language maintenance was still unknown. The new version therefore made little impact, and historians might have bypassed it, as they did its predecessor, had it not been for the watchful eye of William F. Mackey, who suggested the present English version.

It gives me great pleasure to say a word of thanks to those who helped make this new book possible. First of all, Professor William F. Mackey was the first to envisage this project. He succeeded in finding a publisher and, through him, a translator. He also spent considerable time and effort on editing the manuscript.

My thanks go also to Professors Henri Dorion and J.-G. Savard who as directors of the International Centre for Research on Bilingualism consented to have this book become an ICRB publication, to the publisher, Newbury House (Rupert Ingram and his staff), and to those secretaries who carefully helped prepare the final manuscript, especially to Mrs. Marta Grimard (née Hamm) in Quebec City and to Mrs. Erika Reufsteck in Mannheim (Germany).

Quebec, 1975   Heinz Kloss

*T*he *A*merican *B*ilingual *T*radition

INTRODUCTION

Since by far the larger part of the present book had to be translated from a foreign language (German), its terminology was unavoidably influenced by the language of the original. The task of translating the book was complicated by the fact that the original German text contained some concepts that were first introduced by the author and therefore are not in previous German writings, let alone in dictionaries.

While this is not the place to comment on all technical terms used in the present English version, the recurrent use of some key concepts and "master terms" throughout the book makes it necessary to explain them briefly and define them in advance.

The term *nationality* is, in the context of this volume, almost never used to indicate juridical nationality, i.e., citizenship. It refers rather to "ethnic nationality," a concept quite common in European sociological and political writings, where it denotes an ethnic group held together either by a mother tongue shared by all members of the group or by a language-centered feeling of ethnic identity shared even by many persons who no longer speak the ethnic tongue.

American writers, when speaking of *minorities,* frequently think in terms of racial rather than of language groups, having in mind American Negroes, rather than, for example, Scandinavian immigrants. Even where a referential group—e.g., the Chicanos—is separated from the majority by both language and race, the

American author is more concerned—inwardly at least—with the color of their skin than with the way they speak.

With European authors it is usually different. When political scientists mention that a certain nation is beset with a minority problem, they usually mean language minorities, unless otherwise specified. Throughout the present book the term *minority* is admittedly used in this way.

Language rights for ethnic groups may be either *promotion-oriented* (or *"promotive"*) or *toleration-oriented* (or *"acquiescent"*). Promotive rights imply that public authorities—at the federal, state, or municipal level—are trying to promote a minority tongue by having it used in public institutions—legislative, administrative and educational, including the public schools.

Conversely, toleration-oriented nationality law implies that federal, state, and municipal governments do not interfere with efforts on the parts of the minority to make use of the ethnic tongue in the private domain—e.g., newspapers, religious life, secular associations, and most important, private schools. More will be said in Chapter Three about this distinction, which, incidentally, has been accepted by a number of European specialists.

In most countries, a description of the rights of language minorities, their history, and their present station must revolve around the language policy pursued by the central government. This does not hold true for the United States. Here the evolution of language rights was and still is conditioned by three salient features.

First of all, the United States is neither an authoritarian nor a totalitarian state. Numerous areas of cultural life which in nondemocratic countries are under tight governmental control are left to the initiative of the citizens: the press, the publishing houses, the production of films, the founding of societies and federations. The United States, in this respect, surpasses even most European democracies where, for example, all radio broadcasts are the concern of the government while in the United States it is possible to found, and run, private stations without interference.

Second, the United States is not an unitary state but a federation consisting of 50 component states. Language rights have therefore been largely the concern of the various states—or "territories" as these polities were designated in prestatehood days—rather than of the central government, most emphatically in the field of education.

Third, Americans throughout their history have been more willing to grant language rights to old-established groups than to more recent immigrants (a rule which for a number of reasons was never applied to the Amerindians). The "old settlers," i.e., the descendants of immigrants who had come to North America before or simultaneously with the advent of the Anglo-Americans, had a fair chance to see their languages not only tolerated but actually promoted.

The sequence of chapters in the present book is largely determined by these three basic features. It was normal that the first chapter be devoted to an outline of the constitutional and ethnolingual background and an overview of the main categories of language rights. Logically the next step had to be a description, in Chapter Two, of the extent to which the central government, since the days of the Constitutional Congress, has or has not made use of and promoted languages other than English. The record is interesting but not altogether momentous, the 1967-68 Bilingual Education Act notwithstanding. Probably the most remarkable and at the same time the least known parts of this record are the cases where territorial legislatures over which the federal government had full control initiated and ran a bilingual self-government without interference on the part of Congress or the federally appointed territorial governors.

The language policy of the central government—President, Congress, and U. S. Supreme Court—however, constitutes but a small segment of the picture of language rights in the United States. Far more convincing and at times dramatic is the tale told, in Chapter Three, of American achievements in the realm of toleration-oriented minority rights—truly a challenge to other democracies. And even the record, in Chapter Four, of promotive minority rights granted to postindependence immigrant groups, while certainly not as bright as the pre-1901 record of acquiescent rights, is indeed impressive.

All this, however, is less remarkable than the events recounted in the core of this book—in Chapters Five and Six. They describe the promotive language rights meted out in what statisticians call the "conterminous U. S.," i.e., the mainland area without Alaska, to large "old settler" groups, and to smaller "old settler" groups. This story is followed by sections dealing with outlying areas, with possessions which have achieved statehood (including the Philippine independence), with possessions which did not reach that status, and with some (Bonin and Ryukyu Islands) which are no longer under American control.

One cannot help considering that the story related in these chapters constitutes a splendid record, in spite of unavoidable weaknesses and setbacks. One cannot write about this without a feeling of admiration for American farsightedness and practical wisdom.

Bilingualism had become the cinderella about which little is spoken. It was discussed—and embraced—as a possible way of enriching the cultural life of a nation.

Whether the movement will last we cannot yet know. But we do know that it is in keeping with similar changes in other parts of the Western Hemisphere where we observe innovations in the field of language policy.

To the north we see the French language in Canada acquiring, in 1969, full equality at the federal level and in the province of New Brunswick and striving for a near-monopoly in the province of Quebec (1974).

To this has to be added Canada's program, from 1971 on, to promote multiculturalism by aiding ethnic groups of non-English and non-French mother tongue, a program which between 1971 and 1974 led the three Prairies Provinces to enact laws admitting all minority tongues to the public schools. From this, both pre-Columbian and immigrant languages have derived considerable benefit.

In Greenland, long the country with the Western Hemisphere's most advanced language policy, no basic changes were needed to keep up with this spirit of the times.

To the south we notice an increasing regard for Indian and creole languages. Mexico took the lead some decades ago by adopting the "bridge approach" in schools and Brazil in 1970 and Peru in 1972 proclaimed bilinguality for schools serving the Indian population. In a number of countries nondominant languages have even become official or semiofficial. In the Netherlands Antilles, Papiomentu since 1956 has been the second official language of the islands of Curaçao, Aruba, and Bonaires; Haiti's constitution, as of 1964, recognized Franco-Creole ("créole") as a working language in fact though not in name; Paraguay's 1967 constitution recognized Guarani as a national language (both in fact *and* in name), while Peru in 1975 made Quechua the nation's second official language—in name to begin with; much has still to be done to implement this law.

Until recently it was possible to venture an admittedly crude generalization regarding the global issue of language maintenance vs. language shift. Africa and the Americas, so the statement went, were leaning toward language shift in order to reduce the number of tribal tongues and, in the New World, also of immigrant tongues. In Europe and Asia, on the other hand, the psychological climate was held to be more favorable to language retention. This juxtaposition is beginning to get blurred, chiefly because so many American nations are moving in the direction of greater freedom for the maintenance and—as a concomitant—for the unfolding of nondominant languages.

Therefore, many events in the history of American language policy will have to be seen and interpreted in a new light. Certain seemingly romantic and superfluous acts of generosity committed at various periods of American history in various parts of the country actually anticipated some modern trends in the field of language policy, being in keeping with the best aspects of other emancipatory American traditions of the American Dream.

CHAPTER ONE

The Nation, National Minorities,
and Minority Rights

1-1 THE CONSTITUTIONAL DEVELOPMENT OF THE COUNTRY

Spheres of Jurisdiction

The United States of America is a federal state whose territory is divided into three basically different parts: (1) the national territory proper, whose individual parts are fully incorporated so that the Constitution is effective within these areas without limitations; (2) the unincorporated territories, which are clearly and exclusively under the sovereignty of the United States; and (3) territories under American jurisdiction which are not under American sovereignty (see Section 7-1).

The territory proper of the United States consists of fifty component states (of which one, Hawaii, lies outside continental America), and the Federal District of Columbia, which comprises the federal capital of Washington.

The unincorporated polities include the free associated Commonwealth of Puerto Rico, the organized Territories of the Virgin Islands and Guam, and the possession of American Samoa. American sovereignty over the Philippines, another unincorporated polity, lasted from 1898 to 1946.

Under the control and jurisdiction, but not the sovereignty, of the United States are the Canal Zone, leased from Panama in 1903 for an indefinite period of time, and the Trust Territory of the Pacific Islands, administered under a trusteeship of the United Nations since 1947. After World War II, two more island groups were for a while under American control: the Ryukyu Islands (1945-1972) and the Bonin Islands (1945-1968).

The American sphere of jurisdiction is divided according to continents into (1) North America—the entire incorporated territory with the exception of Hawaii; (2) Central America and the West Indies—Puerto Rico, the Virgin Islands, and the Canal Zone; (3) Oceania—Hawaii, Guam, American Samoa, and the Trust Territory of the Pacific Islands; (4) (until recently) Asia—the Ryukyu Islands.

The Federal Government

The United States first adopted a constitution for a confederation (1777) and later (1789) a constitution for a federal state. The characteristics of the governmental system based upon this constitution are familiar.

The executive power (Article 2) rests with the President, who is elected by the people. The President unites the functions of head of state with those of a prime minister. He is independent of the confidence of the people's elected representatives and names the secretaries forming the Cabinet (which is not provided for in the Constitution). Beside the President stands the Congress, an elected representative body consisting of the Senate and the House of Representatives, which exercises the legislative power (Article 1). The President, with the approval of the Senate, appoints the Supreme Court members (Article 3). According to American concepts, the executive, legislative, and judicial organs collectively form the government. What in Europe is usually known as "the government" is generally called "the administration" by Americans. The Supreme Court established its right to declare invalid federal laws found to be in violation of the Constitution in 1803 in *Marbury* v. *Madison*. It later applied this principle to laws of individual states. The first time this was done was in 1810 against Georgia in *Fletcher* v. *Peck* (Commager, 1958, 1, 191ff., 205 ff.).

State and Local Authorities

All matters which are not included in the federal powers according to Article 1, Section 8, of the Constitution are reserved to the states, whose administrative autonomy is limited by Article 1, Sections 9 and 10. The everyday life of the United States citizen today still takes place primarily in the sphere of competence of state authorities or local governments, both of which are responsible to him. Certain basic features are common to the constitutions of all states. The executive power rests with a governor elected by the people. With him there is also an elected representative body which consists of a senate and a house of representatives. Of all the states, only Nebraska, in 1934, adopted a unicameral system. The administration of justice is handled at the lowest level by justices of the peace, at the second level by regular courts known by different names in various states, and at the highest level by a court of appeal called in most states the supreme court.

Local government is based on the county (in Louisiana called the *parish*) as the largest territorial unit and on townships (in New England, *town*) as the smallest territorial unit, with recognition of the special status of the city. A variety of differences in detail exists; for example, in Virginia the city is not incorporated into the county but exists side by side with it; in New England the township and not the county forms the nucleus of local government; the city of New York is divided into several counties; and the county does not exist in Alaska. As a rule, local officials are not appointed by the state but are elected by the people of the particular district, which results in great diversity in the formation and handling of local administration.

From the standpoint of minority rights, it is especially important that education is a concern of individual states and not of the federal government. At the community level, education is only seldom placed under authorities established for general administrative functions; education is either subject to the authority of an independent school district or, in the framework of a town or county administration, is under a board of laymen elected by the citizens specifically for purposes of school government.

In its work, this board of education is not subject to interference from other organs of the town or political community. Independent school districts are controlled also by such an elected school board (Kloss 1950, 676-683). The authority of such school boards is extensive. They employ teachers. (Today, of course, the school boards usually follow the professional advice of the school superintendent, who is appointed by the board.) The school board can expand or restrict the curriculum; most importantly, a decision by the State Supreme Court of Illinois in 1874 (*Stuart* v. *School District of Kalamazoo*, 30 Michigan 69) confirmed the right of school boards to introduce the teaching of non-English languages in public schools (see also Section 4-4).

The Institution of the Territory

The basic features of American state and local government are widely known. However, more information should be provided about an administrative institution—the territory—which has played an important role in American history but which exists today principally in remote areas (the Virgin Islands, Guam) and is unknown outside the United States. The word territory has two meanings in American English: (1) the general meaning "region" and (2) the meaning "territory" in an administrative sense. American administrative practices create confusion at times by neglecting to distinguish between these two meanings. For example, the term trust territory is misleading for the Pacific regions that have been given in trust to the United States (Farrand 1900, 676-681).

The term territory denotes a region directly under the jurisdiction of the federal government. (Government is used in the American sense of executive plus legislative plus judicial branches.) In placing the territory under the jurisdiction of the federal government, Congress passes an Organic Act that determines the main features of civil administration and administration of justice.

Farrand (1900, 681) offers the following definition: Territory is an American possession which has an elected representative body and is scheduled to become a future state. Puerto Rico, however, has a long way to go before becoming a state, and the Virgin Islands and Guam are even today not thought of in terms of their elevation into states. Also the territories listed in the first and second categories (Table 1-1) had no elected representative body.

The Organic Act of Congress referred to above prevents possible arbitrary rule by executive authorities appointed by the federal government. At the same time the territory possesses its own organ for legislation, which is not necessarily elected or limited to this one task (Farrand 1896; Willoughby 1905). Subordination under Congress meant that military authorities were in all cases at once superseded by civil authorities.

The Union was first founded by only thirteen of the fifty states. Before attaining statehood, the remaining thirty-seven states were originally territories or parts of territories except for Maine, West Virginia, California, and Texas. Furthermore, the District of Columbia had a constitution between 1871 and 1874 that was similar to those of the territories.

All territories have a governor who is appointed by the President with the consent of the Senate and serves as supreme executive authority. Likewise all territories have several similarly appointed federal judges who serve as highest administrators of justice. Unless specified differently by the federal government, the authority of the territorial legislatures extends as far as the authority of the legislatures of the regular states. Their legislative acts must be reported at fixed intervals to the President, however, and can at any time be invalidated or changed by the federal government, a prerogative repeatedly exercised against the Mormons in Utah (Farrand 1896, 49).

In 1884, the Supreme Court (*Murphy* v. *Ramsey*, 114 U. S. 15) stated that Congress possesses nearly unrestricted authority over territories, although Congress was limited by the Constitution in dealing with the fully incorporated territory of that time (Story 1873, 200; Pomeroy 1888, 403; and Farrand 1896, 52-53).

A second, more indirect means of federal control was the veto power of the governor appointed by the federal government. From the beginning in some territories this veto could be overcome by a two-thirds majority of the elected representatives. This procedure was incorporated in other territories by later provisions. For instance, the governor had unlimited power in New Mexico, 1850-1868; in Colorado, 1861-1863; in Arizona, 1863-1873; and in Oregon and Utah throughout the territorial phase.

Vital differences concerning the legislative branch existed within the framework common to all territories (Table 1-1).

The unicameral legislatures of Guam and the Virgin Islands are the result of the small populations of both territories, which made a comprehensive legislative structure irrational.

The territories of the first and second categories, territories without an elected body, contrast with those of the third and fourth categories, territories with an elected body. Historically speaking, the second category is the later branch of the first category and the fourth category is the later branch of the third category. In many territories of the third category, the election of the upper house was subsequently introduced. This is what happened in Mississippi in 1808; in Indiana, 1809; in Missouri, 1816; in Florida, 1826; and in Michigan, 1827.

In many territories of the fourth category the election of the governor was later introduced (Puerto Rico, 1947; Guam, 1968; Virgin Islands, 1968). While we have, diachronically speaking, four main categories of territories, only the last named would be recognized in the second half of the twentieth century as meeting the standard of what constitutes a territory. In 1909, the United States Supreme Court defined the word territory thus (*Kopel* v. *Bingham, cited in Documents on the Constitutional History of Puerto Rico* 1964, 290): "A portion of the country not included within the limits of any state, and not yet admitted as a state into the Union, but organized under the laws of Congress with a separate legislature, under a territorial governor and other officers appointed by the President and the Senate of the United States." Today the definition would be even shorter and would end after the words "and other officers," for in all the territories the governor is now no longer appointed but elected.

The first territorial government was established by Congress on July 13, 1787, by the "Ordinance for the government of the territory of the United States northwest of the river Ohio" (cf. Thorpe 1909, 957-962, and Commager 1958, I, 128-132). This ordinance provided for territories of the first and third categories.

This provision, the Northwest Ordinance, proved to be successful and became famous. Among American historians, the Northwest Ordinance is considered the general model for the step-by-step development of administration of thinly populated areas and for the education of their people for self-government. The two territorial categories were not only applied to all single territories carved out of the Northwest Territory, but until approximately 1820, they were applied also in all other newly established territories (with the exception of Louisiana, called the Orleans Territory). After the Great Ordinance of 1787, practically all areas within the boundaries of 1783 were mere territories or parts of territories before their elevation to full statehood. The exceptions are Maine and West Virginia, which were parts of other states (Massachusetts and Virginia, respectively) before becoming states. Before becoming territories or parts of territories, the areas incorporated into the United States after 1783 were, as a rule, under the control of military governors. It was an exception when a preterritorial framework was expressly designed by Congress (as for Hawaii in 1898) or when the region was even given its preterritorial Organic Law, as with Alaska in 1884 (Section 7-2), which at that time was organized as a "district."

The territory is an important creation of American constitutional law which afforded Anglo-Saxons and inhabitants who were not Anglo-Saxon the opportunity to gain experience in the exercise of far-reaching self-administration and self-government. Where this stage was omitted, as was the case in California in 1850, the young state suffered for this omission at a later time (Farrand 1896, 54). From an educational viewpoint, a similarly sound and important intermediate stage before achieving statehood in the United States was provided in 1934 by the

Table 1-1   Characteristics of Territorial Legislatures

Territorial Category[a]	Legislative Power	Territory and Year of the Organic Act[b]
First	Governor[c] Three judges appointed by the President	Northwest Territory, 1787 Mississippi, 1798 Michigan, January 11, 1805 (Louisiana Territory) Arkansas, 1819 (temporary provisions)
Second	Governor[c] Council appointed by the President[d]	Louisiana, 1804 (Orleans Territory) Florida, 1822
Third	Governor[c] Lower House elected by the people Council appointed by the President	Indiana, May 7, 1800 Mississippi, May 10, 1800 Louisiana, 1805 (Orleans Territory Missouri, 1812 Arkansas, 1819 (permanent provisions) District of Columbia, 1871 Puerto Rico, 1900 Philippines, 1902
Fourth	Governer[c] Lower House elected by the people Type A: Upper House elected by the people Type B: no Upper House	Type A: Arkansas, 1820 Wisconsin, 1836 Iowa, 1838 Oregon, 1848 Minnesota, 1849 New Mexico, 1850 All Territories, 1850-1917 except Puerto Rico 4/12/1900 including Hawaii 4/30/1900 Last of these Organic Laws: Alaska, 1912 Philippine Islands, 1916 Puerto Rico, 1917 Type B: Virgin Islands, 1936 Guam, 1950

Table 1-1 footnotes:

^aTerritory of the First Category, Second Category, etc., and the Types A and B are my own terminology.

^bAll Organic Acts before 1909 are found in Thorpe (1909).

^cIn all four categories, the Governor is appointed by the President of the United States.

^dMembers of the Council were not nominated by the territories.

^eIn Hawaii the Upper House was called the Council; in Alaska and Puerto Rico it was called the Senate.

United States before the Philippine Islands were made an independent nation state (Section 7-5). That the actual independence of other new nations was not directed with equal care after 1945 will possibly prove disadvantageous in many cases.

A stage that sometimes preceded territorial status was the administrative "district" (Farrand 1900, 681). The district has existed in isolated instances (Missouri in 1804; Washington, D. C., since 1874; and Alaska in 1884) but not with sufficient regularity to enable one to speak of a fixed category in the administrative structure.

1-2   THE NON-ENGLISH MINORITIES

The non-English minorities are divided into two categories: (1) those who settled in the area before the United States came into existence (1776) or before it was incorporated into the United States and (2) those who immigrated to their place of settlement at a time when it already belonged to the United States. Table 1-2 offers a survey of the first category, which may be referred to as that of the original or established settlers.

The relatively small numbers of most groups do not at all foreshadow their future importance. The Spaniards of New Mexico, for example, have increased their number tenfold, primarily by a higher birthrate.

Among the settlers already established in the United States by 1776 are the Germans (figures for 1790) in Pennsylvania, 141,000; Maryland, 24,000; Virginia, 28,000; New York, 26,000; and Ohio, 1,000, where German settlers appeared first in 1776. All United States language figures for 1790 in this book are taken from the American Council of Learned Societies, *Report of the Committee on Linguistic and National Stocks in the Population of the United States.*

A rapidly increasing mass immigration from Europe and Canada began around 1830. Table 1-3 presents the numbers of immigrants to the United States who were born outside the United Kingdom (including Ireland) between 1850 and 1880. Based on the data in Table 1-3, the percentages of foreign-born persons speaking a non-English tongue are shown in Table 1-4.

In 1850, the Germans were the only important immigrant group; 30 years later, several other major groups had emerged. The mass immigration from eastern

Table 1-2   Numerical Strength of Original Settlers at Annexation

Area	Year of Annexation	Size of Minority Population	
New Netherlands New York, Delaware and nearby areas	1664	6,000	Dutch
Midwest, east of the Mississippi River	1763	5,000	French
Louisiana	1803	15,000	French-speaking whites
		20,000	French-speaking Negroes
Missouri	1803	3,000	French
Florida Northern Maine (St. Johns Valley)	1821	3,000-5,000	Spaniards
Texas	1845	6,000	Spanish-speaking people
		13,000	Germans
New Mexico	1848	25,000	Spaniards
California	1848	5,000	Spaniards
Alaska	1867	500	Russians
		1,000	Creoles
		10,000	Eskimos
		(5,000	Indians)
Hawaii	1898	39,000	Hawaiians, among them 10,000 of mixed lineage
		25,000	Japanese
Puerto Rico	1898	885,000	Spanish-speaking people, among them 380,000 Mulattoes and Negroes
Philippine Islands	1898	7,000,000	Filipinos
Guam	1898	9,000	Chamorros
East Samoa	1899	5,000	Samoans

and southern Europe began after 1880. The overall result of these immigrants is evident in the language statistics of 1940 (Kloss 1953, 220-225, and the Sixteenth Census).

Table 1-3   Immigrants with Place of Birth Outside the United Kingdom

Year	Total	English Mother Tongue	Non-English Place of Birth
1850	900,000	100,000 primarily born in Canada	800,000 among whom were: 584,000 from Germany 40,000-50,000 from French Canada 54,000 from France 13,000 from Switzerland 13,000 from Mexico 13,000 from Norway 11,000 from Flanders and the Netherlands
1880	3,900,000	500,000	3,400,000 among whom were: 2,000,000 from Germany 200,000 from French Canada 194,000 from Sweden 182,000 from Norway 107,000 from France 124,000 from Austria, among whom were 85,000 from Bohemia of whom 70,000 were Czech 89,000 from Switzerland 68,000 from Mexico 58,000 from Holland

Table 1-4   Percentage of Foreign-Born People Speaking a Non-English Tongue

Native language	1850, %	1880, %
German	15	60
French	13	9
Scandinavian	1.5	11

During the censuses of 1910, 1920, and 1930 the mother tongue of the foreign-born persons was ascertained; during the 1910 and 1920 censuses the languages of the native-born children of foreign-born parents was ascertained. In

Table 1-5   Numerical Strength of the Most Important Language Groups, 1940

Language Groups of Over 200,000	Total	Foreign Born		American Born with One or More Foreign-Born Parents		American Born of Only American-Born Parents "Old Settlers"	
		Total	%	Total	%	Total	%
German	4,949,780	1,589,040	32.1	2,435,700	49.2	925,040	18.7
Italian	3,766,820	1,561,100	41.5	2,080,680	55.2	125,040	3.3
Polish	2,416,320	801,680	33.2	1,428,820	59.1	185,820	7.7
Spanish	1,861,400	428,360	23.0	714,060	38.4	718,980	38.6
Yiddish	1,751,100	924,440	52.8	773,680	44.2	52,980	3.0
French	1,412,060	359,520	25.5	533,760	37.8	518,780	36.7
Swedish	830,900	423,200	50.9	374,040	45.0	33,660	7.1
Russian & Ukrainian, Table 1-6	668,680	372,480	58.7	259,440	38.8	16,760	2.5
Norwegian	658,220	232,820	35.4	344,240	52.3	81,160	12.3
Czech	520,440	159,640	30.7	279,040	53.6	81,760	15.7
Slovak	484,360	171,580	35.4	283,520	58.6	29,260	6.0
Magyar	453,000	241,220	53.3	198,000	43.8	13,180	2.9
South Slavic, Table 1-6	331,720	146,160	44.1	174,580	52.6	10,980	3.3
Dutch, Table 1-6	321,480	134,600	41.9	121,080	37.7	65,800	20.4
Greek	273,250	165,220	60.4	104,620	51.6	6,160	2.3
Lithuanian	272,680	122,660	45.0	140,620	51.6	9,400	3.4
Finnish	230,420	97,080	42.1	118,460	51.4	14,880	6.5
Danish	226,740	122,180	38.8	95,460	42.1	9,100	4.0
Portuguese	215,860	83,780	38.8	120,500	55.8	11,580	5.4
Total, 19 Groups, Table 1-7	21,591,160	8,124,860	37.6	10,560,580	48.9	2,905,720	13.5
English plus Celtic	93,039,640	2,506,420	2.7	12,181,040	13.1	78,352,180	84.2

Table 1-6   The Divisions of Groups Shown in Table 1-5

Category	Subcategory	Total	Foreign Born	Native "Old Settlers"	%
Russian and	Russian	565,080	356,940	13,980	2.4
Ukrainian	Ukrainian	83,600	35,540	2,780	3.3
South Slavic	Serbian	37,640	18,060	1,280	3.4
	Croatian	115,440	52,540	3,290	3.4
	Slovenian	178,640	75,560	5,780	3.2
Dutch	Holland (Dutch)	267,140	102,700	61,200	22.9
	Flemish	54,340	31,900	4,600	8.5

1940 the Census Bureau attempted (not repeated in 1950-1960) to determine the language distribution among the total white population. Only a representative number, however, of the 5% of the population was questioned. Although only 5% of the population was questioned, the Census Bureau maintains that the resultant error is below 5% for figures over 10,000, less than 10% for figures between 5,000 and 10,000, and below 20% for those between 2,000 and 5,000. For figures below 2,000 the results differ from the actual figures by less than 10% in most cases, and only sporadic differences occur above 20%.

The mother tongue was defined as "the principal language spoken in the home of an individual in his earliest childhood," that is, not the present domestically used language but the childhood language, which in most other countries is considered the mother tongue. In the United States especially, many persons in whose parental home a non-English language was dominant use, as adults, English primarily or exclusively in their own families. Many of them have only an imperfect command of their childhood language today. Therefore, the figures presented convey a picture falsely favorable to the non-English languages. According to the method employed, the following percentages were determined for 1940:

1. English (or Celtic) language for 93,040,000 whites, 81%
2. Non-English (and non-Celtic) languages for 21,996,000 whites, 19%
3. Whites for whom information about the language was available, total 115,036,000 whites, 100%.

According to the proportion of natives of native parentage (Tables 1-5 and 1-6, right-hand columns) we get the following order for language groups. An asterisk (*) denotes that the language group settled partially in linguistic enclaves.

1. *Spanish	6. *Norwegian	11. Swedish
2. *French	7. Polish	12. Danish
3. *German	8. Finnish	13. Arabic
4. *Dutch	9. Slovak	14. Croatian
5. *Czech	10. Portuguese	15. Lithuanian

16. Serbian	20. Rumanian	23. Magyar
17. Italian	21. Yiddish	24. Russian
18. Ukranian	22. Armenian	25. Greek
19. Slovenian		

The South Slavic languages were often counted with Slovak; Dutch and Flemish were always listed separately, but undoubtedly many Flemings gave their mother tongue correctly as Dutch.

According to Table 1-5, the Dutch with 20.4% ranked in third place, ahead of the Germans. In this case 24,040 natives of native parentage in Pennsylvania and Ohio, being so-called Pennsylvania Dutch "old settlers," must in reality be added to the German column. Thus 297,440 remain for the Dutch, among them, 51,760 or 17.4% "old settlers." Therefore, the Dutch occupied the fourth rank and the Germans the third. Actually, it would have been more accurate to list the Pennsylvania Dutch as an individual language group instead of treating them as part of the German group (Kloss 1952, chapter on *Pennsilfaanisch*).

Language groups with a strong rural segment stand at the head of the list. Within this group the farmers lead, the Czechs showing five times, the Germans

Table 1-7   Percentages of Natives of Native Parentage
in Rural and Urban Localities

Language Group	Urban, %	Rural-farm, %
Czechs	6.3	32.6
Germans	8.0	31.3
French	22.8	72.1
Norwegians	6.1	19.0
Poles	6.5	19.4

four times, the French, Norwegians, and Poles three times as many native-born individuals among rural as among urban inhabitants on a percentage basis (Table 1-7). As a rule the percentages for the rural nonfarm population are between those for the city and those for the rural farm population.

As has been pointed out elsewhere, "It is certain that in the future the group of American-born individuals of American-born parents will form a considerably larger percentage of the non-English population than it does today" (Kloss 1942 II, 878). Those language pockets which developed during the colonial period seem to have retained their substance best, particularly the enclaves of Spaniards in New Mexico and Colorado (265,000 old settlers), the French of Louisiana and Texas (313,000 old settlers), and the Germans of Pennsylvania (157,000 old settlers). The approximately 735,000 old settlers of these three language islands comprised only 3% of all those who are not Anglo-Saxons; but they represented a full quarter of the number of old settlers. Next we find the French Canadians of the Northeast, who immigrated after 1800, the Mexicans of the Southwest, and the language pockets of the Germans, Czechs, and Norwegians in the Middle West and Texas which came into existence during the nineteenth century.

None of the midwestern language islands reached the 100,000 mark. Furthermore, dialect divided the Norwegian language pockets, and both dialect and denomination divided the Germans. Among the purely urban groups, the French Canadians of the Northeast were the most tenacious in retaining their language and the Poles were next. The survival of larger Italian and Yiddish groups in several states is mainly the result of a projection of the statistics, for with a minimum share of only 2.5% of old settlers all groups of more than 400,000 persons must each have over 10,000 old settlers. Spaniards and Frenchmen represented a total of 15% of whites who were not English-speaking, but they represented 42% of all the old settlers; while Italian and Yiddish represented a total of 26% of all non-English groups, but only 6% of the old settlers. The Swedes, in spite of the existence of several language pockets, did not reach 10%, or the 10,000 mark for old settlers in any state. In Minnesota, among 164,560 Swedes, 9,540 old settlers were found; no more than 4,000 could be counted in any other state.

As for language retention, the Germans were above average; at least their older groups were slow to give up their language. But the French were the most persistent. In the Midwest they retained tiny pockets of their language spoken in colonial times (19.8% of a total of 5,860 French-speaking in Indiana and 32.7% of a 6,300 total in Missouri). In New England they even managed to preserve purely urban groups. The figures for foreign language concentrations in California, concentrations which are frequently very young and of low cohesion, were disproportionately prominent.

The 1970 census yielded the mother-tongue data in Table 1-8, some of them rather startling.

The term mother tongue in this context refers to the language spoken in the person's home when he was a child. But for the vast majority of originally non-English persons English has since become the principal language. This is revealed by the 1969 figures in Table 1-9, even though they are based on a restricted sampling.

Members of a national group may be called *solitary original settlers* if they arrived before the Anglo-Saxons, or they may be called *original cosettlers* if they arrived at the same time with them. During the course of centuries all groups of late settlers became established settlers. In New York City the Dutch were once the original settlers, the British the late settlers. The descendants of both groups were established settlers during the nineteenth century in relation to the Germans, Italians, Eastern European Jews, etc. On the other hand, members of a national group were *solitary late settlers* in Anglo-Saxon settlements where they were the only large non-English group of late settlers, and *late cosettlers* when they were one among several foreign language groups of late settlers (Kloss 1940, I, 14-26, 38). If we include the foreign language minorities (to which the Irish do not belong), we arrive at the following:

Table 1-8 Mother Tongue in the 50 Component States: 1970

Language	Total	Natives of Native Parentage	Same in % of Total
1. Spanish	7,823,583	4,171,050	53.3
2. German	6,093,054	2,488,394	40.8
3. Italian	4,144,315	605,625	14.6
4. French	2,598,408	1,460,130	56.1
5. Polish	2,437,938	670,335	27.5
6. Yiddish	1,593,993	170,174	10.7
7. Swedish	626,102	113,119	18.0
8. Norwegian	612,862	204,829	33.4
9. Slovak	510,366	86,950	17.0
10. Greek	458,699	56,839	12.3
11. Czech	452,812	148,944	32.9
12. Hungarian	447,497	52,156	11.7
13. Japanese	408,504	82,886	20.2
14. Portuguese	365,300	62,252	17.0
15. Dutch	350,748	90,713	25.7
16. Chinese	345,431	30,764	8.9
17. Russian	334,615	30,665	9.1
18. Lithuanian	292,820	34,744	11.9
19. Ukrainian	249,351	22,662	9.0
20. Serbo-Croatian	239,455	24,095	10.0
21. Finnish	214,168	58,124	27.1
22. Danish	194,462	29,089	15.0
23. Arabic	193,520	25,766	13.3
24. Solvenian	82,321	9,040	11.0
25. Rumanian	56,590	5,166	9.1
26. Amerindian languages	268,205	254,859	96.2

1. Solitary original settlers (Spaniards in the Southwest and Puerto Rico; Frenchmen in Louisiana; Dutchmen in New York; Russians in Alaska).

2. Original cosettlers (Germans in the chain of states from New York to Georgia, and in Ohio, West Virginia, and Texas).

3. Solitary late settlers (approximately 1830-1850) (Germans in the Midwest).

4. Late cosettlers (since 1850) [French Canadians, Scandinavians, Dutchmen, Czechs (since 1880) eastern and southern Europeans, Mexicans].

These four types of ethnic groups correspond to a scale of claims, pretensions, or demands with which these groups wittingly or unwittingly confronted the Anglo-Americans, and to a scale of esteem or respect which the

Table 1-9   The Six Leading Immigrant Languages in the
               United States in 1969

	Mother Tongue		
Language	Native Born	Foreign Born	Total
1. Spanish	4,878,000	1,822,000	6,700,000
2. German	4,809,000	1,025,000	5,934,000
3. Italian	3,147,000	1,218,000	4,365,000
4. French	1,801,000	378,000	2,179,000
5. Polish	1,982,000	399,000	2,381,000
6. Yiddish	1,142,000	478,000	1,620,000

Principal Languages
(percentages based upon the number of
mother-tongue claimants of each language)

Native Born, %		Foreign Born, %		Total, %	
1. 3,104,000	63.6	1,581,000	81.2	4,685,000	69.9
2. 256,000	3.2	159,000	15.5	415,000	7.0
3. 165,000	5.2	493,000	40.5	558,000	12.8
4. 254,000	14.1	160,000	42.2	414,000	19.0
5. 66,000	3.3	163,000	40.7	229,000	9.7
6. 20,000	1.8	106,000	35.8	126,000	7.8

Anglo-American extends to the vital rights of these ethnic groups. Demands and esteem are highest in the case of the solitary original settlers and lowest for the late cosettlers. The foregoing groupings are not intended to be inflexible structures by which all settlers can be judged, for other factors must sometimes be considered. For example, the Germans who settled in the Midwest in the nineteenth century were later settlers from the point of view of the nation at large, but they were original settlers, along with the Anglo-Saxons, from the point of view of the respective territories and states.

1-3   NATIONALITY LAW

Definition of Minority Law

In this book all state and local regulations, measures, and patterns of behavior based on prescriptive law which regulate the living together of groups of citizens of different mother tongues in the same state are called *nationality law.* Even though the problems of certain religious minorities occasionally overlap those of ethnic minorities, they do not belong to the topic of this book. Nor do the problems of racial groups, such as those of the twenty million American Negroes, receive consideration in this volume. The problems facing racial minority groups are often the opposite of those facing the foreign-language groups. Foreign-speaking minorities can achieve equal status with the English-speaking majority groups only when they are able to cultivate their own language through separate public or private institutions. On the other hand, the struggle of racial groups has little to do with language differences but is directed toward abolishing special institutions established by the state for this racial group, particularly toward abolishing separate schools.

A difficult and tense double polarity exists where separate ethnic groups differ from Anglo-Americans by both language and race, as is the case with the Hawaiians among the original settlers and the Mexicans among the late settlers. In their racial policy the Mexicans must demand admission to the general public schools, even though several factors would speak in favor of separate schools at least in the first generation.

The Indians are not treated in this book, even though originally they spoke non-English languages and quite a few still speak one today. The largest Indian language group in the United States, the Navajo, is estimated to be 120,000 persons. American Indians were always fragmented into a variety of small language groups which were without a system of writing, with notable exceptions. The Cherokees have and use their own script, devised by Sequoya, and other written forms exist beginning with John Eliot's Indian grammar of 1666 in Massachusetts and the earlier work in this field by the French Jesuits in Canada. The fragmentation and the different degree of civilization between the whites and the Indians were the principal reasons why English was instituted as the language in federal institutions for Indians. The regional scattering of the Indians and in many cases their intertribal aversions prevented them from dealing with the whites as an unified group until well into the twentieth century. The history of the relations between Indians and Anglo-Saxons belongs more in a treatment of racial than nationality law and is so vast a topic that it would have to be dealt with in a separate book, for which other sources than those used in this volume would have to be consulted.

Where terms like "nationality," "ethnic group," or "minority" are used here, they refer always, unless expressly stated otherwise, to a group speaking a non-English language. Part of the American literature about minority questions suffers from the fact that the terms "minority," "race," "ethnic group," etc., are used within the framework of one and the same book to refer to language and racial groups. It is not always clear in such books that the needs of these two separate groups are opposite nor how complicated and confusing the situation becomes especially where one group, for example, the Mexicans, belongs to both types.

The minority laws deal basically with groups of persons who are citizens of their country of residence. Neither the immigration laws, the alien laws, nor the naturalization laws are part of the minority laws. These three laws deal with the stages through which the foreign-born members of a minority must pass before they are citizens of the United States and members of a minority. The immigration laws regulate the question of whether and under what conditions they are permitted to enter the country. The alien laws regulate their legal position after their immigration as far as it differs from that of American citizens. The naturalization law finally opens—or perhaps impedes—the process for obtaining American citizenship. Immigrants constitute a national minority only after having become American citizens. Incidentally, the naturalized citizens, unlike the native-born, are still subject to some legal restrictions. These three laws include also those immigrants whose mother tongue is English but who, after naturalization, do not form a language minority, for example, immigrants from Finland or English-speaking Canada. The separation of minority law and the three above-mentioned laws cannot always be clearly maintained. For example, a Pennsylvania law of 1895 provides that in counties with 40,000 inhabitants born in the German Empire, certain notices must be published in German (Section 5-3). No distinction was made even though these people had in the meantime become American citizens.

Naturalization laws assume considerable importance with respect to minority laws where groups that do not speak English are denied the right to become American citizens, for they are thereby also prevented from becoming an ethnic group, a minority in the narrower sense of the word. This denial became reality on several occasions not because of the immigrants' native language but because of their race. As late as 1922, the Supreme Court ruled that a Japan-born Japanese "being clearly not a Caucasian" could not be naturalized (*Takao Ozawa v. United States, 260* U. S. 178) and that already naturalized foreign-born Japanese are not legal citizens (*Yamashita* v. *Hinkle,* 260 U. S. 199).

Even American-born children of Asians needed a decision of the Supreme Court (1898) to rule that they were citizens according to jus soli (*United States* v. *Wong Kim Ark,* 169 U. S. 649). As for the Mexicans, a federal district court decided in 1897 that they could become citizens regardless of their racial affinity (In re *Rodriquez, 81* Fed. 337=1 Dec. Dig. 61) because the treaty of Guadelupe Hidalgo (1848) granted citizenship to all Mexican inhabitants of the newly annexed territories regardless of their race. But as for naturalizing Canadian and South American half-breeds and Indians, the courts repeatedly issued negative decisions.

During the course of this century the United States granted the right of naturalization to several ethnic groups, among them the Chinese and Indians, until the Immigration and Naturalization Act of 1952 (66 Sta. 239, sec. 311; U. S. Code 1422) abolished all racial limitations.

A New Structural Principle for Minority Rights

Minority law may be subdivided according to several criteria. A really useful division (and one which, as far as can be seen, has not been carried out systematically in other literature) is the one into tolerance-oriented and promotion-oriented minority rights. Tolerance-oriented minority rights are the sum of those legal norms, customary laws, and measures with which the state and the public institutions dependent upon it (especially the public schools) provide for the minorities and which, if need be, protect for the minorities the right to cultivate their language in a private sphere, namely, in the family and in private organizations. For further information on the concept of private self-government, see among others Kloss 1961a (61-93, especially 70-73). Further information on the application of private self-government to minority rights may be found in Pernthaler (1962, 50-89, especially 75-79).

In contrast to tolerance-oriented minority rights, promotion-oriented minority rights regulate how public institutions may use and cultivate the languages and cultures of the minorities. In a democratic state, tolerance-oriented minority rights may be derived from the principle of formal equality whereas promotion-oriented minority rights can be derived only from the principle of material equality.

A meaningful example of a distinction between tolerance-oriented and promotion-oriented minority rights is found in Article XIX of the Austrian Constitution of December 21, 1867, which in the opinion of most legal experts in Austria is still in force (Ermacora 1963, 530, 532). Article XIX states (Hugelmann 1934, 81-82):

1. All ethnic groups of the state enjoy equal rights, and each ethnic group has an inviolable right to the preservation and cultivation of its nationality and language.

2. The equal status of all regionally customary languages of the empire in schools, offices, and in public life is recognized by the state.

The first paragraph concerns the preservation and cultivation of their separate identity by the minorities themselves and is therefore a tolerance-oriented minority right. The second paragraph promises them the recognition and use of their languages by the organs of the state and is therefore a promotion-oriented minority right. The second part of this paragraph, however, limits this right to the languages common in that specific area. This led to the Czech language's being tolerated *and* promoted by the Austrian Empire in Bohemia and Moravia, where it was indigenous, but not in Vienna, according to a decision of the Reichsgericht of October 19, 1904, where the Czech language had been carried by later migrations but had not yet become customary (Hugelmann 1934, 448-449). The toleration granted in paragraph 1, on the other hand, applied without restrictions to the Czechs in Vienna.

Tolerance-Oriented Minority Rights

In certain instances tolerance-oriented minority rights must be established by explicit legal provision. But here too the content is passive toleration, not active enforcement by the state. As soon as the law is established, the same principle applies to it that applies to the remaining toleration-oriented minority rights: it is heard of only when violated. "If an intervention of the state is demanded, the real desire is always directed only toward the restoration of the free sphere; materially speaking, it is not a positive content that is at stake, but a restoration of the conditions for the unrestricted acts of persons in the sphere which is free of state control" (Raschhofer 1931, 106). The following belong to the tolerance-oriented minority rights (Raschhofer 1931, 84, 104-105):

1. In the widest sense: the trinity—as distinguished in America— of *natural* rights such as life, liberty, property, of *civil* rights such as contracts and competence, and of *political* rights such as the right to vote and the right to hold office.

2. In a wide sense: the right of the individual to use his mother tongue at home and in public.

3. In a narrow sense: freedom of assembly and organization, the right to establish private cultural, economic, and social institutions and to use one's mother tongue in these.

4. In the narrowest sense: the right to cultivate one's own language in private schools.

In the widest sense the concept of tolerance-oriented minority rights assumes that members of an ethnic group have the same needs as do all other citizens; it represents no favored treatment of the ethnic group and does not concern matters of a specifically ethnic and lingual nature. In a wide sense, tolerance-oriented minority rights also affect only individual concerns, but in an area where the individual runs much more risk of being affected, particularly in his capacity as a member of an ethnic group. Certain rights which concern local institutions of an ethnic group, such as organizations and newspapers, represent the third group, the narrower sphere of tolerance-oriented minority rights. But the toleration of an organization of a minority does not automatically include the toleration of the language of the minority. In even as exemplary and generous a state as was the Austrian Empire with respect to minorities, instances are known where members of an ethnic group were permitted to establish private organizations but not to cultivate their language in them (Hugelmann 1934, 441). Finally, the rights in the narrowest sense are distinguished by permitting the cultivation of the mother tongue in private schools. Only by tolerating foreign language schools, i.e., in the narrowest sphere of tolerance-oriented minority rights, does the state accommodate itself to the continued existence of the particular language among future generations. Consequently, the toleration of private foreign-language school instruction represents the most important part of the tolerance-oriented minority rights and, at the same time, its most sensitive part, against which attacks by the dominant speech community are most likely to ensue even in a tolerantly governed state.

Toleration of "Outside Promotion"

In some cases the host country will allow the kin-state of an ethnic group to promote institutions designed to serve the cultural life of a resident minority group, particularly the development of ethnic schools. An ethnic group may have several kin-states; for the Mexicans there are Mexico and Spain, for the French of New England, Quebec and France. Since this promotion comes from outside the host state, it may be called *outside promotion.*

Simple Promotion-Oriented (or "Promotive") Rights. The host state keeps its own state language as the language of official communication to all groups within the state. Nevertheless, minority languages are permitted in texts flowing from public offices and institutions which deal directly with or serve the minorities as, for example, in legal notices. In some instances, simple promotion-oriented law also permits publication of pending or enacted legislation in the language of the minority. Such publications are read by the members of the minority with benefit; their relationship to the state is thereby improved both individually and collectively. But other inhabitants who speak other languages are not obliged to take notice of these publications; the relationship of these other inhabitants to the state is not affected by such publication, especially since these translations have no legal standing.

We should point out that special public funds must be earmarked for the printing of documents in minority languages. Such funds have often been appropriated for such publications as, for example, to pay the cost of printing the non-English versions of law collections (Sections 2-1, 4-2, 5-2, 5-3, 6-3). To trace such cases in detail would go beyond the scope of this book; it would, however, make a useful minor study to compile a chronicle of such resolutions from a single state, such as New Mexico, Pennsylvania, Louisiana, or Ohio.

It is not always easy to determine how far the instruction in non-English languages in the United States is part of minority law. As a rule of thumb we may say that so far as instruction in German, French, and Spanish is concerned, it is part of minority law only in the following cases:

1. In grade schools when the students or at least their parents speak primarily German, French, or Spanish

2. In high schools and colleges when the language is cultivated not only as a subject but also as a tool of instruction

The teaching of languages that enjoy less frequent international usage, such as Czech or Swedish, may be considered part of minority rights when they are taught in high schools and colleges, if their inclusion in the curriculum is caused by the presence of a large group of people who use these languages in their daily lives. This was generally the case in the United States until the middle of the twentieth century.

Certain special problems of toleration-oriented rights are closely interlaced with promotion-oriented rights, for example, the special problem whether, within the framework of general civic equality, access to official positions is open to members of the ethnic group in the same way that it is to Anglo-Americans and whether consequently "officials" and "citizens" speak the same language.

Expansion of Promotion-Oriented Minority Rights. Simple minority rights may be expanded in two ways. First, the state can grant the minority the right to care for its internal affairs through its own public organs, which amounts to the state's allowing self-government for the minority group. These organs in such case, of course, use the language of the minority side by side with or even in place of the language of the country. Such a public self-government of an ethnic group may either be direct and on a personal basis (rare in the United States) or on an indirect and regional basis.

Such self-governing, sometimes self-ruling, areas in which most of the population speak a non-English language have not been hard to find in the United

States. Even where the ethnic group in a certain administrative unit forms only a minority, it has a concern in the granting of regional self-administration, since it can press its special claims better with the government of a region than with the federal government.

Another expansion of promotion-oriented minority rights consists of the state's using the minority language in its relations not only with the minority but also with the total population. In this case those citizens who are not members of the ethnic group come in contact with the language of the minority. In such cases we may speak of complete equality of minorities. When the language of an ethnic group is being used not only in publications of the legislature but also in its deliberations, all representatives who speak other languages come directly into contact with the language of the ethnic group. They have to listen to speeches made in it, but only those of them who have a command of this language will be able to become speakers of the legislative body. The same thing happens when the texts of laws in languages of various minorities are declared authentic so that, before handing down their decisions, judges who are not members of a particular ethnic group will have to consult the version in the language of that minority. This equal status of minority languages may be achieved especially easily in places where the ethnic group has received regional self-government via the indirect minority law, as discussed at the beginning of this section.

Expediency-Based Promotive Rights. Promotion-oriented (or "promotive") rights are usually more favorable to ethnic groups than are tolerance-oriented rights. However, although the concept may be elevated to higher forms of civil and legal self-government or of equality among nationalities, it may on the other hand also be restricted to elementary forms which are actually of less value to the ethnic group than are those of the tolerance-oriented minority rights. Such elementary forms are designed to serve certain ends of the government rather than the concerns of the minority. We may speak in this connection elliptically of *expediency-based promotive* law. Such purposeful promotion occurs, for example, when the state generally ignores the languages of the ethnic groups but makes use of them in sending its non-English-speaking citizens tax notifications, or when the state grants a modest and insufficient promotion to the language of an ethnic group in its public schools because it hopes to lure students away from private schools which are predominantly or partially conducted in the language of the minority.

We may add to this category also instances in which certain time-limited promotion-oriented measures are tied to the presence of a minimum number of foreign-born members of a given language group. In these instances public notices or laws in languages of the minority are in effect only for a limited time.

CHAPTER TWO

Federal Promotion-Oriented
Minority Laws

2-1 CONGRESS AND THE GERMAN LANGUAGE

The German Language during the Continental Congress

During the years of the War of Independence, the Continental Congress had German translations printed of many of its proclamations (Journals of the Continental Congress; Seidensticker 1878, 309-316; Seidensticker 1893). The first publication was available in 1774: *Auszüge aus den Stimmungen und Verhand-lungen des Amerikanischen Congresses vom Vesten Lande. Gehalten zu Phila-delphia . . .* ("Excerpts from the Votes and Deliberations of the American Continental Congress Held in Philadelphia . . .").

Some of the later documents of which the Continental Congress had German versions printed were: a circular letter to its constituents of December 10, 1776; a report of 1777 about the behavior of the enemy armies (4,000 English, 2,000 German copies); a declaration of April 23, 1778, concerning the treatment of such American citizens or such immigrants who would come over from the British to the American side (500 English, 200 German copies); and a circular letter of September 13, 1779, to the voters.

On June 28, 1775, the Congress agreed to print and distribute a letter (naturally in German) of the Lutheran and Reformed clergy of Pennsylvania and other prominent persons "of that nation" to their friends and countrymen in the colonies of New York and North Carolina appealing to the Germans in those two contested areas to join the cause of freedom. Likewise according to a decision of

July 6, 1777, the Congress had printed in German at its own expense an appeal of the representative body of New York to its constituents.

The most important German publication of the Continental Congress was the German edition of the Articles of Confederation, which had the following German title: "Artikel des Bundes und der immerwährenden Eintracht zwischen den Staaten von New Hampshire, Massachusetts Bay . . . ." The official recognition of the German language in the publications of the Continental Congress corresponded to a strong and enthusiastic participation of most of the German minority in the armed rebellion. This participation assumed almost the character of a regular participation of the minority when the Congress decided to form purely German troop units, for example, as on May 25, 1776, "one battalion of Germans," and in implementing this decision, on June 27, 1776, "four companies of Germans . . . in Pennsylvania and four companies in Maryland." The term "German" refers in this instance clearly to the young, almost exclusively American-born, generation of German-Americans. The language of command in this battalion was undoubtedly German. Strange to say, the Continental Congress during the later years of its existence, from 1780 to 1788, issued no more German publications, the reasons for which are unknown. But the use of German by the Continental Congress during the years 1774-1779 meant a relatively vigorous beginning of the American minority law on the federal level.

The Continental Congress between 1774 and 1777 issued also a few French publications. They were not destined for the few French-speaking inhabitants of the rebellious colonies, but for the inhabitants of the present province of Quebec, who were, among others, addressees of three special circular letters of the Congress. It was still hoped at that time that they could be induced to join the rebellion. In this instance minority rights are involved insofar as the French Canadians were addressed not as foreigners but as expected future citizens of the United States. Of the first of these imprints, a "Letter to the Inhabitants of Quebec," dated October 26, 1774, there appeared official editions in English, French, and German. It was followed by two more letters dated May 29, 1775, and January 24, 1776. A French translation of even the Articles of War adopted November 7, 1775, was ordered to be sent to Canada, the delegates obviously cherishing hope that eventually French-speaking units from Quebec might join the American army.

However, the relationship between the rebels and Quebec was ambiguous. In October of 1774 the Continental Congress in three great demonstrations came out against the so-called Quebec Act of June 22, 1774, in which Great Britain made concessions to the French in present Quebec in regard to the exercise of the Catholic religion, an act which was taken by the Continental Congress as a threat to the Protestant religion in North America. It is far from certain whether the French Canadians would have been able to preserve their identity within the framework of the United States as easily as they did under the British crown (Kloss 1940, 82-85).

The Attempt of 1794-1795 in Congress

At the beginning of 1794, German citizens of Augusta County, Virginia, petitioned the Third Congress to always print a certain number of German copies of federal laws (Kloss 1940, 86-92; Lohr 1931, 283-290). A Congressional committee consisting of Daniel Hiester and F. A. Muhlenberg, Representatives from Pennsylvania, and F. Preston, Representative from Virginia, proposed this measure to the House on April 1, 1794; however, it was not voted on. Again, at the end of that year a new three-man committee (Hiester, Moore, Baldwin) took up the matter and recommended at the beginning of 1795 that 3,000 copies should be printed of the previously enacted federal laws and that as many copies in German ought to be printed of all future session laws as were requested by representatives from districts with "German citizens."

The matter came to a vote on January 13, 1795. The Speaker of the House, F. A. Muhlenberg, vacated the post to Representative David Cobb of Massachusetts, who presided over the vote. Forty-one votes were cast in favor and forty-two against the recommendation. The names of the supporters and opponents are not known. It is, however, certain that the outcome was extremely close. It is certain, furthermore, that Muhlenberg vacated his post and just, thereby, got the chance to tip the scales. It is, therefore, very likely that Muhlenberg was responsible for the outcome of the vote to the disadvantage of the German language. This likelihood becomes a certainty insofar as the later varying and inconsistent oral tradition almost exclusively points to F. A. Muhlenberg as the man responsible for the defeat of the German language. However, a contemporary, Helmuth, whose testimony would suffice as proof, does not name Muhlenberg directly; he only speaks of "a German proud fool . . . who deliberately thwarted the best interest of his nation and his constituents."

On February 16, 1795, the question was raised again in the plenary session, Representative Hartley of Reading, Pennsylvania, strongly favored the publication of a German version of federal laws; other representatives opposed it. For example, Elias Boudinot and William V. Murray (Maryland) declared that in England laws were never published in Welsh. A new vote does not seem to have been taken. That was probably the last reading of the matter.

During the nineteenth century the events of 1794 and 1795 gave rise to the so-called Muhlenberg legend. According to this legend, Congress—or according to another version, Pennsylvania—during or soon after the War of Independence wanted to abolish English as the official language and to replace it with German; but this action was thwarted by Muhlenberg's vote. Obviously, this legend stemmed from a confusion of the events of 1794-1795 in Congress and those of 1837 in Pennsylvania (Section 5-3).

In 1798 a new attempt in favor of German seems to have been made. The message of President Adams of April 7, 1798, dealing with directives given to and messages received from American representatives in Paris, appeared in a German version (Seidensticker 1893, 150). The documents of the session provide no clue, however, as to whether or nor this was an official publication. On April 6, 1798, two requests by Brook and Williams for the printing of a larger number of copies of the message than had been originally planned were rejected after a rather long debate without mentioning a German edition. Nevertheless, it becomes evident that the number of copies was disputed; the incident would merit a thorough investigation as far as the language question is concerned (*Debates and Proceedings of the Congress of the United States 1851, col. 1337-1380*).

An Attempt in 1843: Its Forerunners and Follow-Ups

During the 1830s the number of German immigrants increased considerably. Among them were small groups of adherents of political liberalism who had left Germany more or less involuntarily. Several of these "30ers" worked with great vigor to have the German language granted a high degree of minority status in those states with strong German elements. They also established several nationwide organizations. The Allgemeine Schulcommission der Deutschen in den Vereinigten Staaten (the general school commission of the Germans in the United States) called in 1839 for the establishment of a teachers' seminary and reported that, among others, President Van Buren and the governors of Ohio and Pennsylvania had made contributions. The Pennsylvania legislature in 1840 granted a charter to the "German convention for promoting education" which was to be the sponsor of the seminary and whose members, "citizens of the U. S. being native Germans, or descendants of Germans," were entrusted with the task "to promote the cause of education particularly among the German population" (Kloss 1940, 287-288).

As early as 1835 Congress was petitioned by German liberals to publish its deliberations and decisions in German (Kloss 1940, 94-95). On December 11, 1843, the Pennsylvania German Whig Representative Henry Frick (died 1844) moved in Congress that the annual message of President Tyler also be published in a German edition (*Congressional Globe I*). Representative Ramsay of Minnesota (later its first governor) demanded that the reports from the departments attached to the annual message be printed also in German. (His mother was Pennsylvania German.) Representative J. Slidell of Louisiana proposed to include French also. Three times in the course of a long debate it was moved to table the proposal, a move which was rejected by 53 to 134 votes the first time, and by 84 to 99 votes the second time. The third time, with votes deadlocked 86 to 86, the issue was decided against the non-English languages by the vote of the Speaker W. Jones.

An analysis (Table 2-1) of the last vote shows the voting pattern. If we take all Midwestern states (including Ohio) and Pennsylvania as the once so-called German Belt, we find the regional voting pattern shown in Table 2-2, while Table 2-3 shows the voting pattern according to political party membership.

A comparison with the first vote, which was favorable to the language proposal, shows that 41 Representatives changed their vote; i.e., they voted at first in favor and at the third time against the proposal—15 from New York, 10 from the southern states, 6 from New England, and 5 each from New Jersey and Ohio. In 1844, 1845, 1846, and 1847, Representative Robert Smith of Illinois

Table 2-1   Votes on Subject of Publishing Presidential Message
in Non-English Languages

Regions Represented	In Favor	Against
New England States	3	19
Middle Atlantic seaboard states and Ohio (Pennsylvania 22:1)	41	34
Midwest without Ohio	19	0
Southern States	23	33

Table 2-2   Votes of German Belt Compared with
Other States

Regions Represented	In Favor	Against
The German Belt	55	5
The remaining states	31	81

Table 2-3   Votes According to Party
Membership

Party	In Favor	Against
Democrats	59	58
Whigs	27	27
Others		1

(supported in 1844 by his fellow Representative from Illinois, John Wentworth) proposed the publication of a German edition of the Presidential message. This proposal was rejected each time without debate or formal vote (*Congressional Globe II*).

When in 1853, the "30er" Heinrich Roedter planned a German edition of the *Congressional Globe*, the Congressional Committee in charge of the matter decided to subscribe to one copy per Representative, but the project was limited to two or three installments at most (Rattermann 1911, 283-284). H. A. Rattermann's statement (Rattermann 1911, 334) that the *National-Zeitung*, edited by Alfred Schücking, "published the laws of the United States in the German language at the time of Daniel Webster" is highly dubious, since the *National-Zeitung* began publication in April 1843, and Webster was Secretary of State only until May of that year (Wust 1959, 41-42; Arndt-Olson 1961, 13-16).

The Attempt of 1862 in Congress

The Civil War broke out in April 1861. As during the War of Independence, many German-speaking American citizens joined in the fighting. According to W.

Kaufmann there were in the armies of the North 216,000 German-born soldiers, 300,000 sons of German immigrants, and numerous grandsons and later descendants of German ancestry (Kaufmann 1911, 182-190). While special German units were formed during the Civil War, specific acts of Congress authorizing the establishment of separate German units (similar to those for the War of Independence) cannot be found in the literature. Of the 216,000 German-born soldiers about 36,000 served in purely German regiments. Of these approximately 10,000 formed a purely German division. Regiments which consisted entirely of German immigrants or their sons have been found in New York (10), Missouri (7), Ohio and Pennsylvania (4 each), Wisconsin (3), Illinois (2), and Indiana (1), in addition to 18 regiments in Pennsylvania which consisted entirely of American-born Germans. In most, but not all, German regiments the language of command was German.

At this time another attempt was made to obtain the right for German-speaking American citizens to have federal publications in German (*Congressional Globe III*). On April 24, 1862, Republican Cyrus Aldrich of Minnesota proposed to print 25,000 German copies of the Report on Agriculture for 1861. He was seconded by his fellow Republican William S. Holman of Indiana and just as vigorously by E. B. Washburn of Illinois, a Whig, who pointed out that it was also customary in his state to have official reports printed in German. A Democrat of Pennsylvania, S. E. Ancona, declared that Aldrich in his proposal anticipated Ancona's own proposal. Aldrich's proposal was approved by fifty-seven to fifty-one votes. Suddenly the German language had gained—even though only to a minuscule extent—minority status on the federal level.

But only for twenty-four hours! On the following day Representative E. P. Walton brought before the House a resolution of the printing committee asking that the decision of the previous day be reversed. Walton argued that if Aldrich's proposal were put into law it would be necessary to hire special German printers and typesetters and to purchase special types. Furthermore, it would hardly be confined to this isolated case of a government publication in German, and, he stated, "I submit the question whether we are to have a national language or not." A proposal by Washburn to reject the resolution—he questioned that it was permissible under House rules—was overruled by seventy-one to forty votes, and this killed the attempt to have German admitted as an official language.

If we analyze the voting of April 24, 1862, by the principles we applied to the vote of 1843, we get the figures in Table 2-4. Disregarding the fact that in 1862 most of the Southern states were not represented, the new figures coincide very closely with those of 1843. This time, too, the New England states voted mostly against, the Midwestern states mostly in favor of German, while the middle zone (Middle Atlantic seaboard states and Ohio) were divided. The majority which the border region (northernmost Southern States and Far West) could muster against German in 1862 exceeded the total of the Southern states in 1843.

In part politics the trends are more evident in 1862 than they had been nineteen years before. The Republicans, like the earlier Whigs, are approximately evenly divided but the Democrats show a clear majority in favor of German, and

Table 2-4   Votes in 1862 Concerning Governmental Publications
              in German

Representatives Voting	In Favor	Against
According to regions		
New England	4	14
Middle Atlantic seaboard states and Ohio		
(Pennsylvania 6 for, 4 against)	26	21
Middle West	22	3
Border states (Va., Del., Ky., Md., Tenn.,		
Cal., Oregon)	3	17
German Belt (Midwest and Pennsylvania)	40	11
Other states	15	44
According to parties		
Republicans	31	28
Democrats	19	11
Splinter parties	6	11

the splinter parties, most of them from the border states, show an even clearer majority against German.

Permission for official publication in their own language which Congress denied in 1862 to the German farmers was granted in following years to European peasants as an inducement to immigrate to the United States. Several times between 1867 and 1870 Congress had printed in various languages of the European mainland the annual report of the General Land Office about the free government lands that were open to immigrants. On January 3, 1867, however, Senator Ramsey stated that copies designed for use by Congress would continue to be exclusively in English. Such a strategy to attract immigrants as also conducted by several states, especially those of the Midwest, is not part of the concept of minority rights or law (Kloss 1940, 128-129). According to Pochmann and Schultz (1953, number 4657), a speech of Representative D. B. Henderson on farmer protection appeared in 1888 as a German pamphlet. I was told by the Library of Congress that the records of the session contain nothing which would indicate a corresponding decision by Congress.

In 1874 German Mennonites from Russia—40,000 to 50,000 people— petitioned Congress to be permitted to settle in compact areas in the prairie states of the United States in order that they might not become "Russianized in language and religion" (Correll 1946, 178-222, especially 186, 210, 216). In the elaborate debate over the corresponding bill, House Resolution 2121, the ethnic problem was touched on only occasionally. Senator Edmunds spoke (April 14) against compact denominational areas, and his colleagues Carpenter (April 22) and Sargent (April 23) spoke against compact non-English areas of settlement. Carpenter asked what would happen if 100,000 German Protestants or 20,000

French Communards were permitted to form their own settlements.
not pass, and most Mennonites moved to Canada, which was more ob
Mennonite settlements did spring up, larger ones especially in Kansas,
ones in other prairie states.

2-2 LANGUAGES OTHER THAN ENGLISH IN THE FEDERAL GOVERNMENT DURING THE TWENTIETH CENTURY

The question of communication between the federal government and non-English-speaking citizens continued into the twentieth century and became prominent during World War I. The government, faced with the problem of reaching thousands of citizens who did not speak English, tried various ways of doing so. The Foreign Language Division of the Bureau of Publicity of the Treasury Department, founded in May 1917 (Daniels 1920, 318-320 Americanization Conference 1919, 201-209), advertised the four Liberty Bonds in every sort of reading material in every language used in the United States, including posters, pamphlets, newspapers, etc. The federal government utilized the language of even the minutest ethnic group. At the time of floating the third bond, for example, the Foreign Language Division contacted more than 40,000 organizations of non-English nationalities. In each Federal Reserve District "racial group committees" were established which numbered from 18 to 37 in each of the various districts and which represented a total of 43 nationalities.

The result was that the Foreign Language Division could point to no fewer than 7 million purchased bonds, 41½% of all purchases, while the foreign-born (immigrants and immigrant children) formed at that time only one-third of the population. It should be taken into account, however, that these purchases amounted to only 17¾% of the total value of the purchases. Similarly, the United States Food Administration established local committees of 19 nationalities in 115 municipalities at that time. Their directives in Massachusetts alone (Americanization Conference 1919, 395) were distributed in Armenian, Finnish, Italian, Lithuanian, Polish, Portuguese, and Arabic (Syrian). In 1918 the federal government established a press service which soon served 745 newspapers in 14 languages and which received its materials from the various federal agencies. In 1921 it ceased to be a governmental agency and became an independent private agency. From 1928 on it published *Interpreter Releases*, a newsletter dealing with American legislation and practice concerning immigration and naturalization. In 1937 it changed its name to Common Council for American Unity, which was not a "public-supported agency" (Common Council on American Unity letters).

In 1917 something was apparently attained which one would never have thought possible in 1862. In 1862 great efforts were made for the one-time consideration of a single language, German; in 1917 the federal government appealed yearlong in thirty-four languages to the inhabitants of the country. Is any proof necessary that this was only a device that suited a temporary need of the state?

Characteristically, the first Americanization Conference met in 1919, one year after the end of the war, sponsored by the Department of the Interior in Washington, and that marked the beginning of sharp suppression of almost all foreign languages, as will be discussed in the following chapter (Section 3-4).

In the 1930s Roosevelt's administration made use of the non-English press of the country to broadcast its social and economic policy. In 1937 four lengthy articles dealing with the Social Security Act of 1935 were translated by the government into twenty languages "from Yiddish to Chinese" and distributed to about 1,000 non-English newspapers. The Public Relations Division of the Public Housing Administration at that time distributed its press service, among others, to 682 non-English papers (High 1937, 34).

Also during the 1930s the Federal Theater Project of the Works Progress Administration (WPA) subsidized theaters conducted in minority languages, e.g., in New York City a German theater (1935-1937) under J. E. Bonn and a Yiddish theater (McDermott 1965, 325-334).

As far as we know, the Social Security Administration in the Department of Health, Education, and Welfare was in 1960 the only body which regularly distributed information to the domestic press in languages other than English. The other departments distributed their information for the press only in English.

The Department of Health, Education, and Welfare went on distributing non-English information and is responsible for a program which goes beyond a mere momentary promotion narrowly prescribed by time and purpose.

In the 1950s America awoke to two stirring insights: that its educational system, in quality, was in danger of falling behind that of other countries, notably that of the Soviet Union, and that particularly the level of the knowledge of foreign languages was completely inadequate. This led to three major operations.

First, the United States Office of Education in collaboration with, for example, the Center for Applied Linguistics in Washington and the newly created Languages-of-the-World Archives in Bloomington, Indiana, launched a number of projects by means of which it tried to conduct surveys of all living languages in the world and to locate experts for all major languages which so far had not commonly been taught in the United States.

The *second* measure was a Survey of Language Resources of American Ethnic Groups which was conducted by the United States Office of Education after 1960 in cooperation with the University of Pennsylvania. The man in charge of this survey, Professor Joshua A. Fishman, distributed as early as 1960 a circular letter to the editors of non-English papers which contained, among other things, the following passage: "The maintenance and preservation of your mother tongue is important both to you and to the country at large. What steps can be taken to perpetuate the language and culture of your ethnic group in this country, how can difficulties that stand in the way be overcome, how can greater interest in and awareness of this problem be secured?"

The basic thought is that in its ethnic groups America has a hitherto unused reservoir of bilingual persons who could render the country great services through their knowledge of non-English languages. As a result Fishman submitted a

Table 2-5   Language Instruction in U. S. Public Schools, 1960,
              Kindergarten through Eighth Grade

Language	Instruction by Teacher	Television Instruction	Total
Spanish	485,825	232,810	718,635
French	184,651	101,421	286,072
German	17,535	1,951	19,486
Russian	1,384	1,199	2,583
Italian	1,188		1,188

mimeographed report, *Language Loyalty in the United States* (1964), containing contributions by a number of experts. Two years later a condensed version appeared in book form. In a chapter, "Planned Reinforcement of Language Maintenance," Fishman suggested innovations such as the creation of a federal Commission on Biculturalism (or Bilingualism) in American Life or a Language Maintenance Section in the U. S. Office of Education. He advocated government aid to schools of ethnic groups engaged in formal instruction of the mother tongue. Where the constitutional restrictions concerning the separation between church and state prevent this, private foundations might step in. However, several private colleges and universities as well as hundreds of periodicals, radio broadcasts, and cultural institutions of American ethnic groups are untouched by religious complications and might receive assistance, "whether by tax exemption, by direct support, or even by indirect facilitation and encouragement."

Other possible remedies mentioned by him were a network of language camps for selected children and youths; guidebooks and textbooks for parents and children; the coordination of FLFS programs with the (few) remaining non-English language islands. Even "old country" contacts with immigrants and their children might be fostered.

Third, the United States Office of Education promoted the spread of the so-called FLES (Foreign Languages in Elementary Schools) movement for the expansion of foreign language instruction in the elementary schools (Zeydel 1961, 301-303; Kloss 1967a; Dieckhoff 1965, 18-33, 95-96; Andersson 1969). It is generally considered that this movement began with the introduction of French instruction in the elementary schools of Cleveland in 1922. The first impetus came when, during World War II, various cities of the Southwest and South introduced Spanish as a sign of "hemispheric solidarity." The real growth of the movement, however, took place in the 1950s. The number of pupils receiving foreign language instruction had mounted to 270,000 by 1955 and to over a million (Breunig 1961, 2, 6, 38) by 1960, with Spanish and French leading by far (Table 2-5).

Here and there language minorities have profited by the movement. For example, Spanish was introduced into public schools in West Las Vegas, New Mexico, in 1941 and in Las Cruces, New Mexico, in 1949, and French was introduced in Beaux Bridge, Louisiana, in 1932 and in Van Buren, Maine, in 1942. The benefits to people speaking a minority language have usually accrued because Spanish or French was introduced in a Spanish or French enclave or in a city with a strong infusion of residents who are native speakers of the language (see Table 2-5). More rarely, languages have been introduced which are internationally less widespread, such as Japanese or Italian.

In 1955 there were 506 students of Italian and about 35 each of modern Greek, Norwegian, and Polish on the mainland; in 1960, 1,188 of Italian (among them 772 in grades seven and eight), 53 of Norwegian, about 35 each of modern Greek and Swedish. In Hawaii there were 673 students of Japanese, 283 of Hawaiian, and 214 of Chinese.

This movement spread in a manner characteristic of America. The state governments contributed relatively little, even though the school system is primarily under their authority. The FLES movement spread primarily through cooperation between the relatively independent school districts (Section 1-1), the Modern Language Association, and, as third partner, the federal government. The United States Commissioner of Education, McGrath (1953, 115-119), started the campaign with a speech in St. Louis in May 1952. The United States Office of Education promoted the movement in various ways during the following years. In 1958 a federal act, the National Defense Education Act (NDEA, Publ. L 85-864), provided considerable funds for subsidies to public schools (Section 303a5 of the Act) and loans to recognized private schools (Section 305a of the Act) for the promotion of the teaching of foreign languages (and other subjects) in elementary and high schools. Since then, the United States Office of Education has assumed half of the cost for the purchase of modern teaching materials and has published printed guides for language teachers. It also has organized 133 workshops since 1959 which in 1964 had already trained 15,000 elementary and high school language teachers in modern methods of instruction (Mildenberger 1961, 402-409; Dieckhoff 1965, 7). A special National Council of State Supervisors of Foreign Languages was established. The United States Office of Education subsidized a Franco-American institute at Bowdoin College in Brunswick, Maine, which accepted as students exclusively French-American teachers of French—mostly teaching at Catholic parochial schools—to introduce them to modern teaching methods. In 1961 about 40 were enrolled. The NDEA, which at first was to expire in 1962, was later repeatedly extended.

In the United States, the Bilingual Education Act (BEA) of 1967 (Public Law 20-24) became even more important than the National Defense Education Act (NDEA) for the minority languages. Interest in the Mexican-American child had been on the increase ever since the 1960 census had revealed that in the five southwestern states the population with Spanish surnames had completed an average of only 4.7 years in school compared to 8.1 for the nonwhite and to 12.1 for "Anglo" students fourteen years of age or over. In October 1966, the National Education Association sponsored a conference in Tucson, Arizona, on The Spanish-speaking Child in Schools in the Southwest, which in turn triggered a series of conferences and actions, especially in Texas.

On January 17, 1967, Senator Ralph Yarborough (Democrat, Texas) introduced a bill to provide assistance to local educational agencies in establishing bilingual schools for Mexican-American and Puerto Rican children. It was later reworded so as to include all Spanish-speaking children. Then California Congressman Hawkins and Rayball introduced bills including the French-speaking population.

Finally Congressman James Scheuer of New York rewrote Yarborough's bill, including all children who do not speak English and emphasizing teacher training, development of materials, and demonstration programs. This bill, merged by a committee into a single measure with Yarborough's bill, became the BEA, and therefore no special vote was taken on it. It constitutes Title VII of the Elementary and Secondary Education Amendments of 1967 (ESEA) and provides (Section 703) $85,000,000 to be spent over a period of three years in order to meet "the special educational needs of the large number of children of limited English-speaking ability in the United States" (Section 702), who are defined as "children who come from environments where the dominant language is other than English." It will be seen that this definition broadens the terms of reference, for a child may come from a predominantly non-English home and yet already be familiar with the English tongue. According to Article 705a (8) and 705b (4), nonprofit private schools are to participate in this program.

"My purpose in doing this," Yarborough declared in the Senate on December 1, 1967 (Congressional Record, p. 34703), "is not to keep any specific language alive. It is not the purpose of the bill to create pockets of different languages throughout the country . . . not to stamp out the mother tongue, and not to try to make their mother tongue the dominant language, but just to try to make those children fully literate in English." He thus left open the question of whether the purpose of the new program was to perpetuate minority tongues or to speed up assimilation by a deft shortcut.

At first the House refused to fund the new law, rejecting by 96 to 95 a government request for five million dollars, but late in 1968 Congress appropriated seven and a half million dollars. Among the 76 projects that the United States Office of Education thereupon subsidized, roughly 90% fostered Spanish. Among the non-Spanish projects were two with Chinese (San Francisco and New York City) and one each with Portuguese in Hawaiian Gardens, California; French in Wilton, New Hampshire; Cherokee in Talequah, Oklahoma; and Navajo in Blanding, Utah. One program in Honolulu fostered Japanese, but only in grades 7 to 12.

In 1968 bilingual programs across the United States enrolled 26,000 students. By the end of 1972 this figure had risen to some 112,000. At that time estimates claimed that about five million school-age youngsters—nearly 10% of the total—spoke a first language other than English; four million of these were of Spanish origin.

In 1974 there were some 220 bilingual programs wholly or in part BEA-supported. About the same number of bilingual programs had either received BEA funding in former years or may be supposed to have been "stimulated by the

Act indirectly" (Fishman, 1974, p. 38). Supposing attendance in bilingual schools or sections of schools to have averaged 500, attendance in some 450 schools would have totaled 225,000.

Of 340,000 pupils receiving bilingual public education in 1974-75 under ESEA Title VII grants 292,200 attended schools where Spanish was the only non-English language being taught and used, while 20,400 attended schools where the only other tongue was French (4,200), Navajo (3,600), or some other non-English language. Besides 26,600 were in schools offering and using more than one non-English language; here too Spanish was usually represented. The states with the greatest numbers of bilingual students in 1974-75 were New York (78,200), Texas (72,200), California (63,900), Florida (36,000), and New Jersey (13,400); all others were under the 10,000 mark.

Small numbers were to be found even on Guam (240 Chamorro-English), the Trust Territory (55), and the Virgin Islands (135, Spanish-English).

Probably the earliest Spanish-English programs in the South were the following: in Florida, Miami (1963); in Texas, "Laredo United Consolidated" (1964), Edinburg (1965); in New Mexico, Pecos (1965), Las Cruces and Silver City (both 1967). "Laredo City Schools," sometimes listed as the earliest starter (1960), actually taught Spanish just as a subject matter. But in 1972 Laredo became the first city school system in the United States to conduct all schooling bilingually.

In New York City the East Harlem Block schools became bilingual in 1965, followed by other city schools in 1968, chiefly in the Bronx. In kindergarten the child started with 85% of his instruction in his native language and 15% in the second language. Through the years the second language is used more and more, so that in grade six the child receives 50% of his instruction in his second language. Besides those schools in which the total student population was enrolled in the bilingual program, other New York City schools had numerous other bilingual programs in which only a partial group within the student population was enrolled. In 1972 the predominant language in most of the programs was Spanish. However, some attempts were being initiated at that time to establish bilingual programs in French (for Haitian pupils), Italian, Chinese, and Greek.

Local procedures have varied enormously. In some school systems bilinguality of teaching was meant only for children of non-English mother tongue; in others it was for all pupils. Some schools aimed at preventing or at least slowing down assimilation; others aimed to accelerate it by a deft detour via the mother tongue (cf. Kjolseth 1972). In some schools all branches of learning (except native language skills) are taught bilingually, whereas in others English only is used for some of the branches and the minority tongue only for the rest of them. Use of the minority tongue in some cases terminates with grade two, and in others it may last through grade six.

While most bilingual teaching was done in elementary schools, there were also bilingual public kindergartens and bilingual secondary and college-level institutions such as the Bilingual Upper Grade Center (grades five to eight) of the

Lafayette School in Chicago (1968), where Spanish was the teaching tool for mathematics, science, social studies, and health. The Bilingual Science Program (1970) maintained 10 junior high and 2 intermediate schools in New York City.

For the first time in the history of the United States there existed, if only rudimentarily, an integrated language-oriented program covering Indians, indigenous white minorities (chiefly in New Mexico), and recent immigrant groups. Other bilingual schools for Amerindians (American Indians) were being sponsored by the United States Bureau of Indian Affairs, notably the Navajo-English school at Rough Rock, Arkansas, which became bilingual in 1968, two years after its foundation. Some of these bilingual projects seem to have aroused high hopes among the Indians, some of whom have dreams of "Red Power," of self-determination, and even of statehood, at least for the Navajos.

This shows how easily language movements can change their goals. From the point of view of the federal authorities, the BEA was primarily of socioeconomic relevance, part of a large program to aid the underprivileged masses, whether they were monolingual English-speaking poor whites, or bidialectal Negroes, or Spanish-speaking workers. In the process of collaboration between the local authorities and the parents, this program in most groups retains a purely cultural aspect while in others it may lead to political nationalism.

Incidental mention may be made of the fact that the United States has at least one "Spanish immersion" program (Culver City, Calif., 1972) where monolingual English-speaking grade-school pupils are being taught exclusively (grade one) or chiefly (grades two to four) through the medium of Spanish (Cohen 1974 and 1975). This challenging project, while bound to strengthen the prestige of the minority tongue, obviously does not fall into the category of minority rights. But it certainly would if a similar "English immersion" program with its concomitant regard for mother tongue skills were to be applied to a group of Chicano pupils.

Leibowitz (1969, 44-46, 50-51) rightfully points out that the linguistic segregation made possible by BEA may easily be abused as a pretext to bring about racial segregation.

Besides the BEA, other federal laws have in recent years been used for funding bilingual programs, for example, Title I of the Elementary and Secondary Act of 1965 (ESEA), the Migrants' program; Title III of the ESEA, designed to meet the "educational needs of low income families"; and, insofar as teachers' training is concerned, the Educational Personnel Development Program (EPDEA), and the NDEA of 1958.

Among the many programs subsidized outside the BEA was FLICS (Foreign Language Innovative Curricula Studies) with headquarters in Ann Arbor, Michigan, a statewide program in Michigan drawing on Title III of the ESEA. It was doing three major projects, namely:

1. Dutch Language and Heritage: Christian Reformed (parochial) schools, Holland, Michigan.

2. Polish Language and Heritage: Orchard Lake, Detroit, Hamtramck, and Warren, Michigan.

3. Hispano-American Language and Culture Program: Flint and Adrian, Michigan.

The first-named includes nonpublic schools and even high schools. Another project, under Vera John at Yeshiva University, New York City, dealt chiefly with the kindergarten stage. Most bilingual experimentation, however, goes on in the Southwest, chiefly in California and Texas. With so many programs underway it becomes necessary to know to what extent state legislation is in favor of or stands in the way of bilingual schools. The reader will find in Table 4-6 indications of the present state of affairs.

2-3   THE ETHNIC HERITAGE STUDIES PROGRAM

A federal law dated 6/23/1972 (P. L. 89-10, title IX 901: = subch. VI, 900-900a in title 20—Education; 86 Stat. 346-348) appropriated means for the study of the ethnic heritage of the various groups of the nation. Its preamble read: "In recognition of the heterogeneous composition of the Nation and of the fact that in a multiethnic society a greater understanding of the contributions of one's own heritage and those of one's fellow citizens can contribute to a more harmonious, patriotic, and committed populace, and in recognition of the principle that all persons in the educational institutions of the Nation should have an opportunity to learn about the differing and unique contributions to the national heritage made by each ethnic group, it is the purpose of this subchapter to provide assistance designed to afford to students opportunities to learn about the nature of their own cultural heritage, and to study the contributions of the cultural heritages of the other ethnic groups of the Nation."

Each program assisted under this law was to develop and disseminate relevant curriculum materials for use in elementary and secondary schools and in higher education, to provide training for persons using or preparing to use these materials, and to cooperate with persons and organizations with a special interest in the ethnic group in question. The United States Commissioner of Education, in implementing the Act, was to be assisted by a National Advisory Council on Ethnic Heritage Studies the members of which were to be appointed by the Secretary of the Interior.

The curriculum materials thus prepared were to bear on "the history, geography, society, economy, literature, art, music, drama, language and general culture" of the group or groups concerned and with "the contributions of that group to the American heritage." The wording of the Act leaves open the question of whether the emphasis is to be on the identity and survival of a group or on its contributions to building the American nation. While it is not certain that the Act per se will greatly contribute to the linguistic survival of non-English minorities, it will undoubtedly help create a psychological climate which will be more favorable to language maintenance.

2-4   LANGUAGES OTHER THAN ENGLISH
IN THE DISTRICT OF COLUMBIA

Special mention should be made of the legal situation in the District of
which since 1874 has been directly administered by the federal gove
almost without the participation of the inhabitants. The status of the Disl
Columbia has changed frequently. From 1802 on, the Federal District h
bicamaral elective council. In 1820-1871 it elected its own mayor, and during
period 1871-1874 it was like a territory. Not until 1961 were the inhabitan.
granted the right to vote in presidential elections. Here too we find isolated cases
of promotion of minority languages. For example, German was admitted as a
subject of instruction in elementary schools in 1860, and in 1886 one public
school had 226 students of German (Pempeit 1932, 93-94; *Amerikanische
Schulzeitung* 1870, 39; *Deutscher Pionier* 1866, 50ff.). During the 1930s, public
school buildings were made available for private evening schools in minority
languages (Kloss 1942, 737). There is no legal provision that makes the use of
English mandatory in the public schools of the District. Quite a number of
children attend private schools where a non-English language is used and which
receive subsidies from foreign governments; some of these schools are, however,
on the outskirts in the adjacent counties of Maryland or Virginia.

There seem to have been no official announcements in the minority press
(Wust, personal communication). On the other hand, K. G. Wust (1959, 50-51)
tells us that N. H. Miller obtained "substantial subsidies" for the *Täglicher
Washingtoner Anzeiger*. It is possible that part of these subsidies came from public
funds as well as from party funds.

2-5   OTHER FIELDS OF ACTIVITY OF THE FEDERAL GOVERNMENT

No survey of the minority policy of the federal government would be complete
without taking the following aspects into consideration:

First, the speed and the extent to which the federal government granted
territorial status with an elected representative body and later statehood to areas
with a majority or a strong minority of the inhabitants and voters of non-English
languages. Insights into the struggle for the status of a self-governing territory may
be derived from the reports concerning Louisiana (see Section 5-1), Alaska
(Section 7-2), Missouri (Section 6-1), and Michigan (Section 6-1). Of the struggles
for statehood, those concerning New Mexico (Section 5-2), Alaska, Hawaii
(Section 7-3), and Puerto Rico (Section 7-4) are the most interesting. Sometimes
Congress acted as quickly as the advocates of minority rights could have wished.
But even where Congress hesitated for decades—as it did with New Mexico,
Alaska, and Puerto Rico—the final result nevertheless has to be judged positively.

Second, the extent to which minority law developed inside the territories.
Only part of these regulations originated with the President-appointed executive
and even fewer with Congress. For examples of Congressional initiative in New
Mexico see Section 5-2, in Hawaii see Section 7-3, in Puerto Rico see Section 7-4.

ɪven regulations which originated with the representative body elected by the inhabitants of the territory were subject to the veto of the governor and of Congress. Under these circumstances it is remarkable that minority language promotion was permitted to develop in New Mexico and Puerto Rico during their territorial phases, 1850-1912 and 1900-1952, respectively (Sections 5-2 and 7-4).

Third, the legal situation within the present territories and other possessions of the United States. As a result of this promotion, non-English languages have found entrance into federal publications in recent times. For example, Congressional publications which contain the statute of American Samoa (House of Representatives Committee on Interior and Insular Affairs 1961) and publications of the 1960 census which exclusively concern Puerto Rico (United States Census 1960) are all bilingual.

Fourth, the important role which the Supreme Court and the United States District Courts played in the actual formation of the minority law. In two particular areas the Supreme Court was the real decisive factor: since 1900 in the clarification of the legal status of those possessions which were originally not part of the continental United States (Section 7-1) and since 1923 in the protection of the private schools and the instruction in minority languages which takes place in them (Sections 3-4).

Fifth, regard for and use of non-English languages by the political parties, which are firm, indispensable supports of the state's framework and which have made use of minority languages, especially orally in their election campaigns but also to an appreciable extent in writing, for example, by issuing leaflets or founding or supporting non-English newspapers, again especially during elections.

2-6 TOLERATION OF PROMOTION FROM ABROAD

American law on ethnic groups has a special feature in that the toleration of assistance is not unknown, so that private and even occasionally public institutions serving the culture of ethnic languages are promoted by foreign governments.

In Alaska the Tsarist government for many decades assisted Greek Orthodox schools for Russians and Creoles, which for a long time were more numerous than the English-speaking public schools (Section 7-2).

In San Francisco the Spanish government supported a Spanish private school until the outbreak of the Civil War in 1936 (Brown and Roucek 1937, 391).

The French government, or the Alliance Française subsidized by it, for five decades (about 1908 to about 1958) gave funds for the assistance of French instruction in the public and private elementary and high schools of New Orleans (Kloss 1940, 187) and after 1931 for the private schools of the Union St. Jean Baptiste d'Amérique in the New England states (Mallot 1934, 15); also in 1935 it founded in New York City a private French school, the Lycée Français, which gave instruction entirely in French and for a long time offered grades 1 through 12 (France in New York 1950, 22), but since the 1950s has offered its students only grades 7 through 12. Of the approximately three hundred students in 1956 almost three-fifths had French parents, more than one-fourth were from "American" homes, and the remainder were from various other backgrounds.

The Hungarian government supervised and supported between 1900 and 1914 a Magyar elementary school in Bridgeport, Connecticut.

During the rule of Fascism the Italian government donated prizes and thereby promoted to a considerable extent the teaching of Italian in private elementary schools as well as in public and private high schools (Brown and Roucek 1937, 692; Cosenza 1933-1934 Sections 15-20; 1934-1935, 29). Several of the new states which were created at the end of World War I followed this example: the Baltic states (especially Lithuania), Poland, and Czechoslovakia. No doubt a good many other examples of promotion from the outside could be found. It is especially remarkable that the German-American school system, which at times operated on a gigantic scale, seems to have managed completely without official German promotion.

In the 1960s a considerable number of schools supported by foreign governments sprang up, for example, about six to eight French private schools and, in Washington, D. C., one German-language school. Here is what a prominent American scholar, Joshua A. Fishman (1966, 379), has to say about this issue: " 'Old Country' contacts with naturalized American citizens and their children should be fostered under favorable international circumstances. Italian governmental efforts to keep Italian language, literature, and customs alive among Italo-Americans may be thought of as a form of reverse lend-lease and may very well be a form of debt repayment. . . . Surely there is sufficient ingenuity in American governmental circles to enable us to initiate, control, and (if need be) discontinue activities of this kind as international conditions dictate. For the sake of language maintenance it would seem to be worth our while to institute agreements concerning such activities, at least with a few 'safe' countries, at the earliest opportunity."

Agreements similar to those envisaged by Fishman have since been arranged by Louisiana through the "Council for the Development of French in Louisiana" (Codofil) with the governments of France, Quebec, and Ottawa. According to Codofil chairman James Domengeaux (personal communication of April 21, 1970) "All of our agreements have been made on an informal basis. As we need their particular help and advice on matters which we consider essential to the accomplishment of our program, we agree on a particular subject and have it cleared through the Department of State in Washington." (For details see Section 5-1).

The toleration of this form of promotion is the more noteworthy, since generally the ethnic groups living in the United States were economically better off than those in their kin-states so that this promotion from outside could not in most cases be justified on economic grounds.

CHAPTER THREE

Tolerance-Oriented Rights

3-1 THE WIDEST SPHERE OF TOLERATION

In the introductory remarks about promotion-oriented and tolerance-oriented (or "acquiescent") minority rights, we distinguished four spheres of tolerance: the widest sphere of human, civil, and political rights; a wide sphere of the right to use one's native language; a narrow sphere of the freedom to assemble and organize; and the narrowest sphere of the right to a private nationality school.

Little is generally heard about tolerance-oriented minority rights as long as they are observed, but much is heard as soon as they are violated. Our record may easily create a wrong impression, since it deals for the most part with negative interference. It is, therefore, all the more important to realize from the very beginning that the sphere of civil law, and with it the scope of possible toleration, is incomparably larger in nontotalitarian states than in totalitarian states and that it extends farther in the United States than in many other democracies.

Tolerance-oriented minority rights have been handled very generously in the United States. Only the narrowest of the above-mentioned partial spheres, the right to schools conducted in the mother tongue, had become controversial at the end of the nineteenth century. The three remaining spheres of the tolerance-oriented minority rights remained by and large untouched throughout the nineteenth century. Even if we should later uncover isolated early cases of encroachments in one of these three spheres, they would hardly be important.

The widest sphere of tolerance-oriented nationality rights is under the protection of the first ten amendments to the Constitution (1789-1791), especially Amendments IV to VII which protect life, liberty, and property by guaranteeing the individual a definite form of legal procedure, the essence of which was made binding for the individual states in 1868 by an additional amendment (XIV), and by the First Amendment, which protects freedom of religion. As will be shown later, these amendments were also utilized to protect other spheres of tolerance, including protection of the narrowest sphere: the private foreign-language schools.

In the widest sphere of tolerance-oriented nationality rights, members of national minorities are seldom directly discriminated against because of such membership. To be sure, there are cases where life, personal liberty, property, and freedom of religion or belief of members of national minorities were endangered, but these did not occur because the persons belonged to a particular national minority. When in the nineteenth century the Mormons were prohibited from practicing their religiously motivated polygamy, some non-English members of the sect were affected by this, but not on account of their nationality.

Occasionally, however, creed and nationality overlap. During World War I members of the Christian communist sect of the Hutterites (Mennonites), which was composed of Germans only, were tortured to death in prison because they refused to serve in the military (Ewert 1919; Hartzler 1922; H. C. Smith 1927, 269-293). If the members of the sect had been English-speaking nationals, perhaps they would have been persecuted less severely. Certainly time and again members of a national minority were murdered, and their murderers were not punished. During the violent suppressions of workers in mines or heavy industries by a semipublic factory police, as was common before World War I, people of non-English mother tongue often became the victims of arbitrary acts. There are cases where the murderous assault was deliberately aimed at members of a certain national minority. In 1891 the lynching of several Italians in New Orleans by a mob cast a definite shadow on the diplomatic relations between Italy and the United States; in 1914 several Italians were also lynched in southern Illinois (Foerster 1919, 408; Pisani 1957, 186-187). Nevertheless, lynchings and other kinds of mob outrages have almost always been directed only against people of a different race, and it has been secondary whether these people spoke English or a foreign mother tongue. In the years from 1882 to 1903, in addition to numerous Negroes, 45 Indians, 28 Italians, 20 Mexicans, 12 Chinese, 1 Japanese, 1 Swiss, and 1 Czech were lynched (Cutler 1905, 171-172). We know, on the other hand, that foreign-born persons of every color were punished for many offenses with sentences which were on the average higher than those for American-born whites and even for Negroes, and this we assume was not necessarily because the victims were foreign-born but rather because they spoke a foreign language (Sellin 1935-1936, 212-217).

In the three cases where an entire nationality was denied political, civil, and even natural human rights, special circumstances played a part every time. Either a state of war existed with the kindred state of the particular nationality or else a non-English ethnic group was at the same time also of a different race.

Both factors worked together in the bad treatment of the Japanese Americans who lived on the west coast during World War II. Some 110,000 of these were forcibly resettled in 1942 (Postown 1945, 193-200; Thomas and Nishimoto 1946; Bloom and Riemer 1949; Marden 1952, 171-196; Broom and Kitsuse 1956; Rabl 1958, 91-92, 136-137) on the basis of two executive orders and a law of that year (Executive Orders 9066, 9102; Law of March 21, 1942). Not only were the foreign-born Japanese considered security risks, but also their American-born children, the so-called Nisei, of whom about 10,000 (the Kibei) had been educated for a time at schools in Japan, were thought to be potentially dangerous to the security of the country (Marden 1952, 180ff.). All these forcibly resettled people were removed to relocation centers in the interior, which were under the special control of the War Relocation Authority. In September 1944, there were 18,700 Japanese in Camp Tule Lake, which accommodated only those who had either refused to serve in the American army or refused to formally renounce their citizen's allegiance to Japan. While 61,002 lived in other camps, 28,900 had been given indefinite leaves of absence from the camps. The Supreme Court in a decision of December 18, 1944, ruled that these acts were not unconstitutional under the special conditions of a state of war (*Korematsu* v. *U. S.*; *Hirabayashi* v. *U. S.*; *text in Commager II, 645-650*). The minority view of the Supreme Court justices, however, sounds more convincing to us today. Judges Jackson and Murphy declared that the treatment of the Japanese was racial discrimination. They repudiated the argument that there was not enough time for an individual investigation of all Japanese. In Great Britain, they pointed out, 74,000 enemy aliens had been investigated within six months and detention had been ordered for only 9,000 of them while for 64,000 of them no restriction of their freedom of movement was deemed necessary. The forcible evacuation of the Japanese-Americans was begun four to eight months after Pearl Harbor and was not completely executed until after eleven months. Also on December 18 the Court decided that individuals found to be loyal had to be released at the request of the detained person (*Ex parte* Endo; Rabl 1958, 136). Implicitly in this decision and expressly in the dissenting opinions of Judges Murphy and Roberts, the question was answered in the affirmative as to whether an American citizen who had been removed from his permanent residence by illegal procedures was entitled to return to that place.

Evacuation, not detention, had been the purpose of this legal act. On December 17, 1944, the War Department had canceled the relocation order effective January 2, 1945. On December 18, 1944, the War Relocation Authority ordered all camps to close until January 2, 1946. In the years 1948-1950 courts invalidated also the state laws of California and Oregon that had been directed against the purchase of land by Japanese of foreign birth (*Oyama* v. *State of California*; *Namba* v. *McCourt*; *Fuji* v. *State of California*).

War with the homeland of the ethnic group, not racial aversion, gave rise to special laws pertaining to German-Americans in World War I but not in World War II. There were numerous cases in which German-speaking American citizens were attacked, beaten, injured, tarred and feathered, or deprived of their freedom, and where the cattle of farmers were driven away and private and community houses (including churches) of German-speaking people were damaged. The tarring and feathering, which occasionally resulted in death, became a "kind of popular open-air sport" in some states of the Far West, according to G. Creel (Wittke 1936, 188). The most important source for the terrorism against German-Americans during World War I is Wittke's chapter "Furor Americanus" (Wittke 1936, 163-196). Two sources which were not available are Deitz (1949, 97-121) and *Language Development in Action* (1960).

Federal authorities disapproved of this form of suppression, which therefore cannot be considered to be part of national policy. But the institutions of local self-government (in the wider sense of the word government, which also includes jurisdiction) sanctioned the suppression. They could do so as a result of the strong decentralization in self-government—so characteristic of the United States—which leaves considerable leeway to the local authorities. The actual absence of legal protection which existed at that time in many places for members of the German minority with respect to their life and property can therefore be described neither as a state of law created by the federal or state governments nor as pure anarchy. It is rather a state of law, limited in its very nature by time and place, which was created arbitrarily by the institutions of local self-government at the lowest levels.

Supposing that the charges levied against Germany at that time had been justified, it still must be stressed that no criticism about the homeland of a national minority should have made this national minority atone for that kin-state as an act of collective responsibility. No amount of irritation toward Spain would entitle Washington to restrict the use of the Spanish language in Puerto Rico any more than the conquests of Napoleon I would have justified Great Britain in revoking the privileges of the French in Canada.

One of the driving forces of this puzzling eruption of hatred was, as Zeydel (1961, 298-299) said, a long-time resentment that had been building up among the Anglo-Saxon Americans about the slowness with which some of the German Americans gave up their language and about the prominent place that Germans occupied in the curricula of many big cities. This was in effect a resentment about the results of America's own generous policy toward nationalities.

Even more important, because it was a lasting situation in some parts of the country and not tied to an isolated, exceptional historical situation, is the actual absence of legal protection for many Spanish Americans, especially Mexicans. An extensively documented bibliography about the Spanish Americans and their legal position has been prepared by Charles C. Cumberland (1960). Some early important case studies were Kibbe (1946), Tuck (1946), and Perales (1948).

With alarming frequency we find the claim in the literature that in certain parts of the country Anglo-Americans did not have to fear legal prosecution for killing a Mexican (Taylor 1930, 480; Marden 1952, 142; McDonaugh and Richards 1953, 181). The absence of legal rights for this group of immigrants—in the 1930s alone half a million Mexicans were forcibly deported—became among other things the subject of a petition on April 17, 1959, to the United Nations which pointed out that even Mexicans born in this country were not always protected (Petition of the American Committee 1959, 275-305). This bad treatment was not meted out to the Mexicans because of their foreign language but rather because of their different racial background. Presumably they would have to suffer extensive social discrimination—similar to that against the Negroes—even in cases where English was their mother tongue.

In addition to the human rights claim for protection of life, liberty, property, and opinion and to the civil right to free activity of the individual in the civil order of the country (whether as a partner to a contract or as a plaintiff in legal proceedings), the democratic claim to equality extends also to the political right of the naturalized ethnics to freedom of activity in those domains to which they as citizens should have access. Here belong the exercise of the right to vote as well as the admission to positions as officers and officials in the civil service. This part of the widest extent of toleration seems to have been curtailed only rarely before World War II.

To be sure, naturalization in the United States is made dependent upon the capacity to understand English and in the State of New York the voting right was made dependent upon the ability to read and write English by an amendment (first proposed in 1894) in 1921 and a law of 1923. For many state or honorific offices a command of English is required. Such prescriptions represent a "nonpromoting" but not a "nontolerating" attitude. These two should not be mistaken for each other. Nontoleration would have existed, for example, if it had been required that the candidates for an office have English as their mother tongue.

When, as will be shown later, Spaniards were excluded from a jury in New Mexico, it was presumably not because Spanish was their mother tongue but either because they had no command of the English language or because they were considered to be of a different race. This does not mean to deny that the nonpromotion of his native tongue could often bring the member of a national minority into a difficult situation. This nonpromotion will arouse particular bitterness in cases where an exception is made in favor of some other non-English language, as for example, in New Mexico and Hawaii. In places where a large coherent group of people speaking a non-English tongue settles and where the individual hence has no opportunity to acquire a fluency in English, nonpromotion may of course equal nontolerance in its results.

If, for example, in Puerto Rico the occupancy of all government positions had been made dependent on a fluent mastery of the English language, formally the Spanish language would certainly not have been promoted, but the individual member of the group would not have had his civil rights curtailed. In fact, however, such a regulation would have amounted to the exclusion of almost all Puerto Ricans from government positions, because, outside of the capital, San Juan, most of them had absolutely no opportunity to acquire sufficient oral fluency in the use of the English language.

In such cases, however, Anglo-Americans have in general not been narrow-minded. Where, as in Puerto Rico, the simple toleration of the non-English language was not sufficient, they have promoted it; that is, they have recognized it officially. An attempt by Congress in 1912 failed to curtail the political rights of the New Mexico Spaniards, who in their isolation remained monolingual and were becoming acquainted with English only by great efforts.

As of 1961 in thirty of the fifty states the right to vote was not made dependent upon language qualifications. In four of them this was particularly stressed by special clauses. The constitution of New Mexico (1912) expressly stated that the voting right must not be withheld on account of unfamiliarity with the English language; that of Louisiana put the ability to write in other languages on an equal footing with that of English. In North Dakota people who had no command of the English language were permitted to let themselves be helped either by persons chosen by them personally or by the election officials (Section 16. 1208 Cent. Code 1960). In Indiana instructions designed to inform the voter had to be printed, in addition to English, in any language deemed necessary (Sections 27-5011, 1949 Statutes).

Of the twenty remaining states, four (Alaska, New York, Oregon, and Washington) demanded in general a command of English; Hawaii made a command of Hawaiian, which immigrants do not know, equal to that of English. Five states required that persons be able to read and write parts from the federal Constitution (three states) or from the state constitution (two states): Alabama, Georgia, North Carolina, South Carolina, and Oklahoma.

Ten states required only that the respective voter be able to read sections from the federal Constitution (three) or state constitution (four), or from both (three): Arizona, Connecticut, Delaware, California, Maine, Massachusetts, Mississippi, New Hampshire, Nevada, and Wyoming (Margolin 1961).

Requirements unfavorable to immigrants could therefore be found primarily in most of the New England states and the states of the Old South as well as all Pacific Coast states; fourteen of the twenty states are coastal states. The relatively stricter demands for an ability to read and write were made especially by some Southern states where they were obviously aimed more at the Negroes than at non-English nationalities. In most of the classical immigrant states—the entire Midwest, Texas, New Jersey, Pennsylvania—this requirement was unknown. Among the twenty states mentioned above only a few are typical immigrant areas: parts of New England, Hawaii, California, and above all New York.

Especially in New York City, hundreds of thousands of Puerto Ricans, who did not know English but who had come into the country as American citizens, were affected by the New York voting qualification. Newspaper reports speak of 200,000 people in New York City alone who have no knowledge of English. Of the Puerto Ricans who came to the mainland during 1958, 43% had no knowledge of English.

A Puerto Rican merchant, Jose Camacho, charged in 1958 that this New York provision violated the Constitution, but he was turned down in all courts, the last time in October 1959 by a federal court in New York (*Washington Post* October 22, 1961; Hancock 1960, 152). During the trial before the court of appeals in Albany all lawyers were provided by the American Jewish Congress; they referred to the Constitution as well as to the United Nations charter and the General Declaration of Human Rights (Section 8-7).

In 1965 the situation was remedied by Congress in Section 4(e) of the Voting Rights Act which declared what was necessary to secure the rights under the Fourteenth Amendment of persons educated in American-flag schools in which the predominant classroom language was other than English: "No person who demonstrates that he has successfully completed the sixth primary grade in a public school in, or a private school accredited by, any State or territory, the District of Columbia, or the Commonwealth of Puerto Rico in which the predominant classroom language was other than English, shall be denied the right to vote in any Federal, State, or local election because of his inability to read, write, understand, or interpret any matter in the English language."

An exception was made for states in which a different level of education is presumptive of literacy and where therefore the same level may be held to be indicative of literacy in American-flag schools which do not have English as their major language.

This provision has been contested by the government of New York State, which held that Congress had power to enact such a law only if and after the judiciary had decided that the English literacy requirement was incompatible with the Equal Protection Clause of the federal Constitution. Actually as late as 1959, the Supreme Court had decided that an English literacy test was allowable under the Constitution (*Lassiter* v. *Northampton Election Board*). They won their case in the Federal District Court of the District of Columbia but lost on June 13, 1966, before the Supreme Court (*Katzenbach* v. *Morgan*) where Judge Harlan gave a dissenting opinion. Concerning the whole issue, see Leibowitz (1969, 30-35). He holds that the original intention of New York's English literacy clause at the time of its adoption (1915) was to prevent 1,000,000 Yiddish-speaking Jews from voting.

On the same day as the decision in *Katzenbach* v. *Morgan,* the Supreme Court held that it was constitutional to subject to an English literacy test a woman who had been born in Puerto Rico and who was literate in Spanish but who could not submit evidence that she had successfully completed the sixth grade of a Commonwealth school (*Cardona* v. *Power*). Justices Douglas and Fortas, however, held that she should have been permitted to pass a Spanish literacy test.

Obviously the introduction of the new concept of American-flag schools, while a convenient expedient for the legislators, cannot be considered wholly satisfactory. It seems to discriminate invidiously against those American citizens who, while equally unfamiliar with the English language and equally literate in another language—perhaps even Spanish—happen not to have attended an American-flag school. It is open to dispute whether this arrangement is compatible with the Constitution (384 United States 656-657) and with the Covenant on Civil and Political Rights adopted by the United Nations in December 1966. Against this view some will hold that such discrimination as there was cannot be considered arbitrary and invidious, since a person educated in an American-flag school may be supposed to be better grounded in American history and civics than one who received his training in a school other than an American-flag school and therefore it is fair to assume that he is better qualified to cast his vote with a grasp of the issues at stake.

It is, of course, not sufficient that immigrants obtain the right to vote; they must also be permitted to exercise it. The Mexicans—similarly to the long-established conditions with Negroes—have been prevented time and again from exercising this right. As a result, by far the greatest number of foreign-born Mexicans did not bother to become naturalized since the process had no practical value (Walker 1928-1929, 465-467; Bogardus 1930-1931, 74-88; Bogardus 1940-1941, 166-174; Humphrey 1943-1944, 322-355).

This discrimination consequently prevented the Mexicans from developing into a genuine national minority which possesses the citizenship of the host country. "If you become a citizen but are treated as a foreigner, what have you gained?" was the typical complaint (Bogardus 1940-1942, 168). It should not be overlooked, however, that naturalization is frequently not coveted because the immigrant, following his Mexican and Latin tradition, considers problems of government and the community as something that has to be cared for by officials who are paid to do this (Walker 1928-1929, 466). Authorities, on the other hand, often treat even members of the second generation as aliens (Bogardus 1940-1941, 171).

The withholding of political rights is incidentally subject to the same considerations as that of human rights: the Mexicans are affected by such withholding not because they speak a foreign language but because they have a different color of skin.

In individual cases knowledge of the English language was made a prerequisite for ordinary vocational positions which were in no way connected with politics. An 1897 Pennsylvania law required that laborers occupied in mines who intended to become miners had to take an examination during which they, among other things, had to prove their command of English; this was designed to keep out the Slavic workers (Warne 1904, 87-88). Much more frequent than is evident from such isolated state regulation were cases of actual discrimination against members of non-English groups in the open labor market. But in such cases society, and not the state, discriminated; such discrimination is not directly related to the legal status of linguistic minority.

3-2   THE WIDE SPHERE OF TOLERATION: THE USE OF THE LANGUAGE

The wide sphere of tolerance-oriented nationality rights concerns the toleration of the use of the mother tongue. Since mother tongue use within homeland and family can hardly be prevented, this refers primarily to use of the mother tongue in public (on the streets, on the railroads, on the telephone, in meetings) or even its use on signs by private business.

Freedom of assembly borders closely on the freedom of organization and belongs, therefore, partially within the narrower sphere of toleration. Use of the language, however, goes beyond this sphere because it refers also to participation by members of a nationality and use of the nationality language in meetings which are not held by an ethnic organization. Freedom of assembly is protected in the First Amendment (1789-1791).

During World War I several attempts were made to prevent the use of the German language completely. The driving forces behind this attempt were the so-called councils of defense. Through federal law a National Council of Defense was established on August 29, 1916, to which similar councils of individual states, cities, and counties were gradually attached and subordinated. A decree issued by the Victoria County Council of Defense in Texas in 1918 reads as follows: "The National and State Councils of Defense request that the use of the German language be proscribed among us. . . . We call upon all Americans to abandon the use of the German language, in public and private, as an utmost condemnation of the rule of the sword."

As impossible as it was to suppress the use of German in the private sphere, thorough and successful attempts were made to suppress its use in public. In Findlay, Ohio, the town council levied a fine of $25 for the use of the German language in the streets (Wittke 1936, 186). In Turner County, South Dakota, the County Council of Defense passed a similar decree (Wittke 1936, 187). On May 19, 1918, an appeal was put before the House of Representatives by the select and common councils of Philadelphia to outlaw the use of the German language in public meetings throughout the United States (House Journal, 65th Congress, 2d Session, p. 394).

Before the end of the war, nevertheless, several of these measures began to turn not only against German but against all minority languages. In May 1918, Governor W. S. Harding of Iowa issued a proclamation which prohibited the use of a language other than English in public places, over the telephone, and on the railroad; public speeches could be given only in English; church services for those who did not know English had to be held in private homes (Kloss 1942, 942-944).

This proclamation, which was also directed against instruction in non-English languages, led to heavy protest from the Czechs and Danes of Iowa. The regulation did not remain on paper. In Scott County, which was almost exclusively settled by people from northern Germany, four women had to pay a fine to the Red Cross on orders from the Scott County Council of Defense because they had held telephone conversations in German (Wittke 1936, 186-187).

A 1919 law of the state of Nebraska went not quite so far when it prescribed the use of English for meetings which concerned themselves with any public affair other than churches and lodges (Thompson 1920, 296-297; Kloss

1942, 699). Proposed bills against the use of non-English languages in business signs and advertisements in the State of New York in 1919 failed because of the objections made by the New York Bar Association (1919, Memos 158-159; Kloss 1942, 700, 710). All this passed by rather rapidly; it had a lasting effect on the use or, rather, the increasing decline of the German language, but not on the general legal situation.

The right to use non-English languages in accounting books of firms was protected by the Supreme Court in a decision of January 1, 1926 (*Yu Cong Eng* v. *Trinidad*), which invalidated a Philippine language, thus attempting to force the Chinese in the Philippines to abandon their bookkeeping in Chinese. The Territorial Supreme Court in Manila had tried to save the law by an interpretation which cannot be derived from its wording: it prescribed the use of one of the named languages only in addition to and not instead of Chinese. The decision was formally made on the basis of the Philippine Bill of Rights, especially its due-process-of-law clause; but the same court had already stated in 1907 that this clause had to be interpreted exactly in the sense of the American Bill of Rights (*Serra* v. *Mortiga*; cf. also *Kepner* v. *United States*).

3-3   THE NARROW SPHERE OF TOLERATION: MINORITY ORGANIZATIONS OTHER THAN SCHOOLS

Associations and Church Congregations

Toleration of minorities in the narrow sense concerns the group institutions of minorities. This refers, first of all, to secular associations of any kind as well as to church congregations and church synods. To this we add three (in America very widely spread and important) private institutions: press, movie theaters, and radio. In Western and Central Europe, press and movie theaters are also private institutions while radio, on the other hand, is normally in public hands. That radio remained in private hands in the United States led to an immense quantitative variety as far as programs in English are concerned; this result is even more noticeable with respect to non-English programs.

Even though the press, movies, and radio, economically speaking, usually are not community enterprises but rather are profit-making enterprises of single persons or groups of persons, nevertheless they are in function and essence community-creating and community-promoting institutions.

We also consider as part of this sphere of tolerance-oriented rights the toleration of those private schools which are founded not by associations but by individual persons as means of profit making. It may happen in this connection that a minority may be permitted to maintain its community institutions but not to cultivate its own language in these institutions.

Freedom of assembly also belongs for the most part to this category, that is, meetings which are held by members for members of an ethnic group, especially those of organizations of an ethnic group.

The First of the Amendments to the Constitution, added 1789-1791, guarantees freedom of assembly and freedom of the press. Freedom of organization, however, which is so vitally important to ethnic groups, is guaranteed nowhere, neither in the Constitution nor by federal law. Freedom of organization has always been taken for granted since the establishment of the Union (Freund 1904, 516-521). The Commonwealth Constitution of the Philippines of May 14, 1935, which was drafted under American control, includes in Article III, paragraph 6, among the basic rights of citizens the "right to form associations or societies."

Only three kinds of secular organizations (private militias, labor unions, and the so-called secret orders or oath-bound organizations) have encountered difficulties at certain times and in certain regions, difficulties which were suffered also by those nationalities which intended to create such organizations. The trade unions partially originated among the Germans in the United States and remained for decades primarily a concern of the immigrant groups. Long after World War I, for example, the Mexican farm workers in the Southwest and the Asian plantation workers in Hawaii still encountered the greatest of difficulties in their attempts to organize unions.

The right to establish religious organizations stands under the special protection of the First Amendment of the Constitution. Freedom of religion occupies a special place within the framework of the world view that found its expression in the American political and social order, since religion was the reason for the establishment of the Puritan colonies in New England (1620). It, therefore, became to an especially high degree a sustaining and moving force of American developments (Stimson 1923, 147).

Until about 1800 the religious congregation itself was promoted in many instances as an institution that was a quasi necessary institution from a political viewpoint. This was the attitude also toward church schools so that these institutions assumed semi-public status.

During the first large-scale sales of land in Ohio in 1787-1788, the sixteenth section in every township was set aside for schools and the twenty-ninth section for church use; and similarly, as late as 1795 Connecticut set aside the income from the sale of the Western Reserve and added it to the school fund for the "schools and the gospel."

Federations of associations and congregations encountered in principle as few difficulties as did individual associations and congregations—even such gigantic organizations as the Deutsch-Amerikanische Nationalbund (1901-1917) which temporarily organized over two million people in over seven thousand associations. The cooperation between associations of different ethnic groups was also not impeded. In Chicago the United Societies for Local Self-Government, which comprised German, Czech, Polish, Italian, and other associations, operated after 1906 (Kloss 1937, 260). In Nebraska a statewide Interracial Group worked for the non-English press of the state, 1934-1935.

Since World War I when the purchase of Liberty Bonds and other matters was at stake, it has become a common practice of the state, and even more of the local authorities, to establish such interethnic organizations, or at least they were promoted with the purpose of increasing the interest of the minorities in the goals, ideas, and way of life of America.

Beginning in 1921 an English-language tutelary organization for the leading organizations of the non-English nationalities of America existed in the Common Council for American Unity. After 1928 it published twice a week the newsletter *Interpreter Releases* (Section 2-2), an information service about American legislative and legal practices concerning questions of immigration and naturalization. Furthermore, it distributed twice weekly a multilanguage news service to the approximately 600 stations throughout the United States which have regular broadcasts in non-English languages and a weekly press service in 23 languages to the 850 non-English newspapers of the country. In 1959 it merged with the American Federation of International Institutes, an organization of aid and advisory centers for immigrants in 40 cities, to form the American Council for Nationalities Service, which continued the old activities of the Common Council without changes but at the same time also fulfilled tasks on the local level.

The toleration of group institutions of non-English nationalities was strongly emphasized by the fact that the legislatures of the various states, or at times even the Congress of the United States, granted them the status of legal persons, and often the ethnic function of the association was openly stated in their charter.

In 1819, in the Dartmouth College Case, the Supreme Court guaranteed freedom from state interference to organizations which have received a charter but which were threatened, not in spite of the charter but because of it (*Trustees of Dartmouth College* v. *Woodward*). The charter made these institutions private corporations, which are under the control of the legislatures. A legislature occasionally went so far as to grant an ethnic group a legally binding corporate status and with it indirectly legal autonomy (Section 2-1). As an example of the recognition given by Congress to an umbrella organization of a minority, we may cite the charter which was granted to the Deutsch-Amerikanischen Nationalbund in 1907 (Kloss 1937, 256; *Mitteilungen des Deutschen Pionier-Vereins von Philadelphia* 1908, 27).

Often charters were granted which defined the continued cultivation of the language of the ethnic group as the function of the organization. This was especially frequent with respect to church congregations. Sometimes such charters contained the provision that these language clauses should never be changed, a provision which proved impossible to realize in practice. Consequently, it was specified in Ohio by an 1868 law that in church organizations such language clauses could be changed at any time by a majority vote of the adult members of that particular language group (Kloss 1942, 704).

Press, Radio, Movies

In 1960 there were in the United States approximately 19,000 news publications, 11,000 newspapers, and 8,000 magazines. Among them were 620 non-English publications. There were approximately 4,000 radio stations, among them 547 which had regular non-English broadcasts. This number does not take into account the 42 broadcasts devoted to language instruction, 19 for French, 9 for Spanish, 7 for German, 4 for Italian, 2 each for Yiddish, Polish, and Scandinavian. In reality these broadcasts benefit the particular language groups even though they are normally not addressed to those groups.

In 1958 there were approximately 13,000 movie theaters, of which 550 showed in 1960 almost exclusively non-English movies.

Of these three categories, the press is by far the oldest. The first German newspaper in the United States was edited by none other than Benjamin Franklin (1732); the oldest newspapers that were still existing in 1960 stem from the first half of the nineteenth century: *New Yorker Staats-Zeitung*, German, 1834; *Crespusculo*, Taos, New Mexico, Spanish, 1835. A survey of the German press may be found in Wittke (1957) and in Arndt and Olson (1961). For the entire press of the country, including the non-English press, see Rowell (1869-1908); Ayer (1880-); and Fishman (1966, 51-73).

In 1880, 770 newspapers were listed, among them 620 (80%) German; in 1960, 650 newspapers, among them 60 (9%) German; 101 (16%) Spanish; 43 Italian; 40 Czech; 38 Polish; 34 Magyar; 26 each French and Scandinavian (13 Norwegian, 10 Swedish, 3 Danish); 24 Yiddish; 19 Lithuanian; 17 Yugoslav; 24 Ukrainian (among them 8 Carpatho-Ukrainian); 14 Russian, 13 Chinese, 12 Japanese, 11 Armenian. In addition to these there were 4 to 8 each Arabic, Bulgarian, Dutch, Portuguese and 1 to 3 each Estonian, Hebrew, Lettish, Welsh, and White-Buthenian newspapers.

The freedom of the non-English press has, however, been endangered several times, particularly during World War I (Section 3-3).

The non-English radio of the United States offers the imposing panorama in Table 3-1.

In addition there were three stations with emission in Amerindian languages (other than Cherokee, Navajo, and Ute), Finnish, Irish, Pennsylvanish (2 listed under "Dutch," 1 under "German"), Russian: two stations each with Armenian, Cherokee, Hawaiian (KLEI, Kailua, Hawaii, the other in Angola, Indiana 2 hours, Hindi, Korean, Rumanian, Ute); one each in Albanian, Arabic ("Lebanese"), Créole of Haiti, Dutch, Eskimo, Estonian, Gaelic. The number of stations given in Table 3-1 excludes the purely educational broadcasts that were mentioned in the first paragraph of this section. Other tables giving information about non-English radio broadcasts are to be found in Fishman (1966, 77-79) and in the German edition of this book (1963, 59-60).

It is important that the languages of the Indian population are broadcast: a total of 27 stations in Navajo, 2 each in Cherokee and Ute, 4 in other Amerindian tongues, and 19 Eskimo. The Tlingit and Eskimo are broadcast in Alaska. Japanese and Filipino broadcasts are almost exclusively in Hawaii.

As early as 1942 there were regular broadcasts in 26 non-English languages from 205 of the 915 stations that existed then, broadcasts for an estimated 15 million listeners, among them 3 million with no knowledge of English. In May

Table 3-1   Non-English Radio Broadcasts in the U.S.A.
(Source: 1970 Broadcasting Yearbook, pp. D58-D60. Figures from Puerto Rico excluded.)

Languages	Number of Stations	Station with Highest Number of Hours per Week
Spanish	234	11 exclusively Spanish (3 Arizona, 3 California, 2 Colorado, 3 Texas); KABQ in Albuquerque, N.M., 111 hours.
Polish	116	WOPA, Oak Park, Ill. 28½ hours.
Italian	87	WEVD, New York, 18½ hours.
German	80	WMIL, Milwaukee, 26½ hours.[1] (KWYN, Mynne, Ark., "88%"; WICR-FM, Indianapolis, either 75 or 7.5 hours).
French	64	KFJZ, Ft. Worth, Texas: 24 hours.
Greek	25	WEVD, New York: 10 hours.
Portuguese	21	KBRG-FM, San Francisco: 15 hours.
Japanese	13	KTRG, Honolulu: 28 hours.
Slovak	13	KFRD, Rosenberg, Texas: 8 hours.
Scandinavian Languages[2]	12	KWDM, Des Moines, Iowa: 3 hours.
Hungarian	10	KMAX-FM, Arcadia, Cal. 3 hours
Navajo	9	KYVA, Gallup, N.M.: 35 hours.
Yiddish[3]	9	WEVD, New York: 33½ hours.
Filipino languages	8	KORL, Honolulu: 80 hours.
Ukrainian	7	4 stations, 1 hour each.
Serbo-Croatian[4]	7	3 stations, 2 hours each.
Lithuanian	6	WEVD, N.Y. and WHIL, Boston: 1 hour each.
Czech[5]	5	KMIL, Cameron, Texas: 7 hours.

[1] KWYN, Wynne, Ark. "88%"; WICR-FM, Indianapolis, either 7.5 or 75 hours.

[2] 11 stations "Scandinavian," 1 "Norwegian."

[3] In the Yearbook called "Jewish."

[4] 3 Croatian, 3 Serbian, 1 "Yugoslavian."

[5] 2 Bohemian, 3 "Czechoslovak."

1942, the broadcast industry established the Foreign Language Radio Wartime Control as an agency of self-control, which had its code approved by the federal government in May 1942 and incorporated into the wartime regulations in July 1942 (Brown and Roucek 1945, 384-391).

We are far less well informed about the non-English movie theaters than about the radio. We may cite as an example that there were 30 Spanish movie theaters in New York City in 1960. There were eight German movie theaters in 1954, among them three in Greater New York City with others in Baltimore, Chicago, Milwaukee, Los Angeles, and San Francisco (Kloss 1954, 118).

The case of the non-English movie theater is different insofar as it requires the existence of a country which continuously produces movies in the language of the particular minority, a producing country from which these movies may be imported into the United States. This supply is missing, for instance, in cases of Basque, Eskimo, Yiddish, and the Indian languages. The numerous ethnic groups coming from countries which are communist today, from the Chinese to the Poles, certainly encounter difficulties getting films in their mother tongue.

Radio and movies which cater to language minorities are under less competitive pressure from television programs than are radio and movies which cater to Anglo-American audiences, since television programs are so difficult and expensive to produce that only a few minorities can afford them.

Some Special Institutions

In conclusion, we may characterize several special institutions which are particularly notable to the European observer:

Court Jurisdiction. To take some of the pressure from the regular courts, the state of New York had established permanent private courts of arbitration. Based on this provision, a Jewish Court of Arbitration was formed in New York City in February 1920. It was composed of rabbis, professional judges, merchants, and lawyers. It was particularly advantageous that the members of the courts have a command of the non-English languages spoken by the parties involved, in most cases Yiddish (Claghorn 1923, 217-218). In Section 5-2 there is reference to special jurisdiction by the Penitentes in New Mexico.

Militia Units. As early as July 1775, there were the Deutschen Füsilier (German Fusiliers) in Charleston, South Carolina; in 1842 one company each of artillery and riflemen; in 1859 a second artillery company and a company of hussars. Before the outbreak of the Civil War six companies existed (*Deutscher Pionier* 1871, 37, 167, 214). We have proof that in the year 1839 there were several militia companies with German as the language of command: in New York (among them one artillery company), Philadelphia, Pittsburgh, and Baltimore (*Deutsche Vierteljahresschrift* 1839, 69). A Deutsches Militärkorps (German Military Corps), consisting of fusiliers, dragoons, and artillery, came into existence in St. Louis in 1842 (*Deutscher Pionier* 1871, 301). Among four companies documented for 1845 in New Orleans, one was mounted, the Louisiana Dragoons (1831). German companies were officially dissolved in 1854 in Louisville, Kentucky, proof that they were not considered merely harmless rifle clubs (*Handwörterbuch des Grenz- und Auslanddeutschtums*, III, 1938, 282, 408). These companies played a military role, for example, in the Mexican War (1846-1848). In addition to the few examples of German militia units cited here, there existed less frequently units of other nationalities, such as Polish (Thomas and Znaniecki, II, 1927, 1582).

Local Institutions of the Old Country. Immigrants attempted here and there to transplant local institutions of the old into the new country. Catholic Germans from the Volga introduced into their new settlements in Kansas in 1876 such administrative institutions as the Gemeindevorsteher (mayor), Büttel (bailiff), and Gemeindeversammlung (town meeting). However, since these institutions stood outside of the established American administrative system, they had no authority whatsoever (Sallet 1931, 66; Laing, II).

The Japanese in Hawaii were more successful in transplanting the mura, the village organization of their home country. However, during this transplant the mura was transformed from a political institution into a private body in charge of language schools, welfare, and leisure time activities (Lind 1939, 207).

Publishing Houses. As a rule the development of private publishing houses is naturally a matter of commercial undertaking. One can comprehend what it means for ethnic groups to be able to establish private publishing houses when one considers that in the countries of eastern Europe publishing is controlled by the public authorities, so that there exclusion of an ethnic language from the assistance program of the state automatically brings the publication of books to an end, as, for example, was the case with Yiddish in 1949 in the U. S. S. R. From time to time among several language groups who emigrated to North America, literary life developed more quickly and more richly than it then did in the country of origin as, for example, in Albanian, Yiddish, Lithuanian, and Syrian Arabic.

Theater. The theater is as unrestricted in its development in the United States as are the movies, and its history is much older. A fully developed theater with professional actors existed especially in the German language (Zucker 1943, 255-264) and, after 1890, in Yiddish. The original French opera in New Orleans also deserves mentioning. All things considered, the American climate was and is not too favorable for the theater in any language, but for reasons which do not concern minority rights.

Television. Television in the languages of the nationalities is as free of restrictions as is radio but is, of course, far more difficult and expensive to establish so that so far it has not even approximately reached the same proportions. Furthermore, there is no agency which gathers information about it. A television station in New York City (WOR) televises Spanish movies with English subtitles daily. There was for a time a weekly program in Pennsylvania Dutch in Reading, Pennsylvania. There was also a weekly telecast in German around 1956 in St. Louis, Missouri. These are random finds.

Libraries. Since the public administration was very generous in the field of public libraries there was little need for the minorities to develop their own (Section 4-6), although this would have been possible within the legal framework. Some of their organizations and institutions did establish important specialized libraries for the history and literature of the respective ethnic groups, but their holdings (for example, those of the German Americans) were neglected and even lost after the lingual absorption of the ethnic group.

In addition to libraries and archives we also find museums of individual nationalities, for example, the Polish museum in Chicago (1928).

Minority Languages in Anglo-American or General Institutions

In America more than in Europe, institutions can be found which are in the hands of neither the state nor a municipality but which fulfill functions which are designed to benefit all inhabitants equally. Here, too, we find many instances of the use of minority languages. To cite three out of hundreds of examples:

1. Numerous transportation and utility companies, which in Europe are mostly in public hands, are purely commercial enterprises in the United States. As late as 1937 signs in Italian and Yiddish appeared on the platform of a subway line in Philadelphia.

2. The Wisconsin Historical Society published in 1856 and 1857 some yearbooks in German and Norwegian.

3. Perhaps the most impressive example is the one offered by the nineteenth century banks which issued bilingual banknotes. From some time in the 1830s, about the time of the expiration of the charter of the Bank of the United States in 1836, until the Civil War, we find an almost unrestricted freedom on the part of individual private banks in issuing their own banknotes. German notes were issued by an Allentown, Pennsylvania, bank which collapsed in 1842 and by a bank in Canton and Wooster, Ohio (Kloss 1937, 209). They were preceded in March 1833 by the Western Bank in Philadelphia, Pennsylvania. The five-dollar notes of this bank depicted William Tell's apple shot, while its ten-dollar notes had a picture of George Washington (according to the Reading, Pennsylvania, *Adler* of March 5 and March 11, 1833). Among the periodicals which at that time kept the public continuously up to date about the authenticity of the banknotes were several in German, for example, Kennedy's *Banknoten Reporter* (1853-1858) and Gerhard's *Banknoten Reporter* (1856-1865). See the Reading *Adler* for November 16 and December 21, 1858, and for June 21, 1859, and Arndt and Olson (1961, 364, 378).

Attempts at Oppression around 1920

During World War I the authorities of many states began to prohibit the use of all non-English languages, even in organizations and church congregations. The stiff proclamation of Governor Harding of Iowa dated May 23, 1918, has already been mentioned (Section 3-2). In Iowa, Missouri, and Texas the State Councils of Defense solicited information on all clergymen who still dared to preach in German (Wittke 1936, 187; Kloss 1942, 698, 704). The statement by M. R. Davie (1936, 502) that German sermons were prohibited by law in Missouri does not seem to hold.

According to a federal law of October 6, 1917 (Kloss 1942, 706), the non-English press was forbidden for the duration of the war to publish news and articles about the war and foreign policy without first submitting an English

translation to the post office at the place of publication (Park 1922, 440-441;
Wittke 1936, 173-174). The Postmaster General could exempt newspapers from
this duty, and did so for 650 newspapers, among them 74 in German. Attempts
broke down in Congress to bring about a total prohibition of foreign-language
newspapers, whether in an "enemy" language (German, Magyar, Bulgarian) or in
all non-English languages. On the other hand, in Oregon a law of January 20,
1920, was in effect until 1927 which obligated all non-English papers to print
their contents simultaneously in full English translation (Kloss 1942, 706-707). A
similar draft, which was submitted in the State of New York on January 26, 1920
(No. 278, Thayer Bill), failed as a result of a memorandum submitted by the New
York Bar Association (Kloss 1942, 707-710), which based its opposition on the
provisions of Article I (8) of the state constitution about freedom of opinion and
the press, on the due-process-of-law clause of Article I (6) of the federal
Constitution, and on Article I (8) of the federal Constitution which protects
interstate commerce. The memorandum contained the important statement:
"that the enjoyment by a citizen of his rights, whether he be native-born, or
naturalized, cannot be made dependent upon his ability to speak, read, or write
the English language."

The opportunities offered by the widest, the wide, and the narrow spheres
of the tolerance-oriented minority rights have been utilized by all nationalities
(see Section 4-8). Great differences in details may of course partially be explained
by varying numerical strength. A Polish movie theater presupposes that a certain
minimum number of Poles live in the same community and, if in a large city, in
the same part of the city. Equally important is the character of the nationality—
there are more sociable and less sociable ethnic groups. Even more important is
the level of education. Among the two million Mexicans, for example, there were
so many illiterates that their press long remained underdeveloped.

The issue underlying American policy regarding the use of non-English
languages in private activities has aptly been summed up by Leibowitz (1969, 14):
"The author would question neither the existing official character of English nor
the desirability of an open articulation of the language's status. What should be
clarified is what follows from such an assumption or articulation. An official
language would properly regulate governmental proceedings and establish a
customary norm for the country. It should not, however, imply or require statutes
aimed at regulating business or social adjustment."

3-4   THE NARROWEST SPHERE: THE PRIVATE SCHOOLS

The Position of the Private Schools in General

The Early Public-Financed Private School. The ideal private school for its
sponsors is the one which is free to combine the major advantage of the private
schools (the self-administration of one's own problems free from state interference) with the major advantage of the public school (financing by public funds).

In the United States schools were at first financed by private funds. When
the idea of using tax money for the support of the school system gained ground,

several states at first adopted the policy of supporting the existing private schools with these public funds. This provision is, for example, contained in three school bills of the State of New York from 1795 to 1813 (Kloss 1942, 719, 720), in a bill of 1854 in Texas (Section 6-2), and in 1855 in Indiana (Kloss 1942, 948). Other states granted only assistance for needy children, as is shown in bills passed in Pennsylvania in 1802 and 1804 (Kloss 1942, 722-723). In New York the subsidized school had to be predominantly English (a nationality language could be taught only as a subject); Indiana and, at the beginning, Texas knew no language clauses. In Pennsylvania the German private school was even granted equal status with the English school.

The Separation of Parochial and State Schools. In New York City the private nondenominational Public School Society (1805) gradually managed to gain control over the entire school fund. This caused the Catholics there to rebel in 1840, but they found no allies among the Protestant church groups. At the end of the 1830s German groups joined the Catholic opposition. Inspired by the examples in Ohio, these German circles wanted separate German schools, or at the very least they wanted German introduced as a subject. Governor Seward, a Whig (who later became Secretary of State in the federal government), declared in his message of 1840: "As a result of obstacles which arise from differences of language and religion, children of immigrants are all too often robbed of the advantages of the public educational system. . . . Therefore I do not hesitate to recommend the establishment of schools in which they are taught by teachers who speak the same language and confess to the same creed as they do."

Encouraged by this statement, the Catholics first petitioned the city administration and later the state legislature for a partition of the school fund. They were joined by a Scotch-Presbyterian and a Jewish congregation, while the Methodists, Baptists, Episcopalians, Dutch Reformed, and the Reformed Presbyterians sided with the Public School Society. The state legislature did not reply until 1842 (April 9). It replied with a bill which provided for the establishment of nonparochial public schools and which definitely rejected the Catholic efforts (Cubberley 1934, 235-237; O'Gorman 1894, 369-374).

The Catholic defensive struggle—and it was defensive and not offensive in nature—roughly coincides in time with the successful introduction of a part-German public school in Ohio and with the unsuccessful first agitation for public teaching of German in New York. All these cases involved the question as to whether or not the public elementary school system of the United States was to be unified and uniform or articulated and varied in structure. At that time the fight was won with respect to language (by the Germans in Ohio) and lost with respect to the denomination (by the Catholics in New York): the public separate German school was introduced, the public or semipublic separate Catholic school was rejected.

The attempts of the Catholics to preserve for themselves separate public Catholic schools were confronted by attempts of certain Protestant circles to give all public schools, be they attended by Protestant, Catholic, or students of other denominations, a Protestant character. Their opposition was primarily broken by the confrontations in 1838-1846 during which Horace Mann, the eminent State School Superintendent of Massachusetts, fought back their attacks on the articulated schools in his state. The last to give up were the Episcopalians.

In other places the public schools still resembled Protestant institutions for decades. For example, until 1875 it was generally customary in the schools of Rochester, New York, to have Bible readings and to sing from Protestant hymn books (Zwierlein II, 1926, 142, 151). As late as 1890, the public elementary schools in many rural towns of Georgia and of other Southern states are said to have been Protestant church schools without the existence of a legal basis for this (*Report of the United States Commissioner of Education* 1889, 434). Similarly, the nonofficial public church school existed in Utah for a long time. Here the Mormons, a semi-Christian group which originated in America and which, in addition to the Bible, venerated its own holy scripture, the Book of Mormon, did not permit the establishment of public schools in place of church schools until after 1880. In many places the Mormons turned these schools into places for the cultivation of their faith. Around 1890 the separation between parochial and state schools progressed rapidly in Utah (*Report of the United States Commissioner of Education* 1889; 434; *Dexter* 1922, 145-146). This strong denominational orientation of public schools is reported also from southern Idaho, which is inhabited by Mormons (*Report of the United States Commissioner of Education* 1890, 710).

In the territory of New Mexico all denominational schools were completely supported by the territory until 1891 (McGee 1955, 45). As late as 1875 a bill against the use of tax money for denominational schools was rejected in New Mexico. The same conditions returned in the State of New Mexico until a decision of the State Supreme Court in 1949 put an end to it, the so-called Dixon case (*Zellers* v. *Nuff*). Even the mission schools among the Indians were for decades subsidized to a great extent by the federal government until the Protestants, at first, gradually discontinued this practice. In 1897 a federal law put an end to all subsidy. But it remained possible, according to a decision by the Supreme Court in 1907, to grant federal funds to Catholic mission schools out of the federally administered Treaty and Trust Funds (Ackerlund 1950, 178-241).

Against all these persisting tendencies, however, after the New York school battle of 1840, the policy gradually prevailed that demanded a purely secular public elementary school. In a number of states this separation of church and state is handled somewhat more loosely in certain detailed questions:

Bible reading, for example, was permitted in some states; thus it was permitted by the State Supreme Court in Maine in 1854 and was customary in seven states in 1940, but it has since been declared unconstitutional by the United States Supreme Court (*McCollum* v. *Board of Education*, see below).

Catholic sisters in their robes may teach in state schools. This was so in 13 states in 1946. Where state law prohibited the wearing of robes by the Catholic sisters, they were upheld by the courts, e.g., in New York in 1906.

Students of private schools may be given free bus transportation and free school lunches. Free bus transportation was provided in 16 states (*Everson* v. *Board of Education of Ewing* 1947). Free school lunches for all students of private schools are provided for according to a federal law of 1937, since this is considered a social and not a pedagogical measure.

Denominational schools may be granted free textbooks (*Cochran* v. *Louisiana State Board of Education* 1930).

Denominational schools in school districts without public schools may receive tax funds. A positive ruling on this is a Texas law of 1874 (Brown 1912, 50), and a negative ruling was in 1932 by the State Supreme Court of Nebraska (*State* v. *Taylor*; cf. also *Ritchter* v. *Cordes*; Kloss 1942, 726, 948-949; Ackerlund 1950, 178-241).

The most important, and particularly for the ethnic groups the most consequential exception is that even the schools of denominational orphanages, homes for crippled children, and similar institutions may be supported by state funds. In 1938 this was permitted in 7 states, but in at least 2 of these only for nondenominational schools (Kindred 1938, 200-211).

In 1948 the Supreme Court ruled in *McCollum* v. *Board of Education* that, if students of public schools were given religious instruction during regular school hours and on school grounds, this would violate the concept of separation of church and state as provided in the Constitution of the United States even if participation is voluntary and the teacher of religion is not paid from tax money (*McCollum* v. *Board of Education*; Commager II 1958, 726-728). Four years later this kind of religious instruction was permitted when given during regular school hours but outside of the school building (*Zorach* v. *Clauson*; Sorauf 1959, 777-791). Finally on June 25, 1962, the same court ruled that prayers recited in the school during regular hours violate the concept of separation of church and state even if those prayers are nondenominational in character (*Engel* v. *Vitale*).

In 1947 the Supreme Court allowed states to finance bussing for parochial school students (*Everson* v. *Board of Education of Ewing*). In 1968 it approved free textbooks for secular courses (*Board of Education* v. *Allen*). In 1968 a Pennsylvania law permitted the state to reimburse all nonpublic schools for nearly all expenses (teachers' salaries, textbooks, teaching aids) that were incurred by the teaching of four specified subjects, among them modern foreign languages (nonpublic Elementary and Secondary Education Act). This law was imitated soon after by Rhode Island, Connecticut, and Ohio. The Rhode Island law of 1969, Chapter 246, effective July 11, 1969, was more important than those of either Connecticut or Ohio because of the many fully bilingual schools in the state (Section 3-4).

In the law suit following the Pennsylvania law, the defendants were, besides the State Superintendent of Public Instruction and the State Treasurer, several Roman Catholic schools, two Jewish schools, one Lutheran academy, and the Ukrainian Catholic Holy Ghost School in Philadelphia. The constitutionality was upheld 2 to 1 on November 28, 1969, by a federal court in Philadelphia. Former

Virgin Islands Governor Hastie, an Afro-American, was the only dissenter. On June 28, 1971, the United States Supreme Court in *Lemon* v. *Kurtzman* (403 United States 602) invalidated the 1968 Pennsylvania law. Three years later, on April 4, 1973, this was supplemented by a decision concerning payments made under the 1968 law during the 1968-1971 period. And on June 25, 1973, the same court, in the three decisions *Levitt* v. *Committee*, *Committee* v. *Nyquist*, and *Sloan* v. *Lemon* (413 United States 825), declared unconstitutional a law enacted by Pennsylvania subsequent to the 1971 decision and a New York state law (1972, ch. 414), both of which provided for tuition reimbursement to parents of children attending nonpublic schools. The New York law, incidentally, affected about 2,000 schools attended by some 700,000 to 800,000 students, quite a few of whom were taught in or used languages other than English. All these decisions were based on the constitution's Establishment Clause according to which Congress and the states "shall make no law respecting the establishment of religion." And all these decisions served to curtail, if only indirectly, the teaching of minority tongues. Still this adverse effect was partly balanced by the expansion, within the same period, of bilingual teaching in the public schools (cf. Sections 2-2 and 4-4).

The overwhelming majority of the Protestant church groups have come to terms with secular elementary schools since the last third of the last century. Only four larger bodies maintained schools in their congregations: one of Anglo-Saxon origin, the Seventh-Day Adventists; one of Dutch origin, the Christian Reformed; and two of German origin, the Lutheran Missouri Synod and the Lutheran Wisconsin Synod.

The schools of the three last named groups remained bilingual far into the twentieth century. It is highly characteristic of the orthodox Lutherans that they do not ask that their schools be supported by public funds, but rather they even specifically reject the idea as being an undesirable amalgamation of church and state. Only in isolated instances do we hear that schools of Protestant congregations strove for support from the public school fund, as did, for example, the school of the German Lutheran Trinity Church in St. Paul, Minnesota, in 1864 (Pempeit 1932, 84).

On the other hand, the Catholics repeatedly attempted to obtain public funds for their schools; they considered it unjust that the members of their congregations, who overwhelmingly belonged to the poorer strata, had to maintain their own schools and at the same time pay the full tax contribution to the state school system. But since the final switch of almost all Protestants into the camps of the advocates of a secular state school in the 1840s, Catholics have not striven for the denominational public school as the basic form, but only as a subvariety. This led to heated arguments in the 1850s. In Massachusetts, Catholics and Episcopalians joined ranks in 1848 to protest. Their struggle ended in 1855 with a constitutional provision for the nonsectarian public school. Similar provisions were adopted into the constitutions of New Jersey (1844), Michigan (1850), Ohio (1851), and Iowa (1857), etc. The Catholics opposed this on a large scale, as in Michigan in 1853, where in 1808 P. Richards' attempt to obtain territorial or federal funds for the French parochial schools had failed; in Ohio, where the city council elections in Cincinnati centered around this issue; and in Kentucky and other states, where, as in Texas in 1854, they scored a decisive victory in favor of private schools. In St. Paul, Minnesota, Monsignor Cretin signed a petition to the state legislature in 1853 that the only Catholic parochial school existing there be granted state school funds.

The Catholic efforts in turn led to a dramatic increase in the Know-Nothing Party, whose platform of 1855 contained a plank against the parochial school. Much earlier it had been one of the major objectives in founding the Native American Party in 1841 "to prevent the amalgamation of church and state," which was at that time the issue in New York (Cubberley 1934, 238-239; for Minnesota, Pempeit 1932, 76; for Michigan, Section 6-1). In San Francisco a court decided in 1855 that only nonsectarian private schools with teachers certified by the state could claim money from the school fund (Dexter 1922, 147).

The Catholics were repeatedly tossed about in the following decade. A corresponding petition was made to the school board of St. Paul, Minnesota, in 1867, which was rejected notwithstanding a favorable report by the committee (Pempeit 1932, 76). In Missouri in 1870 a draft bill which provided that parts of the public school fund be diverted to parochial schools barely missed passing (*Deutsch-Amerikanisches Conversations-Lexikon* VII, 1872, 411-412). In Georgia a law of 1866 which granted a separate Catholic school to Savannah and the surrounding Chatham County remained valid until the 1890s. Article VIII (5) of the state constitution of 1877 protected these schools (Kloss 1942, 728). Such Catholic public schools also existed in Augusta, Georgia, and in New Haven, Connecticut.

In many cases the Catholics, instead of separate schools, strove for schools which would be a mixture of a private Catholic and a public secular school. For example, in 1873 the following system was established in Poughkeepsie, New York: the Catholics built the school building, provided the teachers (sisters), and paid them for giving instruction in religion; the state certified the teachers, paid them for the entire secular curriculum, and paid a nominal rent for the use of the school building for the time of this secular instruction (Zwierlein II, 1926, 147-148). Equal or similar procedures were adopted at that time in many other towns. The most famous was the compromise solution which was arranged by Archbishop Ireland of St. Paul with the local school boards of Faribault and Stillwater in Minnesota in 1891 and which resembled closely the Poughkeepsie plan. A detailed description of the Faribault plan is in Zwierlein III (1926, 163-164) and in Gisler (1912, 101-102). Ireland was at this time the leader of an influential wing in the Catholic hierarchy. This wing consisted predominantly of men of Irish birth or descent who rejected private parochial schools primarily because these schools frequently had become bastions of non-English languages but also because these men desired a closer coordination of the operation of the Catholic church and the liberal state. (For more about Ireland, see Section 3-4.)

Disregarding the French and Spanish groups, which were limited to clearly defined parts of the country, most of the Catholics in the United States were of either Irish or German descent until about 1880. The Irish were frequently more liberal in doctrinal matters than the Catholic Germans were. Furthermore, they generally had no need to defend a separate language, but used the English language exclusively or predominantly from the beginning. Consequently they were less eager to establish schools for their congregations than were the German Catholics. The Germans were more conservative in church matters and therefore were more interested in the establishment of their own schools but also hoped to preserve their language and native culture in these schools.

The German Catholic organizations were particularly well developed at the end of the 1880s. In 1886 approximately 165,000 students attended bilingual parochial schools. After 1855 a vigorous tutelary organization, the Centralverein, was developed, and to this were added in 1887 a Press Association, Presseverein; Priests Association, Priesterverein; and the beginning of annual meetings, Katholikentage (Kloss 1937, 149-150). Ireland hoped to render superfluous the maintenance of the separate sectarian school by promoting a school that was a blend between state and parochial schools.

In this controversy the school policy of the German-speaking Catholics was called Cahenslyism after Peter Paul Cahensly, the founder of the Raphaelverein in Germany. Finally the controversy over the school policy of the German-speaking Catholics reached Rome, and all Ireland was able to obtain for the Faribault plan was a "Tolerari potest." While Catholic circles were apprehensive that the Catholic influence in the compromise schools created by Ireland would be too weak, liberal circles were apprehensive about a "Catholization" of the state school. For example, the North American "Freidenker" spoke of a "sneaky parochialization of the school" (Erziehungs-Blätter für Schule und Haus 1892, 9). Consequently, the compromise school died out very soon. There were also instances where the same type of school was established by members of local ethnic groups, for example, in Jaspers, Indiana (Indiana Magazine of History, 12, 1916, 340).

Isolated Attacks before 1914. Here and there the existence and freedom of nonpublic day schools came under attack before World War I. In 1853 a bill was introduced into the Ohio legislature which would make it mandatory for all children of school age to attend public schools for three months annually. This bill, which was rejected, was designed to have the private day schools operate only part of the year.

In 1873 the State Supreme Court in Columbus, Ohio, had to annul an attempt by authorities of Hamilton County (which includes Cincinnati) to handicap local Catholic schools through taxation (Lamott 1921, 279-280).

In Minnesota the parochial school existed for years without a legal basis, but not until 1911 were the Germans and Scandinavians able to have a bill passed that granted equal status with the public schools (Mitteilungen des Deutsch-Amerikanischen Nationalbundes 1911, no. 5).

In Nebraska a bill was rejected in 1911 which was intended to damage the nonpublic day school in the same manner as was the 1853 bill in Ohio (*Mitteilungen des Deutsch-Amerikanischen Nationalbundes* 1911, no. 2). It seems safe to assume that many other instances of local struggles could be found.

The Attack of 1922. In Oregon a harsh law against the non-English press had been passed in 1920 (Section 3-3). Then on November 7, 1922, a new law provided that, from 1926 on, all children from their eighth to their fifteenth years had to attend public schools exclusively (text in Kloss 1942, 782). This bill was imitated at the end of 1924 in proposals which were put before the voters in Florida, California, Ohio, Oklahoma, Michigan, Montana, and Washington.

The matter did not come to a vote in these states, however, because Catholic organizations protested the Oregon law, and the Supreme Court decided on June 1, 1925, in their favor (*Society of Sisters* v. *Pierce*; text in Kloss 1942, 784). Among the arguments cited in his defense by the accused Governor Pierce was that the state should have the right to ensure the assimilation of its immigrants; the "objectionable part of the Nebraska bill was that it prohibited the instruction in living languages in regular as well as in supplementary schools" (see Section 3-4). In the case of Oregon the nationality question did, therefore, play a part, even if only a minor one.

Struggles for Private Ethnic Schools ("Nationality Schools")

The Attack from 1889 to 1890. In 1889 the first movement against the private day school began, which more or less strongly affected the entire country. It was also the first conscious attempt to end the special activities of these schools in the fields of language and ethnic culture. All earlier movements either attempted to destroy the private day schools altogether or were directed against their sectarian character.

Laws which prescribed that private schools should use English exclusively existed at that time in only three states, all located in New England: in Connecticut (from 1872), in Massachusetts (from 1873), and in Rhode Island (1883-1887). A fourth state, New York, required that English grammar be taught in private schools. Nowhere else did language requirements exist for private schools. (See the *Report of the United States Commissioner of Education* for the year ending June 30, 1891, pp. 34-37. The text of the laws in their 1889 version is in the Report for the year ending June 30, 1889: 482 Massachusetts, 488 Connecticut, 501 Rhode Island.) Since the laws were frequently revised between the years of their adoption and 1889, it is possible that in one or the other the language requirement was added only after the year in which the law was adopted.

In the year 1889-1890, other states attempted to prescribe the use of English in private schools (Hense-Jensen and Bruncken II, 1902, 144-169, 278-299; Kellog 1918-1919, 3-25; Whyte 1926-1927, 363-390; Schafer 1926-1927, 455-461; cf. also *Reports of the United States Commissioner of Education* for these years and Babcock, 161ff.; Thwaites 1908, 405ff.; Schulze 1926, 457-472; Hattstaedt 1928, 71-75; Gross 1935; Wyman 1968). The states which attempted to prescribe the use of English in private schools at this time were New York, Ohio, Illinois, Wisconsin, Nebraska, Kansas, and in 1890 the newly established states of North and South Dakota (Hense-Jensen and Bruncken II, 1902, 144). Massachusetts is listed here too, but this may have represented an amendment of rounding out the existing laws.

In New York, Governor Hill vetoed a bill (Hense-Jensen and Bruncken II, 1902, 145), which stipulated that children be permitted to attend only those schools in which English alone and no other language was taught (Hense-Jensen and Bruncken II, 1902, 294). The bill also prohibited the teaching of minority languages even as subject matter.

The major battles were fought in Wisconsin and Illinois. On April 18, 1889, the so-called Bennett Act was passed. It prescribed that children 8 to 14 years old who attended private or public schools had to be instructed by the use of English in the following subjects: reading, writing, arithmetic, and American history. The Edward Act, passed in Illinois on May 24, 1889, contained the same provisions but added geography. These acts were primarily directed against the parochial schools of the German-speaking Lutherans, who at that time were in the Republican camp because of tradition rather than because they were politically influenced by their church leadership. At this time, however, the Lutheran Synods began to interfere in politics; the German Lutherans went over to the Democratic camp en masse; here they found also the Polish and German Catholics, who had always been overwhelmingly Democratic because of their denomination, the majority of the Scandinavian Lutherans, and the German freethinkers (Kloss 1942, 745-746). However, all the latter groups were far behind the German Lutherans in zeal and solidarity.

The Democrats won the 1890 elections in both states, and the acts were soon repealed. It is possible, but hard to prove, that these events also contributed considerably to the Democratic victory in the midterm elections of 1890 and the Presidential election in 1892. Gerhard attributes the election of Cleveland directly to the Republican school policy (1915, 7).

The attacks of 1889 to 1890 left their impact on the German parochial schools. The Bennett and Edward Acts were in operation for several years in Wisconsin and Illinois, and the schools had tried to adjust to them: as early as 1890 the Milwaukee press reports that henceforth English would be given more room in the curriculum of the Lutheran schools. This footing that English gained was not taken back even after the repeal of the Bennett and Edward Acts. A position once gained by the English language among an ethnic group in the United States is not easily lost again. The Lutheran schools in Wisconsin had heretofore partially taught English only as a subject matter. From this time on, English became in general an equal tool of instruction. An example of how this worked is a Lutheran school in Johnson Creek, Wisconsin (*Kirchenblatt* 1935, 7). The Catholic schools, which had already given more room to English, at this time reduced the German language here and there to the position of a subject matter except for its use in the teaching of religion.

It is very likely that a secret organization, the American Protective Association (APA), was behind the 1889-1890 attacks against the parochial schools of non-English groups (Davie 1936, 183-184; Stephenson 1926, 145-147; Hense-Jensen and Bruncken II, 1902, 144-145; Davie refers to Williams 1932; see also Kloss 1942, 736-738). There is also some indication that the APA was behind the attacks on the teaching of German in public schools which occurred at the same time. The teaching of German was discontinued, among other places, in St. Louis (1888); in Louisville, Kentucky (1889); and shortly thereafter in San Francisco and St. Paul. In other cities, for example, Milwaukee, Indianapolis (1890-1891), and Cleveland, it came under attack.

In these years the reports of the State Superintendents of Public Schools of Minnesota and the Dakotas (Section 4-4) are full of attacks. In Missouri the same report which opposed the use of German in public schools also opposed the appropriation of public funds for sectarian (mostly ethnic) schools in Missouri.

Consequently, it appears to me not unlikely that, during those years, especially from 1889 to 1891, a centrally organized attack against non-English, primarily German, instruction in all elementary schools, private and public, did indeed take place. That this did not become better known or understood by the public can surprise only those who are unaware how thoroughly separated propaganda and real motive can be kept in the United States and how completely the American press—usually very news-conscious—can bypass actual motivations and connections if publication and public debate is not desirable on these points.

The movement attacked on two fronts: against the languages which were considered alien and against the churches which were considered alien. In its opposition to certain churches it may, under certain circumstances, very well have attacked certain schools which were not objectionable because of the language of instruction, for example, the Irish-Catholic parochial schools. In its opposition to non-English language groups the APA may have also attacked schools and other forms of instruction which were not church-affiliated, e.g., the secular German-English private schools.

A third movement against non-English instruction in elementary schools came into existence during these years. Side by side with the political attack against public and private non-English instruction, the struggle over Cahenslyism (see Section 3-4) raged within the Catholic church. At this time some of the English-speaking clergy attempted to restrain the parochial school and its non-English instruction. Was this movement, too, connected with the APA? This seems impossible at first glance, since the APA originally had been anti-Catholic. But suddenly we read that Archbishop Ireland, the principal figure in the struggle against the German Catholic school and creator of the compromise solutions of Faribault and Stillwater, publicly defended the Republican party in 1894 in the State of New York after it had rejected a resolution against the APA (Zwierlein III, 1926, 228). We learn that he, in a letter to Republican Governor Hoard of Wisconsin, approved the Bennett Act which restricted the parochial school in that state and against which at that time the entire Catholic hierarchy of the state, mostly German-speaking, was fighting (Whyte 1926-1927, 385). Several factors seem, therefore, to indicate that the APA-initiated movement indeed allied itself with a small but vociferous and influential liberalized wing within the Catholic church; indications, however, do not constitute final proof.

Attacks in the Years from 1917 to 1920. After the United States entered World War I, measures were taken in many states against private as well as public instruction in German. It was prohibited in Louisiana for all educational institutions, ranging from elementary schools up to universities, by a law which remained in effect from 1918 to 1921. In Iowa German was prohibited by a gubernatorial proclamation (text in Kloss 1942, 749, 942-944); in South Dakota by the State Council for Defense; in Nebraska by a resolution of the legislature, which constituted more a recommendation than a directive. After the end of the war a systematic campaign against all non-English languages began. The Americanization Department of the United States Bureau of Education established the following program in 1919 (*Proceedings of the Americanization Conference* 1919, 374): "We recommend urgently to all states to prescribe that all schools, private and public, be conducted in the English language and that instruction in the elementary classes of all schools be in English. But our office does not oppose the conduct of church services in other languages, and also not the instruction in other languages as long as thereby the right of the child to acquire an elementary knowledge of the English language and to receive his education in it is not violated."

This sounds harsh today but was rather moderate in the atmosphere that prevailed at the time. And public statements of leading Catholic and Lutheran circles essentially agree with these demands, e.g., the statements by the National Catholic War Council in May 1919 and in the *Lutheran School Journal* in 1921 (Thompson 1920, 301; Gross 1935, 72-73; Kloss 1942, 769, 950). The school laws passed by the individual states differ widely, depending upon the existence or nonexistence of a strong German-speaking group in the state. In the New England states the Germans were unimportant, the French Canadians being by far the most important nationality there (Kloss 1942, 756-762; Lemoine 1921; Sargent 1925, 730-742; Thompson 1920, 137-143, 292-295; Wessel 1931, 22-23; Rumilly 1958, 312-377). They succeeded in Vermont and Connecticut in thwarting attempts to restrict the use of French in parochial schools before laws could be passed. Rhode Island passed a bill in 1922 (Kloss 1942, 758) requiring private schools to teach all subjects in English, with the exception of instruction in foreign languages and those subjects which were not taught in state schools, such as religion. That legislation was mild compared to many laws passed in the Midwest during those years (see below), but was still considered by the French as going too far and was replaced, at the instigation of Representative Henri Nesbitt and Senator E. Belhumeur, in 1925 by the following provision which is still in force today (1970): "Reading, writing, geography, arithmetic, history of the United States, history of Rhode Island, and basic principles of American government have to be taught in the English language to the extent that it is required for the instruction in public schools. The instruction in English and the other subjects listed here must be thorough and effective. But nothing contained in this regulation should be interpreted as or be effective in denying private schools the right . . . to teach one of the above-mentioned subjects or any other subject, apart from the English instruction hereby prescribed, also by means of any other language."

This left private schools in Rhode Island in a much more favorable position than those in Illinois and Wisconsin under the school laws of 1889 (see above), for it permitted the fully bilingual school.

The French were not quite so successful in two other New England states. In New Hampshire according to a law of 1919 (Kloss 1942, 759-760), regular elementary school subjects, including music and drawing, could be taught only in English; but the teaching of one non-English language and the holding of non-English prayers were expressly permitted. In Massachusetts supervision over private schools was considerably tightened; it seems that a milder proposal failed initially, as a result of French Catholic opposition, and was later replaced by a harsher one. It is typical for America that the school struggle of the Catholics, which was primarily conducted through mass petitions, was completely ignored in the press of the state and that a belated treatment of this struggle in the magazine *Forum* (Sargent 1925, 730-742) dealt only with the church-related aspects of the case and not with the ethnopolitical aspects.

Ethnic groups in the Midwest, where we find a large German-speaking population, fared much worse. The Norwegian-American historian Norlie (1925, 389) writes about this time: "There prevailed an almost morbid hostility against any foreign language, which resulted in the dissolution of many Scandinavian classes." A 1919 study about the Poles in Cleveland at first contrasts the tyrannical treatment of their culture in European countries—including Austria!—with the generous treatment in America, only to complain in the subsequent chapters about the Polish parochial schools. It expressed the hope that the new school law in Ohio would correct this "overemphasized nonadjustment" (Coulter 1919, 8, 20).

Typical school laws were also passed in 1919 in Ohio, Iowa, and Nebraska (Kloss 1942, 752, 768). They all prescribed (Iowa only for "secular subjects") the use of English as language of instruction below the ninth grade (Ohio below the eighth). Iowa and Nebraska, in addition to this, prohibited for these grades any teaching of a foreign language; Ohio prohibited only the teaching of German.

It was not clear if these regulations applied also to the supplementary schools as well as to the regular schools. The State Supreme Court of Nebraska ruled in 1919, in response to a suit filed by the German Lutheran Missouri Synod, that supplementary schools were not affected by this law (*Nebraska District* v. *McKelvie*). Even the elementary schools were permitted to teach foreign languages outside of regular school hours. Subsequently, a new law, the so-called Norval Act (Kloss 1942, 772), was passed in Nebraska in 1921 according to which students who had not yet reached the ninth grade could generally not be taught a foreign language. Only the so-called Sunday schools (which teach religion through a foreign language but do not have these languages themselves as a subject) were exempted.

The German Lutherans filed suit against the school laws of Nebraska, Iowa, and Ohio. On June 4, 1923, the Supreme Court ruled (*Meyer* v. *Nebraska*): "Forbidding the teaching in school of any other than the English language, until the pupil has passed the eighth grade, violates the guaranty of liberty in the fourteenth amendment of the Federal Constitution, in the absence of sudden emergency rendering the knowledge of the foreign language clearly harmful." On the same day the Supreme Court annulled also the language laws of Iowa and Ohio (*Bartels* v. *Iowa* and *Bohning* v. *Ohio*).

This decision of 1923 represents a Magna Charta for the private nationality school and put the United States far ahead of most countries in the New World. It enables all immigrant groups to cultivate their languages as a subject matter in private elementary schools; no nationality must be put into an inferior position through a discriminating special treatment.

Entirely un-European is the justification given by the court for this cornerstone of American nationality law. A European court would have justified permitting on the elementary school level the study of a language other than the official one.

1. Either on account of the right of a group: as the claim of a national minority to cultivate its ethnic tongue in addition to the official language or

2. On account of the right of an individual: be it the right of the parents to have their children instructed in the parental tongue in addition to the official language or be it as a claim of the child to be trained in his home or mother tongue in addition to the official language.

But the United States court initially ignored the fact that the domestic language of parents and students was concerned, and treated the case exactly as if the parents would have had their children taught Sanskrit or Latin. It protected:

1. The right of the children to learn any desired "foreign language."

2. The right of the parents to have their children instructed in any subject matter which does not constitute a threat to the state.

3. The right of language teachers to exercise their profession.

Instruction in the mother tongue was basically considered foreign language instruction and was, therefore, included in the comprehensive term "language instruction." The court stated expressly: "The protection granted by the Constitution extends to all—to those who speak other languages as well as to those who were born with English on their lips."

The language rights of the immigrants were, therefore, indirectly protected not because the justices were particularly understanding or even sympathetic toward these rights but because, out of their commitment to a liberal constitution and social order, they were compelled to protect even activities of the citizens which they deemed insignificant, odd, or even perhaps undesirable. In a free and lawful order the rights of the individual are protected even in cases where values are involved which are not appreciated by the prevailing public opinion (in this instance the mother tongue) because the freedom of the individual can be restricted only where it clearly endangers the public interest.

The decision was based on the Fourteenth Amendment to the United States Constitution (1868), whose due-process-of-law clause protects the citizen against illegal acts of state governments and state authorities. It could not therefore have a straight effect on the territories, which were under the federal government. This gap was closed when, on February 21, 1927, the Supreme Court decided (*Farrington* v. *Tokushige,* see also Section 7-3) that the Fifth Amendment (1791) was violated by a 1920 law of the Territory of Hawaii that restricted the foreign language schools (supplementary schools operating on weekdays) that were maintained by the Japanese and Chinese. The Fifth Amendment extends the same guarantees to inhabitants of federally administered areas as the Fourteenth Amendment does to inhabitants of the states.

Present Legal Situation. Since World War I the decisions of 1923 and 1927 have lost their immediacy. On the one hand the number of students in private schools with non-English instruction has decreased considerably (in the case of the Poles from 300,000 to 40,000). On the other side, the federal government has demonstrated with the FLES Movement and the Language Resources Project (Section 2-2) that it at least temporarily does not favor a further disappearance of non-English languages. It also took positive steps for the promotion of private schools with non-English instruction.

Table 4-6 states with reasonable accuracy the state of legislation as of October 1969 in the fifty states with regard to languages prescribed or admitted as media of teaching in both public and nonpublic schools. Near the end of Section 2-1 there is a summary of voting rights of those who have no knowledge of English.

In many states the right to cultivate the languages of the minorities in private schools was restricted to language and religion classes. This restriction has occasionally been under heavy criticism. As H. B. Lemaire (1962, 48) says, "Private schools were tolerated if they were, in short, public schools." The criticism is correct insofar as the private minority school, in which only religion and minority language do not have to be taught in the official language, represents by no means the ideal type of an unrestricted immigrant school. Those private elementary schools may be considered ideal which primarily use the minority language in the lower grades and which teach bilingually in the sense of the 1925 Rhode Island law in the intermediate and upper grades. The United States private nationality school fares well when compared to those in other immigration countries, such as Australia, Brazil, and Argentina. Two examples may serve to show how much can be achieved under the existing regulations. In the French-American schools in New England (approximately 80,000 students) until about 1956 most of the secular subjects were taught in the morning, which was reserved for English, but in the afternoon French instruction was given in the

French language itself, religion, music, art, penmanship, and biblical history, according to information received from the Reverend Mother Raymond de Jesus, Putnam, Connecticut.

In the conservative majority of the Jewish (private) schools from the first grade on, half of the school hours are reserved in similar fashion for Hebrew. Here, too, most of the secular subjects are taught only in English, and only religion and Hebrew lessons are given in the second language, a fact which prolongs regular school hours. Only in a very few Jewish schools—the so-called progressive schools—is Hebrew instruction reduced to one hour daily and begins only with the second grade. One can see that here, following old French and Jewish traditions, much is demanded of the student, even in matters of time. Not many ethnic groups in the United States had the determination and discipline to carry out such programs. An example is the Jewish school in Los Angeles which I was permitted to visit in 1956. Half of the classes had instruction in Hebrew between 9:00 and 11:30 a.m. and English instruction from 12:30 to 3:30 p.m. The other half had their classes in reverse order.

To fully appreciate the legal status of the private nationality school, the following three facts have to be considered. These apply to private elementary schools. The status of private colleges is even more secure.

1. Many institutions were granted a state charter, and such a charter often made the goal of cultivation of a specific language very clear. An example is the charter for the school in Hermann, Missouri (1849), which according to Hawgood (1940, 121) provided that the school should "remain forever a German school" in which all subjects would be taught in German. According to a Supreme Court decision of 1819, the state is not entitled to deduce a right to increased intervention and supervision from the very act of granting the charter (*Dartmouth College* v. *Woodward*; text also in Kloss 1942, 946 and Commager I 1958, 220).

2. All educational institutions, including private ones and those without a charter, generally enjoy tax exemption, which a court in 1904 granted even to a German athletic association (*German Gymnastics Association of Louisville* v. *City of Louisville*).

3. The state repeatedly recognized the work of the nationality groups in their cultivation of the nationality languages by delegating highest officials to their educational meetings or celebrations. For example, in 1890 the United States Commissioner for Education gave a lecture at the meeting of the leading organization of German teachers in the country (W. T. Harris on the meeting of the National Deutsch-amerikes Lehrerbundes in Cincinnati; see Viereck 1903, 240), and in 1908 the Vice President of the United States participated in the opening of a Polish parochial school in Chicago (Thomas and Znaniecki II 1927, 1556).

Practices of the Individual Nationalities

The various nationalities made different uses of their opportunities to establish their own schools. Contrary to the cliché opinions prevailing in Germany, the

Table 3-2   Number of Students Studying German in Elementary Schools

Year and Type of School	Number of Schools Private	Public	Number of Students Private	Public
1886:				
Public elementary		70		150,500
Private secular "independent"	119		15,800	
Protestant	1,119		99,300	
(Illinois 22,944; Wisconsin 14,900; others under 10,000)				
Catholic	825		164,800	
(Ohio 30,835; New York 22,682; Pennsylvania 16,688; Indiana 15,595; others under 12,000)				
Total, private schools	2,063		279,900	
1900:				
Public elementary		143		231,700
(739 high schools with 45,700 pupils)				
Private secular "independent"	871		18,700	
Protestant	2,067		105,800	
Catholic	1,046		193,600	
Total, private schools	3,984		318,100	

German Americans did attempt to preserve their native language. They can hardly be compared to other immigrant minorities since the German Americans were the only group for which the public school played an important role side by side with the private school. Table 3-2 gives a survey of German schools (Wollfradt 1886, 50-55; Viereck 1903, 215).

Actually German students exceeded 600,000 in 1900, since for 1894 an official report found 165,000 in Protestant schools alone, 147,100 in Lutheran, and 17,900 in United Evangelical schools (*Report of the United States Commissioner of Education* 1894-1895, 1670-1671; Handschin 1913, 79); so that we may also count on at least 160,000 for 1900. The approximately 600,000 German students constituted 4% of the approximately 16 million elementary school students at that time, 32% of the students in private schools, and 1.5% of those in public elementary schools.

The chairman of the committee of the Teachers Association, Director E. Dapprich, who compiled these surveys, considered the figures for 1900 still incomplete. "If we had received complete reports from the local school authorities, the total number of students receiving instruction in German would by far have exceeded the one million mark" (Viereck 1903, 215).

Of the other larger immigrant groups the French Canadians and the Poles made the most intensive use of those possibilities that were offered within the framework of the tolerance-oriented nationality rights as they applied to schools. Least intensive were the Italians and Spanish Americans, the latter closely followed by the Swedes and the Yiddish-speaking Eastern European Jews. The Czechs, Norwegians, Dutch, and Lithuanians occupy a middle position.

Around 1900 the Germans, Scandinavians, and Poles were leading; around 1935 the Poles and the French Canadians.

In 1900 the number of students in private nationality schools was estimated at 600,000, of which 350,000 (58%) were in German schools; 80,000 in Scandinavian; 70,000 in Polish, and most of the rest in French (New England), with the smallest number in Czech and Dutch schools (Kloss 1942, 795, 806, 717-718).

For the twentieth century the data in Table 3-3 are available. The data for 1955, for which only Catholic figures are available, are from a survey by Sister Annunciata of Edgewood College, Madison, Wisconsin, and the data for 1960 are from Breunig (1961, 59, 93).

In the figures for 1960 we see the impact of the FLES movement (Section 2-2). We may presume that in the case of all students of Russian, most students of Spanish, and almost all students of French in "independent" schools, we are dealing with normal foreign language teaching not influenced by the students' ethnic background.

In 1900 approximately a half of the 1.2 million, and in 1935 approximately a quarter of the 2.2 million students in private elementary schools attended nationality schools in which a non-English mother tongue of the children or their parents was either a second language of instruction or a subject taught from the first grade on. In 1900 the mother tongue of the nationality group was at times the first language of instruction.

In 1900 all and in the 1930s most of these schools were normally bilingual; most of the subjects were taught in the official language of the country *and* in the minority language. However, in 1955 only the non-English language and religion were taught via the respective "foreign" language.

In 1960 there were still numerous schools, particularly among the French in New England, which spent half the regular school hours teaching French or teaching in French (see above). The textbooks for the afternoon classes were printed either in Quebec or in France and were based on the assumption that French was the mother tongue of the students. This assumption became inaccurate in more and more places, however, and consequently in 1956 new textbooks had to be introduced in the Diocese of Worcester. These books had been written in the Diocese itself, and they taught French as a foreign language (*The Holy Ghost French Series*).

Most of the Jewish elementary schools are also bilingual in nature, with

Table 3-3   Students of Foreign Languages in Nonpublic Elementary Schools, 1935–1960

| | 1935 | | | 1960 | |
Language	Group	Totals	1955*	Group	Totals
Polish					
Independent	12,000				
Catholic	280,000	300,000	40,000		10,636
French					
Catholic	100,000		90,000	101,155	
Independent				25,139	
Lutheran				484	126,778
Slovak					
Catholic	41,000				
Lutheran	2,000	43,000	3,000		
Italian					
Catholic		23,000	15,000		4,075
German					
Catholic	1,000			2,537	
Lutheran	19,000	20,000		2,037	
Independent				491	5,065
Lithuanian					
Catholic		10,000	8,000		864
Spanish					
Catholic				24,234	
Lutheran				858	
Independent				5,186	30,278
Russian					
Catholic				473	
Independent				62	535
Ukrainian					
Catholic and					
Greek Orthodox		5,000	2,000*		

*Roman Catholic only.

instruction half in English and half in the "foreign" language, Hebrew. In earlier days these schools were scarce: in 1935 there were about 3,000 students. Since the founding of the central school association, the Torah Umesorah in 1944, however, they have grown rapidly and in 1956 were attended by 30,000 and in 1961 by about 50,000 grade school pupils.

The oldest of these schools was established in 1730, and only 7 existed in 1853. In these early days the language of instruction was a dead language, comparable to the teaching of Latin in other schools. Since Hebrew has again become a living language in Palestine, however, the intention and the effort of these schools have also gained a certain importance with respect to nationality policy in the narrower sense.

Private High Schools and Colleges—Private Supplementary Schools

In addition to the elementary schools, private high schools as well as colleges, seminaries, etc., have been and are permitted. But competition with the extraordinarily well-developed Anglo-American high schools and colleges was much more difficult for the nationalities than it was at level of the elementary school, even though the law allows private schools more freedom with students who have advanced beyond the compulsory school age than is allowed private elementary schools.

Following the establishment of the bilingual Franklin College in Lancaster, Pennsylvania, in 1787, dozens of bilingual colleges came into existence during the nineteenth century. The following German institutions pioneered in this field: Teacher seminaries: *secular* seminaries in Philippsburg (today Monaca), Pennsylvania (1841 to 1842) and Milwaukee (1878 to 1919); *Lutheran* in Addison, Illinois (1864), New Ulm, Minnesota (1884), Seward, Nebraska (1894); *Catholic* in St. Francis, Wisconsin (1871).

Theological seminaries: *Lutheran* in Columbus, Ohio (1830), St. Louis (Concordia, 1847), Dubuque, Iowa (1853); *United Evangelical* in St. Louis (Eden Seminary, 1850); and *Catholic* in St. Francis (1856), Columbus (1888).

In addition, numerous German colleges and/or secondary schools were organized. Institutions established early by the Scandinavians were: the colleges in Rock Island, Illinois (1860), St. Peter, Minnesota (1862), Lindborg, Kansas (1881), all of which were established by Swedes; and by the Norwegians in Sioux Falls, South Dakota (1860), Decorah, Iowa (1861), Northfield, Minnesota (1874); and by the Danes in Blair, Nebraska (1884); and by the Finns in Hancock, Michigan (1894).

Especially interesting examples were the "Folk High Schools" which were maintained by the Danes in Nysted, Nebraska (1887), and Tyler, Minnesota (1889). During the middle of the 1930s the Poles maintained three Catholic colleges (in Chicago; Erie, Pennsylvania; and Orchard Lake, Michigan), a secular technical college in Cambridge Springs, Pennsylvania (1912), and 40 high schools (Brown and Roucek 1937).

The New England French had 1 college in Worcester, Massachusetts (1903), and 15 high schools; the Lithuanians, 1 college in Thompson, Connecticut (1931), 1 seminary in Hinsdale, Illinois, and 7 high schools; the Czechs, 1 college in Chicago and 4 high schools (3 Catholic, 1 Protestant); the Slovaks, 3 high schools; the Ukrainians, 2 high schools; and the Slovenes, 1 high school. The French Collège de l'Assomption in Worcester, which was granted the right to award degrees by the legislature in 1917, refused until about 1952 to admit students who did not have French as their mother tongue.

While figures of the number of private elementary schools maintained by the nationalities are hard to come by, those for supplementary schools are even harder. We may set the German Americans' lower limit for 1876 at 350,000 students. But this figure indicates more the approximate minimum than the actual number of students. For the middle of the 1930s it can be ascertained that, among others, 70,000 students received German, 32,000 Ukrainian, 21,000 Yiddish, 20,000 Polish, and 10,000 Czech or Slovak instruction in supplementary schools of this type. Today the Jewish supplementary schools have by far the largest number of students. In 1962 about 300,000 children received Hebrew instruction five times a week. The Japanese supplementary schools in Hawaii may have over 10,000 students (Section 7-3). Between the end of World War II and 1961, 23 German supplementary language schools with about 2,000 students who are instructed once a week were reestablished. To this we may add a presumably larger number of German church-based Sunday schools.

At certain times public authorities supported some of the supplementary schools. Probably the most frequent type of support was the permission given for classes to be held in public school buildings, but sometimes they provided textbooks or even gave financial support. For example, in 1936 private evening classes in German, Esperanto, French, Irish, Yiddish, Polish, and Spanish were held in public school buildings in Washington, D. C. This is only one of many such cases.

CHAPTER FOUR

Promotion-Oriented Nationality Rights for Immigrants

4-1 IMMIGRANTS BEFORE AND AFTER 1880

In this chapter I call immigrants only those persons who entered the United States when it existed as an independent polity, fully developed in most of its regions, and who arrived at a time when the specific regions in which they settled already belonged to the United States.

Among these immigrants we distinguish two main types: immigrants who entered the country after 1880 and immigrants who came before 1880. Those who came after 1880 found an almost completely opened country where they could not easily establish themselves as farmers. A well-known example is the Poles in Connecticut. The majority of the immigrants who came after 1880 became city dwellers, even though most of them, the Italians and Polish, for instance, had been peasants in the old country. To these "sole late settlers" belong the members of most of the southern and eastern European people and nationalities; most prominent among these were the Italians, the Poles, and the Eastern European Jews.

The Germans, French Canadians, Scandinavians, Czechs, and Dutch who immigrated between 1830 and 1880 settled for the most part in regions which had just been opened by the white man and which were therefore only partially settled by whites. Two characteristics distinguish these older immigrants from the immigrants who came after 1880: (1) They could for the most part still settle in the countryside and form compact language pockets where in the farming districts and small towns their language was automatically retained longer than in the larger cities. (2) They were, as far as the entire United States was concerned, "mere" immigrants. From the point of view of the state or territory in which they lived, however, they belonged to the original settlers, whose claim to cultural toleration and promotion by the state was second to that of the Anglo-Saxons but greater than that of the later arrivals (Kloss 1940, 23).

Among those early immigrants the Germans often occupied a special position, since they constituted for decades the only foreign language immigrant group of any importance. Calculations for 1850 (Table 1-3) show that, among the 800,000 foreign born with a non-English mother tongue, 75% were German speaking and 13% were French speaking, which represents a total of 100,000 French-speaking people, the upper limit. The rest were splinter groups, 1 to 1.5% each of Spanish, Dutch, and Norwegian. Among the 3.4 million non-English foreign born in 1880, there were 60% who were German speaking, 11% who were Norwegian and Swedish (380,000), 9% French, 2% each of Czech, Dutch, and Spanish (mostly Mexican).

There are spheres of promotion-oriented nationality rights which essentially were enjoyed only by the immigrant groups who arrived before 1880. The most important was the printing of government documents and the cultivation of the mother tongue in public elementary and high schools.

4-2   GOVERNMENT PUBLICATIONS

Official publications have been printed to a considerable extent for the older immigrant groups in their own languages. We must distinguish between such publications which served only to inform the population and those which served also the internal business of the civil authorities.

To the latter category belong the laws, to the former the state constitutions and the annual or biennial executive messages. Of the laws only German versions are known to me, disregarding editions in languages of original settlers such as the French in Missouri (1843) and the Spanish in Texas.

The following is based on Kloss (1942, 605-608, 934) and on information (1961) from the Indiana State Library and from the Legislative Reference Library in Madison, Wisconsin.

Some complete translations were called private endeavors of the translators, namely, the editions in Illinois (1839) by G. Körner, in Ohio (1839) by G. Walker, and in Iowa (around 1855) by H. R. Claussen. Sources for this are, for Illinois, *Deutscher Pionier* 1871, 233, and Körner 1909, 430; for Ohio, Rattermann 1879, 217-218; for Iowa, Fiböck 1900, 414. It seems likely, however, that these men could risk these editions only because the state legislatures guaranteed the purchase of a certain number of copies or granted a subsidy for the printing, which would have to be proved for each individual case. On the other hand, the state legislature directly ordered, for example, the German edition of the civil laws of Colorado in 1877 (Section 6-2) and that of the Revidierten Gesetze des Staates Indiana (Revised Laws of the State of Indiana) in 1853, two volumes of 650 and 830 pages, respectively.

In addition to such law collections in German, German editions of the annual or biennial legislative laws also existed as they are documented, for example, in Missouri for 1843, in Wisconsin for 1849, in Indiana for 1857, 1859, 1861, and 1867; in Colorado for 1876 to 1900. Much remains to be discovered in this field, however. The source material is discussed in the following letter from the Wisconsin Legislative Reference Library, which is dated September 29, 1961, and signed by R. Theobald. The original is in German.

"Partially it may be gathered from the annual reports of the department heads during the first decades of our state—approximately from 1850 to 1870 (the favorable attitude toward nationalities changed as early as during the Civil War)—that publications were made in non-English languages. But it would require time-consuming historical research to determine exactly all the publications in all languages.

"The annual report for 1850, for example, reports (page 19) that $1,000 was paid to 'Schoeffler, Fratney & Herzberg, for Publishing Laws in German, 1849.' Unfortunately, no information is given after 1850 about the purpose of such expenses but only about the receiver of the money. So appears, for example, on page 34 of the Annual Report for 1852, the entry, 'No. 190—Fratney & Herzberg—27.35'; but it is not related why check No. 190 for $27.35 was made out to Fratney & Herzberg.

"I remember having seen several years ago a copy of an address by the Governor to the Legislature in German—but cannot remember the date or the name of the Governor. Let me summarize: since 1917 for certain, but perhaps even since 1870, all public documents in Wisconsin have been published in English only, except for information pamphlets for immigrants. We do not know much about nor does our otherwise excellent Historical Society incidentally—what was formerly published and in which languages. It is certain that the Session Laws as well as the Executive Messages have from time to time been printed in German; it is possible—but not proved—that they appeared in other languages also. During the 1850s many Scandinavians and Welshmen settled here; it is quite possible that several translations in those languages were made by the State. Our codified legislation has always been published only in English; the language of the courts, and with it also the language of the lawyers, was apparently English from the beginning."

Many of the German editions of the annual or biennial legislative laws have actually been used also in the practice of the lower courts. The 1852 Indiana law which ordered the German version of the complete collection specified clearly that one copy be made available to the clerk of each circuit court.

Körner (1884, 424) writes: "Before the lower courts, where it occurs quite frequently in the Western states that justices of the peace, contestants, and witnesses are all Germans, the trial is conducted in German while in all protocols, subpoenas and all court orders—for the sake of all appeals—the language of the country is used."

In this connection judges and lawyers certainly used the German version of the laws quite frequently for the instruction of the contestants and witnesses. Concerning the executive messages, I know of German verions in Indiana for 1851 and 1869; in Missouri for 1843 and for the period from 1859 to 1917 (a total of sixteen); from 1901 to 1917 they are recorded for every second year (with the exception of 1911). A Czech edition existed in Missouri for 1903, a Norwegian one in Wisconsin in 1847, Welsh editions in Ohio in 1838, in Pennsylvania in 1879. But these are accidental findings from among a certainly much larger number of non-English editions.

A considerably larger number of immigrant languages was considered in connection with the printing of a new state constitution. For example, according to the records of the respective sessions, the respective constitutional assemblies had the following numbers of their creations printed in non-English languages (Kloss 1940, 393, 529; 1942, 606, 608, 394, 928-929, 930):

Wisconsin	1848:	5,000 in German; 5,000 in Norwegian
Minnesota	1857:	5,000 in German; 2,000 each in Swedish, Norwegian and French
Iowa	1857:	3,000 in German; 1,000 in Dutch
Illinois	1870:	15,000 in German; 5,000 each in Scandinavian and French
Texas	1875:	5,000 in German; 3,000 in Spanish; 1,000 in Czech

Notice that French and Spanish (and in Texas German also) were the languages of the original settlers. In several instances (Wisconsin in 1848 and Minnesota in 1857) there were also moves to publish in several Indian languages—whether made seriously is difficult to determine.

As had the federal government, so also did several states have certain pamphlets printed in German, Scandinavian, etc., for the purpose of propaganda in the emigration countries of Europe. Wisconsin was one such state. Since about 1869 the Wisconsin Board of Immigration has made such pamphlets available, but the publication of these pamphlets does not constitute nationality law.

4-3   OFFICIAL ANNOUNCEMENTS

Official announcements appeared frequently in newspapers in the languages of all larger immigrant groups. This was primarily because the authorities out of practical considerations wanted to make the contents of their announcements known to as many citizens and noncitizens as possible. Here we find a genuine attempt to help the ethnics which at the same time helped the immigrant papers as well, for they often profited considerably from these official announcements.

In another chapter of this book, laws of Pennsylvania are mentioned which favored the papers in German, Italian, and Yiddish, and laws of Ohio which favored the papers in German, Czech, and Polish (Sections 5-3 and 5-4).

In Illinois a law of 1867 prescribed that in Chicago all official city regulations, records, and announcements should also appear in a German daily newspaper (Kloss 1942, 936). Concerning this matter, the State Supreme Court ruled that, since the state constitution prescribed English for all official announcements, local authorities were permitted to have their regulations published only in English, even in a German paper (*Chicago* v. *McCoy*; Kloss 1942, 936-937). Analogous decisions were made in 1916 and 1917 (*Perkins* v. *Board of County Commissioners of Cook County*; *People* v. *Day*).

In New Jersey a law was in effect from 1876 to 1919 according to which official announcements, whenever printed in English in a German newspaper, could also appear in German (Kloss 1942, 609). The law was repealed in 1918. On the other hand, the State Supreme Court ruled in 1891 that only announcements could be printed in German; laws or ordinances had to appear only in English (*State of New Jersey* v. *Mayor, etc., of Orange*; Kloss 1942, 935). The State Supreme Court of New York permitted the treasurer of Long Island City to print his announcements in a German paper, without saying anything about the language of this publication (*Kernitz* v. *Long Island City*; Kloss 1942, 938).

Wisconsin seems to be the one state where, even today, laws provide that the county board of supervisors may publish notices in foreign languages in addition to English in certain cases and where county court notices must be printed in English but may be published in newspapers that are printed in any language (Wisconsin Stat. Ann. 59.09(4); 324.20). In North Dakota (North Dakota Cent. Code 1960), "official newspapers must be at least 3/4 English." Leibowitz (1969, 63, 67), from whom these facts come, lists eight states where the law explicitly prescribes English newspapers: Arizona, California, Indiana, Louisiana, Maine, Massachusetts, New Jersey, and Washington.

Numerous confrontations centered around these non-English announcements, especially since local authorities and courts at times held the view that such practices had to be expressly permitted by state laws (Section 5-3). In 1911 in Minnesota Germans and Scandinavians succeeded together in having non-English newspapers put on an equal footing with English newspapers as far as official announcements were concerned. And in 1935 in Nebraska a law dating from World War I which excluded the non-English press from these announcements was repealed. There are still a good many facts and incidents to discover on the level of the states, even more on that of municipal government.

4-4   RIGHTS CONCERNING SCHOOL LANGUAGES

Laws

Sources for the laws regulating school languages for immigrants are more abundant than those for questions of official publications, even though much still remains to be uncovered.

So far as schools are concerned, we must distinguish clearly between the laws of the state and the practical implementation of the affairs in individual communities. The development of the legal framework and the local practice are two curves which at times approximately coincide but at times also differ widely from each other.

In many of the earliest school laws the language question is not touched upon (examples: Missouri, 1817, school law for St. Louis; Illinois, 1825; Michigan's first school laws after statehood between 1835-1837; Iowa, 1841) because the exclusive acceptance of English was taken for granted. In other instances quite the reverse, because no possibility was seen of excluding the minority language. But individual laws may be found which, without excluding other languages as subject matter, do establish English as the dominant language (Indiana School Laws 1824). Among those laws in which the admission of non-English language is referred to, we must distinguish during the nineteenth century between (1) those which allowed only German; (2) those which permitted all languages, and (3) those which permitted all but name specifically one (German) or several.

Equally important is the differentiation as to whether the "foreign" language is permitted as a tool of instruction or merely as subject matter. A third possibility, which I encountered only once, in a Minnesota school law of 1877 (see below), allowed the oral use of an auxiliary language in elementary grades to explain unfamiliar English to the children.

As a tool of instruction sanctioned by state law, we shall meet German in the public schools of the immigrants in Ohio and Colorado (Sections 5-4 and 6-2). All non-English languages were permitted by two Wisconsin laws of 1846 and 1848 (text in Schafer 1927, 219; Kloss 1942, 617). The first applied only to Milwaukee and prescribed that a school, in order to be recognized as public, had to teach English at least as subject matter; the second permitted the bilingual public school. An Oregon law of 1872 permitted purely German public schools in Multnomah County (including the city of Portland) if it was demanded by at least one hundred voters (Kloss 1942, 660).

Much more frequent, of course, were school laws which allowed ethnic languages a place only as subject matter within the framework of a basically English public school. Such laws were passed as those shown in Table 4-1.

Some of these laws (Wisconsin 1854, Minnesota 1867 and 1877, Nebraska 1913) limited this instruction to one hour a day. An expert opinion by the Wisconsin Supervisor of Education (1905, 58) states that the purpose of the 1854 law was to restrict the cultivation of foreign languages in elementary schools, not to encourage them. Haugen (I 1953, 245) attributed this Wisconsin law to the Norwegian American political leader Knute Nelson. In other instances the executive authorities of the state considered the status granted by the law rather as a minimum. In Nebraska, for example, in the operational regulations for the 1913 law, according to which the minority language had to be introduced in the town schools at the request of the parents of 50 students, it was stated that the same could be done in rural schools at the request of the parents of only 25 students (Kloss 1942, 766). While in Nebraska in 1913 the instruction was limited to the upper half of the elementary schools (from the fifth grade up), the other laws included all grades.

Table 4-1   School Laws That Stipulated the Teaching of Languages

Page in Kloss (1942)	Year	State	Non-English Languages	Requested by
618	1854	Wisconsin	All	School Board
620	1857	Illinois	All	
616	1861	Iowa	"German or other Languages"	Majority of school district voters
625	1867	Kansas	German	50 parents
623	1867	Minnesota	All	School Board
615	1869	Indiana	German	25 parents
621	1872	Illinois	All	School Board or citizens of the school district
624	1877	Minnesota grade schools	All	School Board (unanimous only)
765	1913	Nebraska for towns only	All	Parents of 50 students
626	1935	Wisconsin	All	Mandatory at request of parents of 50 students. Otherwise optional

In 1891 the State Supreme Court of Indiana ruled specifically that, if the parents of a school desired the teaching of German in all grades, this could not be denied on the grounds that German had already been introduced in another school of the town in the upper grades (*Board of School Commissioners* v. *State ex rel. Sander*).

The external framework of these laws was that the non-English tongues were considered to be a foreign language; their toleration in state schools was officially considered not so much a minority right as progressive educational policy. This attitude became more pronounced through the decades. It also occurred that German—the only "foreign" language which really became widely taught in elementary schools—was initially even taught via English as was the case until 1870 in Evansville, Indiana (Kloss 1942, 639). In Illinois it had to be expressly permitted by a (1872) law that for the teaching of "foreign languages" these languages themselves may be used at the same time as tools of instruction (Kloss 1942, 621).

Several of these regulations were short-lived. In Kansas, for example, German was tolerated only from 1867 to 1874; in Nebraska non-English languages were taught only from 1913 to 1918. But others managed to survive for many decades, and the regulations in Wisconsin (1854) and Minnesota (1877) survived even World War I, with the latter still in effect in 1969 (Minnesota 1959 Laws). This does not exclude the possibility that they were forgotten. In Milwaukee, for example, the non-English languages were permitted again by a new law in 1935, even though the old one was still nominally in effect.

Local Practices

As important as these laws are as a yardstick for the attitude of the English-speaking part of the population, the developments in the individual communities are more important. Two reasons account for this.

During the pioneer decades of the young territories and states of the Midwest and Far West, the external prerequisites for a centralized direction and shaping of the events were still lacking. In the farming districts and small towns of the newly developing non-English-language pockets, the inhabitants initially had no teachers at their disposal who were familiar with English, and during the first years there was little practical need for a command of English.

Even after the central authorities and institutions—such as teacher seminaries—had been established in the states, their influence remained restricted by the principle of educational home rule. The administration of the local educational system lies normally not in the hands of the state or the general local authorities but in the hands of a popularly elected lay body, the school board. In about half of the states the school board is the organ of a legally independent school district existing side by side with the municipal unit; in the other half of the states it is one of the institutions of municipal government that is generally of an equal standing with other local administrative organs and is not subordinated to the city or county council. The Supreme Court of Michigan decided in 1874 in the Kalamazoo case that school boards were authorized on their own volition to introduce new subjects into the curriculum (*Stuart* v. *School District of Kalamazoo*):

"The right is upheld of the school authorities in the school districts of this state to levy taxes on the public for the purpose of maintaining high schools and in this way to permit the instruction of children in non-English languages free of charge. There is nothing in the policy of this state nor in its constitution which would restrict the elementary school districts in respect to the number of subjects which they may wish to have taught."

Another important question was answered in 1881 by the State Supreme Court of Illinois: Can the school board introduce foreign language instruction in the elementary school in places where the laws do not explicitly permit instruction in foreign languages as subject matter and where these laws demand a so-called English education? The court ruled: Yes (*Powell* v. *Board of Education*).

"According to provisions of the school law which permit instruction in 'those additional subjects, including music and art, which may be suggested by the chairman or the voters,' every modern language may be taught. . . . An education received via English is an 'English education'; if the same subjects were to be taught via the German language, this would constitute a 'German education.' Education receives its special character from the language used as the tool of instruction . . . and not from the individual subject taught. . . . The mere fact that the German language belongs to the prescribed subjects does not deprive an institution of its character as an English school. . . . The fact is that, in our elementary schools, instruction in modern languages has existed too long to change it, if at all, other than by action of the legislature. It should not be done by judicial interpretation."

Among the older immigrant groups public elementary instruction in non-English languages developed in two phases which at times merge into another, but which in other instances were separated in time by an intervening phase where English alone prevailed in the schools. During the first phase, which remained confined to compact language pockets, the Middle and Northern European settlers established public schools in their own languages because other possibilities were nonexistent. This has been documented for the Scandinavians, a concrete example being Arendale, Filmore County, Minnesota (Norlie 1925, 109). But among them this first phase came rapidly to an end. It gave place to a period in which there were purely English public schools, which initially taught only for three to four months annually so that in many places parochial schools conducted in their mother tongue managed to survive side by side with them. Blegen (1940, 244-245) reports an exceptional case where the public district school taught for three months while the community mother tongue school taught for six months.

Individual Nationalities

Germans. Two phases may be distinguished in the large German-language pockets in the Midwest. One was the instinctive cultivation of German. This merged without sharp borders with the second phase of conscious retention. The first phase is reflected in the report for the years 1886 to 1888 of the State Supervisor of Public Education for the newly settled territory of the Dakotas. It states that the law did require the schools to instruct in English, but the "foreign population" was so strong that it could elect not only the local school boards but even the county superintendents. The following report of the State Supervisor of Public Education of the State of Missouri for the years 1887-1888 takes us into the second phase (Handschin 1913, 67-68):

"In a large number of districts of the State the German element of the population greatly preponderates and as a consequence the schools are mainly taught in the German language and sometimes entirely so. Hence, if an American family lives in such a district the children must either be deprived of school privileges or else be taught in the German language. In some districts the schools are taught in German for a certain number of months and then in English, while in others German is used part of the day and English the rest. Some of the teachers are scarcely able to speak the English language."

In the next annual report of the State Superintendent (Kloss 1942, 631), it is expressly stated that this condition exists without legal basis and could be changed by court order at any time; "this injustice will not be tolerated for much longer."

In the larger cities there could be no such "instinctive" establishing of German public schools. From the very beginning we find conscious actions which, disregarding rare exceptions, never aspired to a purely German school but at best to a bilingual school patterned after the Cincinnati and Baltimore examples (Sections 5-4 and 6-3).

In this context a remarkable shift of aims is noticeable in the Midwest. In the beginning German was a language of instruction in bilingual schools; then German became a subject from the first grade on; later German was taught as a subject in the upper grades of the elementary school.

In the long-settled East, where the large groups of German immigrants constituted a purely urban minority and even more in the South with its scattered Germans, often only the third objective (German in the upper grades of the elementary school) was aspired to from the beginning. For example, in 1854 German was introduced in New York from the seventh grade on; in 1872 in Nashville, Tennessee, it was offered in the upper grades. But, perhaps because of the more favorable position of German in the Midwest, the goal of having German instruction in the lower grades was occasionally included in the educational programs of later years. In some places, for example, in New York, this goal was actually attained.

Running parallel to the goals pursued in connection with the introduction of German were shifts in the arguments used to justify this introduction. Initially the desire to preserve the German mother tongue, born out of considerations of nationality policy, was openly expressed. But after 1870 and even more after 1900, this expression was replaced by the argument that German has a high educational value as a foreign language; and in 1875 this was advocated publicly during a great protest demonstration in which the Germans of New York City protested against the announced abolition of German (Bagster-Collins 1930, 19; Viereck 1903, 180).

This reason for teaching German led logically to an increasing shift away from demanding German as a subject for lower-grade children of German-speaking parents and toward advocating German instruction for the children of Anglo-American parents as well, a program which came close to the present FLES movement (Section 2-2). A variety of languages was brought into the country by Eastern and Southern Europeans after 1880. While the introduction of these new languages into the public schools was rarely attempted, their very presence made it necessary to find novel justification for the retention or introduction of German, a justification which would not apply equally well to the other immigrant languages. At this time it was believed that this justification was found in the high educational value in the German language, and around 1900 it enjoyed a maximum of international prestige. The Deutsch-Amerikanische Nationalbund founded in 1901 also adopted this argument. Professor Marion D. Learned (1901, 88), one of its leading members, declared:

"All public schools in America should recognize English as the official language of the school and general instruction. No foreign language should be taught in the public schools of America merely because students and parents of the school speak the particular language. If this is not accepted, we would not only have to have German schools, but Magyar, Polish, and Italian schools as well. Of all living languages German deserves the first rank on account of its cultural as well as its economic value."

After 1900 German was newly introduced or reintroduced almost exclusively in the upper grades of the elementary schools; for example, 1910 in Frankfort, Kentucky; 1911 in Elizabeth, New Jersey; 1912 in Altoona, Pennsylvania; 1914 in Ann Arbor, Michigan; 1914 in Jonesboro, Illinois; and 1914 in Portland, Oregon. An exception to this was in Mt. Lebanon, Pennsylvania, where in 1914 German was taught from the third grade on.

The introduction of German as a mere subject and, if possible, only in the upper grades of the elementary school was also desired by numerous Anglo and some German-Americans for still another reason. The private schools perished. For the most part they had been purely German or bilingual German-American elementary schools, and most of them had been church schools. When German was successfully introduced as a subject in the upper elementary grades, many Anglo-Americans welcomed the introduction as a blow against the church. This is discussed in detail in Kloss 1942, 668-674.

In several cases the undermining of the private German schools even led to a temporary strengthening of the German language in public schools. Often private German elementary schools, especially secular schools, but occasionally also parochial ones, were taken over by the public school system and there retained their particular character for a while, especially their curriculum and their teachers. Occasionally German-Americans later complained that they had been deceived and that their previously private school had been radically Anglicized after a few months.

German instruction spread very rapidly to the larger cities during the 1860s, especially after the Civil War, as indicated by the following dates for the introduction of German: Buffalo: 1839, Louisville, Kentucky: 1852, New York City: 1854, Chicago: 1865, Indianapolis and Washington, D. C.: 1866, San Francisco: 1867, Cleveland and Milwaukee: 1869, Detroit: 1875.

In several instances, German disappeared rather quickly: before 1900 in Detroit and St. Paul, Washington, St. Louis (1887-1888). In most instances, however, it prevailed. Especially impressive was the development in Indianpolis, which, after Cincinnati and Baltimore (Sections 5-4 and 6-3), became the third major American city in which bilingual public schools survived up until the time of America's entry into the First World War. According to Ellis (1954), German was taught as a branch of study in grades 2 to 5; grades 6 to 8 (after 1882) were dual-medium grades. When in 1890 the local authorities decided to suppress

Table 4-2   Teaching of German in New York and Chicago

New York		Chicago	
From Grade	*Since Date*	*From Grade*	*Since Date*
7	1854	1	1865
1	1870	5	1875
5	1876	3	1885
3	1890	5	1893
6	1897	7	c.1903
8	1903 to 1917	5	1910 to 1917

Table 4-3   Highest Number of Students Who Studied German

City	*Date*	*Number*	*City*	*Date*	*Number*
St. Louis	1881	21,800	Cincinnati	1902	17,200
Chicago	1893	44,000	Buffalo	1914	12,000
New York	1895	23,500	Milwaukee	1915	32,000

German in grades 2 to 5, the Germans appealed successfully to the courts (cf. *supra*). In 1909 in Indianpolis 6,500 students participated in German instruction; and in 1915 Indianapolis was called "an Athens of German culture in America" (Heim 1915, 182; Kloss 1942, 639-640; Ellis 1954; Andersson 1969, 70-79, 209-213).

In other cities German instruction survived only from day to day, one day extending to many grades, the next restricted to a few. The two largest cities of the country, New York and Chicago, are representative of the Midwest with its more influential German population and of the Middle Atlantic States with their rootless German immigrant population (Table 4-2). The number of German students who existed temporarily in such cities may be gathered from the counts shown in Table 4-3. This teaching of German was by no means designed only for children with German as their mother tongue. On the contrary, it was soon extended to students from English-speaking homes, particularly in places which were almost exclusively inhabited by a German-speaking population. We learn, for example, that around 1900 between 90 and 100% of all elementary school students participated in German instruction in towns like Carlstadt, New Jersey; Hermann, Missouri; New Braunfels, Texas; New Ulm, Minnesota; and Tell City, Indiana. It is thus obvious that the children of non-German descent also studied German. More important is the percentage of children of non-German tongues who studied German in several large cities (Table 4-4, Kloss 1942, 633, 661; 1940, 471, 495).

The threefold division used to describe German students in Chicago is open to various interpretations. German may mean either German speaking or German

Table 4-4   Elementary School Children Studying German Who Did Not
                    Have German as a Mother Tongue

City	Year	Percent	Comment
St. Louis	1867	24	
	1875	33	
	1877	30	6,341 children
Cleveland	1873	33	1,200 children
Baltimore	1884	25	Approximate
Louisville	1870	15	But 75% of the German- speaking children participated
Chicago	1898		15,020 "German" children, 12,195 "American" children, 12,788 "other" children
Columbus	1911	30	800 children

born; American may mean American born in general or excluding those of German descent. "Others" presumably refers to foreign-born Swedes, Poles, Italians, etc. (*Pädagog. Monatshefte* 1899-1901, 47). The data for Columbus are found in *Monatshefte* 1911, 246.

After 1913 when German was introduced in the elementary schools of smaller towns of Nebraska, we find among them almost purely Anglo-Saxon communities like Aurora. In Lincoln, Nebraska, a German-teaching elementary school was located in a purely English-speaking part of the city (Werkmeister 1931).

Even if we are to assume that the national average of students from non-German homes came to only 25%, their total number would already have reached approximately 60,000 (out of 232,000 students) around 1900; but in reality their total was probably substantially higher.

To this we must add, particularly since 1900, a steadily increasing number of students who came from German-speaking homes but who themselves could not speak German. This partial Anglicizing of the grandchildren and greatgrand-children of immigrants is documented, for example, in Cleveland in 1901 and 1905 (Kloss 1940, 472); in Erie, Pennsylvania in 1913 (Kloss 1940, 281); in Milwaukee in 1915 (Kloss 1942, 645). Whenever instruction was given as if German were the mother tongue, i.e., an oral competence was presupposed and a written competence was aspired to, the results were increasingly unsatisfactory. Shortly before World War I separate studies in Erie and in Buffalo determined that what the elementary school had been trying to achieve for many years with little success could be achieved much more quickly and easily on the high school level (Kloss 1940, 281; Kloss 1942, 655). Taken as a whole, the teaching of German prior to 1914 was more than instruction in the mother tongue. Among the arguments used in justification by the German Americans were those pointing out the progressive pedagogical methods and the high value of German as an international language of the educated. When in 1870 the independent (secular) German elementary school was handed over to the local authorities in New Albany, Indiana, the previous proprietors made it a condition that not only its language but also its pedagogical structure was to be retained because "teaching by demonstration, instruction in reading and spelling based on the phonetic system, arithmetic without the memorization of rules, grammar instruction by analyzing sentences, in short, the modern achievements in the field of teaching methods are an indigestable diet for the larger number of public schools" (*Amerikanische Schulzeitung* 1871, 439; Kloss 1942, 665).

Scandinavians. Among the Scandinavians decades of purely English elementary school instruction seem to have passed between the time of the cultivation of their language in elementary schools that was forced by circumstances (Section 4-4) and the phase of conscious cultivation.

At the beginning of this century a movement was generated in the western parts of the Midwest that were heavily settled by Scandinavians. The aim was to introduce into the public schools Swedish, Norwegian (Riksmaal), and, in isolated instances, Danish. The first successes were achieved in high schools. Norwegian appeared in the curriculum in 1900 in Story City, Iowa; in 1905 in Grand Forks, North Dakota; and Danish in Minneapolis, but not until 1910 (Meixner 1941, 73; Benson 1952, 365). After 1906 these attempts, thanks to the efforts of Professor J. N. Lenker, seem to have been extended also to the public elementary schools (Kloss 1942, 648-649; especially Norlie 1925; Lenker 1915). Interestingly enough, these efforts for elementary school instruction in the Scandinavian languages were not included in the previously mentioned works by Meixner (1941) and Benson (1952).

In 1914 in Minnesota alone approximately 150 elementary schools, in addition to 50 high schools, taught one of the Scandinavian languages, and the teaching of these languages began to spread into the two Dakotas, Wisconsin, Illinois, Iowa, Nebraska, and the state of Washington (Lenker 1915, 7; Kloss 1942, 649). Lenker gives a complete list of all localities where Scandinavian was being taught as, for example, in Minnesota, in 18 rural schools in Pope County, 13 in Waseca County, 12 in Stearns County, 11 in Norman County, etc.

Dutch. The Dutch in the Midwest had Michigan as their main center of settlement. As early as the end of the 1870s, a determined movement, started by H. Doesburg, was demanding the introduction of their language in the district schools. In 1880, Dutch was taught in the district schools of seven communities in Michigan, partially during the regular term, partially during the summer months (Lucas 1955; 590).

Czechs. The Czechs succeeded in introducing their language primarily in their pocket settlement in Texas, where Czech was even specifically named in the school laws and where it was again admitted after World War I (Section 6-2. For a list of localities in Texas that had instruction in Czech in 1932, see Kloss 1940, 403-404). Czech was very likely taught in the elementary schools of several communities in the Midwest; for example, in 1913 Czech was introduced in an elementary school in Omaha, Nebraska (*Monatshefte* 1913, 383).

Poles and Italians. Polish in 1907 and Italian a few years later were instituted in Milwaukee initially in the upper grades and later in all grades of the elementary schools when 75% of the parents demanded it. In 1913, in five schools 2,387 students learned Polish and in one school 770 learned Italian. Attendance was large in grades one through four, but in grades six through eight decreased to insignificant numbers (Bagster-Collins 1930, 26; *Monatshefte* 1912, 85; 1913, 273). Rarely did languages of the most recent immigrants find access into the public elementary schools. The later immigrants generally had to be satisfied that their languages were tolerated in private schools.

Spanish Americans. The school problem of the Spanish-American immigrants from Cuba, Spain, Mexico, and Puerto Rico differs from that of the Middle European immigrants in five ways.

1. The high-water mark of their immigration lies after 1924, while that of the Middle and Northern Europeans was before 1880. In the 1950s Spanish-speaking immigrants were numerically larger than other non-English immigrants to America, as the Germans had been one hundred years earlier.

2. They were in the vast majority simple farmhands or unskilled laborers.

3. They instinctively held onto their language very stubbornly but showed little initiative in establishing private schools or even in bringing their language into the curricula of the public schools.

4. They formed huge aggregations so that by force of circumstances in many public schools over 80% of the students, including those of the big cities, had Spanish as a mother tongue. This situation resulted in special pedagogical tasks and possibilities.

5. The strong admixture of Indian and, among the Puerto Ricans, some Negro blood led to racial tensions with their Anglo-American environment.

Even though they themselves did not press for the establishment of public Mexican or Puerto Rican schools, such schools were frequently established, partially by force of circumstances because of their local concentration. In the case of the Mexicans in the Southwest, school districts were deliberately carved out so that the Mexican sections formed separate districts, a situation similar to that of Negroes.

Racial policy, not language policy, formed these separate schools. But naturally there were resulting effects on the language policy. For example, Spanish remained the language of the children in the schoolyards, and many teachers attempted to use Spanish as an auxiliary language in the lower grades. This practice developed into a regular system for Puerto Rican children in New York City (Morrison 1958; and *The Impact of Puerto Rican Migration* 1957) where as early as 1953 there were 53,900 Puerto Rican students out of the city's total student population of 588,200. The Puerto Rican students were enrolled in so-called C classes, or orientation classes, where they were taught by substitute auxiliary teachers (SATs), who were usually Spanish-Americans who had difficulty finding positions in regular schools because of their accent. The office of a Puerto Rican Coordinator was established in junior high and elementary schools to inform the teachers of special problems of their Puerto Rican students. This coordinator was usually an SAT. But all these efforts did not make the public elementary and high schools bilingual, even though Spanish classes in high schools grew considerably in numbers and quality as a result of the influx of Puerto Rican students.

The special schools for Mexicans in the Southwest had similar effects. These schools have repeatedly been declared illegal where they did not come into existence as a result of settlement patterns but were created artificially. In 1929 this type of forced segregation was ruled illegal by the California Attorney General (Bogardus 1934; Kloss 1940, 423) and in 1945 by the United States Circuit Court of Appeals (Menendez case; see also Section 6-2). Teachers in the Southwest, however, have quite often made use of the opportunities offered by the special schools to teach the Mexican students the fundamentals of English with the help of their own mother tongue.

The Texas Educational Survey declared in 1925 that special schools and the separation of English-speaking and Spanish-speaking students were justified where they had been introduced for educational reasons and where they had led to determined efforts to have students of non-English mother tongues be taught by specially trained teachers and with special teaching aids (text in Kloss 1942, 680). The federal District Court for Texas followed suit and in 1948 permitted this kind of segregation at least for the first grade (The Delgado case; Marden 1952, 149). Individual public experimental schools went far beyond the use of Spanish as a mere tool of instruction in elementary education. Both English and Spanish were used together in all grades in a high school in San Antonio, Texas, during the 1920s (Reynolds 1933, 57, 62).

Table 4-5   Spanish Teaching in Elementary Schools

City	Year Introduced	Grades	Number of Students
Corpus Christi, Texas	1940	3-6	16,000
Gainesville, Florida	1942	3-6	120
Los Angeles, California	1943	differed	81,000
San Antonio, Texas	1943	3-6	3,000
San Diego, California	1944	4-6	8,000
El Paso, Texas	1951	1-5	7,700
Miami, Florida	1953	1-6	49,000

All these efforts received a new impetus from tl (Section 2-2). This movement was started entirely by Anglo of introducing Spanish on the elementary school level was re Anglo-Americans in cities with large Spanish-American mino

Table 4-5 gives figures to demonstrate the spread of tl in public elementary schools throughout the South (l.. Section 5-2). In El Paso this instruction was put under the supervision of a Spanish-Texan, Carlos Rivera (see, among others, Rivera 1954, 493-496). It seems a reasonable guess that in many instances the introduction of Spanish at the elementary school level aided the retention of the Spanish language.

Present Legal Status of Bilingual Schooling

Since the passage of the Bilingual Education Act (BEA) in 1967-1968 the problem of bilingual schools, buried and almost forgotten since World War I, has gained new significance (Section 2-2).

Table 4-6 gives a first outline of state legislation concerning schools with two languages as media of instruction as of January 1970. This table, however, tells only half the story. Underlying the silence of the laws we find in a good many cases a stubborn conviction that it "goes without saying" that all teaching has to be done through the English language. To this group belonged Hawaii, the states of the Old South, and both Massachusetts and Nevada, where the statutory provision prescribing English as the medium of instruction in nonpublic schools makes sense only if we assume that the same stipulation was taken for granted with regard to the public schools. In Hawaii a former provision making English mandatory was dropped in 1965 because it was believed to state the obvious. On the other hand, Alaska, Florida, Maryland, and Ohio interpreted the silence on the part of the statutes as indicative of a broadly permissive attitude. Kentucky, New Jersey, and Wyoming were known to permit at least the use of a non-English language (Spanish) in order to facilitate the transition from the mother tongue to English.

In those few states where we have explicit permissive legislation, it was in most cases of quite recent origin (1967-1969). Only in Minnesota (1877) and Rhode Island (1925) are these provisions several decades old. Moreover, most of these laws envisage merely the goal of promoting the acquisition of English by use of the mother tongue. Minnesota's law of 1877 and the amendments enacted in 1968 in New York State and in 1969 in Arizona, Colorado, and Maine all fell into this category. On the other hand, there were states which obviously permitted children to acquire equal ability in handling both their mother tongue and the English language. To this group belonged California, New Mexico, Texas, and (for nonpublic schools) Rhode Island. The recent permissive laws of Illinois, New Hampshire, and Pennsylvania left the question open but may be construed as giving leeway for fully bilingual programs.

Since 1970 a number of other states have enacted laws permitting and promoting bilingual education. Some of these aimed at paving the way for

6   State Legislation for Schools with Two Languages as Media for
           Instruction, January 1970

Legislation	Public and Nonpublic Schools	Public Schools Only	Nonpublic Schools Only
English required as medium of teaching	Alabama Arkansas Connecticut Iowa Kansas Michigan Minnesota Nebraska Nevada North Carolina Oregon South Dakota West Virginia	Idaho Indiana Louisiana North Dakota Oklahoma Wisconsin	Massachusetts Nevada
The statutes are silent	Alaska Delaware District of Columbia Florida Georgia Hawaii Kentucky Maryland Mississippi Missouri New Jersey Ohio South Carolina Tennessee Utah Vermont Virginia Wyoming	Arizona Colorado Massachusetts Nevada Rhode Island	Idaho Indiana Louisiana North Dakota Oklahoma Wisconsin
Permissive legislation	California (1967, 1968) Illinois (1969) Maine (1969) Minnesota (1877) New Hampshire (1969) New Mexico (1969)	Arizona (1969) Colorado (1969)	Rhode Island (1925)

Table 4-6 (continued)

New York (1968)
Pennsylvania
Texas
Washington

"organic assimilation" by using the mother tongue as a springboard for the acquisition of English. This holds, for example, for a Massachusetts law of 1971 (ch. 1005 = Gen. L. ch. 71 A) for providing "Transitional Bilingual Education" and an Illinois law as of 1973 (P.L. 78-727 = art. 14C school code) which even set up a State Department of Transitional Bilingual Education. Other post-1970 bills fostering bilingual education have become laws:

1972 in Alaska, California, Virgin Islands.
1973 in New Mexico and Texas.
1974 in Colorado.

They will be dealt with in the chapters on these six polities.

Finally, there has recently emerged in the United States a third movement in the area of bilingual teaching. Basically it has more to do with the teaching of foreign languages to English-speaking children than with language maintenance among non-English groups. Educators have become aware of the fact that teaching Spanish to "Anglo" children may become vastly more effective if the second language is not merely taught as a subject matter but is used as a medium for the teaching of some of the branches in learning, e.g., world history or even botany. This "content teaching" through the foreign languages has long been a practice in the Soviet Union (Ornstein 1958, 382-392). It has been tried out in a good many high schools in various parts of the United States (Christian 1967, 22-56; Caldwell 1967, 50-56). At least two state laws explicitly authorize this particular method (California 1967 and Pennsylvania 1969). Needless to say, this content teaching through target tongue while originally designed for English-speaking children, may become an efficient instrument in strengthening the mother tongue among students who happen to be native speakers of this "foreign" language.

After a bilingual public school was set up among Cuban refugees in Miami, Florida, in 1963 a strong movement to create Spanish-English schools all over the Southwest came into being. It gained nationwide significance and quickly reached a first climax with the passage in 1967 of the federal Bilingual Education Act (BEA, about which see Section 2-2). Some of these local Spanish-English experiments—a majority of which were started in Texas and California—were genuine attempts to bring about a fully bilingual and even bicultural education. Others simply and modestly tried to speed up Anglicization by the temporary use and teaching of the mother tongue; i.e., they constituted a new, enlightened brand of TESL (Teaching English as a Second Language) programs.

High Schools and Colleges

In the case of the cultivation of non-English languages in public high schools, colleges, and universities, one has to distinguish carefully between the cultivation of German, French, and Spanish on the one hand and that of all other languages on the other. The three languages enjoy a high status in the United States, although this has been true of Spanish only since the early twentieth century, with only 5,000 high school students studying Spanish in 1910 and 32,000 in 1915, while by 1928 there were 296,000. Because of the high prestige of these languages in the United States, their introduction as a subject is not necessarily related to the presence of an ethnic group that speaks German, French, or Spanish. In several instances, however, such a connection is quite obvious.

That Spanish became a compulsory subject in the public high schools of New Mexico in 1919 was primarily the result of the presence of the large Spanish-speaking population in that state, not because of the common border with Mexico. That French became a compulsory subject in the high schools of Massachusetts between 1857 and 1898 was, however, not the result of the presence of the large French Canadian element in the state. The teaching of German in the high schools of German settlements of the Midwest was occasionally so organized that German became more than a mere subject. In fact it is no exaggeration to say that many of these schools were bilingual (Section 5-4).

It was an exception, though hardly the only one, that at Washington University in St. Louis one of the five courses on German culture was intended for German Americans only while another one was for advanced Anglo-Saxon and freshman German American students (Viereck 1903, 146). At the University of Pennsylvania, German was recognized for some time as the second language of instruction (Section 5-3). There, around 1900, Professor M. D. Learned held lectures (presumably in English) about German-American topics. In the evening classes at the University of Cincinnati, beginning in 1908, H. H. Fick lectured in German about German-American literature. (For an outline of his lectures see Kloss 1940, 468-469.)

Where other living languages appeared in higher education, the respective immigrant ethnic groups were almost without exception responsible for their introduction. For example, the Scandinavians had chairs founded for Scandinavian languages at the University of Minnesota (1883) and at the University of North Dakota (1891). The Czechs too got chairs for their language and literature at the University of Nebraska (1907) and at the University of Texas (1915).

At the University of Hawaii in Honolulu a conscious and systematic program encourages students to study the language of their ancestors in their last years of study. For example, the students of East Asian descent are encouraged to study East Asian languages (Section 7-3).

4-5   MUNICIPAL GOVERNMENT

The languages of most recent immigrant groups were extensively used by the authorities and public institutions in two areas: in local administration and, even more, in public libraries.

In the case of city and county administrations we have to distinguish between the use of non-English languages as internal official languages and their use in the relation between civil servants and the residents of their city or county. The authorities almost without exception used only the languages of those groups which enjoyed the prestige of original settlers and which perhaps even lived in compact areas of settlement.

The long-time official use of minority languages by institutions of local administration in the old Spanish, French, and German areas of settlement in New Mexico, Louisiana, and Pennsylvania was quite natural. In many localities these languages were frequently the language of the overwhelming majority of the residents or in some instances of all of them. German was for some time the second official language in many language islands of the Midwest which came into existence during the nineteenth century. In Tell City, Indiana, which was founded in 1858, the members of the city council deliberated in both languages until about 1894, and also city ordinances were published in both English and German (*Indiana Historical Magazine* 1918, 124). The official language used in Hermann, Missouri, founded in 1837, was German until at least 1905 (Bek 1907, 147). In the city council of New Braunfels, Texas, German was used until 1890 (Eikel 1954, 16-17). Similar facts could perhaps be uncovered for several Czech communities in Texas and Scandinavian communities in the Midwest.

During the nineteenth century when they constituted the only very large immigrant group, Germans succeeded in winning comprehensive recognition for their language in many communities where they did not even form a majority. Schläger (1874, 22-23) wrote in 1884 concerning the time after the Republican ascendancy to power in 1860: "It was the rule in the large cities with many German-speaking residents to publish the records of the city council meetings and even the annual reports of the various city boards as, for example, the three-hundred-page report of the St. Louis Board of Education, in a German translation in a German newspaper (in New York City even in several) at the expense of the city. As a result those newspapers received an additional income of thousands of dollars, a fact which is of great importance for explaining the extraordinary political power of the newspapers which were favored in this manner."

As the above-mentioned example of the St. Louis Board of Education report proves, these German publications were not only notices in newspapers but also separate publications which were most likely printed by the printing houses of the German newspapers. Schläger's report should, however, not be taken to imply that there had been no local notices in the German language prior to 1860. The city council of Louisville, Kentucky, for example, decided in 1856 to resume the publication of its minutes in a German newspaper of the city, a practice which had been discontinued only the previous year because of nativist riots (Stierlin 1873, 178).

Smaller publications of local authorities were frequently printed in languages other than German. This was the case not so much with respect to official measures and ordinances but rather with respect to pamphlets intended to influence the residents in a certain direction, be it in connection with educational or social measures. In 1907 the City Health Board of Chicago published a pamphlet *Care of Infants and Young Children during the Hot Season* in English, German, Italian, Yiddish, Lithuanian, Polish, Swedish, and Czech and in 1917 a pamphlet *Our Babies . . . ,* in the same languages plus Croatian and Serbian (see *Chicago and Cook County*). Other pamphlets were printed for one particular ethnic group alone. For example, the Chicago Welfare Board published in 1919 a pamphlet *The Italians in Chicago* in English and Italian. A more detailed study of local official non-English language publications would have to include those semiofficial institutions which, without being integrated into or subordinated to the institutions of local government, use public funds and fulfill public functions, and which are given state-owned or city-owned property or housing, or on whose board of directors the government is represented as the result of specific laws. In Chicago we may count among these semipublic institutions the Historical Society, the Zoological Society, the Academy of Science, the Institute of Art, the Municipal Museum, and the Chicago New Charter Convention (Hodgson, p. iv). The Historical Society of Wisconsin in 1856 and 1857 published several annual volumes in the German and Norwegian languages.

At present, owing to the immigration of Puerto Ricans, New York City has become partially bilingual. The City Administration has undertaken to publish in Spanish various notices, posters, and leaflets issued by the City Departments of Fire, Health, Police, Sanitation, and Welfare. Placards urging pedestrians to cross the streets only with green traffic lights are written in both languages. Many policemen carry a Spanish dictionary as part of their equipment. Not a few have graduated from the police academy's courses in Spanish and in the history and culture of Puerto Rico. Also around two hundred Puerto Rican policemen had been recruited.

4-6   PUBLIC LIBRARIES

The numerous public libraries in America are a matter of municipal responsibility. Of course, there are state and privately financed libraries as well.

The extensive holdings of non-English books in the public libraries represent one of the most outstanding and, at the same time, least known American achievements in the field on nationality policy. Purchases of non-English books for public libraries constitute an altruistic promotion of ethnic groups because practical considerations on the part of the local authorities play no role.

While the purchase of some German or Spanish classics does not constitute intentional promotion of ethnic groups, numerous municipal libraries bought German books to an extent which went beyond a mere cultivation of certain generally valuable literature, and was clearly intended to promote the interests and the mother tongue of the German-speaking residents of the city. Even books in less frequently spoken languages were also often available in large numbers.

The New York Public Library once had one reading room each for Slavic languages and for Yiddish and Hebrew literature. The Chicago Public Library published special catalogs, among others, in 1929, a catalog of its Lettish books (63 pages); its Russian books in 1890, 1902, and 1918; its German books in 1912 (only new acquisitions since 1909); its Polish books in 1926; its Scandinavian books in 1913 and 1929; etc. (*Chicago and Cook County* 172-173). In 1961 the same library had 90,000 non-English books, among them 20,000 German, 13,000 French, 9,000 Polish, 7,000 Spanish, 6,000 Yiddish, 5,000 Russian, 4,000 Italian, etc.

As of 1961 the foreign-language department of the Los Angeles Public Library (not counting the numerous non-English books of the branch libraries) held 20,000 to 24,000 German, French, and Spanish volumes; over 9,300 Russian; 6,000 Italian; 4,700 Yiddish; 2,800 Swedish; 2,700 Magyar; 1,800 Polish; 1,300 Hebrew; 1,200 Dutch; 1,100 Czech; 1,000 each Danish and Norwegian; 500 to 900 each Arab, Finnish, Japanese, Portuguese, Serbo-Croatian; and 200 to 400 each Armenian, Chinese, Greek, Lettish, and Lithuanian volumes.

The corresponding figures for the Cleveland Public Library are: 24,700 German; 19,700 French; 10,600 Magyar; 9,200 Spanish; 8,100 Russian; 7,700 Italian; 6,500 each Yiddish and Czech; 6,300 Polish; 4,300 Ukrainian; 4,000 Slovak; 3,700 Slovene; 2,900 Hebrew; 2,700 Swedish; 2,300 Finnish; 2,000 Lithuanian; 1,600 to 1,900 each Arab, Croatian, Dutch; 1,100 to 1,500 each Danish, Greek, Portuguese, Rumanian, Serbian; 800 to 1,000 each Armenian, Bulgarian, Lettish; 200 each Chinese and Estonian.

While in all these cities the non-English holdings are considerable, there are others where we find them to be rather slender if compared with the number of immigrants. The St. Louis Public Library owned in 1968, 46,400 non-English books, whereof 15,500 were German; 11,900 French; 5,700 Spanish; 4,000 Italian; 1,300 each Latin, Russian, and Yiddish; 600 Polish; 700 in Classical Greek; 400 each in Modern Greek, Hebrew, Dano-Norwegian (probably. Danish plus Riksmaal); between 200 and 250 in Portuguese, Rumanian, and Dutch; and 150 in Chinese. No other language is represented by more than 89 titles, i.e., the number of Czech books. The almost complete absence of books in Slavic languages, other than Russian, is particularly striking. Our findings are worse in Milwaukee, where in 1968 of 21,000 non-English books, 11,600 were German; 2,100 Polish; 1,600 French; 1,200 Spanish; 800 Italian; 700 Hungarian; 500 Serbo-Croatian; 400 Russian; 300 each Lithuanian (plus Lettish), Swedish, and Dutch with no other language getting beyond the 245 mark reached by Modern Greek. The most obvious neglect is the lack of Yiddish books, with only 43 titles. The picture is worst in Cincinnati (1968): 5,600 German books, 2,600 French, 570 Spanish, 520 Italian, 250 each Hungarian and Russian, 100 Polish, with all other languages remaining below this mark. Thus it cannot generally be said that all public libraries are promoting the various immigrant languages with equal zeal.

In public libraries of communities inhabited by a predominantly non-English population, English books sometimes even formed a minority. In 1907, of the 1,300 books in the school library of Hermann, Missouri, 705 were in German (Bek 1907, 147), and in 1900, of the 23,000 books in the Belleville, Illinois, public library, 13,000 were German (Steuernagel 1936).

When the Wisconsin Free Library Commission (founded in 1895) established traveling libraries, one of their major functions was to serve "communities whose libraries have a large number of Scandinavian, German, Bohemian, or Polish patrons" (*Blue Book of Wisconsin* 1909, 735).

4-7   PUERTO RICAN OFFICES ON THE MAINLAND

The Puerto Ricans occupy a special position among the more recent immigrant groups. Their number was estimated in 1960 at 850,000, of whom 640,000 were island-born persons. Their major periods of immigration were the 1940s and particularly the 1950s. During these decades the immigration of other ethnic groups decreased to a degree which justifies calling the Puerto Ricans the "sole immigrants." They came from an area (until 1952 a territory, since then an associated state) where Spanish is the language of practically all the inhabitants and enjoys equal official status with English.

The large number of Puerto Ricans in New York City made it inevitable that Spanish be used from time to time by New York City authorities. For example, the notices of the city's Bureau of School Lunches are bilingual (*The Impact. . . .* 1957, 41). Puerto Rico has always had an official Resident Commissioner in Washington, D. C. After mass immigration to New York was under way, the Puerto Rican Ministry of Labor established in 1948 an office in New York City to aid Puerto Ricans in locating jobs and housing. In 1949 a similar office was set up in Chicago. Both in 1951 were put under the control of the newly created Migration Division of the Ministry of Labor in San Juan. In the year 1956 branch offices were opened in Cleveland and in seven eastern cities so that there were now branch offices in: New York State (Newburgh and Rochester), New Jersey (Camden and Keyport), New England (Boston, Massachusetts, and Hartford, Connecticut), and the Midwest (Cleveland, Ohio, and Chicago, Illinois). Hanson (1960, 37-39) gives a very different list of names.

The New York office, under Joseph Monserrat, is the head office while the Cleveland and Chicago offices are regional offices for the Lake Erie area and the Midwest region, respectively. As official agencies of the Puerto Rican government, they provide support, advice, and guidance to Puerto Rican immigrants in their mother tongue. These offices also sponsor night classes in English and organize Puerto Rican clubs. Small wonder then that these immigrants, despite their often miserable economic circumstances, are frequently more self-confident and determined than are other non-English groups and that in New York City Puerto Ricans frequently acted as spokesmen to the city authorities for groups composed of various ethnic groups, for example, speaking for Puerto Rican, Polish, Negro, or Italian tenants in the city's slums (Hanson 1960, 39).

Table 4-7   Chief Ethnic Institutions in American Cities

Groups of People	Educational Institutions	Information and Entertainment
Associations	Public library	Newspapers
Congregations	Private school	Magazines
		Radio programs
		Movie theaters

4-8   A CROSS SECTION: MIAMI

Up to now we have listed in systematic order those individual institutions which were established on the basis of either promotion-oriented or tolerance-oriented nationality rights, by the immigrants or for them. Using the example of a single city, we will now demonstrate how these institutions operate at present. We have chosen a city with relatively simple conditions, since a study of a larger city with many immigrant ethnic groups would take up too much space.

In the average American city the five major private institutions which adult members of a minority group may establish on the basis of tolerance-oriented nationality rights are associations, church congregations, newspapers, radio stations, and movie theaters. These are joined by important institutions like the foreign-language departments of public libraries, and the private, mostly parochial, elementary schools where the language of the minority is the language of instruction.

If we group these institutions together, we get the pattern of Table 4-7. Of course magazines and radio programs are not necessarily tied to the city but can also operate outside the city limits. Because of the FLES movement in recent years, the public elementary schools have surpassed the private elementary schools as an important means of cultivating minority languages.

According to *The New York Times* (January 1, 1961) and letters received from Miami, in 1960 about one-tenth of the 292,000 inhabitants of Miami, Florida, had Spanish as their mother tongue. (Miami is the county seat of Dade County, which had a population of 935,000). They are all recent immigrants. No descendants of the Florida Spaniards from the period before 1819 are among them (Section 6-2). Spanish won additional importance for Miami because many visitors from Latin America make the city (the nearest airport in the United States) their first stop during visits to the United States and because many thousands of political refugees from Cuba have settled in Miami. The following description of ethnic-linguistic conditions obtained in Miami around 1960 will serve to illustrate the potential possibilities inherent in the overall legal situation in the United States. I deliberately chose a city situated in a state which is not noted for a particularly marked bilingual tradition.

Among others, the Spanish-Americans in Miami enjoyed the following institutions which were based on tolerance-oriented nationality rights: numerous associations (for example, "Centro, Hispano Catolico," a "Centro" for business-men, "Casa de las Americas"); a bilingual daily newspaper, *Diario de las Americas* with 17,000 copies in 1953; a Spanish column in the English-language Catholic weekly; three movie theaters; 52.5 hours of Spanish-language radio broadcasts per week, station WMIE; 14 hours of television broadcasts per week from one television station.

In 9 of the 35 Catholic congregations sermons were held in English and Spanish. In the vast majority of the Catholic elementary schools of the city Spanish was taught as a subject, usually beginning with the fourth grade; but nowhere was Spanish used as the language of instruction.

The extraordinary development of Spanish in the public schools will be described in the section on Florida (Section 6-2). The other major non-English-speaking group, the German-speaking minority, had its own weekly newspaper (*Florida Echo*, since 1925). There were also four German-American clubs. The oldest of them, the Steuben Society, dated from 1946, and one of the four was a club of German Jews, dating from 1957. German movies were shown from November to April at the university. German-language church services were held until about 1959 in a Lutheran church.

In the area of promotion-oriented nationality rights we may point to the 800 to 850 German books in the public library. German is taught, however, only at senior high schools. The *Deutscher Verein* at the university, dating from 1925, is the oldest German-language organization of the city.

Radio station WMIE, in addition to its Spanish-language programs (see above), also broadcast weekly 2.5 hours in Italian, 2 hours in Yiddish, 1.5 hours each in Greek and Magyar, 1 hour in Polish, and 0.5 hour in Arabic (Syrian). It should, however, be taken for granted that many of the listeners to non-English language broadcasts live outside the city of Miami and Dade County.

The above figures are intended to demonstrate those features of Miami which are typical for the manifold opportunities and forms of cultivating immigrant languages in larger American cities. For this reason, we ignored nontypical features which in the case of Miami appeared in recent years when Miami became the center of Cuban exiles from the Castro regime, with approximately 200 of their organizations, including their main organization, "The Cuban Revolutionary Council," under Dr. Jose Miro-Cardona, Castro's first prime minister.

CHAPTER FIVE

Promotion-Oriented Nationality Law
for Large Old-Settlers Groups
in Mainland States

5-1 LOUISIANA

Background

As the first white settlers, the Spaniards set foot on Louisiana soil not later than 1542. In the year 1682 La Salle claimed the area for France, and in 1718 New Orleans was founded. From 1719 on Negro slaves were imported, who later became French speaking. In 1762 Louisiana was ceded to Spain, which had to assert itself against the armed resistance of the local Frenchmen. Louisiana was returned to France in 1800 and purchased by the United States in 1803.

The French-speaking population of Louisiana is composed of three groups (Kane 1943; Smith and Hitt 1952; Ficatier 1957, 261-293; Tisch 1959):

1. The Creoles are French-speaking people who came directly from Europe. They originated predominantly in France but have also absorbed large groups of Germans ("German Creoles") who settled between 1718 and 1721 up the river from New Orleans (Deiler 1909) and Spaniards, who entered the country during the Spanish rule. According to Tisch (1959, 29), Spanish is still spoken in isolated instances by the older generation, for example, at the Bayou Teche. Tisch points out also (1959, 48, 57) that many Anglo-Saxon mountaineers were absorbed by the French element during the nineteenth century and a number of Italians during the twentieth century.

2. The Acadians are the French Canadians who came to Louisiana around 1765 (having been expelled from the Maritime Provinces) and who settled west of the Creoles.

3. The French-speaking Negroes (and Mulattoes) are scattered throughout the French language area as pointed out by Desdunes (1911), himself a Negro.

The safest way to demarcate roughly the area of French settlement is by making use of the parish figures for the proportion of Roman Catholics (cf. map in Kloss 1942, 1001).

In the past the Creoles have furnished the majority of the intellectual and political leaders of the French element, especially since they were frequently reinforced by later immigrants from France during the nineteenth century. In 1860, French-born persons numbered 14,900. This element furnished a large part of the French-writing journalists and authors. The Acadians retained their language more stubbornly, however, and extended the French-speaking area into Texas. In recent times the slowly emerging middle and upper class Acadians are gaining the upper hand against the declining Creoles.

In 1940, French-speaking whites numbered 298,000, of whom 97% were the children of American-born parents and who at that time constituted approximately one-fifth of the entire white population. To this figure may be added as of 1940 some 100,000 French-speaking Negroes. At present estimates run from a few hundred persons to more than a million; the figure 500,000 should be reasonably near the truth.

Three kinds of French can be found in Louisiana: (1) the standard Louisiana French of the Creoles is a variety of standard French (Read 1931; Lane 1934, 323-333). (2) Acadian is spoken in the southwest of the state and is a twin sister of the French dialect spoken in New Brunswick (Ditchy 1932; Phillips 1936). (3) Gombo is often confusingly called Creole and is the language of most of the French-speaking Negroes (Tinker 1935; Broussard 1942).

The French element reached its cultural height during the first half of the nineteenth century when a substantial literature (Caulfield 1929; Tinker 1932) and a vigorous press (Tinker 1933) were flourishing. This time also marked the peak of French political influence. The leading paper was the daily *Abeille* of New Orleans (1827-1923).

During the first half of the twentieth century, the remainders of the French press have disappeared, and the literature continued to be cultivated only in the annual *Comptes Rendus* of the Athénée Louisianais in New Orleans, an independent academy, founded in 1876 for the protection and cultivation of the French language and still existing.

The French element participated early in the political leadership of the state (Newton 1933-1934; Klein 1940). For many years the election results followed the language patterns rather clearly. For example, in Howard (1957) compare the maps with the election results of 1828 and 1831 and, to a lesser degree, also of 1834, 1850, and 1852. In the year 1816 Villère was elected the first French governor; and until 1846 there was a majority of French governors, among whom Mouton (1843-1846) was the first Acadian. Derbigny (1828-1829) was born in France, Thibodeaux (1824) in New York State, and the rest were Creoles.

Until about 1831 the ruling party was the Democratic, which had been called the Democratic-Republican Party until about 1825. After that the Whigs held power as a result of the views of most of the French sugarcane planters, who favored protective tariffs. Then again in 1843 the Democrats, primarily supported by the Anglo-Saxons of northern Louisiana and of the city of New Orleans, won the upper hand. Most governors were by that time Anglo-Saxon, but the equal legal status of the French language was guaranteed by the state constitutions during this same period (see below).

The secession from the United States of 1861 was strongly supported by the French element with A. Mouton acting as chairman of the secession convention. The French were sparsely represented among the Republicans who ruled after 1864 and who based their strength for the time being strongly upon the Negroes. When the whites and the Democratic party returned to power with the help of the White League, founded by Alicibiade De Blanc, the French element was again represented among their ranks, but seldom in leading positions. However, maps showing the election results may still occasionally reveal the special position of the French south toward the rest of Louisiana. For example, in Howard (1957) compare the charts of the elections of 1900, 1916, 1924 (Huey Long elected by the northern part), and 1928 (when the southern part voted for Catholic Al Smith).

Gradually the position of the French language was shaky, particularly among the Creoles in the eastern part of the originally French area where Anglicization has made considerable progress. However, the opinion of Ficatier (1957) is too pessimistic when he says that only a few hundred Creoles still use French as their main language. The French language survives more vigorously among the Acadians of the Southwest, even though it is predominantly in the form of a dialect. The dialect was also used by many of the eleven radio stations (1961) which broadcast regular French programs for the French-speaking areas: in Abbeville, 20 hours weekly; in Crowley, 20 hours; in Eunice, 13 hours; in Houma, 11 hours; in Jennings, 7 hours; in Lafayette, two stations, 1 hour and 2.5 hours; in Lake Charles, 1 hour; in Marksville, 2 hours; in Opelousas, 20 hours; and in Thibodaux, 1 hour. Until recently broadcasts were almost exclusively in the Acadian dialect, but now efforts are under way to give more room to standard French.

The relatively small groups still active in the twentieth century in their endeavors for the preservation of the French language have received support from France and Canada.

The French government financed until about 1958 the teaching of French at a number of public elementary schools in New Orleans. The Comité France-Acadie in Paris created a France-Louisiane section. Only a few years after it was established, scholarships were granted to bring students from Louisiana to France.

Since 1930, when an Acadian delegation from Canada discovered the Acadians in the South, relations between Louisiana and French Canada, particularly between the Acadians of both countries, have become much closer.

Apart from the French element, the German element in Louisiana also enjoyed temporarily certain language rights (Kloss 1938, 402-405). Nevertheless the descendants of the German immigrants of the eighteenth century were absorbed by the French element after 1800. But in the nineteenth century numerous Germans immigrated and in 1860 there were 24,600 German-born persons (19,800 in New Orleans). In 1910 there were 29,000 first or second generation persons of German lineage, of whom only 8,900 were born abroad.

For the German element the Deutsche Gesellschaft (1847 to 1928) and the *Deutsche Zeitung* (1848 to 1907) were particularly important, the latter, together with the *Abeille*, being for a long time the most influential non-English newspapers of the state.

The Struggle for Self-Government

The treaty of October 21, 1803, stated in Article III that the inhabitants of the territories newly ceded to the United States should "as soon as possible . . . enjoy all rights, privileges, and legal protection of citizens of the United States." But by the Organic Act of March 26, 1804, the area of present Louisiana was made a territory of the second category (Table 1-1) under the name "Orleans," with a governor appointed by the President and a council whose members were required to have lived in the territory for only one year and who were also appointed by the president. This arrangement offered no guarantees to the French element that it would participate in the government of the territory at all.

The plan met with heavy opposition during the debate in Congress (E. S. Brown 1920, esp. 129-146). In the Senate, John Quincy Adams denied the authority of the federal government to take such a step. The people of Louisiana had not been asked to give that authority, and the people of the United States could not grant it since they had not been informed in advance about the treaty and were therefore no party to it. Congress was obliged to propose an amendment to the Constitution, to submit it to the states for approval, and to ask the inhabitants themselves about their wishes. In detailed criticisms, John Quincy Adams pointed out the absence of a separation of powers and of a provision which would automatically grant the territory the right for an elected representation in Congress once a certain population had been reached. Similar views were voiced in the House of Representatives and by the press. One New York newspaper spoke of "a form of government as despotic as that of the Turks."

As early as 1804 members of the French population of the Orleans territory listed their complaints in a detailed petition to Congress. The petition was drafted by Livingston and was presented in Washington by three French-born inhabitants; Derbigny, Destrehan, and Sauvé (E. S. Brown 1920, 146, 155-156).

On the basis of the new Organic Law, Louisiana could perhaps be considered a province of the United States but not a component part, because this would presuppose a republican form of government. Consequently, Louisiana had not yet been incorporated into the Union—an argument which anticipated the topic of the controversies beginning in 1900 and 1917 about the status of Puerto Rico and other new acquisitions (Section 7-1).

On January 25, 1805, Representative J. Randolph of Virginia answered the petition for a Congressional committee. He denied the charges made in the petition that Congress had failed to fulfill the obligations toward the French in Louisiana which had been specified in the treaty of annexation, but he recommended urgently that Congress voluntarily make concessions to the French of Louisiana.

"Your committee at the same time earnestly recommend that every indulgence, not incompatible with the interests of the Union may be extended to them. Only two modes present themselves, whereby a dependent province may be held in obedience to its sovereign state—force and affection. The first of these is not only repugnant to all our principles and institutions of Government, but it could not be more odious to those on whom it might operate, than it would be hostile to the best interests, as well as the dearest predilections, of those by whom, in this instance, it would have to be exercised. The United States are not the property of an hereditary despot, or the rich prize of a military adventurer ... but they form the patrimony of a free and enlightened people, who control, while they constitute, the only fund from which the men and the money of which military power is composed can be drawn. It can never be the interest, therefore, of the people of the United States to subject themselves to the burthens, and their liberties to the dangers, of a vast military force for the subjugation of others. The only alternative, then, which presents itself, is believed to be not more congenial to the feelings, than to the best interests of the Union. So long as their authority pervades the Territory of Louisiana, so long as their laws are respected and obeyed therein, your committee are at a loss to conceive how the United States are more interested in the internal government of that Territory than of any State in the Confederacy. By permitting her inhabitants to form their own regulations the voice of discontent would be hushed, faction (if it exist) disarmed and the people bound to us by the strong ties of gratitude and interest. The spirit of disaffection, should it be excited at any future period by ambitious and unprincipled men, would be in direct hostility to the obvious interests of the people of Louisiana, whilst the ability of the Union to repress it would remain unimpaired."

This report is one of the most important American and Western documents concerning the question of how a state should treat the ethnically different inhabitants of a province which had been annexed without prior consultation of these inhabitants. For this reason, it would merit inclusion in Commager's *Documents*. (The text appears also in Kloss 1940, 159-160.)

On the basis of a corresponding Congressional resolution of the same day which expressly granted the inhabitants of Louisiana the right of self-government, Louisiana (still called Orleans) on March 2, 1805, received a new Organic Act which took important steps forward with regard to all three points listed above: an elected territorial legislature, a council whose members were appointed by the President in conjunction with the Senate on the basis of suggestions made by the territorial legislature, and last, but not least, the promise of statehood as soon as the census should show a population of 60,000 free inhabitants, a provision which corresponded to the Great Ordinance of 1787 (Section 1-1).

For the first time in the history of the United States, self-government was granted to a newly annexed territory that was inhabited by a strong majority which was not Anglo-Saxon. For 1806 the population was estimated at 26,000 whites, 3,400 free colored inhabitants (thus a combined total of about 30,000 free inhabitants), and 25,600 slaves. Of the white inhabitants, 13,500 are estimated to have been born in Louisiana, only 3,500 in the remainder of the United States, and the rest in Europe (Germany, France, England, Ireland, Spain). Jefferson is reported to have contemplated in 1807 a plan to have the government settle 30,000 Anglo-Saxons in Louisiana and thereby create an English-speaking majority (E. S. Brown 1920, 165). As early as 1810 the census showed the required minimum number of free inhabitants.

Thus, in 1812 Louisiana could be admitted as a regular state on the basis of an 1811 Enabling Act of Congress which permitted from then on the election of the senate and the governor. Also in 1812 the area of Louisiana was enlarged by the former Spanish West Florida which, however, was at that time predominantly Anglo-Saxon. There is no doubt that a strong French majority still existed in Louisiana at that time. As late as 1830, there were an estimated two Creoles for every American in New Orleans.

In 1968 the French element had been given, through law no. 409, a central coordinating agency, the 50-member "Council for the Development of the French Language in Louisiana" (CODOFIL). Through its activities, close collaboration with the governments of Canada, Quebec, New Brunswick, and France had been established which aimed at reinforcing the hold of French on the inhabitants of southwestern Louisiana.

Language Provisions in the State Constitutions

The state constitution of 1812 did not mention the French language a single time. In Article VI (12) it was stated that state laws, official documents of the state, and court and legislative records should use the language "in which the Constitution of the United States is written." This provision was adopted from the Enabling Act of Congress of February 20, 1811, and was, with only insignificant change, repeated in the state constitutions of 1845 (Article 103) and 1852 (Article 100). The language provisions of the latter were identical with those of the 1845 constitution. But, in addition, the two later constitutions contained several articles which expressly addressed themselves to the French-speaking inhabitants:

Article 132 of the 1845 constitution (Article 129 of 1852) reads: "The constitution and laws of this state shall be promulgated in the English and French languages."

Article 104 of 1845 (Article 101 of 1852) stated: "The Secretary of the Senate and clerk of the House of Representatives shall be conversant with the English and French languages and members may address either house in the French or English language."

According to Article 140 of the 1845 constitution (Article 141 of 1852) amendments to the constitution had to be made public in each county in at least one newspaper in each of the two languages.

Louisiana's defeat on the side of the other southern states in the Civil War led to a new state constitution in 1864. It omitted all 1845 and 1852 pro-French-language provisions; reiterated the provision of the three earlier constitutions about English as the language of the laws, documents, and records; and stated in Article 142 that instruction in the public elementary schools had to be given in English. The earlier constitutions did not concern themselves with the language of instruction.

According to Article 155 the constitution was to be published in three newspapers of the state; two of them were to publish it in English and French and one in German. That German was taken into consideration was presumably the result of the fact that among the numerous Germans of the state (particularly of New Orleans) there were relatively more partisans of the North than among the Anglo-Saxons and French. Of the ninety members of the constitutional assembly of 1864, twenty had names of German origin; the assembly almost decided to have its records published in German in addition to French (Kloss 1940, 170). The first Republican governor of the state (1864-1865) was Bavarian-born Michael Hahn.

The constitution of 1868 retained all the provisions of its predecessor, which had been unfavorable to the French language, and added the provision (Article 109) that no law should require that court procedures be held in any language other than English.

After the Democrats regained power in the state in 1877, a new constitution was adopted in 1879. It again granted certain privileges to the French language. According to Article 154, the state legislature could order that laws be published also in French and that court announcements also be made public in French in certain towns and counties which were to be specified by name. Article 226, even though again prescribing English as the language of instruction in public schools, added that, in counties, or towns of these counties where French was predominantly spoken, the elementary subjects could also be taught in French "provided this would not cause additional expenses."

Here we have the bilingual school in which all subjects could be taught in both languages. In contrast, the constitution of 1898 brought several restrictions; according to Article 251 "French could be taught" in predominantly French towns and counties; i.e., French was permitted as a subject only, not as language of instruction.

The constitution of 1913 retained the language provisions of its predecessor. In the constitution of 1921 (in force until 1974) all references to the French language had disappeared. The existence of a language problem in Louisiana was only hinted at in Article 197 (3), where it is stated that any applicant is permitted to write his petition, asking for the right to vote, in English "or in his mother tongue." This provision put French into the same category as the immigrant languages. During the constitutional convention, Silas Ponder proposed inserting "French language" instead of "mother tongue" (Kloss 1940, 167).

On January 1, 1975, a new constitution became effective which, while not mentioning the French language, confirmed in article XII (4) the right of inhabitants "to preserve, foster and promote their respective historic, linguistic and cultural origins."

Summing up the language provisions in the ten constitutions of the State of Louisiana, we can note the following: the constitution of 1812 ignores the French language; those of 1845 and 1852 grant positive recognition; those of 1864 and 1868 deny recognition; those of 1879, 1898, and 1913 again grant recognition; that of 1921 denies recognition definitely; that of 1975 seems to reopen the door to formal recognition. A basic difference exists between the two periods of recognition. Under the constitutions of 1845 and 1852 the French element enjoyed fully equal status; under the constitutions of 1879, 1898, and 1913 it was granted just simple nationality rights. During the later period it was taken for granted that the language of the state was English. French found consideration as a supplementary language only, with provisions permitting French but not making its use mandatory, often with clear reference to the special needs of the French-speaking areas. During the period from 1845 to 1864, on the other hand, French enjoyed equal status with English. It was mentioned side by side with English and, in two instances, even before English. The provisions in favor of French do not regulate the special needs of an ethnic group; rather, they touch the life of the state in its totality. They affect as well, therefore, the Anglo-Saxon population. No Anglo-Saxon, for instance, who was unable to speak French was allowed to be secretary of the senate or clerk of the house of representatives.

This attitude toward the French language is evident even in the constitution of 1864, which is otherwise characterized by its anti-French character. Though Article 155 provided that the constitution be published in the newspapers in English, French, and German, two different methods were prescribed for the French and German verions. The German version was to be published by itself (which could only be done in a German newspaper). The French version, on the other hand, was to be published in two newspapers together with the English version; it was therefore presented to the Anglo-Saxons as well.

As in the case of the periods of recognition, the three periods of nonrecognition of the French language also differ considerably in character. We can speak of a direct campaign against the French language only during the middle period, 1864 to 1879. In the period after 1921, the French language was less the object of a direct campaign against it but rather was dropped as superfluous. During the period from 1812 to 1845 French could be bypassed, but not directly be attacked. We will see later that during those years a considerable number of laws already respected the importance of French. Generally speaking, the legal as well as the actual conditions were not so drastic during the three less favorable periods as may be supposed from the wording of the constitution. For example, the 1864 constitution stated that the English language should be taught in the elementary schools. It is no accident, however, that in the constitutional convention the plenary session rejected the phrase, "the English language only shall be taught," as was suggested by the committee for education (Kloss 1940,

169). The constitution of 1921 also speaks of English instruction, but French has nevertheless always been taught as a subject at individual public elementary schools (see below).

French Administration and Legislature

The constitution of 1812 provided that the laws and government publications be printed in English—but not that they be printed *only* in English. In the example of the school language article of the 1864 constitution in the preceding paragraph, I showed what importance the members of the constitutional assembly placed on the word "only." We may assume that very early, perhaps as early as 1812, the laws and government publications appeared either in a special French edition or, more likely, in bilingual editions. The latter possibility is known to me, for example, in the case of the 1825 Civil Code (after it had been decided the previous year that the English and French texts were to be printed on opposite pages) and in the cases of the 1825 Code of Practice and of two militia laws of 1834 and 1842 (Kloss 1940, 190-191, 171-172). The journals of the legislature were printed in bilingual editions during the years 1812-1867 (*American Notes and Queries* 1943, 173).

A comprehensive regulation, however, is known only from the period of the 1845 constitution with its favorable treatment of the French language. A law of 1847 provided: "The laws shall be published in the English and French languages, in the same manner as heretofore, the English upon the odd and the French upon the even page. . . . There shall be 250 copies of the journals of each house, in book form, in the English and French languages, in the same manner as heretofore. . . . Bills and resolutions shall be printed on foolscap paper in the English and French languages unless otherwise directed. . . . Of every bill and resolution which have been ordered printed by either of the two houses, 200 copies shall be printed."

Under the anti-French constitution of 1864, a law was passed which changed the situation: Official prints were not mentioned; only English was prescribed for bills and resolutions, but the arrangement was retained as far as promulgation of the laws and printed editions of the session records were concerned. It was also added that the current session records should be published daily in both languages in the official journal.

It was not until 1868 that a law was passed (No. 8) which prescribed only English editions of the laws and session records.

During the year of the Democratic victory, however, a law was passed on March 12, 1877, according to which the state laws had to be continuously published in French and German in a French and a German daily. The provision existed for only four years. Law No. 6 of 1881 (in Paragraph 19) restricted this continuous publication of laws to one French daily; i.e., it eliminated the German publication; furthermore, it ruled (Paragraph 13) that the compiled edition of the laws should occur in hard cover in the English language and in soft cover in the French language, while the publication of the session records continued to occur in English only. The regulation of 1881 was incorporated into Law No. 184 of

Table 5-1   Number of Copies Prescribed in English and French for
Publications of Certain State Offices

Office	English Copies	French Copies
Swampland Commissioners	800	200
State Comptroller	1,500	500
School Superintendent	1,000	500
Director of the School for the Deaf, Dumb, and Blind	250	250

1908 concerning official publications. But this 1908 law was replaced in 1912 by a new law (No. 141) which no longer contained any mention of French.

Until 1950 a law of 1856 remained in force which prescribed the publication of French editions for four state offices as shown in Table 5-1 (Louisiana 1950; Wolff 1920, II, sec. 1558).

The Courts

In no other part of the United States did a non-English language play such an important role in the judicial system as in Louisiana. The importance of the French language was increased by the fact that the written law of the state is based primarily on the Code Napoleon. The oldest collected statutes under federal rule, however, which appeared in 1808, were still primarily based on Spanish law, which had prevailed in Louisiana, but some of its ideas had already influenced these oldest statutes.

As late as 1819 an edition of the Spanish Siete Partidas, which were still valid at that time, could be published at the instigation of the legislature. In the year 1824 Livingstone presented a Criminal and Penal Code which he had drafted in French and English at the order of the state legislature. This Code was published in 1833 but never became effective. At approximately the same time a committee, of which Livingstone was also a member, completed a Civil Code which was ordered printed in a bilingual edition with the English and French versions on opposite pages (Pierce, Taylor, and King 1852, 147).

The Civil Code appeared in 1825. In the same year a Code of Practice was also published which became important for ethnic groups since it contained several language provisions (see below). In 1936 the bilingual texts of both codes were newly published following a 1935 resolution of the state legislature and a request of the State Bar Association of Louisiana (Louisiana Law 286; Besou Letter; Lauvrière 1939, 430). A law of 1828 repealed all laws which had been adopted prior to the time the 1825 code went into effect.

The Civil Code of Louisiana is based almost entirely upon the Code Napoleon, while in other parts of the legal system the English common law dominated as, for example, in the Penal and Commercial Codes. The fact that the law frequently went back to French legal sources gave the French version of the laws an importance which exceeded that of equal validity. In 1826, for example, Articles 179 and 959 of the English version of the Code of Practice were especially adapted to the French version by law (Pierce, Taylor, and King 1852, 147; Fuqua 1867, 144). Greiner declares in his 1841 preface to his *Louisiana Digest* that the French text is generally more precise and consequently of more value to him. Article 952, for example, is said to be completely nonsensical in its English version (Greiner 1841, vii).

As time went by, the French version naturally became less important. Nevertheless, occasionally French decisions are still quoted in legal textbooks of the twentieth century (Edwin and Merrick 1925, 466).

During the first decades, the mingling of Latin and Anglo-Saxon ways of administering justice led to the most curious difficulties. The spirits of the two legal concepts were completely different. The Anglo-Saxon were unable to reproduce the concepts of the Code Napoleon, and the Anglo-Saxon institution of the jury was completely incomprehensible to the French. The French Louisianan Charles E. A. Gayarré has given a convincing and entertaining description of the clash of these two worlds within the same legal framework (Speranza 1923, 34ff.). In general, the French reluctantly adopted the institutions of Anglo-Saxon self-government. The frequent elections alone were repugnant to them. An excellent description of the Creole attitude toward the Anglo-Saxon way of life is given by Charles Sealsfield (1846, 250-273).

The barrier created by their different ways of life and ethnic characteristics was further accentuated by the lingual separation. This was particularly true during the first decades when the French seldom had a command of English and when the courts did not yet make use of the French language to the extent that it was used in the years following 1825. A description by Judge F. X. Martin is given in King and Ficklen (1893, 159) and is typical of the reports of these years: "The courts employed interpreters of the French, Spanish, and English languages. They interpreted, when need arose, the proofs and charges of the judges, but not the pleas of the lawyers. The proceedings were opened in the English language, and those jurors who did not understand English were permitted to retire to the lobby. If the lawyer pleaded in French, they were again called back, and if the remaining jurors were American and could not understand French, they in turn were permitted to retire. They went together to the jury room where everybody would declare the plea he had heard best, and finally they would agree upon a verdict as best as circumstances permitted."

The language provisions of the 1825 Code of Practice were omitted in the 1870 edition, though they could still be found in the 1867 edition. The language provisions, disregarding paragraphs dealing with official announcements which will be discussed below, applied to the following areas: it was necessary to draft in both languages according to Article 172 the petition of the plaintiff and according to Article 177 the subpoena of the justice of the peace to the defendant, if one of the two parties involved was of French mother tongue; according to Article 179 the subpoena to the defendant, if the defendant was of French mother tongue;

according to Article 178 the reply of the defendant, if the plaintiff was of French mother tongue; according to Article 626 the writ of execution, if the losing party was of French mother tongue.

With respect to the last provision the courts ruled in 1848 that acceptance of a petition drafted only in English (Article 172) would not constitute an abrogation of bilingual draft of the court order on the part of the debtor (*Dubroca* v. *Favrot*; Kloss 1940, 195). In 1851 it was ruled that the debtor could forgo a French version of the court order without given the creditor cause for complaints (*Le Blanc* v. *Dubroca*; *Lafon* v. *Smith*; Kloss 1940, 196).

Still valid is a provision of 1855: "Any act or contract made or executed in the French language is as legal and binding upon the parties as if it had been made or executed in the English language" (Phillips, *Revised Statutes*; Kloss 1940, 214; *Louisiana Revised Statutes*).

Official Advertisements

The oldest law known to me dates back to the year 1817. It regulated announcements concerning real estate and slave auctions in Jefferson Parish (including New Orleans) and made the basic bilingual character (which was presupposed) more elastic by permitting the possibility of having the announcement published in one language only—even in French. The texts of all the laws discussed here are in Kloss (1940, 196-213).

The 1825 Code of Practice stated in Article 293 with respect to provisional distraints: "The sheriff must give this notice, by advertisement, published in English and French, three different times, in at least one paper if any be published in the place or by affixing the same at the usual place if there be no newspaper published in the place."

A similar regulation was provided in Article 669 for the sale-and-purchase commission of property sold under a *writ of fieri facias*; Article 668 also stated that these sales should be announced by bilingual handbills on the church or court building of the place of confiscation.

A similar dual order (handbills and newspaper advertisement, both bilingual) appears in Articles 968 and 969 of the Code of Practice for announcements concerning trustees for unclaimed inheritances and absentee heirs. Like the language provisions of the Code of Practice named above, these regulations disappeared in 1870.

The manner in which the bilingual texts had to be handled was the object of several laws after 1825. According to a law of 1834, it was sufficient in Orleans Parish when the announcements of the inheritance court appeared in English and French in two New Orleans newspapers (no matter of what language). The court, therefore, could make use of two English, or perhaps two French, newspapers. Since this was obviously not adequate, an 1835 law ordered that all official announcements of any kind had to be published in at least one purely English and one purely French newspaper. However, in 1850 this law was superseded by another which made it mandatory for the French version of an official announcement to appear in a bilingual paper. According to an 1847 law, the governor had to announce general elections in both languages in the *State Gazette*.

The connection between the language of the announcements and of the newspapers once more occupied the legislators. It was stated in 1866 for the entire state that French legal advertisements should not appear in a purely English newspaper if a French or bilingual newspaper existed in the particular parish. English announcements were to be handled correspondingly.

As late as 1868 a law ordered the Secretary of State to publish all official announcements required by law for Orleans Parish in the official journal "be it in the English or in the French language or in both." Even at this late date, the possibility of a monolingual French announcement was still taken into account.

These laws and others such as the 1850 law concerning Vermillion Parish (Kloss 1940, 206) which on the basis of the 1825 Code of Practice presuppose the equal status of both languages offer no surprise. Much more interesting was a series of laws in which this equal status was abolished step by step through special laws in certain parishes long before it was abolished officially for the entire state in 1870. We will have to assume that the northern parts of Louisiana, still largely unpopulated in 1812, were gradually settled by Anglo-Saxons (and their slaves), that new parish governments were constantly established there, and that the authorities of these purely English-speaking rural parishes found it cumbersome to use French along with English in their administration.

This series of laws, which reduced the official usage of French, began in 1828 with two laws, one dealing with the announcements of sheriffs, police officials, and coroners, the other with court reports in four parishes: East Feliciana, West Feliciana, St. Helena, Washington. A second law of 1830 added the county of Concordia.

The 1830 law provided that announcements and notices of auctions by the court authorities of the parish of Claiborne should generally be made in English, but the announcements had to continue to be bilingual in cases where the defendant whose property was put up for sale was of French mother tongue.

In 1835 a law followed which restricted the use of French with English in Rapides, Carrol, and Concordia parishes to cases in which one of the party was of French tongue. Even this condition was missing in a law regulating the announcements of parish judges and sheriffs of Caldwell and Catahoula parishes. In the following year, however, a law stated that the court officials of these two as well as of three other parishes (Ouachita, Caddo, and Union) would have to announce the sale of property under judicial process as a rule only in English but that they would have to use French also if one of the parties involved was French-speaking and demanded it in writing.

A law of 1845 named seven parishes—Concordia, Tensas, Madison, Carroll, St. Helena, Washington, and Sabine—where so-called monitions would have to be written in English only. A monition is an invitation to anybody to make his intentions known who wants to appeal against a court-ordered auction.

Finally in 1847 a total of twenty parishes were made monolingual—with due regard for the rights of French-speaking parties—among them seven which had not been named in any of the earlier laws: "It shall not be necessary to publish in the

French language any legal advertisements or judicial proceedings whatsoever in the parishes of Claiborne, Bossier, Caddo, Desoto, Sabine, Jackson, Union, Ouachita, Concordia, Livingstone, Catahoula, Madison, Carroll, St. Helena, East Feliciana, Morehouse, Rapides."

In a law of April 29, 1853, the regulation of 1847, as far as it applied to announcements of court procedures or of auctions of court-disputed property, was almost reversed; those parishes were not listed in which purely English announcements were permitted, but those were listed in which it was necessary to continue to make announcements bilingually.

"It shall be the duty of the sheriff or other officer publishing such advertisements (in relation to judicial proceedings, or to the sale of property under judicial process) to publish the same in the English language only except when the defendant in the judicial process or the person directing the sale shall request the said advertisement to be published in the French language also; and provided further that this proviso shall not apply to the parishes of St. Landry, Calcasieu, Lafayette, Vermillion, St. Martin, St. Mary, St. Bernard, West Baton Rouge, St. Charles, Lafourche, Avoyelles, Natchitoches, Plaquemines, St. James, Assumption, Ascension, Terrebonne, Pointe Coupée, Iberville, and St. John the Baptist."

This regulation, however, was repealed in 1855 only to be introduced in 1868 by a new regulation of the same contents but differing substantially in form.

In 1870, the same year in which the new Code of Practice abolished the equal status of French with respect to court announcements, it was decreed by law that in the two neighboring parishes of Orleans and Jefferson certain court notices must also appear in the daily *Deutsche Zeitung.* Hereby French and German were put on an equal status in Greater New Orleans. (See above about the 1868 law concerning French in Orleans parish). But the law of March 12, 1877, which regulated the question of official announcements anew, mentions neither the German nor the French language, but permitted only English.

In the parish of Orleans, however, the French were once more able to obtain a favorable regulation; according to an 1880 law (accessible to me only in the July 12, 1888, version) the announcements concerning court proceedings or court-ordered auctions were to be made in a French daily also. This regulation was appealed in 1914 (effective beginning July 31, 1916).

Laws Concerning Languages in Schools

During the time of Spanish rule there existed only one public school (in New Orleans); it was entirely Spanish according to a report by B. Duvallon in 1803 and Spanish-French according to an anonymous report in 1804 (Fay 1898, 22-23). The Ursuline nuns, who (beginning in 1727) ran a finishing school for girls in New Orleans, did not accept Spanish nuns into their order.

On April 19, 1805, during the territorial phase, a law was passed to establish a college in the city of New Orleans, in which among other subjects "the Latin, Greek, English, French, and Spanish languages" should be taught. Furthermore, in each parish at least one academy was to be established for "the instruction of the male youths in the French and English languages, reading, writing, grammar, arithmetic, and geography." For the female youths special academies were to be established for instruction "in the French and English languages as well as in suitable branches of the belles lettres and the fine arts and skills." It is presumably no accident that French is listed in the paragraph about the college in second place to English but in the paragraph about the academies in first place. For general education English was still not quite suitable at that time; it seemed, however, already suitable for college instruction.

The founding of the College of Orleans in 1811 can presumably be traced to this law of 1805. The college came under rather one-sided French influence, Spanish was not taught, and the chair for English, after it had become vacant, was not filled again. Therefore, the college was dissolved in 1826. And in 1825 a charter was granted to the College of Louisiana in Jackson where English played the dominant role; while Jefferson College, founded in 1831, was primarily to serve the French population.

The Jesuits, who returned to Louisiana in 1835 after having been expelled in 1763, founded two secondary schools (called collèges in French) and the Université Loyola where, according to Tisch (1959, 10), "l'enseignement se faisait toujours en français."

For decades public elementary schools existed only in isolated instances. Instruction was given in private schools or, in the case of rich planters, by private tutors. An elementary school law was passed in 1806 and repealed in 1808. It remained largely on paper and did not contain any language provisions.

The first Louisiana law to create a public school system dates from the year 1847 and does not apply to the question of *whether* French schools could be established but (Article 26) deals with *how* the relationship between French and English schools should be worked out. The school article if we substitute German for French, is identical with a corresponding article in the Ohio law of 1839 (Section 5-4). The article makes clear that the French school could be the only public school of a school district and that it should not have the character of a special school.

The school law (No. 6) of 1870 contained no language provisions but left the decision about the subjects of instruction to the members of the school board, a body of laymen controlling the parish schools (Kloss 1940, 178-180). We have to take into consideration, however, that at the time the constitution of 1868 was in effect, and this prescribed English as the language of instruction (Section 5-1). Thus the school board was at best permitted to include French as a subject.

Yet French obviously disappeared from the schools completely at that time. Dumez (1877) complained in the *Comptes Rendus* of the Athénée Louisianais, which had been founded the previous year: "This (French) language was taught in all parishes of Louisiana before the arrival of the Republican carpetbagger; today it has been expelled from these schools." The protests of small groups of the

French-speaking population met with success: The constitution of 1879 readmitted French (Section 5-1). Article 14 of the 1888 school law repeated almost verbatim the provisions of the 1879 constitution according to which the bilingual elementary school was permitted in predominantly French-speaking parishes and communities if this would not cause higher expenditures. The school law of 1902 adopted this provision in a slightly, but characteristically, altered manner—it no longer spoke of "parishes or communities" but only of the latter. In this form the provision was incorporated into the school laws of 1906 (Article 23) and 1911 (Article 16). It was omitted only in the school law of 1922 which followed logically the constitution of 1921 (see above).

This was not done to replace French because at that time French had practically disappeared from the schools. French never recovered from the impact of the Civil War. Thus A. Mercier (1889, No. 6) declared that in New York French was taught in the public elementary schools, but in New Orleans only at two high schools and only as a foreign language. Two years later A. Fortier (1891, 16) emphasized approvingly that at Breaux Bridge in St. Martin Parish and in the neighboring Lafayette Parish French was taught in the public schools together with English—a proof that this was an exception.

The introduction of French as a subject at the State Teachers College in Natchitoches in 1893 had no noticeable effect on the cultivation of French in the schools. The State Board of Education wrote in March, 1931: "In no school of the state is French used as a medium of instruction. A quarter of a century or more has passed since this custom was abandoned. . . . French is taught in no elementary school class of the state."

Nevertheless in 1908 an Alliance Franco-Louisianaise was founded in New Orleans for the promotion of the teaching of French. It was probably connected with the Alliance Française. (For years the Louisianan Alcée Fortier was chairman of the Alliance Française for the entire United States.) These two organizations defrayed the expenses of about 1,000 students who received French instruction in New Orleans in 1911, in 1931 of 1,200 students in New Orleans and 50 in Breaux Bridge, but obviously outside of the regular school hours. This instruction was subsidized by the French government for decades until about 1960.

During the middle of the 1930s attempts were made to have French taught in all elementary schools, according to Thérist (1940, 344-346). For example, in 1936 a teachers' conference in Monroe, Louisiana, demanded "Romance language" instruction. In 1937 the State Board of Education recommended to the parish boards of education the teaching of "foreign languages." Both meant French. In 1938 the State Board issued a guideline for teachers (Louisiana Board of Education 1938). The major drive behind the movement seemed to have come from the northern part of the state where, for example, French was taught in Oakdale and Monroe (Boudreaux 1940, 427-430. See also Section 2-2 near Table 2-5). While in 1939 approximately 5,500 elementary school students studied French, in 1955 only about 2,200 in seven communities did the same; and of these seven communities all, with the exception of Breaux Bridge, had introduced the teaching of French after 1951 (Mildenberger 1955, 13-14).

In the year 1956 in 57 public elementary schools in Louisiana (15 schools in Baton Rouge, 10 in New Orleans) French was taught to 4,522 students below the seventh grade. In most of the cases French instruction began above the third grade, but in 4 schools it started in the second grade, and in 8 schools in the first grade (Louisiana Foreign Languages 1955-1956). Spanish was studied by 1,049 children in 22 elementary schools and German was studied by 129 children in three elementary schools. The teaching of these tongues was carried out strictly as foreign language instruction; i.e., it was confined to conversation; reading was not begun until the fifth grade, writing only in high school.

In 1960, there were known to be 5,999 students of French in the public elementary schools below the seventh grade, all of them almost exclusively in the French-speaking areas of the state (Breunig 1961, p. 11, Table 6).

In addition, French has recently again been taught in numerous Catholic schools, for example, since 1956 in all schools of the Alexandria diocese (Tisch 1959, 54) and in the eight in New Orleans (Athénée Louisianais, May 8, 1961). This instruction of French handled it only as subject matter.

On the other hand, the spread of school education reduced the support which the French language enjoyed for a long time among the illiterate population; in 1920 the incidence of illiteracy among the white natives of native parentage in nine purely French parishes amounted to between 27 and 45%. In Evangeline Parish illiteracy among the native whites was 44.5% and in St. Martin, 44%. The state average of Louisiana (10.5%) was the highest in the entire United States (Kloss 1940, 189).

In 1968, Act 408 provided for a sensational large-scale comeback of French in the schools of Louisiana. It ordered that: "As of the start of the 1969-1970 school year, all public elementary schools shall offer at least five years of French instruction starting with oral French in the first grade; except that any parish or city school board, upon request to the State Board of Education, shall be excluded from this requirement and such request shall not be denied. A single request for exclusion is sufficient unless a school board later decides to participate in the program. The fact that any board is excluded, as here provided, from participation in the program established by this Act shall in no case be construed to prohibit such school board from offering and conducting French courses in the curriculum of the schools it administers. In any school where the program provided for herein has been adopted, the parent or other person legally responsible for a child may make written request to the parish school board requesting that said child be exempted from this program."

In addition the same law made it binding upon all public high schools to offer, beginning in 1970, a program of at least three years of instruction in the French language, including at least one course in the culture and history of the French populations of Louisiana and other French-speaking areas in the Americas; except that any parish or city school board may request the State Board of Education to be excluded from this requirement and such a request shall not be denied. Moreover, Section 2 says that "educational television operated under the auspices of any public institution in the State of Louisiana shall be bilingual in character, paying due regard to the proportion of French-speaking listeners within the broadcast area of such operations."

Act No. 257 of 1968 provides for the State Board of Education and the Louisiana State University Board of Supervisors to jointly organize, within the framework of general teachers' training, courses authorizing French at the primary-school level. Until then all courses had aimed at preparing French teachers for high schools. In November 1969, the president of the *Conseil pour le développement de la Louisiane française* (M. Domengeaux), during an official visit in Paris, asked the French government to supply up to 3,000 French teachers in order to make the desired restoration of the French language a reality. Formal agreements were signed between the governments of Louisiana and France and later between Louisiana and Québec to give Louisiana the technical assistance it requested. In 1970 the first French teachers came over from France; in 1973 there were, in all, 215 from France and 15 from Québec. Later Belgium also dispatched some teachers. IN 1974 Québec started sending students (junior college) to work as auxiliary teachers of French. Large-scale retraining of Louisiana students, teachers, and other personnel was taking place in France (200 scholarships annually), in Québec (summer courses in Jonquière since 1970), and in the state itself. In 1973, 40,000 elementary school students from Louisiana were studying French; in July 1975, this number had soared to 69,000. At the same time five parishes had bilingual programs, i.e., dual-medium schools with French being not merely a subject matter but one of the two teaching languages.

As early as 1973, the total number of French radio broadcasts had reached 150 hours per week. A permanent official delegate of the Québec provincial government was residing in Lafayette, the spiritual capital of the Acadians.

Act No. 458 of 1968 created a nonprofit French-language television broadcasting corporation, known as *Television Louisiane* and directed by a board of ten appointed by the governor and "empowered to establish, manage, and operate a television broadcasting facility at and in conjunction with the University of Southwestern Louisiana at Lafayette, Louisiana, which operation shall be conducted primarily in the French language."

Reports on these programs in Louisiana have been contradictory. While some are optimistic and enthusiastic, others are skeptical. Here is an ethnic group—the Acadians—where many elderly people are still monolingual French and the bulk of the middle generation are fully bilingual using both standard English and dialectal French. But though most of the school-age children usually are still able to understand French and many even use it when addressing adults, they are more at home in English than in the tongue of their forebears. The situation is similar to that in Alsace with regard to conquering standard French and yielding dialectal German. Whether a concerted effort by three governments will manage to stem the tide and to reverse it in the direction of French has remained an open question. Unquestionably it was to the credit of both Washington and Baton Rouge—the federal and state governments—to permit this unique experiment in bringing about a comeback of an already greatly weakened minority tongue.

It was obvious that these attempts to restore the French language could succeed only if the desired rebirth of French were conceived as part of, or leading to, a general cultural renascence. Few Americans dreaded such a cultural awakening among the Acadians. If they had followed events in Canada, however, they could have become apprehensive as to whether the cultural aspirations may not in turn engender political demands of a less desirable nature. Ante-bellum Louisiana has, however, been both fully binational and completely loyal.

5-2 NEW MEXICO

Background

The Spaniards entered New Mexico in the first half of the sixteenth century. In 1598 they established the first permanent settlement and in 1609 the present capital of Santa Fe. A rebellion of the Pueblo Indians in 1680 forced the Spaniards out, but they reconquered the area between 1692 and 1696. The Spaniards settled primarily in the northern part of the country; their area of settlement was separated from Mexico by a wide, almost uninhabited strip of land. In this geographical isolation the Spaniards of New Mexico developed as a self-contained group. Around 1800 they numbered approximately 20,000.

In the year 1804 the first Anglo-Saxons entered the country, and in 1810 New Mexico sent a representative to the Cortés in Madrid to ask for protection against a threatening alliance between the Indian tribe of the Apaches and the Anglo-Americans. In the year 1821 New Mexico became a part of the newly independent state of Mexico, and in 1822 a provincial government under Francis Xavier Chavez was established and trade religions with the United States begun.

In 1836 those parts of New Mexico which were located east of the Rio Grande River were claimed by the newly established independent state of Texas. After Texas had been incorporated into the United States in 1845, the United States maintained these claims. But only after war with Mexico had broken out in 1846 did American troops enter the area. In the treaty of Guadalupe Hidalgo, the entire area was formally annexed to the United States in 1848. At first New Mexico was under the control of military governors. It became a territory in 1851 and a state in 1912.

In the year 1853 the territory was enlarged in the south by an almost uninhabited strip of land that had been Mexican and which was acquired by the United States in the so-called Gadsden Purchase. To the north, the territory had to cede a large area to the newly created Colorado Territory in 1861 with the new border cutting right through the Spanish area of settlement. Its thinly populated west was delimited and defined in 1863 as Arizona Territory.

The census in 1940 counted 222,000 Spanish-speaking inhabitants of whom 193,000, or 87%, were the children of American-born parents. After 1945 a lively migration from other parts of the country began so that the population climbed to 630,200 in 1950 and to 951,000 in 1960. In 1950 there were 249,000 with Spanish names, 36.5% of the population. In ten counties these constituted more than 50% of the population (Mona 85.2%, Taos 81.0%, Rio Arriba 80.2%) and in three other counties between 45 and 49%. Today the percentage of the Spanish element has dropped below 30%. In 1930 there were 59,300 persons of the first and second generations who had immigrated from Mexico and in 1960 only 34,500 such persons. The number of immigrants from Mexico remained relatively small and, for the most part, did not go into the old area of settlement.

The dialect of the Spaniards betrays their Castilian origin but also shows influences of neighboring dialects, for example, Andalusian, North Austurian, Galician (A. M. Espinosa 1930). Words were borrowed from the Indians and from the Nahuatl in Mexico, and in recent times many English words have entered the language. The first Spanish newspaper, *El Crespuscolo* in Taos, was founded in 1835. Along with it we find in 1960 five bilingual papers with a total circulation of approximately 10,000.

The Spanish-language radio is quite well developed. In 1961 station KABQ in Albuquerque broadcast exclusively in Spanish; 12 other stations regularly, among them 2 (in Santa Fe and Las Cruces) for 18 hours a week each. In contrast to Louisiana, Pennsylvania, and Puerto Rico, a notable native literature does not seem to have developed while popular tradition and folklore still survive today.

Politically New Mexico was ruled during the territorial phase by a lasting alliance between immigrated "Anglos" and a few wealthy Iberian families. Also during this time no Spaniard became Governor, none became Chief Justice, and only 3 (of 21) became Secretaries of the territory. Governor Otero (1896-1906) was born in St. Louis. While among the highest officials and judges Spaniards can hardly be found, they supplied 10 of the 17 delegates who represented New Mexico (with no right to vote) in Congress. In the state of New Mexico, however, the influence of Spaniards was stronger. In 1935, for example, 5 of the 11 popularly elected executive officers were Spanish. The separate political as well as cultural and social life of the Spanish found for decades a strong basis in an association of religious laymen, the Penitentes, which in addition to providing health insurance, assistance in cases of death, etc., provided also legal and political assistance, and even exercised, whenever possible, a private system of arbitration of disputes between members, thus avoiding the official courts (Henderson 1937; Chavez 1954, 97-123; J. E. Espinosa 1960).

The entire life of New Mexico is colored by the coexistence of these two language groups—the Anglos and the Spanish-Americans (Russell 1937-1938, 268-271; Zeleny 1944; Gonzalez 1967). A lingual assimilation has hardly started, even though standard Spanish is no longer spoken by all Spanish-speaking inhabitants. Compared to the assimilation process in Pennsylvania, New Mexico by 1960 had reached approximately the level of one hundred years ago (and to Louisiana, fifty years ago).

The two-way cultural division has become a three-way division by the fact that among the approximately 40,000 Indians of the state we find about 18,000 Pueblo Indians, who among all Indian tribes of North America developed the highest indigenous culture (Fergusson 1952). From the point of view of a language policy, however, they are not important because they are subdivided into six speech communities so that they have long used Spanish and in more recent times English as a means of intertribal communication.

Struggle for Self-Government

As in Puerto Rico, a struggle for self-government also took place in New Mexico prior to American rule (Bloom and Donnelly 1933). Here, in contrast to similar attempts in Texas, it was carried out by a purely Spanish-speaking population. From 1813 on, while still under the rule of Spain, local councils (ayuntamientos) were established. We know of at least fourteen that were established by 1820. In 1824 New Mexico became a territory within the federal republic of independent Mexico. When in Mexico the centralizing tendencies became victorious, however, self-government in New Mexico was severely restricted in 1835, and the area became a mere administrative district (departamento). The dissatisfaction with this situation led to an unsuccessful rebellion in 1837 during which the rebels elected the fullblood Indian Gonzales as governor. In this rebellion influences were felt from Texas, where liberal Spanish Texans participated side by side with Anglo-Saxons in the rebellion. In the year 1846 New Mexico was about to be promoted to the status of a full-fledged member state when the American occupation delayed the move for 66 years.

When the American troops entered the capital, Santa Fe, in 1846, their commander, General S. W. Kearney, declared that the government of the United States intended to grant New Mexico with the least possible delay a free government patterned after those in the United States. Article IX of the peace treaty of Guadalupe Hidalgo (1848) declared that Congress would grant to all inhabitants "at the proper time" all political rights of American citizens. In a unilateral act, Washington replaced this article even before the exchange of the official documents (May 30, 1848) by Article III of the Louisiana Treaty of October 21, 1803, which had promised to grant equal political rights "as soon as possible."

Under American rule, New Mexico was at first governed by military governors. The attempt of a constitutional convention in 1850 to gain statehood immediately failed because of the resistance of the governor. Instead, New Mexico became a territory of the fourth category (Table 1-1) with a popularly elected lower house and a council. After that, it had to wait for 62 years before it was awarded statehood. This is remarkable for many reasons (Bradford-Prince 1910): First, the inhabitants of territories ceded by Mexico had been promised the same treatment as had been granted to the inhabitants of Louisiana, but Louisiana had become a state only 9 years after its incorporation into the United States.

Second, almost all other regions ceded by Mexico became states considerably earlier than New Mexico did: California as early as 1850. Nevada 1864, Colorado 1876, Utah (in spite of its Mormon population which was quite unpopular throughout the Union) in 1896.

Third, other territories had been freed from federal control upon reaching substantially lower population figures. The Great Ordinance of 1787 had specified a free population of 60,000 before the Midwestern territories could advance to statehood. Later, this figure had often been substantially revised downward in its practical application. Minnesota advanced to statehood in 1858 with about 6,000 white inhabitants, Nevada in 1864 with 7,000, Oregon in 1859 with 13,000, Colorado with 40,000. But New Mexico had reached 61,000 white inhabitants by 1850; it had reached 160,000 by 1890 and 327,000 by 1910.

According to a federal law of April 20, 1872, a territory could from then on advance to statehood only if it had a sufficient population to be entitled to a seat in the House of Representatives, a provision which today would make it difficult for Guam, the Virgin Islands, and Eastern Samoa to become states.

Fourth and last, during the entire period in which it fought for statehood, New Mexico had a particularly small immigration from abroad. It could therefore be considered, to an unusually high degree, a community of "native Americans."

Abortive attempts were, of course, not missing: in 1872 and 1890 constitutional assemblies were called to draft a state constitution, and a total of about 50 petitions to this effect were submitted to Congress. So-called accidents have certainly contributed to the fact that nothing was achieved as, for example, in 1892 when the sponsoring Senator fell ill and his bill was not voted on again.

Still, the real reasons for these repeated failures can be found in the unwillingness to create a state in which most of the inhabitants were Spanish-speaking. The problem was repeated in Puerto Rico with its entirely Spanish-speaking population and in Hawaii with its great majority of non-white inhabitants. When, for example, in 1902 Congress established a special committee to investigate conditions in the territory, this committee almost completely ignored the economic and social prerequisites for statehood but concentrated almost exclusively on the use of Spanish in the courts, the schools, the families, and in the streets. The committee ascertained that English was still a foreign language for the mass of the population and declared that New Mexico would finally be permitted to become a state if its population, under the impact of domestic in-migration, became thoroughly acculturated. The New Mexico of 1900 would still have become a state with a Spanish-speaking majority. But in 1910, of 303,000 native-born inhabitants, fully 118,000 or two-fifths were born elsewhere in the Union, whereas in 1900, of the 181,000 native-born inhabitants, only 38,000 (21%) had been born elsewhere in the Union. Together with the descendants of those Anglo-Americans who had come earlier to New Mexico, they formed an English-speaking majority, even though a small one.

The federal government exercised its control during the territorial phase mostly through the governor and in exceptional cases through special pieces of federal legislation as, for example, that which abolished peonage in the territory (1867) or which was directed against the incorporation of the Jesuit Order (1879).

Nationality Rights in the State Constitution

The Organic Act of 1850 contained no provisions which could be grouped under nationality rights. Paragraph 6 granted the right to vote to the male white population.

The constitution of 1912, which is still in effect today, contains a number of protective provisions with respect to the Spanish population: All rights granted to it in the Treaty of Guadalupe Hidalgo should be retained unaltered (Article II, 5); the right to vote should not be abridged on account of race, color, or previous condition of servitude (Article XXI, 5); children of Spanish descent should never be excluded from public schools or sent to separate public schools (Article XII, 10).

Any alteration of these three provisions, designed to protect inhabitants of Spanish descent, was made difficult by a special clause of the Constitution which, as do the provisions themselves, goes back to O. A. Larrazolo, later Governor and United States Senator. The Constitution stated, furthermore, that the legislature should provide training for bilingual teachers for Spanish-speaking students "so as to facilitate the instruction of such students in the English language" (Article XII, 8). Future amendments to the Constitution had to be printed in both languages in those counties where Spanish newspapers were published (Article XIX, 1). The new laws should be printed in both languages for the next twenty years and later at the discretion of the legislature (XX, 12).

On the other hand, we find two provisions which restrict the rights of the Spanish ethnic group. According to Article XXI (4) the public schools should have English as the language of instruction. According to Article XXI (5), all state officials and elected representatives should have a good command of English, so that they would not have to depend upon interpreters. This second and very stringent provision which Congress at that time imposed upon both new states (New Mexico and Arizona) was deleted from the Constitution during the same year that statehood was achieved. Congress may well force a territory to accept political conditions in its Organic Act. The moment the territory has become a state, however, Congressional authority, as confirmed by the Supreme Court, extends only as far as that over all the other states; and the new state is entitled to abolish by a unilateral act any special restriction imposed by Congress during the territorial phase (*Escanaba* v. *Chicago*; *Coyle* v. *Smith*; Beard 1924, 490; Redslob 1914, 312).

Spanish in Government and Legislature

No law from the nineteenth century is known to me which would prescribe that the official publications of the Territory of New Mexico would also have to be published in Spanish. This should not be taken to indicate that no such Spanish editions of territorial laws existed. They were taken for granted and it was not deemed necessary to have them specially authorized by the legislature. A federal law of March 3, 1858, authorized the territorial legislature to hire translators and interpreters for its two chambers as well as two Spanish and two English clerks. This makes it obvious that the session records were kept in both languages; whether they were published and in what language, however, is not known to me. Most English versions of territorial laws printed during the first decades under American rule carry the comment "translation." This raised the question as to whether the Spanish or the English version of laws would generally govern. On January 8, 1874, a law was passed with regard to this question which stated: "Hereafter in interpreting the statutes of this Territory, whether the same be of the Compiled Laws or the Session Laws, the language in which the said law was originally passed shall govern, whether it be Spanish or English. . . ."

This meant in practice that, in general, the Spanish versions of the laws would govern. This in turn made it necessary that every judge in New Mexico, even if he worked in a predominantly English-speaking community, would have to have a certain command of the Spanish language. As late as 1913 the State Supreme Court affirmed in a decision (*New Mexico ex parte de Vere*) that the 1874 law was still in effect, and it remained so until 1915. A federal law of February 14, 1884, had stated that all official publications of the territory should be in English but had carefully refrained from putting "only" before the word "English." Similar to the 1874 provision, a law of January 31, 1889, read: "Hereafter in this territory any person who cannot read and write sufficiently well to keep his own record in either the English or Spanish language shall be eligible to be elected or appointed to or hold the office of justice of the peace, constable, school director, school treasurer, or other such office or position of trust in which writing is to be done or a record is required to be kept."

This provision put Spanish and English on an equal footing as far as all the lower court and administrative offices were concerned and, at the same time, distinguished both languages sharply from all others. Spanish is here granted equal status with English not only for external communication between the authorities and the people but also for internal official use.

No proof is needed that Spanish was used in deliberations of the New Mexico legislature during the first decades. During the 1865-1866 session all 12 members of the Council and 21 of the 22 members of the House of Representatives had Spanish names. The only Anglo-Saxon representative (Ellison from Santa Fe) typically became speaker of the house. On the other hand, during the 1886-1887 session 6 members of the Council had Spanish names and 6 non-Spanish names, but in the House of Representatives still 13 members had Spanish while 9 had non-Spanish names. During the 1860s Spanish was still the general language of the deliberations, and English appeared only in the written documents (Bancroft 1888, 706-709).

What was the development after statehood? The Constitution ensured the publication of Spanish versions of the laws for the first twenty years of statehood. The Compilation of Laws edited by Courtright, which appeared in 1929, contains the provision that it should be printed also in Spanish at the expense of the state.

This twenty-year limit was extended by ten years each in 1931 and 1943

(Law No. 43). The second time this extension was not fully used, however. The last annual Spanish edition of the state laws appeared in 1949.

Spanish was also unable to maintain itself in the House of Representatives. During the 1920s it was still regularly used there; according to Gino Speranza (1923, 62) one-fifth of all the salaries paid by the legislature in 1923 was paid to translators and interpreters. According to information (1935) from the state government (text in Kloss 1940, 341), Spanish was no longer considered an official language of the legislature despite the fact that in the 1933-1935 session 19 of the 42 representatives had Spanish names. During the 1935 session a permanent interpreter was employed for the last time, according to the unprinted proceedings. Whenever a representative chooses to speak in Spanish, which has occasionally happened since that time, a bilingual government official will be called upon to serve as interpreter for the occasion. (This information was received orally in Santa Fe in 1956.)

Still in effect in 1970 was a group of seven provisions from the years 1927 and 1938-1939 which regulate the equal status of Spanish during elections. Individual provisions concerning the use of Spanish on ballot sheets, on instructions for election officials and voters, in registration lists, etc., are: from the year 1927, Statutes 1953 3-3-1, 3-3-7, 3-3-12, and 3-3-20; from the year 1938, Statutes 1953 3-11-15 and 3-11-18; from the year 1939, Statute 1953 3-2-41. In 1967 two laws were enacted making mandatory printing of primary election ballots in English and Spanish (Section 3-11-12.82E(5) and H; Section 3-11-18.3) and permitting the use of Spanish for publications, ballots, and instructions pertaining to school-district bond elections. In 1963 laws were amended involving the printing or preparation of ballots, instructions to voters, poll books, and tally books in English and Spanish (Section 77-15-3, 1953 Statutes), but there was no change in the requirement that the printing be done in both English and Spanish. In 1965 (Chapter 249) Sections 3-3-30 and 3-3-34, relating to assistance in voting and involving forms written in English and Spanish, were repealed.

The Courts

In the lower courts Spanish seems to have been predominantly used in deliberations and records until into the twentieth century. The Beveridge Committee, constituted in 1902, declared in its report concerning this matter (Bradford-Prince 1910; also Beveridge Committee Report, 99, 6): "The justices of the peace practically all . . . speak Spanish, and the proceedings of their courts are conducted in Spanish. The dockets of nearly all justices of the peace are kept almost exclusively in Spanish." The same report states it would be impossible to keep the court machinery running without the aid of interpreters (Beveridge Committee Report, 5; Section 5.2.4). The necessity for court interpreters had already been recognized by a decision of the Territorial Supreme Court in 1887 (*New Mexico Territory* v. *Thomasson*; Kloss 1940, 356). Note also the law quoted in Section 5-2 concerning the hiring of justice of the peace and policemen who have a command of Spanish.

Within the framework of the New Mexican judicial system Spanish has not only been cultivated within the scope of promotion-oriented nationality rights, but Spanish-speaking citizens of New Mexico have been protected also by tolerance-oriented nationality rights. In the year 1915 a jury in Otero County was dissolved by the state because no Spanish-speaking persons had been included in this jury even though 35% of the inhabitants of the county were Spanish-speaking. This dissolution was approved by the State House of Representatives by a vote of 27 to 15. The Democrats voted unanimously against the measure. Of the 27 Republican representatives, 19 had Spanish names. This entire incident belongs to the area of tolerance-oriented nationality rights in its widest sphere, to the protection of the basic political rights of individual inhabitants in their capacity as speakers of a non-English tongue and as members of a non-English ethnic group. Not surprisingly two nineteenth-century laws still permitted the judges and justices of the peace to employ interpreters (New Mexico Statutes 1956-1-6 and 36-5-8). On the other hand it is rather surprising perhaps that many justices of the peace who have no command of the English language have, without express permission, kept their records in Spanish until at least the fifties, perhaps much longer. Again, this information was received orally from the state government in Santa Fe in 1956.

Legal Notices

Laws prescribing the language which is to be used for official announcements are known to me only from the time since statehood was achieved. There is no doubt that in the Territory of New Mexico official announcements could generally be bilingual and in many cases, especially in counties which had only a Spanish newspaper, even monolingual, i.e., Spanish. Practical necessities for a long time made the use of Spanish so natural that it was not even necessary to have it permitted by law.

Of many special laws, which we may assume for the territorial phase, two concerning bilingual public notices are still in effect today, one 1887 law prohibiting firearms in restaurants (New Mexico Statutes 1953, 40-17-10) and one 1905 law concerning trespassing in mines (New Mexico Statutes 1953, 63-2-18). But soon after statehood a law was passed (No. 49 of 1912) which prescribed concerning official notices of any kind: "Except as otherwise provided in this chapter, in countries wherein there is published a newspaper of general circulation with at least 30% of the reading matter in the Spanish language, those publications referred to in this chapter which are required by law shall likewise be published in the Spanish language in such newspaper, provided that publication in the Spanish language shall be unnecessary for all legal proceedings wherein no party to the record is a Spanish-American."

In the year 1919 the participation of the Spanish-language press of New Mexico was again regulated (No. 43): "A legal newspaper qualified to publish any notice required by law to be published or ordered to be published by any state, county, municipal, district, educational or other public official or by any commission, board, or other public body, at public expense, shall be any daily, weekly, or other newspaper now being published in the English or Spanish language or both in the state of New Mexico, at intervals that are not less frequent than once each week. . . ."

This status of the Spanish-language newspapers, basically equal with the English-language newspapers, is typical of the legal status of original settlers and is clearly distinguished, for example, from the status of the German press in Ohio, which, even though it was widely used to publish official notices, nevertheless almost always left the English-language press in a clearly preeminent position (Section 5-4). While these two laws are no longer part of the legal code of New Mexico, the following, no less important 1919 law (No. 72) is still in effect (New Mexico Statutes 1953, 10-2-11): "All publications of proceedings of boards of county commissioners, city and town councils, boards of trustees, boards of education or school directors, and of all other officers of any county, municipality, district, or other subdivision of the state, which are required by law to be made shall be published once only. In all counties, cities, or towns in which the population is not less than 75% English speaking, the publication in English of such notices shall be sufficient; in all counties, cities, and towns where the population is not less than 75% Spanish speaking, the publication of such notices in the Spanish language shall be sufficient. And provided further that, in case of question or disagreement as to the percentage of the population in any county, city, or town using either language, the district judge of the judicial district of which such county, city, or town is a part shall determine such percentage upon such information as he may have without special investigation in the matter, and his opinion and determination thereon shall be conclusive. Provided: there be legal newspapers published in both languages in the county, city, or town by different publishers; otherwise, publication in either language shall be sufficient."

Since we find both English *and* Spanish newspapers only in a minority of the counties, the final provision is practically the most important. In principle, however, the preceding sentences are even more interesting, since they presuppose a knowledge about the relative numerical strength of the nationalities. This is quite normal as far as European governments are concerned but would normally not be expected in the case of state governments in the United States.

In addition to these basic laws, a large number of laws were passed which regulated very special questions. A 1912 law provided for English publication of the annual reports of insurance companies and of the 1923 School Law (Kloss 1940, 357, 360). A 1923 law concerning the creation of Herd Law Districts provided that the necessary announcements be made at the discretion of the county authorities in English, in Spanish, or in both languages (Courtright 1929, 4-404). The following regulations regarding official notices, which all prescribe publication in both languages but do not provide for Spanish publication only, were still in effect in 1960:

A regulation of 1917 concerning drainage districts (New Mexico Statutes 1953, 75-21-3; Kloss 1940, 359).

A regulation of 1919 concerning irrigation districts (New Mexico Statutes 1953, 75-23-4; Kloss 1940, 360).

A regulation of 1927 concerning soil conservation districts (New Mexico Statutes 1953, 75-28-3, 6).

A law enacted in 1965 and amended in 1967 provided that "for the purpose of publishing legal notices in Spanish as required by law for any agencies of the state, the *Santa Rosa News* published at Santa Rosa, the *New Mexican* and the *Santa Fe News* both published at Santa Fe, *El Hispano* published at Albuquerque, the *Alpha News* published at Las Vegas, the *Rio Grande Sun* published at Espanola, and the *Taos News* published at Taos are recognized as official Spanish language newspapers of this state." The 1965 version listed only the papers published in Albuquerque and Santa Rosa plus the Santa Fe *New Mexican.*

Table 5-2   Composition of New Mexican
             Territorial Schools

Type of School	1874		1889	
Purely English	7	(5%)	143	(42%)
Purely Spanish	88	(69%)	106	(30%)
Bilingual	33	(26%)	95	(28%)

Laws Regulating Languages in Schools

The two earliest school laws (of 1860 and 1863) contained no language provisions. The generally prevailing conditions in the territory, however, leave no doubt that the public schools provided for in the laws had a predominantly Spanish character. There were still practically no Anglo-Americans in New Mexico at that time. Both school laws were first drafted in Spanish and translated only later into English, whereby, as shown above, the Spanish text was considered decisive.

According to the annual reports of the territorial school authorities, the composition of the public schools was as shown in Table 5-2.

As late as 1884 a school law was passed which expressly recognized the public Spanish-language elementary school: "Each of the voting precincts of a county shall be and constitute a school district in which shall be established one or more schools in which shall be taught orthography, reading, writing, arithmetic, geography, grammar, and the history of the United States in either English or Spanish or both, as the directors may determine."

This impressive document of American generosity was succeeded in 1891 by a law which stated that (Article 16) in all schools the English language had to be taught, that (Article 13) in school districts where Spanish was the everyday language the teachers would have to be able to speak both languages, and that (Article 7) the Territorial School Supervisor with approval of the Board of

Education should recommend the best English or Spanish and English textbooks. This latter phrase presumably does not refer to bilingual textbooks but to "English as well as Spanish" books for the entirely Spanish-speaking parts of the state.

It is hard to say how serious the provisions of the 1891 law were meant to be. The fact that the Catholic church established a number of Catholic parochial schools in Santa Fe the following year may indicate that the church considered the law a serious threat to the Spanish language. On the other hand, the Beveridge Congressional Committee declared in 1903 with obvious exaggeration, "Until a relatively short time ago, historically speaking, English was not taught in the public schools at all. At the present both English and Spanish are taught in most of the schools" (Beveridge Committee Report, 6; Bradford-Prince 1910, 95).

Close to the end of the second phase, however, we have the report of the Spanish Coloradan Espinosa according to which around 1911 Spanish was completely neglected in the schools of New Mexico. He maintains that the school authorities had an outright animosity toward the cultivation of Spanish, while in Colorado the schools of the Spanish-speaking areas were bilingual (Espinosa 1911, 18). We may therefore assume that between 1900 and 1912, the year in which statehood was achieved, an almost complete removal of Spanish from the schools took place. It is even possible that this was one of the prerequisites for statehood, as had been the heavy Anglo-American immigration after 1900.

The 1891 School Law had a provision that elementary school teachers in Spanish-speaking areas had to have a knowledge also of Spanish. This provision was given considerable impetus by Law No. 97 of 1909, which ordered the establishment of the Spanish-American Normal School in El Rito. Its function was to train young New Mexicans who had Spanish as their mother tongue as English teachers in rural Spanish-speaking communities. This law represents a concession more to the Spanish-speaking population than to the language itself. It opened to young Hispanos the hitherto closed teaching career and, by their employment, facilitated the learning of English for Spanish-speaking students. It did not aim at bilingual instruction designed to promote the Spanish language. In Maine we find a counterpart to the El Rito Normal School (Section 6-1).

Even though after 1900 Spanish was reduced in the schools to the role of an auxiliary language for beginning students and a mere subject of instruction, it retained its equal status in the external relations between the schools and the populace. The School Law of 1891 provided (Article 8) that questionnaires and blanks used in the schools be printed in both languages. According to a law of March 10, 1903, 2,000 copies each in English and Spanish had to be printed of all school laws which were still in effect and of those which should be passed in the future; the same number of copies of the *Directors' Guide* were printed in 1910. According to the annual report of the school supervisor, 2,000 English and 1,500 Spanish copies were printed during the reported period from 1910 to 1912, but 1,700 English and 800 Spanish copies were demanded; obviously many Spanish-speaking persons already at that time preferred English copies.

During the first decade of statehood several laws were passed which were designed to meet the needs of the Spanish-speaking population with regard to their language problems. For example, a law of March 18, 1915, read: "Spanish as a separate subject shall be taught in any public elementary or high school in the State when a majority vote of the board of school directors or board of education in charge of such a school shall direct, provided that the time devoted to such shall be such as shall be provided for by the State Board of Education. . . . Except as herein provided, the books used and the instruction given in said schools shall be in the English language, provided that Spanish may be used in explaining the meaning of English words to Spanish-speaking pupils who do not understand English."

A law of the same day concerning one-year accelerated courses for student-teachers in rural schools was primarily designed to ensure the training of young Spanish-speaking persons for a teaching career with special emphasis on the teaching of Spanish (Kloss 1940, 348), and a 1919 law made Spanish a compulsory subject in all high schools and colleges of the state (Kloss 1940, 348-349). Special precautions were taken to ensure that no person was employed who possessed no more than an elementary knowledge of the language he was supposed to teach, as had happened in the foreign language instruction in other states.

Another law of 1919 stated that in the rural schools English had to be the basic language of instruction, even in Spanish-speaking areas, but that the teachers should have the students translate into Spanish "so that the students will understand better what they read in English." With this law the legislators did not intend to reestablish the bilingual school where Spanish enjoyed equal status.

The second part of the section dealing with the translation from English into Spanish presupposes the student's spoken command of Spanish and is not intended to improve his command of Spanish, but of English. It belongs among those provisions which allow the use of the mother tongue as an auxiliary tool but not as a subject of instruction. To the same category belong the 1909 law concerning the establishment of the normal school in El Rito and a Minnesota law of 1877. This provision, therefore, has the character of a temporary regulation designed not to preserve the old language but to prevent unwise speed in assimilation. Nevertheless, the 200,000 Spanish-speaking inhabitants of New Mexico succeeded in getting this provision included in the statutes, something the one million Pennsylvania Germans of the nineteenth century were never able to accomplish.

It could logically be assumed that during the period from 1915 to 1923 a noticeable improvement in the status of the Spanish language would occur. But this improvement, if it ever did occur, was at least very short-lived. For soon Mary Austin (1921) could not emphasize enough how little the public school satisfied the needs, particularly the spiritual ones, of the Spanish-speaking population. The Spanish-speaking school children learned as little about the early history of New Mexico and its wealth of glorious deeds as, for example, about the plant world of their home state. Their textbooks were usually oriented toward New England, and nothing in the New Mexican school instruction would bring the children into a living relationship with their surroundings and their history. The school thus undermined the self-respect of the Spanish-speaking population, to whom the names of their great pioneers are generally unknown, and did not fertilize their imagination. "In our handling of our Spanish-speaking population we have violated all the fundamentals of folk growth." The problem of schools for ethnic groups does not end with the regulation of the language question. Whether in New Mexico or Louisiana or Pennsylvania, whether in the English language or in their mother tongue, the children should also learn about the spirit and the deeds of their ancestors and their attitude toward life. Mary Austin, for example, mentions the artistic folkloristic traditions of the Spaniards and the natural pride which is common to all of them, while the Anglo-Saxon considers pride a privilege of the wealthy. Not only the language but also the lore of an ethnic group should be taught, but information about such "lore-teaching" is hard to come by. Mary Austin nowhere states expressly that Spanish was not taught in the schools at that time, but this becomes painfully evident from her detailed description of the actual circumstances. If the Spanish-speaking population achieved any serious successes at all between 1915 and 1919, they had obviously again been lost by 1921. It is more likely that the laws of those years never were really put into practice. Mary Austin's writing is particularly singled out because of its value as a piece of literature (see also Gamio 1930, 208-216).

Furthermore, the regulation of 1919 lasted for only four years. The School Law of 1923 listed Spanish among the compulsory subjects for the public elementary schools without giving any further explanations. It was favorable to the Spanish-speaking population in that the teaching of Spanish was no longer expressly restricted to reading, but unfavorable in that the use of Spanish in the teaching of English was no longer contemplated.

This regulation, however, remained on paper. Information received from the State Board of Education in 1931 (Kloss 1940, 354) made it very clear that, in spite of the provision of 1923, which at that time was still included in the statutes, Spanish was not taught in any elementary school. The Board further added that this provision was perhaps included at that time only "to favor some particular person, or section of the state." It was considered a rare exception when, as was reported in 1933, the State University initiated a program in one school in Bernalillo County, where the students in the first two grades were taught how to read Spanish (Reynolds 1933b, 57-58; Kloss 1942, 681).

The teaching of Spanish was given a new chance in the beginning of the 1940s when, under the impact of World War II and the idea of the close relations between the peoples of the Western Hemisphere, comprehensive attempts were made throughout the entire Southwest and Florida to introduce the teaching of Spanish into the elementary schools. A New Mexican law of 1943 (Statutes 1953, 73-4-1b, 73-4-7) created the office of State Supervisor of Spanish, whose function it was to coordinate the teaching of Spanish in the different branches of the state school system and whose title was changed around 1955 to State School Coordinator of Spanish, a title more in line with the more recent concepts about his functions. There had been previously a 1923 law (Statutes 1953, 73-2-1) which provided the State Supervisor of Spanish with a bilingual Auxiliary Supervisor of Spanish.

Above all, a 1943 law (Statutes 1953, 73-17-2) provided that Spanish should be taught in all larger elementary schools (those with at least three teachers and ninety students) from the fifth through the eighth grades, with the specific limitation that the respective school board be given discretion to decide otherwise. It comes as no surprise that until 1955 only about five communities had introduced the teaching of Spanish. By the middle of 1956, however, thanks to the efforts of Medina, the State School Coordinator of Spanish, their number had increased to about forty. (This information was received orally in Santa Fe in 1956.) Breunig (1961, 29) lists only four communities with Spanish instruction at the elementary school level.

The State Board of Education, however, extended the 1943 law by a very important measure. It issued in 1955 a Curriculum Guide for Spanish lessons in all eight grades and stated in its introduction (Medina 1955, 10): "The curriculum guide for the first three grades is mainly designed for students who are not Spanish speaking. . . . In the fifth grade English-speaking and Spanish-speaking students can receive instruction together. Our committee is furthermore of the opinion that it is useful at this level to start the teaching of reading in Spanish."

With this guide, Spanish, as a result of executive action, was introduced into all eight grades—instead of merely the upper four grades—but only for English-speaking students. For Spanish-speaking students the old solution—beginning instruction with the fifth grade—was retained. For them mere instruction in conversational Spanish would have indeed been hardly meaningful. If, on the other hand, they had been instructed in reading and writing during the first four grades, they would have been far ahead of their English-speaking fellow students in the fifth grade, and Spanish lessons in the upper four grades would have had to be continued separately for both groups of students. The school authorities, however, were obviously eager to avoid this segregation.

The 1943 school law (73-17-2) was superseded by law 1967, ch. 16 (77-11-1) which simply provides that "the State Board shall . . . prescribe courses of instruction to be taught in all public schools in the State," without any reference to the Spanish language.

As in Louisiana, the language of the native minority in New Mexico had also been strongly protected in the past by widespread illiteracy. As late as 1920, of those with native Spanish parentage, 11.6% were illiterate. In Rio Arriba County the number was as high as 26% and in Sandoval, Valencia, and Miguel Counties between 21 and 24%.

In contrast to the case in Louisiana, the private Catholic school system contributed relatively little to the preservation of Spanish, since the leadership of the Catholic church rested almost entirely in the hands of Anglo-Americans.

Furthermore, the Church was interested in obtaining public funds by adapting the curriculum of Catholic schools as closely as possible to that of public schools (Section 3-4).

Today the Spanish-speaking minorities on the American mainland are those which have the greatest chance for survival—greater even than the Acadians of southwest Louisiana—even though until recently only a few Anglo-Americans have come out in favor of preserving the Spanish language (Tireman 1951, 211-212, 207). The greatest chances for the Spanish-speaking population lie in the benefits from two new educational policies and decisions of the federal government. Both were already being implemented. One was designed to maintain, for national purpose, groups of bilingual citizens (Section 2-2). The other was based on the premise that it is better from an educational point of view to teach students who have a foreign language as their mother tongue in this mother tongue during the first grades. This principle had been formulated by experts at UNESCO (1935) and it had been applied in Mexico's treatment of Indian languages (UNESCO 1953, 77-86; Kloss 1960, 86-92).

The second solution applies even to communities where the parents of the students are not interested in the continued preservation of their original language. Professor Tireman reports how an attempt to introduce Spanish into a village school failed because of the parents' resistance (Tireman 1951, 211; Tireman 1948).

The two educational principles cited here may possibly supplement each other. Professor Tireman, who wishes to preserve Spanish, advocates nevertheless that the lower four grades of the elementary school be taught entirely in English. In Mexico, quite to the contrary, the Indian languages were cultivated in the lower four grades in order to ensure an organic and surer assimilation.

In later years successful experiments have led to the launching of new local bilingual school programs. For example, starting in 1965, Spanish as a mother tongue was being taught in Pecos, New Mexico, by a native Chilean from grade one upward (Digneo 1968). The legislature in 1969 adopted a law permitting any school district to set up "a bilingual and bicultural program of study" (New Mexico Staf. Ann. Sec. 77, 1-2). A constitutional provision permitting, or requiring (in Article VIII, Section 3) the legislature to provide such programs for both statewide and local option was defeated (December 1969), together with the entire newly proposed constitution, by a narrow margin of the popular vote.

In 1973 the "Bilingual Multi-Cultural Education Act" (New Mexico Stat. Ann. 77-23-1 to 77-23-7) provided for bilingual teaching in grades K to 6 with marked emphasis on K to 3; from the wording of the Act, we may conclude that the lawmakers were thinking not merely of Spanish but also of New Mexico's Amerindian languages, including Navajo. The same year, the legislature adopted an official Spanish version of the flag salute (ch. 185 laws = sen. Bill 286) calling the flag *"el simbolo de amistad perfecta entre culturas unidas."*

In the continental United States no other indigenous group has held onto its language so tenaciously as has the one in New Mexico. All that was needed to ensure its survival was a movement to have the language reintroduced into the schools.

There has been a widespread but mistaken notion that Spanish has again become New Mexico's second official language. This fallacy, which the author has heard even from the lips of persons living in the state, results from a misconception of the term *official language*, which was believed to mean "officially promoted language." Officially promoted Spanish certainly has been. But the session laws are no longer printed in Spanish and the business of the legislature is conducted in English; no provision is made for interpreters, and in recent decades no person has been elected to the legislature who does not speak English. To sum up in the words of a letter from the New Mexico Legislative Council dated August 14, 1975: "Although certain election materials and notices are required to be printed in Spanish and we do have a bilingual education provision, New Mexico is not officially bilingual."

5-3 PENNSYLVANIA

Background

Between 1638 and 1655, small eastern sections of present-day Pennsylvania belonged to New Sweden and, from 1655 to 1664, to New Netherlands. It has been estimated that in 1790 about 3,300 persons of Swedish and 7,500 persons of Dutch descent were living in Pennsylvania. The establishment of British settlements began in 1681. The German immigration commenced in 1683 with the founding of the Quaker community, Germantown, which remained an enclave where High German, Low German, and Dutch were spoken. It was surrounded by Quaker communities where inhabitants spoke English or Welsh.

From about 1710, a large German-speaking area came into existence to the west and north of the Quaker belt. Around 1830 it comprised approximately 5,800 square miles with some English-speaking enclaves in the southwest. There 141,000 Germans lived in 1790, constituting 33% of the 423,000 whites (Meynen 1939, 253-293; Wood 1943; Klees 1950; Meynen 1937).

Throughout this area German was used as the standard language (Wood 1945, 299-314). As conversational language the people used a dialect which originated in America and is close to the dialect spoken in the eastern Palatinate. In English it is called Pennsylvanish or Pennsylvania German, while in German it goes by the names of Pennsilvaanisch or Pennsylvaniadeutsch, which is the basis for the name colloquially used in America, "Pennsylvania Dutch" (Wood 1952, I, col. 785 ff.; Buffington and Barba 1954; Kloss, May 7, 1938, and October 2, 1954). Pennsylvanish survived the disappearance of High German and was still spoken in 1920 by 600,000 to 800,000 people and in 1960 by 200,000 to 300,000 people. It is best preserved among two small highly conservative splinter groups of Mennonites, the Old Order Amish (about 50,000), who are more numerous in Ohio and Indiana, and the Old Order Mennonites (about 10,000), of whom about four-fifths live in Pennsylvania (E. L. Smith 1958).

During the nineteenth and twentieth centuries a huge new wave of German-speaking immigrants settled in Pennsylvania. In the year 1910, 502,000 persons were first or second generation immigrants from the German Empire, and of these immigrants 150,000, a full 30%, lived southeast of the Pennsylvanish-speaking area in and around Philadelphia. Almost 300,000 (about 55%) lived to the west and north of this area, and only some 70,000 (15%) settled in the same area as the older German-speaking groups. In the year 1940, 424,100 German-speaking persons were recorded of whom 157,500 (39%) were children of American-born parents. Outside of Philadelphia and Pittsburgh the proportion of these German-speaking persons of American-born parents ran as high as 48%. In the year 1960 there were still 260,400 first or second generation German immigrants and 76,100 foreign-born persons of German mother tongue.

There exists a great deal of literature of the old German element (Stoudt 1955), which blossomed during the eighteenth century and slowly declined during the nineteenth century. There is also a respectable amount of literature in Pennsylvanish (Reichard 1918; Kloss 1931, 230, 272), which began to blossom with the decline of the German written language (after 1860) and reached a last apex with a translation of the four Gospels (Wood 1968, 7-184). There is also some literature of the more recent immigrants of the nineteenth and twentieth centuries (Jockers 1926). For more about Pennsylvania German literature in all languages, German, Pennsylvania Dutch, and English, consult Robacker 1943.

As a group, the Germans achieved political power with the rise of the Jeffersonian party. In 1808 they furnished the Governor (Snyder) for the first time, and until 1855 all governors, with few exceptions, were German. In the gubernatorial race of 1835 all three candidates were of German nationality, so that a short time later the Scotch-Irish politician Dunlop (1835, 228) complained publicly that people of his background had as little chance to become governor "as if he had been born in Judea or the heathen lands."

This political flowering of the German element came almost a century after its culturally most impressive period. A part of its leadership favored adoption of the English language. The German language had disappeared from the schools by about 1860, by about 1910 from the press, and by about 1940 from the churches. The absolute decline of the German- (or Pennsylvanish-)speaking element was accompanied by a relative decline as a result of the industrialization of Pennsylvania and the resulting immigration of millions of east and southeast Europeans.

A countermovement was attempted with temporary success by the Verein der deutschen Presse von Pennsylvanien, which was founded in 1862 by S. K. Brobst. It joined members of the upper strata of the eastern part of the Pennsylvanish-speaking area with those of the German immigrants, especially in Philadelphia, but became inactive after the death of Brobst in 1876.

Since 1930 a new interest in the surviving folk language, the Pennsylvanish, has arisen in southeastern Pennsylvania which has been expressed by mass attendance at dramatic plays in this language and the establishment of very informal institutions for the cultivation of the folk language, for example, the Fersomlinge (since 1933) and the Grundsow Lodges (since 1934) or for the development of the popular culture in general, for example, the annual festivals in Kutztown since 1950 (Kloss 1952b, 83-87).

It seems, however, that the Anglicization of the younger generations progressed very rapidly during the 1950s. All recent folkloristic organizations of the oldstock Pennsylvania Germans, including the new Pennsylvania German Society, a 1967 merger of the first Pennsylvania German Society (1891) and the Pennsylvania German Folklore Society (1935), pay little attention to the status of the German or the Pennsylvanish language, not even in the area of language teaching. In the year 1960 only two stations continued to broadcast in German: Philadelphia (6 hours weekly) and Erie (1 hour weekly). Two other stations broadcast in Pennsylvanish: Red Lion (¼ hour weekly) and Towanda (1 hour weekly). In 1960 a German weekly (*Gazette-Democrat*, founded 1838, 4,000 copies) still appeared in Philadelphia and a bilingual publication for German societies (established 1838) appeared in Pittsburgh.

Language Provisions before 1776

On the soil of Pennsylvania, German had once been the official language of the New Sweden colony (1638 to 1655) which, however, had its center in present-day Delaware and New Jersey (Lohr 1938, 161-165; Johnson 1911). German was at that time the language of the educated classes in Sweden and at the same time the mother tongue of the inhabitants of western Pomerania, which then belonged to Sweden. The proclamations of the officials were written in Swedish, German, and Dutch. The languages of business accounts and bills were Dutch and German; that of a population census in 1648 and presumably also of the courts was German.

Nothing is known about the legal status of German under British rule. A partial edition of the provincial laws in German, which appeared in 1761 in Philadelphia under the title *Des Landmanns Advocat,* was very likely a private venture. It may, on the other hand, be taken for granted that the municipal authorities in the German areas of settlement used German exclusively in oral and for the larger part in written communications before 1776 since, for a considerable length of time, there were no inhabitants over large areas who had a knowledge of English.

German as Second Official Language

The situation changed with the War of Independence. It should be stated from the beginning that German was not included in any of the state constitutions. When a constitutional convention for Pennsylvania met in 1837, it received from American-born as well as from recently arrived Germans numerous petitions to grant official status to the German language. Most of these petitions asked for the hiring of bilingual court officials, but some demanded also the admission of German in court proceedings and in the educational system.

On November 10, 1837, representative Charles I. Ingersoll proposed the following amendment: "The legislature shall provide by law for the immediate establishment of common schools . . . wherein all persons may receive instruction at the public expense . . . in the English and German languages." This led to a debate of the language problem, which took several days and which is preserved verbatim. During the course of the debate some of the German-speaking representatives, especially William Hiester, attacked Ingersoll so sharply that his proposal was rejected without a vote being taken. In spite of this, Ingersoll proposed on November 15, 1837, again without success, the encouragement of "the establishment of libraries in the English, German, or other languages, at least one in each township."

On January 26, 1838, Representative J. K. Mann proposed that court officials in counties with a substantial German-speaking population should be bilingual, a proposal which was rejected by a vote of 99 to 15. Of the 15 representatives who voted for the proposal, 10 had German names, and 12 came from the area of compact German settlement, particularly from its eastern parts.

In this connection mention may be made of an attempt in 1828 to elevate German to the second official language of the state. Brauns (1828, 368-369) reports "that during the last session of the legislature of this state (1828) a petition was submitted to declare publicly German as being the official language of the state and of equal status with the English language . . . ; the number of those representatives who voted for the introduction of German as an official language of the state was so large, however, that only one vote was missing to bring victory for this petition."

This report is apocryphal; the printed journals do not mention it, and it is hardly conceivable that an attempt was made to create a second official language for the state by a simple law. Perhaps these were attempts to have German introduced into the courts. Brauns (1828, 409) mentions that German would be in a very short time "introduced as official language of the state in the courts" in Pennsylvania and Ohio.

German in Government and the Legislature

The first Constitutional Convention of Pennsylvania decided on July 26, 1776, to publish its records also in German: the official consideration of German in Pennsylvania is, therefore, as old as the state itself. But the session records (journals) of the legislature appeared at first only in English, even though the Convention repeatedly had German versions of individual laws and other documents printed as well. From 1786 to 1856, on the other hand, a German edition of the session records appeared annually. Until 1790 it appeared as *Tagebuch der General Assembly*. From 1791 on, one volume each appeared of the journals of the Senate and the House. Also the special assembly of 1787 for the adoption of the Constitution of the United States and the Constitutional Conventions of 1789-1790 and 1837-1838 had their session records and the constitutions adopted by them published in a German edition. A law of 1805 made possible the publication in 1807 of all state laws which were in effect at that time, and the government was obligated to purchase 1,000 copies (Kloss 1940, 250). In addition, the annual messages of the governor appeared for many years in a German edition.

In the years 1835-1837 a part of the German element was affected by a movement—only partially initiated by recent immigrants—which called itself the Deutsche Reform and which flooded the legislature with petitions in which they asked that court proceedings (*"deutsche Courten"*), regular session laws, and the annual reports of the state authorities be printed in their mother tongue. A law of January 21, 1837 (Kloss 1940, 254), led to the publication of German editions of the session laws and also an incredibly complicated subscription method. This subscription method was simplified by a law of March 31, 1840. At the same time the number of German copies of the laws to be printed annually was fixed at 1,200. This number was reduced to 250 by a law of January 23, 1843; an equal number of German as against 500 English copies of the journals was to be printed.

A law of March 24, 1843 (Kloss 1940, 258), retained the number of session record copies but increased the number of German copies of the session laws to 500. Above all it created the office of "two state printers, one to do the English and one to do the German printing of the Commonwealth." In addition, the government and legislature employed official German translators; cf. for example, the resolution of the legislature of April 29, 1844 (Kloss 1940, 259).

A new regulation was adopted in 1856. It provided for German editions— amounting to one fourth of the entire edition—of the annual reports of only certain state offices, among them the state school supervisor. In 1876 even this remainder of prescribed official publications in German was eliminated. Without legal obligation, however, the legislature continued until 1891 to publish the annual message of the Governor in a German translation. This annual message was at least once also published in Welsh (1879). As a curiosity it may be added that in at least four instances an official publication was printed in as many German as English copies (Table 5-3).

The Courts—Legal Notices

Very early isolated instances are known in which the Pennsylvania legislature decided to have certain information printed in the English and also in the German press. Examples are the Resolution of the Assembly of January 29, 1777, concerning notes about tax delinquency (Kloss 1940, 248); the law of September 29, 1791, about the Schuylkill and Susquehanna Navigation Company which provides for insertion of the law in three newspapers of Philadelphia, one of which was German; a similar law of April 10, 1792, about a navigation company and a law of February 12, 1801, about a turnpike road company (Kloss 1940, 294-295). Concerning the courts, see also Section 5-3.

The first legally binding mention of the German press occurs in a law of March 27, 1824. (The texts of this and all other laws concerning public notices

Table 5-3   Equal Numbers of Official Papers Printed in English
                   and German

Date	Subject Matter	Copies in English and German, Each
November 28, 1778	A Law	5,000
December 16, 1829	Inaugural Address of Governor Wolf	500
February 23, 1832	Washington's Farewell Address	3,000
November 11, 1837	Proceedings of the Constitutional Convention	

may be found in Kloss 1940.) According to this law all sheriffs had to publish notices about taking in execution any lands, tenements, or inheritances in all counties outside of Philadelphia in two or more newspapers of which one "shall" be in the German language, if there be any, a provision which survived for a long time (*Digest Pennsylvania State Law* 1921). The same provision can be found in a law of June 16, 1836, concerning the sale of real estate. Almost 60 years later, on July 2, 1895, this law was altered so that it prescribed publication in a German newspaper only in counties with more than 150,000 inhabitants; in other counties it was merely permitted.

For Philadelphia, which was exempted from the 1824 and 1836 provisions, a law of February 3, 1860, stated that real estate sales could also be announced in a German newspaper. This law differed in many points from the 1836 law—differences which we can call typical for the legal status of recent immigrant groups as compared with that of old established settlers: The 1836 law for all of Pennsylvania, except Philadelphia, made it mandatory that the full text be published in German within the framework of the legally prescribed minimum number (at least two newspapers).

On the other hand, the 1860 Philadelphia law permitted German notice but only as an addition feature, and excerpts from the English text were sufficient. Furthermore, the law of 1860 states expressly that the sheriff would not be responsible for translation mistakes, which he presumably was under the 1836 law.

A law of April 8, 1862, prescribed "three newspapers, among them one German," for announcements of the authorities of Allegheny County, including Pittsburgh. This law did not, however, contain restrictions similar to the 1860 law even though it referred to a county with recent German immigrants.

The entire state area was affected by an amendment to the Concession Laws of the state of April 11, 1862, according to which the announcements of commercial appraisers had to be published in three newspapers of a city or a county, among them a German newspaper if it existed. This provision was partly stymied by a clause which authorized the Auditor General to order a reduction to two newspapers, in which case neither of the two had to be German.

In each instance, all these provisions referred to only a very narrow segment of the entire sphere of official notices. For most of them, no official language regulation existed. A rule of the Twenty-third District Court (Berks County) of 1830 prescribed, unless decreed otherwise by the legislature, that notices and advertisements had to be printed in one English and one German newspaper of the county. But the State Supreme Court ruled in 1855 and 1863 (*Tyler* v. *Bowen* and *Upper Hanover Road*) that, in cases where the legislature did not specifically decree otherwise, English newspapers should always be used.

Probably it is primarily because of the efforts of the Verein der deutschen Presse in Pennsylvanien, which had been founded the year before, that the following law was passed on April 22, 1863: "Wherever any writ, notice, rule or orders shall be required, under any law of this commonwealth, to be published in any newspaper in the counties of Berks, Northampton, Lehigh, Lancaster, Schuylkill, Lebanon, Montgomery, or York, it shall be lawful for the proper court to designate, by general rule or special order, the paper, or papers in which such publication shall be made; and such publication, under such order of the court, in any German newspaper, shall be held to be adequate and shall have the force and effect of a publication in an English newspaper."

This law created for the first time in Pennsylvania a geographical demarcation of the kind which had been established in Louisiana by many laws. For the first time, the area of the ethnic group living in compact settlements was defined by a listing of counties, even though several of them, particularly in the west of the area, were missing. By a law of May 4, 1868, Bucks County was added to the list of counties in which the German press enjoyed equal status. The wording of the 1863 law made it clear that, at least in cases where the publication had to be made only in one newspaper, it sufficed to employ only a German and no English newspaper. For the Twenty-third District Court (Berks County), a court rule of August 24, 1863, decreed that in cases where the law prescribed two newspapers, one had to be in English and one in German. Where only one was prescribed, the party in question was at liberty to choose either a German or an English paper. In *Harrisburg* v. *Dauphin Deposit Bank* (6 Dauphin 4, 1963), the court held that wherever a legal notice was required to be published in "not exceeding three newspapers" it would not suffice to have it published in a German newspaper only, but having it published in one German and one or two English papers would meet the legal requirements.

After a lapse of several decades, the 1890s brought a series of new legal provisions. Two laws of May 16, 1891, and of June 12, 1893, concerned the so-called viewers, court-appointed laymen who mediate in certain disputes between private persons and the authorities. The laws stated that one of the newspapers which announced their meeting "may" be German. More important was a law of June 18, 1895, according to which: (1) in counties where the last census had enumerated at least 40,000 German-born inhabitants, all notices and advertisements prescribed by law should also be published in a German newspaper of that county, and (2) all notices and advertisements of the county authorities could also appear in a German newspaper in counties with 500,000 to 1,000,000 inhabitants according to the last census.

The first of the two provisions was altered on May 3, 1915, so as to have notices and advertisements prescribed by law also appear in a German or Italian or Yiddish daily newspaper of counties with at least 40,000 German-born, 40,000 Italian-born, or 40,000 European-born persons of Yiddish mother tongue according to the last census. This was still in effect at least as late as 1961.

Even in the twentieth century some news laws favored German as the only non-English language. According to a law of April 27, 1903 (repealed on May 3, 1933), one of three newspapers in which the courts announced the names of applicants for liquor concessions could be German. As late as 1915 a law permitted the collector of overdue taxes to publish the names of these tax delinquents in a German newspaper also. This law too was still in effect at least as late as 1961. Since neither daily publication of the newspaper nor a certain number of inhabitants nor a minimum number of German-born persons was prescribed for the county, we may regard this law as the last which benefited the few remaining German newspapers of the colonial German element.

On the other hand, a law was passed on July 19, 1917, which was still in force at least as late as 1961, which to a special degree shows the character of laws for later immigrant groups. It no longer, like the law of May 3, 1915, applied only to specified large immigrant groups but decreed in general terms that all notices and advertisements prescribed by law could "also be published in one or several daily newspapers of the county in question which appear in a foreign language or in several foreign languages."

School Laws and Languages

Long before the War of Independence the Germans in Pennsylvania had built a good private elementary school system on the basis of their church organization. By far the most comprehensive was the school network of the Lutherans and the Reformed churches. In the year 1775, i.e., at the time of the beginning of the War of Independence, 78 Reformed and 40 Lutheran parochial schools were counted. By 1800 the number of the schools of both denominations had increased to a total of 254. In addition, we find schools of German sects. Famous were those of the Herrnhuters, who were the first to develop a secondary school system, in Bethlehem in 1749 and in Lititz in 1755.

Among those who continued their migrations and who after the War of Independence settled in central and western Pennsylvania and in areas more to the west, the parochial school was often replaced by the neighborhood school. As a result of the intermingling of German and Scotch-Irish settlements, these neighborhood schools often showed a less purely German character than did the church-sponsored schools.

A systematic attempt to introduce the English school into the German-speaking areas was made by the London-based Society for the Propagation of Christian Knowledge, which (1754-1763) maintained a number of bilingual schools among the Germans. The number of students never reached 1,000, and when those local Germans who initially had cooperated became aware of the fact that this plan did not have religious but ethno-lingual aims, they went over to the side of the opponents of the project, and the movement failed. Around 1796 a new plan was devised by those Germans who were inclined toward the English language, but this plan was not put into practice.

As far as the private schools had claims to public funds, the purely German schools received their full share. For example, several land grants made by the state to private Reformed or Lutheran schools are documented for 1789 and 1791. When the question of public stipends for the children of destitute parents was regulated by 1802 and 1804 laws (Kloss 1942, 722-724), the second of these laws expressly spoke of "school teachers . . . who teach the English *or* the German language." A proposal of 1817 in the Pennsylvania senate, according to which five-member boards for examining applicants for teaching positions should be established in each of the court districts, spoke expressly of teachers who teach in the English or in the German language.

Between 1764 and 1825 schools were maintained by the small but very education-minded sect of the Schwenkfeldians. These schools were open to children of all denominations without tuition and assumed the character of free public—but not state-sponsored—German schools during the eighteenth century (E. Sch. Gerhard 1943, 5-21).

Remarkable privileges were granted to the Germans during the eighteenth century in the field of higher education. In the year 1780 a chair of German was established at the University of Pennsylvania, which had been founded only one year before. A law of 1785 authorized the incumbent of the chair and the instructors under him to teach the "learned languages" via the German language. Because of the state control exercised in effect by this law, the university can be considered semipublic in nature. When in 1789 the general regulation of 1779 was abolished, the university was divided into five schools, of which one was the German School.

In the meantime the legislature had granted a charter in 1787 for the bilingual interdenominational Franklin College in Lancaster which, however, soon declined to the status of an academy with a merely local student body. When it gradually regained college status, it had long been a monolingual English institution. In 1853 it merged with a Reformed college into Franklin and Marshall College, which still exists and which has played a definite role in the history of the German-American element (Kloss 1937, 207-208, 212).

The school law of April 1, 1834, which established the "free school" for the entire state of Pennsylvania, contained no language provisions. A proposal was made by Cox on April 11, 1834, to expressly grant the right to have German taught in these schools (Kloss 1940, 266). This motion failed. A law of 1837

Table 5-4   Students Studying German in
                 Elementary Schools in Pennsylvania

Year	Number of Students Studying German	Total Number of Students
1845	6,594	327,418
1852	11,901	480,778
1866	5,843	

permitting German free schools is mentioned in the literature by such authors as G. Koerner, A. B. Faust, M. Lohmann, C. H. Handschin, J. Erhorn, and recently (1961) E. H. Zeydel. This law is no more than a legend.

Nevertheless the Superintendents of Public Schools have again and again recognized the right for a German as well as for a bilingual school. The report of the Superintendent for 1836, for example, reads: "Care has been taken during the last year to correct the impression that a German school cannot be a (public) common school." A law of 1838 made it possible to transform those schools which had been maintained by religious groups into public schools with the greatest possible preservation of their special character (Kloss 1942, 948). As a result, the widely known bilingual schools of the Herrnhuters in Northampton County, for example, became public schools.

In the same year a law put purely English and bilingual academies and female seminaries on an equal basis as far as public subsidies were concerned (Kloss 1940, 265).

The annual statewide surveys (by counties) of students learning German in public elementary schools, which extended up until 1866, presumably listed for each county in the state at least occasionally some students who were either German taught or bilingually taught. In 1845 we find that 1,253 of 4,195 students are listed in this survey in Lecha (Lehigh) County and 1,136 of 8,001 students in Northampton County. In 1866 Berks County led with 1,258 students of German, followed by Lehigh with 759, Northampton with 752, and Elk with 551, where during the 1840s new immigrants from Bavarian Franconia had settled. The total figures for the entire state are shown in Table 5-4, but it is certain that only a part of the students of German was included in this survey.

During the years 1868-1870 three consecutive proposals were placed before the legislature to put the German elementary school on a legal basis. The first proposal provided for German public schools in only three counties, Lehigh, Berks, and Montgomery. The second, which was passed by the house in 1869 but failed in the Senate, provided for German or bilingual schools wherever the parents of at least 25 to 30 students demanded it. The third proposal, in 1870, was similar to the second one (Kloss 1940, 270-272).

An especially promising start was made in the field of teacher training. While a private seminary for German teachers existed as early as 1841-1843 in Monaca (then Phillipsburg), in 1870 D. E. Schoedler founded in Broadheadsville a private bilingual Deutsch-Englische Normalschule. Later he received from the state recognition for the school as a regional seminary, but it folded soon. The state teachers' seminary in Kutztown, founded in 1867, at first promoted instruction in German so strongly that by 1874 two-thirds of the students participated. The annually published decisions of the State School Supervisor established the right to teach German in the public elementary school after the year 1866. A decision printed in 1852 but perhaps of an earlier date spoke of the establishment of German schools by local boards of school directors, an elected body of laymen:

"School directors may establish German schools under the common school law, or cause German and English to be taught in the same school, but the board of directors cannot be required to cause German to be taught. They should consult the wishes of the people of their district in this regard, and, if any considerable number of Germans desire to have their children instructed in their own language, their wishes should be gratified. The directors have exclusive jurisdiction over this subject, and from their decision upon it there is no appeal—the Superintendent having only the power to advise. If the voice of the people is not respected by them, the only remedy is to elect persons who will respect it."

This provision was repeated in a shorter version in the edition of the 1857 decisions. In the 1866 edition, however, it was contracted into the short and ambiguous sentence: "Instruction may, however, be given in the German language with the consent of a majority of the board" of directors. This provision remained in the annual edition of the decisions until 1885. Since 1887 it has been missing. I was unable to locate an 1886 edition in either Harrisburg or Philadelphia.

In isolated instances public German instruction continued to be given after 1885, e.g., in North Heidelberg Township, Lehigh County, until 1889.

In the western Pennsylvania city of Erie so-called German schools with entirely German lower grades were established even before 1870. Around 1877 German was introduced instead as a subject of instruction in all city elementary schools so that in 1884, 4,020 students participated in public German instruction. They constituted 97% of all the students of the town and 58% of all the 6,892 students in elementary schools throughout Pennsylvania who participated in German instruction. The remaining 1,519 students came from Philadelphia. As late as 1912, 70% of all students in the elementary schools in Erie (83% in the primary grades) studied German. In the city of Lancaster there remained five elementary schools in 1895 and two preparatory schools which were fully bilingual. This German instruction was discontinued shortly after the turn of the century.

In the years 1912-1914 German was introduced as a subject in some communities (Altoona, Mt. Lebanon) as a result of a campaign by the Deutschamerikanischer Nationalbund. The school law of 1911 excluded non-English languages as a means of public instruction for the most important subjects, and in 1921 they were excluded from private elementary schools.

German found relatively little backing (in contrast to French in Louisiana) in private elementary schools, which became entirely unimportant among the

Pennsylvania Germans. In the year 1886, there were 26,855 students who learned German in private elementary schools. Of these students 18,688 attended Catholic, 8,059 Protestant, and 108 secular schools. Almost without exception these were schools of recent immigrants of the nineteenth century. On the other hand, the contribution of supplementary religious instruction was important for a long time, especially during the time of the Presseverein (1862-1876). Until into the twentieth century the catechetical instruction leading up to confirmation ensured that children of Pennsilfaanisch mother tongue obtained a minimum knowledge of the German written language.

Special mention should be made of occasional attempts to introduce Pennsylvanish, popularly called Pennsylvania Dutch, into the schools. As early as 1873 A. R. Horne, president of the state teacher's seminary in Kutztown, Pennsylvania, and editor of *The National Educator*, recommended teaching Pennsylvanish starting in the first grade—including samples of poetry—and then proceeding from this basis to teaching High German (Horne 1873; Kloss 1940, 279-280).

When after 1930 the Pennsylvania Germans were stirred by a wave of a new interest, or at times even enthusiasm, for their regional culture, various attempts were made to teach Pennsylvanish. It was taught in the night schools in Allentown according to an expressed decision of the city council, in Y.M.C.A. and Y.W.C.A. courses, in Sunday schools (for example, in Lebanon, Neffsville, in the Mahatongo Valley). The Reverend Mr. Swope of Lebanon wrote in the *Lebanon News* of November 27, 1950, that he was the first teacher who—for his high school courses—had received a Pennsylvanish teacher's certificate from the Department of Education in Harrisburg. For years Pennsylvanish was also cultivated at Muhlenberg College in Allentown by Professors H. H. Reichard, P. A. Barba, and R. C. Wood. Since 1946 it had become a regular subject at Pennsylvania State University, taught by Professor A. F. Buffington. Nevertheless the decisive step of introducing Pennsylvanish into the elementary schools was never made.

The FLES movement has not benefited Pennsylvanish at all and German only in isolated instances (for example, Allentown, Bethel Park, Womelsdorf). In general, the Pennsylvania Germans preferred French and Spanish of the FLES languages.

In contrast to the case in Louisiana and New Mexico, the folk-tongue was not supported by continuing illiteracy, which has long ago disappeared in eastern Pennsylvania.

5-4   OHIO

Background

The area of present-day Ohio was traversed by the French at the end of the seventeenth century and since about 1730 by the British. Finally it became British in 1763, part of the Northwest Territory in 1787, and a state in 1802.

Besides West Virginia (Section 6-3), it is the only state in which Germans were the first permanent settlers. Herrnhuters from Pennsylvania founded Schönbrunn and Gnadenhütten between 1772 and 1773. Consequently the first legislative document of Ohio, the *Städtische Verordnung* of Schönbrunn of 1772, was written in German (Kloss 1940, 484-485). In 1788-1789 secular white settlements were established by many Pennsylvania Germans, who until about 1840 formed the great majority of the Ohio Germans. In contrast to an occasionally expressed erroneous opinion (such as that of Trepte 1932, 327), they settled not always jointly with Anglo-Saxons but frequently established vigorous language pockets where Pennsylvanish has not become totally extinct even today (Section 5-3).

The German immigration from Europe grew to gigantic proportions after 1833; large language islands were established, and Cincinnati and Cleveland became particularly favored places of settlement. In the 1880 census, 192,000 persons were enumerated who were born in the German Empire; in the 1910 census, 673,800 persons from the German Empire in the first or second generation; in the 1940 census, 328,000 German-speaking persons were enumerated of whom 73,300 (22%) had American-born parents.

While the Pennsylvania Germans had settled primarily along a northeast-southwest axis in the center of Ohio, the more recent German immigrants settled in the northern and western parts of the state. In 1910 in Cincinnati 125,400 (35%) of the 363,600 inhabitants came in the first or second generation from the German speech community, and over half of the inhabitants were of German descent. In the year 1960, there were 249,900 persons in Ohio who were first or second generation Germans; 71,500 foreign-born had German for their mother tongue.

A flowering German press came into existence; in 1908 German newspapers appeared in 35 communities, in Cincinnati alone 3 dailies, 6 weeklies, and 3 monthlies. German literature during the first decades, even though written predominantly by foreign-born authors, is primarily distinguished from the rest of the German-American literature in that it contained, in addition to fiction, nonnarrative prose in the fields of theology, medicine, history, etc.

By 1960 there remained only two city newspapers, the *Freie Presse* (1863) in Cincinnati and the *Wächter und Anzeiger* in Cleveland with a total edition of almost 5,000 copies, and two church magazines. No literature is produced any more and Anglicization has progressed rapidly even though, in several language pockets, dialects have survived the decline of High German, notably Plattdeutsch (Low Saxon dialect) in Auglaize and Henry Counties.

In 1960 noneducational radio broadcasts in German existed only in two cities—Akron, one hour weekly, and Cleveland, three hours. Educational programs were broadcast in Berea for a half hour weekly and in Columbus for one and a half hours.

That the German element in Ohio enjoyed a particularly well developed legal status of their language can be explained by their deep involvement in the state's history. In this connection, Ohio may be placed side by side with the German element in Pennsylvania and the old settler groups in Louisiana and New Mexico. Beginnings of this legal status were achieved, as in the case of

Pennsylvania, Maryland, and Virginia, by the American-born descendants of German immigrants who had come to America during colonial times. In Pennsylvania the later German immigrants contributed little to the legal status of the German language and in Maryland and Virginia a wide gap existed between the modest language rights of the older and younger German element. That is, no real language continuity had existed in Pennsylvania, Maryland, or Virginia. In contrast, both strata of the German element in Ohio made their contributions, and the later phase of the language laws developed organically from the earlier phase.

Constitutional Law—German in Government and the Legislature

The German language is not mentioned in any of the constitutions of the state of Ohio.

It can be demonstrated in no other field with greater clarity than in the field of official prints that the "new German" immigrants of the 1830s, who came directly from Europe, only continued where the Pennsylvania Germans had prepared the soil for them. On December 11, 1815, a petition "of German inhabitants of this State" was put before the legislature asking that a law might provide for the printing of German editions of the laws and session records. On December 22, 1815, a committee report of the legislature endorsed the petition with respect to the laws and resolutions of the current session, but the plenary session rejected it by a vote of 27 to 26, with the vote of the speaker cast against the petition. A year later new petitions were presented, this time only with respect to the laws. On January 10, 1817, a joint resolution of both houses approved printing in German laws of a general nature, in contrast to the so-called local laws which concerned only questions of a certain part of the state. This success has to be credited clearly to the Pennsylvania German element of the state. However, C. B. Galbraith (1925, II, 250) considers it proof of the presence of many German immigrants from Europe.

Long before 1833 we hear again and again of resolutions of the legislature concerning official publications in German. For example, on February 14, 1829, the printing of a German version of the school law was approved, and on March 12, 1831, "an act authorizing the publication of certain laws of a general nature in the German language" was adopted.

Thus an uninterrupted transition may be established from the official German publications before the 1830s to those that appeared after the 1830s. For example, in December of the years 1832, 1833, and 1834 the printing of 2,000 German copies each of the Governor's annual messages was authorized, while on February 28, 1834, a German edition of the School Law was voted.

Occasionally the two small minorities of the state, the French and Welsh, also were taken into consideration. In March 1838, an attempt failed to have German and French editions made of a law governing the duties of township officials; half a year later the printing was authorized of 2,000 German and 1,000 Welsh copies of the annual message of the Governor. On December 17, 1840, an equal number of German and English copies (2,000 each) of the inaugural address of the Governor was approved.

The printing of official publications in the German language was, therefore, a well-established custom at that time, even though the 1839 edition of the collected statutes by Georg Walker was perhaps only a private publication. The report by H. A. Rattermann (1879, 217-218) that Walker had to contribute much of his own money to this edition, however, does not exclude the possibility that he undertook the printing under a state contract and only miscalculated his expenses. It seems that German editions of the annual reports of the State Board of Agriculture appeared after 1849, for I find that volume 6 of the *Jahresberichte der Landbau-Behörde des Staates Ohio* was published in 1851, and volume 9 in 1854. In 1965 a Dutch bookseller offered me volumes 6-9, 1851-1854.

The law of April 8, 1856, remained silent on the question of German editions, but a law of the following year regulated the business and technical details for the "contractor of German printing" and for all German prints which the legislature may authorize (Ohio *Statutes* 1869; Ohio *Revised Statutes* 1879; Kloss 1940, 443-444). A law of March 12, 1885, regulated individual cases in which German prints were envisioned as follows (in the May 1, 1891, version of the same law): "The reports of the Secretary of State, of the Commissioner of Labor Statistics, of the Inspector of Shops and Factories, and the State Board of Agriculture shall also be printed in the German language. The Secretary of State shall ascertain from each member of the General Assembly how many of the copies to which he is entitled he wishes in the German language, and the aggregate number so determined shall be printed in German and distributed to the members of the General Assembly accordingly." In the version of 1885 a certain number of copies (2,000 of the total of 8,000) was provided for the report on shops and factories; but otherwise only the wording and not the contents differed from the later version.

But this 1885/1891 law presumably did not include all government documents which at that time were regularly or frequently published in German. An idea of the extent to which the German language was used in the official prints of this time may be gathered from the fact that during the 1870s and 1880s a state survey of Ohio of three volumes each on geology and paleontology appeared in both languages. The geographer, Albrecht Penck, reported that Ohio was practically a bilingual state at the time of his visit.

This was possible only because of a continuous strong German representation in the legislature. In the year 1912 a kind of nonpartisan German working group, the Deutsche Legislatur-Klub von Ohio, was formed which was immediately joined by 50 members. The by-laws said, among other things, that the club had as its purpose: "To cultivate German ideals, such as the German language, German gymnastics, German songs, and German lectures as well as liberal convictions. As a first step in this direction be it resolved that all business negotiations be conducted only in the German language; the English language is permissible whenever necessary. Furthermore it is the objective of this club to work with all honest means toward perfecting the teaching of German in the public schools more and more until it has achieved equal status with English in the curriculum. To keep alive the interest in the above-mentioned endeavors, lectures about German and German-American history shall be held in the club. German songs shall be cultivated in the club."

In conclusion, the by-laws read: "This club shall enter into close relations with similar clubs in other states so as to create a national association." A similar but politically less influential club was actually formed soon afterward in the New York state legislature.

How completely the former German official prints have been forgotten in Ohio is shown by official information (Ohio Legislative Reference Bureau, October 3, 1961), "that no official Ohio documents have been printed in a non-English language," information which is in itself a document. Also a letter of the State Supreme Court of August 19, 1961, declares that it knows nothing about laws concerning legal notices in the Polish and Czech press of the state (see below).

The Courts—Legal Notices

As for the courts of Ohio, no provisions are known to me that are in favor of the German or other non-English language. Concerning legal notices in German, which existed at least since the 1830s and possibly much earlier, a law of March 2, 1850, provided as follows (the "court of record" hereunder mentioned, in contrast to the Justice of the Peace, keeps and files court records): "All official notices and advertisements relating to the public business of any county wherein a newspaper or newspapers in the German language are printed and all public sales of property in pursuance of any execution, order or decree of any court of record in such county, now by a law required to be published in any newspaper, shall, in addition to the publication heretofore required, be published in such German newspaper, provided nothing herein contained shall be construed as to authorize 'legal advertisement' to be made in any German newspaper except at the express instance of the plaintiff or defendant in the suit out of which or in relation to which said advertisements are so published; and the party requiring such publication shall pay all the expense attending the same."

Typologically, this provision belongs rather to the later immigrant law since it does not put the German notices on an equal status with the English. An amendment of March 4, 1866, to the code of civil procedure ruled (in Article 1) that the courts were permitted (not ordered) to publish advertisements of court-ordered sales of movable or immovable property in a German newspaper at the request of one of the two parties, but mistakes concerning contents or time of the advertisement, which might occur in this process, should not have any legal force. Article 3 furthermore states: "In all cases in which, under the code of civil procedure, service on a defendant or defendants can be made by publication, the court is hereby authorized to adopt such a rule or rules as to require such notices be published in some German newspaper, if any be printed in the county or, if more than one, in that which has the largest circulation therein."

This law was amended on April 3, 1867, according to which court-ordered sales of land in cities of the first and second classes of an appraised value of at least $1,200 should be announced in a German newspaper; errors in translation would again remain without legal consequences, but failure to make the announcement could lead, upon request, to the annulment of the sales (Kloss 1940, 478). However, the courts were permitted to waive this publication upon a well-founded request.

According to an 1873 law, county officials should publish certain notices—about elections, court dates, new tax and fee rates, and similar matters—in two newspapers of different political views and, in addition, in a German newspaper of the county. In connection with this law several opinions by the Attorney General were issued (*Opinion of the Attorney General 1912, 1916*).

Still, before the turn of the century the State Supreme Court stated on two occasions, 1850 and 1894 (*Cincinnati* v. *Bickett*; *State* v. *Cincinnati*; Kloss 1942, 927-928) that, in places where a state law ordered publication in one newspaper or in two newspapers without mentioning the language, English was intended and that the publication in one English and one German newspaper would not constitute a publication "in two newspapers" within the meaning of the law. In a trial in 1875 the plaintiff maintained, among other things, that always only an English newspaper was intended by the term "a newspaper of general circulation" since a German newspaper would always be referred to as one "of special circulation"; the judge concurred but declared that the experts did not agree on this matter. The term "of general circulation" was expressly applied to non-English papers in many American laws and court decisions; it refers to a general medium of news as opposed to the papers of special professions, organizations, or religious sects.

The legislation about official notices took a completely new turn with a law of April 2, 1891, concerning the sale of land: "In any county wherein a newspaper is published and printed in the German language which has a circulation of at least 550 copies of bona fide subscribers within the county the notice shall, in addition to the publication therein required, be published in such newspaper . . . if the appraised value of the property to be sold exceeds $500. . . . Also in any county the court may, if it deems the interests of the accused require it, direct the publication of the notice in a newspaper printed in the Bohemian language."

This article contained a directive concerning German and a permit concerning Czech newspapers. On April 25, 1894, it was changed so as to put the Czech on an equal footing with the German papers (Kloss 1940, 481). Later, but before 1910, the directive was again limited to the German papers; the permit, on the other hand, now extended also to the Polish papers (Ohio *General Code*, sec. 11, 684).

The provisions concerning the Czech and Polish notices form a counterpart to the provisions about Italian and Yiddish notices in Pennsylvania (Section 5-3). It is significant that, in comparison with the German papers, there is a less advantageous position for those Slavic papers which under certain circumstances had a legal claim to official notices. The later immigrants were thus treated with less consideration than the original cosettlers.

In the same year 1891 which granted official notices to the Czech press in Ohio, the German press was favored by a law of April 25, according to which the amendments to the constitution which were proposed at that time were also to be published in each county in a German newspaper or, in case two German papers of different political affiliations appeared in the county, in both.

A law of April 27, 1893, provided that the county auditors should publish the lists of tax delinquent estates "also" in a German newspaper of the respective county. Again prior to 1910 this provision was changed in a manner which deprived the German publication of its character as an additional (an "also") publication but put it on an equal footing with English publications (Ohio *General Code* 1910, sec. 5,704; Kloss 1940, 483).

Generally speaking, however, the German language in Ohio never acquired a position equal to that in Pennsylvania, as far as official notices are concerned. While in Pennsylvania English and German newspapers were put on a basically equal footing in a number of counties in 1863, this treatment could be found in Ohio in the case of only one single late law (concerning tax delinquency in real estate).

School Language Laws

The Pennsylvania Germans established their own church schools in Ohio as they had in Pennsylvania. The Lutheran preachers of Ohio and western Pennsylvania were at first still under the jurisdiction of the Pennsylvania Ministerium but from 1812 on annually convened in Spezial-Conferenzen. During their 1816 meeting in Lancaster, Ohio, they reached the decision that each preacher had to give at least one sermon annually on the topic of the necessity for having a German school and that a German scholar should be entrusted with the preparation of a "Christian textbook for the use of the German schools in this western country" (*Verrichtungen der 6, Spezial-Conferenzen* 1816, 7).

The Pennsylvania German element in Ohio went so far as to establish German-language higher educational institutions. In 1830 the Lutheran Ohio Synod founded a theological seminary in Canton, which was moved to Columbus in 1833 and to which Germania College was attached in 1841-1842 as a preparatory school.

The later German immigrants soon also founded private schools, but the figures given by Handschin seem exaggerated that Cincinnati had only 400 English-language students in 1831 in addition to 1,500 students receiving German instruction.

The school law of 1834 did not provide for public German instruction. A petition was brought before the Senate in 1837 and a motion in the House of Representatives of January 20, 1838, to support German schools with public funds. These failed to achieve any results: the new School Law of March 7, 1838, made the teaching of German possible only by indirection. This led to vigorous demonstrations by the Germans, and on April 1, 1839, an amendment (Kloss 1940, 449) to the school law was adopted which stated, among other things: "The passage in the said law which requires that subjects of study be taught in English shall be and is hereby repealed. The school board shall have full power to decide what subjects and what language or languages shall be taught in their districts, though the subjects shall be those customary in the elementary schools."

Article 18 furthermore regulated the relationship between German and English schools: "In any district where the directors maintain an English school and do not have the branches taught in German, it shall be lawful for the youth in such district who desire to learn in the German language to attend a district German school; . . . and the same rule shall be adopted and privileges allowed in favor of those wishing to learn the English language who reside in districts where the German language is taught and so of any other language."

This provision was incorporated into the 1847 Louisiana law by merely substituting "French" for "German." (For Louisiana, see Section 5-1; for Ohio, Kloss 1940, 449-450. For a supplementary law of March 7, 1842, Kloss 1940, 452.) As a result, the establishment of German or bilingual public schools seems to have generally spread without trouble. The Whig majority in the Cincinnati School Board, however, claimed that the new law did permit the establishment of such schools but did not prescribe it. Therefore, the following provision was added to the city charter of Cincinnati by a law of March 19, 1840: "It shall be the duty of the Board of Trustees and Visitors of Common Schools to provide a number of German schools under some duly qualified teachers for the instruction of such youth as desire to learn the German language or the German and English languages together."

As to whether or not future schools should be German with English as a subject or completely bilingual, the question was decided in favor of the bilingual school by a study of a three-man committee of the city government (Kloss 1940, 461) and consequently also in practice. At first, separate schools for German children were established. Later separate classes in regular elementary schools were preferred. The number of students receiving bilingual instruction in Cincinnati's public schools is shown in Table 5-5. Between 1886 and 1917, the figure remained almost constant.

After 1853 German was taught in the upper elementary grades and after 1856 in the high schools also. In 1858, 10 of the 15 district schools (grades one through six) and one of the four intermediate schools (grades seven and eight) taught German. In the school year 1907-1908 only one elementary school had no German instruction. The teaching systems varied; for example, in grades 1 through 4, according to the school regulations of 1870, half the time for instruction would

Table 5-5   Cincinnati Public School Students Who
              Received Bilingual Instruction

Year	Number of Pupils	Year	Number of Pupils
1841	327	1886	16,410
1851	1,339	1902	17,200
1860	4,788	1914	14,600
1870	10,440		

be in German, while in grades 5 through 8, only three-quarters to one hour daily were given to German instruction. The conditions were also not uniform in the various schools (Kloss 1940, 466-470). As late as 1910 there seem to have still been isolated schools which cultivated one of the two languages only as a subject.

German elementary instruction was supported by a number of institutions which developed over the years. In November 1863, a German Oberlehrerverein (Senior Teachers Association) was founded which issued a call for the organization of a general German-American Teachers' Association. This was not organized, however, until 1870 (*Monatshefte* 1907, 8: 295). In addition, a Deutscher Lehrerverein von Cincinnati and an organization for women teachers, Harmonia, were formed. It is interesting to read, in *Monatshefte* 1915, 16: 157, for instance, the information about crises in such organizations. In the year 1878, citywide German workshops were started for training teachers in German (Bagster-Collins 1930, 21; United States Commissioner of Education 1878, part 1, 93). In the year 1902, the Deutsch-Amerikanischer Zentralverein organized a group of parents, consisting of knowledgeable men and women, who regularly visited the German classes in public and private educational institutions (*Monatshefte* 1901-1902, 3: 284). In the year 1914 a German Council was constituted which brought together the German teachers of the universities and the intermediate and elementary schools for the purpose of preparing a graded curriculum from the first grade to the final university examination (*Monatshefte* 1914, 15: 357). From 1908 on H. H. Fick, who after 1901 was the city supervisor of German elementary instruction, held lectures in German at university extension level. These were held at the university at convenient times for the general public and were on the subject of German-American literature. This information is contained in a 1935 letter to me from H. H. Fick. From this we may conclude that German was indeed cultivated in Cincinnati to a certain degree as an indigenous language of the educated. Fick's syllabus of lectures is given in Kloss 1940, 468-469.

Prior to World War I Cincinnati had not only the oldest but also the most advanced German instruction of all American cities. Handschin (1913, 72) called it "perhaps the best and most thorough of its kind which exists at the present time in the United States. . . . This system is hardly equalled by any other in the United States." School experts from other places repeatedly visited Cincinnati to study this school system. An impressive number of leading Anglo-American school experts in Cincinnati professed to be warm and convinced friends of the bilingual school.

The legal basis, however, had changed completely during the course of the nineteenth century. The school law of March 14, 1853, still retained the old regulation of 1839: "The township board of education ... may provide German schools for the instruction of such youths as may desire to study the German language or the German and English languages together." In this connection, a decision of the State Supervisor of Schools (1865) ruled that a "German school" could not be a regular common school but would constitute a special school, like the schools for Negroes or like a high school which likewise was established for a certain kind of student and not for all students of the district. (For the texts of the 1853 and 1904 laws, of the decision by the State Supervisor of Schools, and of the proposal of 1912, see Kloss 1940, 455-457.)

The school boards were nevertheless permitted to introduce German as a subject in the regular (English) elementary schools. A law of 1870 changed this right of the board of education into a binding obligation if certain requirements were met: "The board of any district shall cause the German language to be taught in any school under its control, during any school year, when a demand therefor is made in writing by 75 freeholders, resident of the district, representing not fewer than 40 pupils who are entitled to attend such a school."

Later commentaries of the chief state school officer stated (in 1879) that the legislature basically aimed at English instruction and (in 1893) that the 75 petitioners did not have to live within the same subdistrict.

The school law of 1904 finally retained only the right of the school board to introduce the teaching of German, but not its obligation to do so, if petitioned by a minimum number of parents. In the year 1912 a proposal to restore this obligation in cases where the parents of 40 children demanded it was approved by the Senate but failed in the House of Representatives. During the debate representatives pointed out that it would only be fair to apply the same standards to Polish, Czech, and Yiddish too. A school law of June 5, 1919, abolished all foreign language instruction in public schools (Section 3-4).

In contrast to Cincinnati, the development of German instruction in Cleveland, today the largest city of the state, was adapted to the gradually worsening legal situation—even though only hesitantly. German had been introduced in 1869, and, by 1900, in the public schools 17,600 children studied German. With 8,000 students in private schools, they comprised 40% of the entire school population. Grades one through four of the public schools were bilingual. From the fifth grade on, German was only a subject. However, in 1906 German was completely abolished in the lower grades (one through four). While in 1911 as many as 12,400 students were counted in grades five through eight, German was limited to grades seven and eight in 1914.

Bilingual classes in the lower grades of the elementary school flourished temporarily in other cities as well, for example, in Dayton (1844) and Columbus.

Table 5-6　　Rank of Subjects in High Schools According to Enrollment (1906)

High School Location	First Place	Second Place	Third Place	
Minster	German 380	US History 90	Latin	44
New Knoxville	German 129	US History 54	World History	10
			Arithmetic	10
			Speech	10
			Latin	10
St. Henry	German 244	US History 128	Latin	25
			Physics	25

They remained in existence perhaps even longer in many rural communities and small towns. In some of these places the German curriculum was occasionally so expanded that these schools were indeed fully bilingual, even though officially German was taught only as a subject. For example, in 1906, according to the *55th Annual Report of the State Commissioner of Common Schools of Ohio*, the subjects could be ranked in some high schools, based on the number of students, as shown in Table 5-6. The introduction of a language as a subject in the high schools is the minimum concession which can be made to the language of a national minority while the introduction of the language as a means of instruction is the maximum concession.

The example of Minster (Table 5-6) shows that an ethnic group could well change rights of a lower order into rights of a high order by a consistent exploitation of the legal possibilities and thus establish for itself the bilingual public high school. This possibility, however, existed only in rural areas, since in urban high schools the other subjects can never be put aside in favor of language teaching.

Table 5-7 gives a survey of the 1908 conditions of German instruction in certain centers of public instruction. It is compiled from the *55th Annual Report of the State Commissioner of Common Schools* in Ohio and from materials in *Monatshefte* 1909, 10: 276-277. At that time there were 66,400 students of German in public schools who comprised 7.7% of all students in the entire state.

As in Pennsylvania, in Ohio the retention of German was never favored by the existence of any significant illiterate populace. On the other hand, private schools remained strong supporters of the German language until World War I. In 1900 there were 30,680 students enumerated in Catholic, 5,650 in Protestant, and 823 in secular German schools. In the year 1919, a state law prohibited for private schools all non-English languages as a means of instruction and, below the ninth grade, German as a subject. The German Lutherans of Ohio contested this law in two lawsuits, *Pohl* v. *Ohio* and *Bohning* v. *Ohio*. These were decided in 1923 by the United States Supreme Court in favor of the plaintiffs, directly following a similar ruling in the case of *Meyer* v. *Nebraska* (Section 3-4). Nevertheless this

Location	Number of Students Studying German		Percentage of All Students	
	County	Major City	County	Major City
Hamilton	33,810		37.5	
Cincinnati		16,389		42.3
Cuyahoga	14,887		18.2	
Cleveland		13,806		21.3
Franklin	3,277		10.6	
Columbus		3,236		16.8
Montgomery	2,102		9.1	
Dayton		2,041		13.8
Mercer	1,627		26.2	
St. Henry		223		100.0
Auglaize	1,432		22.7	
Minster		378		96.6
Putnam	1,040		14.8	
New Bremen		525		95.0

Table 5-7   Centers of Public School Instruction in German (1908)

favorable ruling was followed by very limited revival of private teaching of German in a few supplementary and Lutheran parochial schools.

The nationality laws of Ohio have to be evaluated in comparison to those of Pennsylvania. The nationality laws of both states differ from those concerning the German element of the other Midwestern states. In the case of Ohio and Pennsylvania a German element dating back to colonial times which already existed laid the foundation for minority rights. In Pennsylvania this foundation laid by the older German element is very comprehensive while the laws caused by the coming of later German immigrants remained very limited. In Ohio, on the other hand, the foundation laid by the old German element is slim, while the center of gravity is to be found in the rights achieved by later German immigrants. The late and sporadic consideration of the Italian and Yiddish languages in Pennsylvania was similar to that of the Polish and Czech languages in Ohio.

CHAPTER SIX

Promotion-Oriented Nationality Rights for Smaller Groups of Original Settlers in Mainland States

6-1 STATES WITH SMALL, LONG-ESTABLISHED FRENCH MINORITIES

The Midwest French

Early History. Throughout the Midwest a number of French settlements were established in the first half of the eighteenth century. These settlers came from present-day Canada.

The settlement first began in the extreme south and north (Section 5-1), where forts were founded at the mouth of the St. Joseph River in 1679 and in Detroit in 1701. They were followed around 1720 by Kaskaskia, Cohokia, and Fort Chartres in present-day Illinois, in 1720 by Fort Orleans, in 1735 by St. Genevieve, in 1764 by St. Louis in present-day Missouri, and in present-day Indiana in 1731 by the military outpost Vincennes where civilians also settled after 1735.

The French settlements in the Midwest formed a bridge between the larger French areas of settlements of Quebec and Louisiana. They came into existence without any territorial connection with the older Anglo-Saxon settlements in the East; the area between the French and Anglo-Saxon settlements—the area of present-day Ohio, Kentucky, and Tennessee—remained entirely Indian country.

In the year 1763 the political fortunes of the French midwestern settlements followed separate paths. Those located west of the Mississippi, together with present-day Canada, came under British rule. Under the British the demand for self-administration of the kind enjoyed by Connecticut was raised at the meeting in Kaskaskia in 1771.

Table 6-1 White Population of Main French Midwestern Areas in 1790

Present Name of State	Number of French Inhabitants	Number of Other Whites
Missouri	1,800	200
Indiana	1,000	500
Illinois	1,000	300
Michigan	3,100	450
Wisconsin	150	0
Ohio	750	3,250
TOTALS	7,800	4,700

In the 1783 Treaty of Paris, England recognized that the midwestern territories east of the Mississippi belonged to the United States, but it did not vacate Michigan until 1796. In the year 1803 Upper Louisiana became part of the United States and from March 26, 1804, when Upper Louisiana was incorporated as a District into the Northwest Territory (at that time called Indiana) until the following year when Michigan (January 11) and Upper Louisiana (March 3) were elevated to the status of separate territories, the old established French element was once again put under one single administration. In 1790 the white population of all these areas showed the composition in Table 6-1. Those listed under *Other* are predominantly Anglo-Saxons, but the number of Germans—primarily in Ohio—can be estimated to be at least 500. The French settlements in Wisconsin were too small to be influential. In Ohio the French were later immigrants who arrived after the Anglo-Saxons and Germans had come. In Indiana the French element was reduced to numerical insignificance earlier than in any other states by mass immigration of Anglo-Saxons and Germans. On the other hand, in Michigan the French were gradually reduced to minority status only after 1820 (Table 6-2).

Illinois and Indiana. After 1776 some of the states raised claims to the vast midwestern hinterland. Congress persuaded these states to cede their claims to the Confederation. Most important was the cession by Virginia of December 20, 1783, which in a special clause protected the "French and Canadian inhabitants" in the "enjoyment of their rights and privileges" and their property (Commager I 1958, 120-121). Only on the basis of these cessions could Congress adopt the famous Great Ordinance of July 13, 1787, which created the Northwest Territory and gave it a constitution. The Northwest Territory became a territory of the first category (Table 1-1) administered by a governor and three judges. As soon as a designated area reached a certain population figure, it would become a territory with an elected legislature and later a state of the Union.

From a practical standpoint this meant that the region would advance to higher forms of self-government as soon as the French were no longer the

Table 6-2   Inhabitants of Originally French-Settled States
                 1810-1830

Territory or State	Inhabitants		
	1810	*1820*	*1830*
Illinois	12,300	55,200	157,400
Indiana	24,500	147,200	343,000
Missouri	20,800	66,600	140,500
Michigan	4,800	8,800	31,700

predominant ethnic element, since the envisioned population increase would primarily occur as the result of immigration by English-speaking people. The Great Ordinance contained no new guarantee of the rights, privileges, and property of the French inhabitants. It stated only that, until the time when the governor and the three judges introduced new laws, the laws and customs concerning the inheritance and transfer of property should remain in effect as they were at that time among the French.

Friction between Anglo-Saxon and French inhabitants was not unknown to the Northwest Territory. In August 1785 two petitions from the French population of Cahokia and Kaskaskia were before Congress which asked for the establishment of a regular county government. The French court of Kaskaskia had been dissolved by County Lieutenant Governor Richard Winston in 1782 while the court of Cahokia still existed. When in 1787 the Anglo-Saxons of Bellefontaine and the French of Kaskaskia established a common court to which each of the ethnic groups supplied three judges, mutual communication proved impossible. The entirely French court, established soon afterward, was not able to continue. On the other hand, the French court of Cahokia as late as September 1787 wrecked an attempt to establish a common Anglo-Saxon court for Bellefontaine and Grand Ruisseauz. However, the French in Cahokia were clever enough to be more amenable to the Anglo-Saxons after this success (Alvord 1922, 368-369, 360).

Under the new constitution a one-month school for children was established in 1794 in Cahokia by the judges following a petition of the population. At that time this school could have been only French in all respects (Alvord 1922, 405). About this time the same judges ordered a translation of the territorial laws into French (Alvord 1922, 405; Allison 1907, 286). The authorities and citizens of Kaskaskia declared in a remonstrance which reached Congress on May 10, 1796, that Judge George Turner denied them "the right reserved to us by the constitution of the Territory, to wit, the laws and customs hitherto enforced with regard to descent and conveyance of property, in which the French and Canadian inhabitants conceive the language as essential." The emphasis put here on language is unusual for the eighteenth century. The French were successful at that time; Turner resigned from his post.

Presumably the French language has also often been used officially in the later Territory (after 1809) and State (after 1818). After all the French supplied in 1818 the first Vice-Governor of the new state, Pierre Ménard, and Illinois witnessed later a considerable French-Canadian immigration (East 1928). Even the Constitutional Convention of 1870 decided to have 5,000 French copies of the new constitution printed in addition to 30,000 English, 15,000 German, and 5,000 "Scandinavian" copies. In the debate it was also mentioned that many immigrants whose mother tongue was not French and who could not read English were nevertheless able to read French (Kloss 1942, 928-929).

Even in Indiana, where the French element had been pushed into the background by the Anglo-Saxons and which became a state in 1816, it has been verified that a French edition of the Governor's annual message was printed as late as 1850. No foundation, however, seems to exist for the assumption that the first institution of higher learning in the state, Vincennes University (1806), was bilingual in the beginning. According to a letter from Professor Thomas W. Kirkconnell (1961) of Vincennes University the institution was founded by an Anglo-American and in the early years was never more than a junior college. From the beginning, French was taught there as a subject.

Michigan. As already mentioned, Michigan was reached by an Anglo-Saxon mass immigration later than its neighbors: There were only 32,000 inhabitants in 1830, but this number jumped to 212,000 by 1840. In the year 1838 John T. Blair estimated that between 10,000 and 12,000 Frenchmen lived in Michigan, practically all of whom still used their old language.

Very early the French had established their own Catholic schools with French as the language of instruction. Their founder was P. Gabriel Richard, who later (1823) became the first representative of Detroit in the United States Congress. In behalf of the French Catholic schools, Richard in 1808 petitioned first the government of Michigan and then the federal government in Washington to which he traveled personally. In Washington he was promised financial support which would have transformed these schools into semipublic institutions, but this support never materialized (McMurtrie 1931, 30-32; *Catholic Encyclopedia* 1913, Schools). In his petition to the territorial government, Richard distinguishes carefully between the two "English" and the seven "other" schools in the territory.

It was this great cultural resistance of the French element which in 1806 inspired Judge A. B. Woodward to put a memorandum before the United States Senate on April 15 in which Woodward expressed opposition to wholesale self-government for Michigan. Almost all inhabitants were French, and by contrast with "new settlements strictly American" it would not be advisable in their case to grant a higher degree of self-government. Instead of a popularly elected body, it would be better to have only appointed judges in addition to the Governor (*American State Papers* 1834, 461-463). Indeed Michigan remained a territory of the first category until 1824, when a representative body consisting of two houses was constituted.

Nevertheless voices were raised very early in favor of a higher degree of self-government, primarily an elected representative body because the first governor William Hull (1805-1812) was very unpopular. He did not come from the Northwest Territory and remained a stranger to the people (Cooley 1905, 148ff., 189ff.). One of the reasons for the tensions between the people and the governor seems to have been the language question, particularly the question of having a French edition of the territorial laws. In general even English publications met with great difficulties in the territory at that time: only after 1809 did a printing press regularly function there, and among other things, for example, the first school law of 1809 has been lost.

When a first collection of the territorial laws appeared in 1806, the twelve members of the territorial grand jury published a report (September 26, 1809). In this report they demanded the translation of the laws into French, since three-fourths of the taxpaying inhabitants of the territory could not understand English. Furthermore, the Governor was heavily criticized in this report for several of his actions (McMurtrie 1931, 113). Hull answered this criticism with a proclamation of October 19 in which he declared that only Congress could challenge the validity of laws issued by him; he had this proclamation printed in French also, and only the French copy has been preserved. Whether Hull also discussed the question of French laws is not evident (McMurtrie 1931, 114).

In the meantime, citizens of Michigan had met on October 16, 1809, and in a series of resolutions demanded a new territorial constitution for Michigan with a representative body consisting of two houses. Their resolutions were likewise printed in an English and a French edition (McMurtrie 1931, 113, 43, 117).

In a petition to President Madison the citizens of Michigan asked for the removal of Hull and, in another petition to Congress, for the elevation of Michigan to a territory of higher category. Furthermore, a petition by several Michigan citizens went before Congress on April 26, 1810, asking that the federal and territorial laws which were in effect in Michigan be printed in a French edition. A committee report (Kloss 1940, 524-526) of April 18, 1810, turned down this latter request, giving as reason that, with the translation into French, a second version would be created which might at times produce different interpretations of the laws. (Bilingual states like Louisiana and Quebec did not suffer much from this allegedly unavoidable double interpretation.)

Further arguments in the committee report were that it would be more important for the people to obtain their views from one single source rather than that a perhaps even larger number of people would use two different sources. Also the courts would be confused by the existence of two versions. (But it would have been easy just to declare the English version as legally binding in cases of controversy.) Finally other ethnic groups (this refers primarily to the Germans) should not be encouraged to cling to their native language by such a promotion of the French language. The arguments of the congressional committee were not only not very clear, they were also not very convincing.

Since the request for the establishment of an elected body had been denied and Michigan continued to remain under the rule of an Anglo-American Governor and three judges, the French language continued to be used only in isolated instances. It was used during the War of 1812 in several Michigan prints, which presumably were addressed more to the Canadian French than to the Michigan French (McMurtrie 1931, 128-130). French was used also perhaps in a proclamation by the Governor (1813) which proclaimed martial law (McMurtrie 1931, 133-134).

A law of 1817 about the founding of the "University of Michigania," also called "Catholepistimiad," provided also for the establishment of branch schools in which French should be a subject for study, but these branch schools did not materialize at that time. Nevertheless in 1818 in a plebiscite most inhabitants of French descent rejected the establishment of a territorial legislature; the legislature was constituted in 1824 but for the time being published its proceedings and laws in English only.

On April 13, 1827, the legislature resolved to authorize the printing of 300 English and French copies of each of three territorial laws (Kloss 1940, 527). The school law of 1827 declared: "Every township within this territory containing 50 families or householders shall be provided with a good schoolmaster or schoolmasters, of good morals, to teach children to read and write, to instruct them in the English or French language as well as in arithmetic, orthography, and decent behavior." This represents an extraordinary moral triumph for the French-speaking population even though the entire law seems to have remained on paper.

According to information received from Michigan, the *Detroit Gazette*, which appeared from 1817 to 1830, published in French some early gubernatorial proclamations and records of the territorial legislature (Michigan State Historical Society 1935). Samples of these French publications are to be found in the Detroit Public Library. McMurtrie (1931, 65), however, claims that the French portion of the newspaper included only synopses of the most important articles and that after a few months it was discontinued.

We have record of the separate French edition in 1830 of a speech by Governor Lewis Cass. Soon after Michigan achieved statehood (1835-1837), the French language seems to have completely disappeared from official use.

Missouri. The French of Missouri (at that time called Upper Louisiana) received a special guarantee of their rights at the time of annexation which went far beyond the wording of the Treaty of Annexation. Captain Amos Stoddard issued a proclamation to the inhabitants of Upper Louisiana on March 10, 1804, which stated (Houck II 1908, 371): "Your local situation, the varieties of your language and education, have contributed to render your manners, laws and customs and even your prejudices somewhat different from those of your neighbors, but not less favorable to virtue and good order in society. They deserve more than mere indulgence; they shall be respected."

Without straining a point, we may well read a differentiation between promotion-oriented and tolerance-oriented nationality rights into the juxtaposition of respect and mere toleration, of active consideration and passive laissez faire.

When on March 26, 1804, the area ceded by France was divided and the south was elevated into a territory of the second category (Section 5-1 and Table 1-1), Upper Louisiana was incorporated into Indiana Territory as a mere district. This action led to bitter complaints among the people of Upper Louisiana. A memorandum dated September 29, 1804, was submitted to Congress (Kloss 1940, 519) asking that all leading officials should, if possible, be bilingual, that county and court records should be permitted to be kept in both languages as in Canada, and that funds should be appropriated to establish in each county a French-English school.

The report of the congressional committee concerned dealt primarily with Lower Louisiana (Section 5-1) and mentions Upper Louisiana only in the introduction, but its favorable attitude toward ethnic groups had also a beneficial effect on this complaint. On March 3, 1805, the district was transformed into a territory of the first category, which in 1812 adopted the name Missouri and which became a state in 1821. From 1804 to 1812 Upper Louisiana had officially been known as Louisiana while present-day Louisiana had been known as Orleans. The French language was still officially used in the new state of Missouri on several occasions; for example, French editions of the annual message of the governor have been recorded for the years 1843, 1858, and 1871. Tiny French-speaking pockets survived well into the twentieth century; in 1935, 90% of the inhabitants of Old Mines, Missouri, were still able to speak French (Dorrance 1935).

Minnesota. That even the smallest French groups found official recognition occasionally is borne out by the fact that in 1848 in Minnesota a French edition was printed of the first territorial governor's first annual message (McMurtrie 1935, 17). This governor was A. Ramsey, who in 1843 had favored German and, to some extent, French in Congress. In 1857 the constitutional convention ordered 2,000 copies of the first state constitution to be printed in the French language (*Debates and Proceedings . . . Minnesota* 1857, 615).

The Far West

The early French groups in the Midwest, even though small in numbers, were still large when compared to the minute French Canadian splinter settlements in the Far West. Yet even here we find attempts at the preservation of the language. When in 1853 the Anglo-American settlers of Oregon formed a government, Père Langlois, speaking in behalf of the 83 French Canadian families in Willamette Valley, sent an address to the assembly in the following year wherein he made the request for some measure of local autonomy for these French Canadians. They feared that they would be completely absorbed by the Americans and sought some guarantee that their customs would be respected (Clarke I 1927, 288-289; Barry 1933).

Maine

The area of Maine was settled by the British in 1607 and was annexed by Massachusetts in 1652-1658. The Peace Treaty of 1783 left the northern border undefined. After that, the area was disputed between Maine and Canada and the border was finally decided in 1842 (Malory 1910, 650ff. and Miller IV 1934, 363ff.). In the meantime Acadians had immigrated at the end of the eighteenth century into the St. Johns Valley (the present-day Aroostook County). As a result of this immigration a small, compact French settlement still exists today in northern Maine (Lawton 1919). To this we may add more recent immigrants from French Canada, mostly Quebec, who have arrived since the middle of the nineteenth century and who in 1910 numbered 617,000 persons of the first and second generations. This new French element, which settled almost exclusively in the urban centers, gave vigor and stimulation to the older predominantly rural French settlement in the northern part of the state. In 1940 there were enumerated 138,300 inhabitants of French mother tongue of whom 36% (50,200) were the children of native-born parents, a percentage which incidentally ran between 15 and 20 in the rest of New England, where its French-Canadian population is largely urban. The only French newspaper, the *Messager* (1882), is being published in Lewiston, outside the compact French-speaking area.

As far as I can see, French was never officially permitted as a tool of instruction or even as a subject in the public schools of the area of French settlement. Handschin (1913, 29) cited a law according to which modern foreign languages should be taught in public schools that had been established before 1880. However, the law relates, as Handschin does not point out, simply to high schools and, in the form cited by Handschin, was in force only between 1880 and 1887. (Details are in Kloss 1940, 509).

On the other hand, teachers were encouraged to use French in the first grades as an auxiliary language to make themselves understood by students who did not speak English. For this purpose a special teacher's seminary was established in 1878 in the area of French settlement. At first it operated for six months each in Van Buren and Fort Kent, but later it was permanently located in Fort Kent, where it still exists today (Kloss 1940, 509-511; Ammoun 1957, 107). This was the only state-sponsored seminary of its kind, aside from the Spanish-American Teacher's school in El Rito (Section 5-2).

It seems logical to assume that the graduates of this school often cultivated French also as a subject and tool of instruction in their practical work, and it is indeed reported of Van Buren in 1920, for example, that its public schools had only in recent years been transformed from entirely French into bilingual institutions (Thompson 1920, 145).

French survived longer in town government; the town meetings of the St. Johns Valley were partially conducted in French until about 1950. But the only private institution of higher learning of the Madawaska French (St. Mary's College in Van Buren, founded in 1859) closed down.

Gradually the French language was completely banned from the school grounds in the St. Johns Valley. This was pushed to such an extreme that both students and teachers were forbidden to use French even during recess, creating problems of morale in the process. Teachers have admitted that the children would revert to French when under the influence of a strong emotion. As a counterweight French was still cultivated well into the 1940s by a considerable number of bilingual parochial schools.

At the Madawaska Training School in Fort Kent graduates were for a long period of time certified to teach in the local area only. It was not until 1934 that a two-year normal school program was established which enabled graduates to teach anywhere in the State of Maine. In 1961 the normal school was changed to a State Teachers College.

For a long period of time the language of instruction has been English. More recently, however, the teaching of a second language (French) has gained popularity in several of the school systems in the state of Maine. In 1942 French was introduced as a subject in the elementary schools of Van Buren (grades three to six with 1,000 pupils in 1955). Many of these programs start at the third grade level. It seemed highly logical that Fort Kent State College should supply the teachers to staff these programs. The entering freshman class is made up of many local students who are bilingual. A program was instituted in 1963 which offered these students advanced work in French along with the methodology of teaching French at the elementary school level.

In 1968-1969 a project for bilingual education in public schools was started. It was funded by the United States government under the NDEA Act (Title III), which is meant to encourage innovations in education. It was designed specifically for School Administrative District 33 (Frenchville and St. Agatha, Maine) of which Martin Daigle was the Superintendent. This project, entitled Project FABRIC (Franco-American Bicultural Research and Innovation Center), was addressing itself to elementary as well as high schools. The laws of the State of Maine actually forbade the teaching of subjects other than foreign languages in a language other than English. On the grounds that their work was experimental, however, the sponsors of the project had an unwritten agreement with the state to allow them to pursue their goals without fear of trouble. Finally (in 1969) the law (Sec. 2 T. 20, 120, sub-16) was amended so as to permit "in areas having high concentration of children from non-English speaking families" bilingual education from pre-school to second grade.

6-2   STATES WITH SMALL, LONG-ESTABLISHED SPANISH MINORITIES

Texas

Background. The Spaniards established settlements in Texas as early as 1690. In 1790, it was estimated that 2,500 Spaniards were in the then province of Texas and 3,500 in the El Paso district, which at that time did not yet belong to

Texas. After 1821 a continuous Anglo-American immigration began which soon left the Spanish-speaking population as a minority.

Mexico returned to centralized and autocratic forms of government. By that time Texas had become largely Anglo-Saxon. Thus when Anglo-Saxon Texas was merged with the entirely Iberian Coahuila into *one* "state," the centralized Mexican government was strange to the Texans, which led to a revolt in 1836 and the establishment of an independent free state of Texas. Among the signers of the Texas Declaration of Independence there were three Spanish Texans and one native Mexican (Zavala), who became the first Vice President of Texas. The revolt centered by no means exclusively around ethnic antagonisms but also around general political principles, such as democratic rule, federalism, and self-government. In the year 1845 Texas joined the United States as a state. The old established Texas Mexicans or Texanos were soon numerically outdistanced by the "Old Mexico-Mexicans."

In 1940, in Texas 738,400 Spanish-speaking persons were counted, among them 272,100 (36.8%) children of native-born parents, and in 1950 there were 1,033,800 persons with Spanish names (13.4% of the inhabitants). Their strongest concentrations in absolute numbers were in Bexar (176,100), Hidalgo (112,400), and El Paso (89,600) Counties, and were relatively strongest in Zapata (94.1%), Starr (89.3%), Kenedy (87.5%), and Webb (84.7%) Counties. Private estimates sometimes go beyond these figures, the highest being two million. In 1960, Texas had 655,000 inhabitants who were first or second generation Mexicans. Their number is difficult to determine and fluctuates considerably since many came into the country illegally and many returned after some time to Mexico or were deported.

The Mexicans, disregarding some of the older Texanos, belong over-whelmingly to the lower classes and a high percentage of them is illiterate. Consequently, the press and schools play a less important part among them than does radio. In 1960 there were three stations (2 in San Antonio, 1 in Corpus Christi) which broadcast exclusively in Spanish and 38 others which broadcast regularly in Spanish as part of their program.

The first German settlement, which was named Industry, was established under Mexican rule in 1831. During the free state period the German element grew rapidly. Vigorous German language pockets came into existence particularly in the city triangle San Antonio-Austin-Houston. Furthermore, for a long time the upper strata of an urban German element enjoyed in San Antonio an almost patrician position. In 1940 in Texas 159,100 German-speaking persons were enumerated, among them 71,100 (44.7%) children of native-born parents, the highest percentage of all the states.

The following circumstances enabled the German Texan ethnic group to develop a specific character of its own: It developed at a time when Texas was not yet part of the Union and consequently entered the Union with a strong spirit of equal political participation. The German Texans lived along the line separating the Ibero-American and Anglo-American language and cultural spheres, in an area where bilinguality was not rare and certain language rights of the Ibero-Americans were almost taken for granted. The German Texans lived far away from the large German-American settlements in Pennsylvania and the Midwest. This distance and also the group's own separate history made them therefore inclined to regard themselves as a separate group and not just as part of "the" German-American element. The Texas German group suffered less than most of the midwestern settlements under the strong tensions between groups of different world views (notably that between Old Lutherans and freethinkers) even though Texas was not completely spared these tensions. Geographically speaking the Texas Germans were concentrated in a relatively small area.

Urban and rural populations were not completely separated as mostly in the Midwest, but in the midst of predominantly German districts there existed small predominantly German-speaking towns with a relatively strong and educated upper stratum which furnished the spokesmen for the rural German element. Finally, an impact was made by a particularly strong desire to ensure the continued use of the German language at the time of the founding of the earliest German-Texan settlements. The German language was so vigorous for a long time that several thousand Wends, who in 1855 had founded Serbin in Lee County, were absorbed into the German element on Texan soil (Engerrand 1934).

It is characteristic of the considerable German-Texan literature that relatively many Texas-born authors participated in it. A German-language press for this language pocket survived there beyond the 1930s—longer than in any other region in the United States. The *Neu-Braunfelser Zeitung* as well as the *Radio-Post* in Fredericksburg remained bilingual until the middle of the 1950s. German radio programs could be found only in New Braunfels in 1960, but here they had the largest number of weekly hours, 15, of all stations in America.

After about 1850, Czech language pockets came into existence in the same areas which already had German pockets of settlement; these Czech language pockets in Texas were the most vigorous in the United States (Hudson 1934). In 1940 in Texas 62,700 Czech-speaking persons were enumerated of whom 26,400 (42.1%) were the children of native-born parents. In 1960 there were Czech radio stations in four communities.

Texas also had always had a small French colony, at first immigrants from Louisiana, then some from France, among them, however, many Alsatians, and after the 1890s, Acadians from southwestern Louisiana, who for the most part settled in and around Port Arthur close to the border of their home state. In 1940 in Texas 18,500 French-speaking persons were enumerated, among them 15,200 (81.6%) children of native-born parents. In Port Arthur there was in 1960 one station with French programs totaling two hours weekly; in addition, some Louisiana stations could be heard (see Section 5-1).

Nationality Rights before 1845. During the time Texas was a part of the state of Mexico a national minority problem existed for the Anglo-Americans who had come into Texas (Lowrie 1932, 121-123). In the winter of 1829-1830 a private English edition of the Mexican laws was published at their own initiative which, however, proved to be unsatisfactory. Thereupon the editor of the *Texas Gazette* suggested in 1830 that a petition be made asking for an official translation of the present laws and those to be passed in the future. But such a translation never did materialize. Even the documents of the municipal authorities, particularly those of the ayuntamientos, had to be written in Spanish, which burdened the communities with the difficult task of finding bilingual secretaries. A law of the "State of Coahuila and Texas" of May 1, 1833, provided for the employment of interpreters by the courts (Gammel I 1898, 332-333). The Code of Civil and Criminal Procedure of April 17, 1834, stated in Article 134 that in case records written in English were presented in an appeal of cassation, these records would have to be translated into Spanish at the expense of the appellant—a statement which presupposed the keeping of English records in the lowest courts. In Article 140 it was stated that the code should be published in Spanish and English "in order to give to this law the corresponding publicity in the two languages spoken by the inhabitants of Texas" (Kloss 1940, 386).

A decree of May 18, 1835, ordered a bilingual edition of all laws of the state of Coahuila-Texas, and the publisher had to put two hundred copies at the disposal of the state authorities. But it was already too late. The Anglo-Texans revolted, but they immediately envisioned the extensive use of the Spanish language in their planned independent state, particularly since a minority of liberal Texan Spaniards was on their side. Five hundred Spanish copies were printed of the declaration about a provisional government that had been agreed upon November 8, 1835, in San Felipe—the so-called Consultation. The actual Texas Declaration of Independence of March 2, 1836, contained many important statements concerning nationality rights, such as: "The Mexican Government, by its colonization laws, invited and induced the Anglo-American population of Texas to colonize its wilderness under the pledged faith of a written constitution that they should continue to enjoy that constitutional liberty and republican government to which they had been habituated in the land of their birth, the United States of America. In this expectation they have been cruelly disappointed, in as much as the Mexican nation has acquiesced in the late changes made in the government by General Antonio Lopez de Santa Anna."

These complaints of disappointed colonists who had once been especially called into the county are well known in Europe too. Even more impressive is the following charge against the Mexican government: "It has sacrificed our welfare to the State of Coahuila, by which our interests have been continually depressed through a jealous and partial course of legislation carried on at a far distant seat of government by a hostile majority, in an unknown tongue; and this too, notwithstanding that we have petitioned in the humblest terms for the establishment of a separate state government, and have, in accordance with the provisions of the national constitution presented to the General Congress a republican constitution which was, without just cause, contemptuously rejected."

As far as nationality rights are concerned, particularly important are the charges contained in these statements, that the Anglo-Texans were governed in a foreign language and that they were not permitted to develop full regional autonomy by establishing a state of their own. This second charge is reminiscent of the decade-long struggle of New Mexico and Puerto Rico for the achievement of internal autonomy and even more perhaps of the complaint of South Tirol to have its autonomy only on the basis of a forced marriage with the Italian-speaking Trentino instead of on an ethnic basis. It is incidentally no accident that at a moment when the North American Anglo-Saxons found themselves in the situation of a suppressed ethnic group they adopted for themselves the term "Anglo-Americans" rather than the less colorful term "Americans."

In the independent State of Texas both houses of the legislature adopted on January 17, 1841, a joint resolution which suspended the printing of the laws in the Spanish language (Kloss 1940, 389), from which we may conclude that Spanish editions had been printed in 1836-1841. The new regulation may be explained by the fact that the Anglo-Texans at that time were not sure of their rule and independence but saw themselves threatened by a huge nation of Iberian character which had never recognized this independence and which was far superior in numbers. The belligerent attitude which had to prevail among them under such circumstances left little room for considerations of a more tolerant nature. That this temporary intolerant attitude was directed against only the Spanish element and not against all non-English groups becomes evident by the fact that the legislature of the sovereign State of Texas on January 27, 1844, granted a charter for a German university (Gammel II 1898, 36). The toleration of private foreign-language secondary schools was no rarity in Anglo-America, but chartering a foreign-language university deserves favorable attention.

Language Policy by the Government and the Legislature after 1845. Never has a non-English language been mentioned in the various constitutions of the State of Texas. Still in isolated instances resolutions were passed authorizing the publication of a particular constitution in a non-English language. The most important of these resolutions, that of April 18, 1846, applied not only to the Constitution but also to the laws: "The Governor is hereby authorized and required to cause the constitution of the State and such general enactments of the legislature thereof as in his judgment the public interest may require to be translated and printed in the German and Spanish languages, and promulgate the same in the counties which embrace German immigrants and Spanish citizens in sufficient quantity for the due administration of the laws of the State."

What is said here of the "administration" of the laws refers to their application by the officials and not just their observance by the people. This interpretation is supported by the law of August 22, 1856, about the Spanish courts in South Texas (see below). It is certain that the law was also applied. A law of September 1, 1856, authorized the governor to have the present session laws printed also in Spanish and German (Kloss 1940, 393). After the constitution of 1875 was adopted, 40,000 English, 5,000 German, 3,000 Spanish, and 1,000 Czech copies were printed.

The special convention which decided the secession of Texas from the Union and the entry into the Confederacy decided also on March 30, 1861, to draft a special message to the population which would contain a summary of the debates and the text of the Constitution of the Confederacy; a tenth of the 10,000 authorized copies were to be allocated each to the German and the Spanish versions. The lively interest of the German Texans in the official prints of the state government is shown by the fact that from 1905 to 1907 a magazine appeared, *Der Deutsch-Texaner* of La Grange, Texas, which carried the subtitle *Monatsschrift, welche die Gesetze des Landes und Gesetz-Vorschläge bespricht,* i.e., "Monthly Magazine Which Reviews Laws of the Land and Proposed Laws" (Arndt and Olson 1961, 620).

During the twentieth century, Mexican mass immigration again forced the printing of state laws in Spanish. In 1920 a Spanish edition of the laws was published which, however, was only a private publication (Patterson and Monroe 1920). Official Spanish translations of government publications were no longer authorized after World War I, according to a letter from the Texas State Library (1961).

The Courts—Legal Notices. An important law was passed on August 22, 1856, on which further information can be found in the decision *Lyles* v. *State.* Section 1 of this law states: "It shall be lawful in the counties west of the Guadalupe River, except for the counties of Nueces, San Patricio, and Refugio, to use the Spanish language in all judicial proceedings, before the Justices of the Peace, when neither the Justice of the Peace nor the parties are able to write or understand the English language." Section 2 of the law stated that, in cases where one of the two parties could speak English only and the other party or the Justice of the Peace spoke Spanish only, the case should be turned over, upon request, to the closest justice of the peace who could speak English. It should be noticed that Spanish was permitted also for keeping the records.

With respect to the German Texans, such provision was less necessary even though they lived in compact areas of settlement, since they possessed from the very beginning their own upper class, and their justices of the peace presumably all could speak English.

As far as I could ascertain, no laws dealing with the publication of legal notices in non-English languages have existed in Texas.

Laws Concerning School Languages. The German municipal schools of New Braunfels are often considered to have been the first public schools in Texas. The texts of the most important provisions of the various school laws may be found in Kloss (1940, 395-402). The school law of January 31, 1854, created a public school fund which should benefit all schools including private schools; the Treasurer of the State apportioned the fund among the different counties according to their school population.

The first, the supplementary law of August 29, 1856, added the provision that the schools would have to teach the English language at least as a subject, and according to another supplementary law of February 5, 1858, English would have to be the principal language at these schools.

The School Law of August 13, 1870, prescribed English as the language of instruction for all public schools but added that the county boards of school directors could permit the teaching of any foreign language in connection with the English branches of education. A law of April 30, 1870, had been even more precise by stating that no person could be employed as a teacher unless the county superintendent had issued a certificate but that this should not be construed as prohibiting instruction in the "German, French, Spanish, or any other language."

In the year 1896, first all the languages permitted were listed, "German, Bohemian (Czech), Spanish, Latin, French, Greek"; then it was added that the teaching of such languages should not be allowed to supersede the use of textbooks prescribed under the provisions of this act. Eight years later (1904) this provision received the following form which was still in force as late as 1961: "Nothing in this act shall be so construed as to prevent the teaching of German, Bohemian, Spanish, French, Latin or Greek in any of the public schools as a branch of study, but the teaching of one or more of these languages shall not interfere with the use of the textbooks herein prescribed."

It should be noticed that the 1896 expression "supersede" was here replaced by the stricter "interfere with" (Vernon 1959, Art. 2,843). A later amendment to Article 2,843 directs the State Board of Education to introduce 3 to 5 subjects each, among them the "Latin, Spanish, . . . German, Czech, and French" languages. Between Spanish and German are listed 8 subjects that are not foreign languages.

A law of 1905 prescribed that, except for the teaching of foreign languages, all instruction in public schools had to be given in English (*Texas Laws* 1905, sec. 102).

It is reported that the Czechs established their first school in 1857 in Fayette County, that this first school was soon followed by six others, and that they all were supported by the state school fund (Hudson 1934, 173-174). Everywhere else in America more parochial than secular private schools were founded by the Germans because the church-oriented Germans were more willing to make sacrifices than those who leaned toward the freethinkers. In Texas, on the other hand, we find in some places more secular than parochial schools among the Germans because private schools were supported by public funds. Olmstedt (1860, 179; also Benjamin, 237) reports that he found in New Braunfels five independent secular free schools, one private "Latin School," and one Catholic school. In Gillespie County there were four secular and two parochial German schools in 1870 (*Amerikanische Schulzeitung* 1870-1871, 71-72, 352). In the year 1868 a German Free School Association was incorporated in Austin just as there had been incorporation in 1860 of the German-English school in San Antonio and the bilingual municipal secondary school in New Braunfels.

Even after 1870 the borderline between public and private schools was not always clear. Hudson (1934, 176) reports a Czech school whose teachers, in observance of an 1870 law, took a state examination, whereupon the school was supported from three to four months per year by the state and the remainder of the time by the parents.

For decades the Germans pressed most vigorously for the cultivation of their language in the public schools. In the year 1886, there were 4,464 children who had German instruction in public and 3,008 in private schools. Of the latter 1,294 attended secular, 1,214 Protestant, and 500 Catholic schools. In the year 1900 all 360 students in New Braunfels had German instruction, 240 in public and 120 in private schools. This 100% participation put New Braunfels at the top of all communities in the United States.

The law of 1904, without being formally abolished, was rendered ineffective by a law of April 3, 1918, which introduced the regulation that all teachers in public free schools should teach in English only and should use only English textbooks. This regulation was quite tolerant in comparison to World War I laws of other states (Section 3-4). The regulation left it permissible also to teach "Latin, Greek, French, German, Spanish and Czech or other languages" in high schools (Vernon 1959, Artc. 2,911 a3).

After the war, the 1918 law was expanded several times by amendments that were favorable to ethnic groups. A provision dated March 28, 1927, allowed Spanish to be taught in the elementary schools of those counties directly located on the Mexican border where, based on the 1920 census, at least one town of over 5,000 inhabitants exists. Legally speaking, Spanish was thus not sponsored as the mother tongue of a part of the population but as a means of communication across the border. Actually the numerous Mexicans who had come into the country after the war were partly concentrated in just these border counties and could therefore benefit considerably from this new law.

In 1933 the German element, after four years of campaigning, succeeded in establishing another amendment that permitted any desired foreign language to be taught above the second grade (Vernon 1933, Art. 288); this provision is no longer in effect. In reality German had already been introduced; for example, in the second half of the 1920s in some rural schools of Guadalupe County and in 1932 in Galveston.

-      Even more active were the Czechs. In Kloss (1940, 403-404) is a list of seven communities in which Czech was taught in the public schools in 1932. In 1915 a chair of the Czech language was established in Austin.

During World War II, the school boards of the entire state were authorized to introduce the teaching of Spanish above the second grade (Vernon 1959, Art. 2911 al). In 1969 an amendment to Article 1893 of the Civil Code permitted bilingual instruction "in those situations when such instruction is educationally advantageous to the pupils." In grades 7 to 9, however, such instruction required express approval by the "Texas Education Agency." Four years later another law made this mandatory for all school districts with a minimum number of children of limited English-speaking ability. (For further details concerning bilingual schools in Texas see Section 2-2).

Colorado

Several Spanish expeditions entered the area of Colorado at the latest during the second half of the eighteenth century. The area, nominally belonging to Spain but not yet settled by whites, fell to the United States in three stages. A part of eastern Colorado was ceded by Spain to France in 1800 and by France to the United States as part of the Louisiana Purchase in 1803. A second part, a small strip of land in central and southeastern Colorado, became part of Mexico in 1821. After 1836 this portion was claimed by Texas and after 1845 by the United States as successor to the Texan claims. In 1846 it was occupied by Anglo-American troops and was formally ceded in 1848 by Mexico in the Treaty of Guadalupe Hidalgo. A third portion of Colorado belonged indisputably to Mexico during the period from 1821 through 1846. In 1846 it was occupied by the Anglo-Americans, and in 1848 it was ceded by Mexico.

In 1806 the first Anglo-American, Zebulon M. Pike, came into the area that is now known as Colorado. After 1828 isolated trading posts were established by the Americans, and in 1857 a mass Anglo-American influx began with the discovery of gold. In 1861 the Territory of Colorado was formed out of various areas which hitherto had been parts of different administrative units. In 1876 Colorado became a state.

In Colorado two ethnic groups assumed a certain importance: the Spanish and the Germans.

The Spanish apparently had already penetrated during the 1850s from the Spanish-speaking areas of what is still New Mexico into the San Luis Valley, which at that time formed a part of New Mexico. Here they settled in clearly defined areas. Numerous Germans came between 1857 and 1862 together with the first Anglo-Saxons. They lived in smaller groups which were scattered all over the state. In 1910 in Colorado 41,500 persons stemmed in the first or second generation from the German Empire. After 1900 Volga Germans came into the northern parts of the state as sugar beet workers. In 1920 the figure for first or second generation Volga Germans was estimated at 21,000.

In 1940 in Colorado 92,540 Spanish-speaking persons were enumerated, of whom 71,800 (77.6%) were children of native-born parents. In the year 1960, there were 20,100 inhabitants who were first or second generation Mexicans.

The first state constitution of Colorado of 1876 prescribed in Article XVIII (8) that the annual session laws until 1900 should be published also in Spanish and German editions. It is certain that the simultaneous German edition of the Constitution, and it is possible that the German edition (1877) of the Code of Civil Procedure "Der Kodex über die Prozeduren in Civilklagen im Staate Colorado" were the result of resolutions of the legislature. We may furthermore assume that between 1870 and 1890 the German press was regularly used for the publication of legal notices. W. R. Hentschel in the *Colorado Herald* (Denver), jubilee edition of October 19, 1930, is of the opinion that German during the 1860s and 1870s had "in a certain sense the character of an official language." Since the first German newspaper did not appear until 1870, however, the situation prevailed perhaps at a slightly later time.

Court proceedings in their own language were out of the question for the Germans, since they did not live in a compact area of settlement. For the Spanish-Americans such court proceedings were obviously quite customary during the first years of the territorial phase. Two decisions of the State Supreme Court, *Dunton* v. *Montoya* in 1868 and *Trinidad* v. *Simpson* in 1879, ruled that in the court record as well as in oral procedures only English was permissible; so did the Code of Civil Procedure (1877, Section 405). Presumably the use of Spanish in the oral proceedings was maintained far beyond these years.

School language legislation developed quite remarkably. According to the school law of 1867 the school boards of school districts with at least 25 German children were directed to establish a bilingual school. In the year 1870 one of the four public schools of Denver was entirely German.

The school law of 1877 was quite different: English was basically the language of instruction in the public schools. Wherever the parents of 20 children would request it, the school boards were permitted to introduce either German or Spanish as a subject and hire suitable teachers for this purpose. Compared to the 1867 law, the reduction of the minimum number, the inclusion of Spanish, and the indirect permission that parents of English mother tongue could also join in the request were more favorable. On the other hand, less favorable provisions ruled that the school boards were no longer "required" but were "permitted" to establish such schools and reduced the status of German from a tool of instruction to a mere subject. But ten years later another provision was added directing the district school boards to hire competent teachers to teach the subjects listed in Section 15 of the law, according to the direction of the school board, in German or Spanish or in only one of the two languages at the request of the parents and guardians of school-age children. In the year 1900, of all elementary students in Denver, 15% were taught German—2,861 in public and 530 in private schools. It has also been documented that Spanish was actually taught in public schools (see Section 5-2).

A School Law of April 9, 1919, excluded the non-English languages completely from the public schools and permitted them only as subjects in private schools. In the wake of the federal Bilingual Education Act, however, Section 123-21-3 of the Revised Statutes was so amended in 1969 as to permit and even to encourage the school districts "to develop bilingual skills" and to help non-English pupils "to make an effective transition to English." In 1974 a new law made bilingual education mandatory.

California

California was reached by the Spaniards in 1542-1543 and occupied in 1769-1770. The administration until 1823 was entirely in the hands of the missionaries but was gradually turned over to secular hands after California became a part of Mexico in 1822; this process was completed by 1840. At about this time American overland migration reached California, which was occupied by American troops in 1846, ceded to the United States in 1848, and admitted as a state (without a territorial phase) in 1850.

The 1848 gold strikes quickly turned the approximately 5,000 Spaniards into a minority. The influx from Mexico remained for a long time very small; in 1880 only 1% of the 865,000 inhabitants was Mexican-born. After World War I, however, huge numbers of Mexicans began to pour into California—many of them illegally or as seasonal workers. In 1940, the census showed 416,100 Spanish-speaking persons of whom only 63,700 (15%) were children of native-born parents. The name count in 1950 showed 760,500 Spanish-surname persons (7% of the population) with 287,600 of them living in Los Angeles County alone; the percentage of Spanish-surname persons was highest in Imperial County (30.2%). In the year 1960 the census showed 695,600 first or second generation Mexicans.

The following first or second generation ethnic groups in 1910 are also important for California: from the German Empire, 161,700; from Italy, 76,300; and from France, 25,700 (next to the French of New York State, the largest French group of European background). California furthermore became the home of considerable groups of Chinese, who immigrated between 1849 and 1884, and Japanese, who immigrated between 1896 and 1924.

In the first state Constitution of California (1849) Article XI (21) read: "All laws, decrees, regulations and provisions which from their nature require publication shall be published in English and Spanish."

Of the first Constitution 2,000 Spanish copies were printed in addition to 8,000 English copies. On the other hand, the Constitution of 1879 in Article IV made English the only official language of the state.

For the implementation of the 1849 language provision the office of State Translator was established on January 31, 1849; the State Translator was elected by the legislature for one year. A law of March 15, 1852, however, directed the Secretary of State to entrust the lowest bidder with the translation of the laws and "other documents." Then a new regulation was adopted as early as May 15, 1852, which reads in its slightly altered version of April 21, 1863: "The translation of the laws into Spanish and their distribution is under the Secretary of State, as follows: During the month of December of each legislative year he must advertise for proposals for the translation into Spanish of such laws as may be authorized by the legislature. The proposals received must be opened on the first Monday in February thereafter, in the presence of a joint committee of both houses of the legislature. . . . The Spanish laws must be distributed in the same manner as the laws printed in English to the counties of San Diego, San Bernardino, Los Angeles, Santa Barbara, San Luis Obispo, Monterey, Santa Clara, Contra Costa, Alameda, Marion and Sonoma and one copy must be sent to each of the district judges of the first, third and seventh districts." This provision, according to which a committee of the legislature joins the Secretary of State and according to which other documents than the laws need no longer be translated, was still included in the 1885 edition of the statutes but was repealed in 1897.

A law of April 3, 1876, about the printing of Spanish laws survived, in frequently altered versions, until 1933 (Statutes 1933, Ch. 988; text of 1921 version in Kloss 1940, 418). The last version stated that the Office of Government Printing should print 240 Spanish copies of each of the laws, resolutions, and memoranda specified by the legislature. The 1968 Vehicle Code (Ch. 955, 1656f) provided for "a synopsis or summary of the Code of which the department shall publish such a number of copies ... in the Spanish language as the director determines are needed. ...." And the department "shall furnish both English and Spanish copies to its field offices and to law enforcement agencies for general distribution."

So far as the courts were concerned, a law was adopted in 1851 which contained provisions that made mandatory the delivery of Spanish summonses and that permitted the use of Spanish in court proceedings. In 1857, the area to which it was applicable was enlarged to Monterey County and reduced in 1863 by the counties of Contra Costa, Santa Clara, and Santa Cruz. The 1863 version reads as follows: "In the counties of Monterey, San Luis Obispo, Santa Barbara, Los Angeles, and San Diego, if the defendant requires it, a copy of the summons or other process must be delivered to him in the Spanish language; and in the counties of Santa Barbara, San Luis Obispo, Los Angeles, San Diego and Monterey, with the consent of both parties, the process pleadings and other proceedings may be in the Spanish language."

Another provision of 1863 decreed for the four counties in which Spanish was permitted as the language for oral proceedings: "Every written proceeding in a court of justice in this state, or before a judicial officer, except in the counties of San Luis Obispo, Santa Barbara, Los Angeles, and San Diego, must be in the English language, and in the excepted counties may be either in the English or the Spanish language."

In recent years a number of legal provisions have been enacted providing for public notices to be published or posted in both English and Spanish. Thus the Labor Code (Ch. 1918, Sec. 1695) made it mandatory for farm labor contractors to "display the rate of compensation the licensee is paying to his employees ... in both English and Spanish"; moreover he is to have available for inspection "a written statement in English and Spanish" containing the same information plus the rate of compensation he receives from the grower with whom he has contracted. A provision was added in 1965 to the Welfare and Institutions Code (Ch. 1784, Sec. 1060) for informational pamphlets and other materials relating to public assistance programs to be printed in both languages. In 1967 (Ch. 1667, Sec. 5325) a provision was made that in all facilities where persons are involuntarily detained for evaluation or treatment a list of the rights of such persons (e.g., to wear his own clothes or to refuse shock treatment) "shall be prominently posted in English and Spanish."

According to Section 316 of California's present Unemployment Insurance Code, "all standard information employee pamphlets concerning unemployment and disability insurance programs" shall be printed in both English and Spanish.

What we have so far learned about California's nationality laws belongs to the category of laws for established settlers based on the moral claim of the long-established Spanish Americans in California. The school language laws are completely different; they are mainly a mixture of laws for later immigrants and the right to a "foreign language." The term "foreign language" is used here in its typical European meaning as a term for languages which are indigenous to areas outside of one's own country, while in America the term has also the meaning of "language of non-English immigrants."

In San Francisco so-called Cosmopolitan Schools were established in 1867 in which particular attention was given to teaching German and French. In the year 1870 there were 13,600 German-born and 3,500 French-born persons among the approximately 150,000 inhabitants of San Francisco. According to the curriculum of 1871 the children in the primary grades learned either French or German for one to one-and-a-half hours per day. In the upper grades they learned both languages together, with almost half of the school hours devoted to these language lessons. In 1871, in the primary grades, 2,305 students learned German and 763 French while 900 students learned both languages in the upper grades.

Around 1873 and again around 1891 the work of the Cosmopolitan Schools seems to have been temporarily interrupted. In the year 1878 the teaching of foreign languages was abolished for the first grade and restricted to oral exercises for the second.

Soon after 1900 the associations of the Germans, French, and Italians, following a suggestion of the German Federation of the City of Los Angeles, joined together in an effort to have Cosmopolitan Schools established in Los Angeles. The opponents to this attempt objected by pointing out that the school law did not provide for such schools and even prohibited them. But in 1909 the efforts met with success by the adoption of a law which made the establishment of Cosmopolitan Schools with German, French, or Italian language lessons mandatory for certain cities; a 1913 amendment added Spanish.

It took forty-six years (1867-1913) before Spanish achieved the same position in the California school system as German and French. In San Francisco a Cosmopolitan Committee was formed of members of the Deutsch-Amerikanischen Stadtverbandes, the Alliance Française, the Italian League, the Spanish League, and five teachers. According to a survey conducted by this committee, out of the 16,104 parents questioned, 7,084 desired German language lessons, 4,613 French, 2,770 Spanish, and 1,637 Italian. From this time on, the living languages were taught in five elementary and three so-called intermediate schools of the city.

Finally the law in its 1929 version was (California Education Code, Sections 660-663): "In every city, which according to the federal census of 1920 has at least 500,000 inhabitants, the school board shall establish and maintain at least one public school in which along with the courses in the English language prescribed and permitted for the elementary schools there shall also be taught French, Spanish, Italian, and German, or one of them."

The following sections of the law permitted the establishment of such schools also for all remaining cities and counties and confirmed the term "cosmopolitan schools." In 1965, however, this law was repealed. During an interlude from 1965 on a law was in force making foreign language teaching mandatory in the uppermost grades of all public schools.

In 1967 an amendment to Section 71 of the Education Code gave latitude to local school boards to "determine when and under what circumstances instruction may be given bilingually . . . provided that such instruction is educationally advantageous to the pupils." Another amendment to Section 71, adopted the following year, provided, "Pupils who are proficient in English and who by successful completion of advanced courses in a foreign language or by other means have become fluent in that language may be instructed in classes conducted in the foreign language." In this way the door was thrown open so that bilingual high school students of both Mexican and Anglo-Saxon stock might be taught partly through the medium of Spanish.

In 1972 the "Bilingual Education Act" (Act B. 2284 = ch. 5.7 Ed. Code) appropriated funds for bilingualizing elementary schools. However, no bilingually conducted class must have more than two-thirds of its students with limited English-speaking ability. Other laws concerned the bilingual assistant teachers at community colleges (1971, sec. 25519.5 Ed. Code) and the needs of non-English pupils in special schools (1972, sec. 6902.085 Ed. Code). At least one city, Culver City, has Hispanized some public schools to the extent of reducing English to a medium restricted to the teaching of English language skills.

California is the state where we find a particularly rich flora of separate public schools, some based on racial differences. A special school for Chinese children was established in San Francisco as early as 1885. A law of 1905 provided for the establishment of special schools for Indian and Mongolian children. When, in the following year, the Japanese children of San Francisco were required to enter the local Oriental School, a conflict ensued between the United States Government and Japan.

On the basis of the Gentlemen's Agreement (Root-Takahira Agreement) of 1907, Japan restricted voluntarily Japanese immigration to the United States, and the Japanese in return were spared enrollment in a special school. The case became quite complicated because the federal government could not easily interfere with the school system of a state (Stephenson 1926, 268-271; Young 1932, 474-475). In other cities of California separate schools were usually confined to Chinese children; these schools were abolished in 1947.

With the beginning of the Mexican mass immigration after World War I many segregated schools for Mexican children were established. The California Attorney General, U. S. Webb, decided on September 7, 1929, that these schools could be established only on a voluntary basis (Bogardus 1934, 71), but this voluntary basis is very difficult to prove, especially since in several cases special schools for Mexican children were established by making the borders of a school district coincide with those sections of a city inhabited by a predominantly Mexican population.

On April 14, 1947, the Ninth Federal District Court decided in the so-called Menendez case (*Westminster School District of Orange County* v. *Menendez* et al.) that separate schools for Mexicans could be established or permitted only by a state law—which, however, did not exist—and never by a mere administrative directive (cf. Marden 1952, 148). One judge (Denman), in his separate opinion backing the decision, attacked particularly the argument that the Mexican schools were desirable because of language reasons: Four generations of long established and two to three generations of more recent Mexican immigrants had attended English schools; a very large proportion of those students, whose parents had been Mexican citizens and who attend schools today, speak English; many students from old established families are no longer able to speak Spanish. The enrollment of such students in Mexican schools would be clearly discriminating. It might, on the other hand, be justifiable to treat differently in the lowest grades children who do not speak English.

It is obvious that these separate schools and classes for children of Chinese or Spanish mother tongue did not have the purpose of promoting ethnic cultivation of these languages. It is equally obvious that bilingual teachers who taught in several of these schools often thought of using the mother tongue of these students at least during the first grades to explain English words or phrases to the children, and conceivably several of these teachers made these languages unofficially a subject of instruction.

Another effect of these separate schools is still more important: they prevented the students for a large part of the day from having contact with English-speaking children and made it, therefore, easy for them to use their mother tongue at least outside of the classroom. Also these schools created a psychological climate which was not favorable to language assimilation. They no doubt have had a delaying effect on the assimilation of these children.

Arizona

Spaniards entered Arizona repeatedly after 1539, but not until the eighteenth century were some missions and settlements established. They were all located south of the Gila River. This part of Arizona was ceded by Mexico to the United States in 1853 in the so-called Gadsden Purchase. The part of Arizona north of the Gila River, which was inhabited only by Indians, had already come to the United States in 1848 as part of New Mexico. For a long time, the entire area formed a county of the Territory of New Mexico. In 1863 it became a separate territory, of the fourth category, with an elected upper and lower house. Finally it became a state in 1912.

The white population, including the Mexicans, amounted to only 2,421 persons in 1860. During the troubled times of the Civil War and Indian uprisings (1861-1863) even this number was reduced, although the estimate of H. H. Bancroft (1888, 529) of 500 to 600 people is almost certainly too low. In a study of the Spanish spoken in the Gadsden Purchase area, A. C. Post (1933, 35-42) informs us that until the early 1870s Spanish was the vernacular used in the streets and at play and that the first Anglo settlers had to learn Spanish. It is, however, certain that of the approximately 435,000 inhabitants in 1930 only a minute number were descendants of the old established Spanish-American element who were in Arizona before the Anglo influx.

During the following years Mexican immigration was quite heavy. In 1880, there were 9,300 (23%) of the 40,400 inhabitants who were born in Mexico; in 1930, there were 114,200 (26%) inhabitants who were first or second generation Mexicans. The language census of 1940 gave 101,900 Spanish speakers, of whom 27,600 (27.1%) were natives of native parentage. The name count in 1950 enumerated 128,000 people (17%) with Spanish names, who, however, formed a majority of the population in only one county (Santa Cruz). This and the fact that the Mexicans did not constitute an old established group but were only recent immigrants caused their position to be psychologically and legally much weaker than in neighboring New Mexico.

Concerning the civil rights of the Spanish-speaking inhabitants who came to be American nationals, the same treaty provisions applied as in the case of the Spaniards of New Mexico.

Despite the minute number of old established Hispanos, the Spanish language was repeatedly used during the first year of Arizona's territorial phase. The legislature adopted in 1864 during its first legislative sessions a resolution which, according to Bancroft (1888, 537, 539) provided for the "publication of laws, etc., in Spanish." It is probable that resolutions as well as laws were included among those texts to be published in Spanish. Among the officials of the first three legislatures, translators are mentioned; only during the fourth legislature (1867) was this no longer the case.

On the other hand, Spanish was excluded from the public schools from the very beginning. The report of the territorial school board for the year 1872 stated that the larger part of the school population was made up of children of Mexican parents and that only a few of them could speak English, but they were instructed entirely in English (*Report of the United States Commissioner of Education* 1872, 365). According to *Educational Conditions in Arizona* (1917, 18), the first public school was established in 1873, two years after the passage of the first school law.

In contrast to New Mexico, from the very beginning Arizona was under a determined Anglo-Saxon leadership. According to a letter from the Governor's office in Phoenix (January 12, 1961), it is customary in some places in the state to give public bulletin board notices also in Spanish. Nevertheless Assistant Attorney General C. L. Huerta (letter of September 25, 1961) points out that this does not constitute a legal claim on the part of the Spanish Americans to the official use of their language.

In 1969, the Arizona Revised Statutes (Section 15-202) were amended so as to make possible bilingual "special classes" in the first three grades of the public school districts.

Florida

Between 1960 and 1967, of the 136,000 Cubans admitted to the United States, 54,000 listed Florida as the state of their future permanent residence.

The history of the Hispanic element in Florida, however, is more than 400 years old. Here the Spaniards founded St. Augustine in 1565. In 1763 Florida became English, but upon its return to Spain in 1783 many of the Anglo-Saxons left the area again. By a treaty of February 1, 1819, the United States purchased Florida. A federal law of March 3, 1819, established provisional government which was appointed by the President. The Organic Act of March 30, 1822, created a territory of the second category with a council which was only appointed. Florida became a state in 1845.

After 1819 a large part of the Spanish population left the area, most of them for Cuba. All the Minorcans who had once been lured into Florida by Great Britain remained. For 1822 the white population is estimated to be approximately 13,000 (8,000 in East Florida, 5,000 in West Florida). In West Florida the Spanish population constituted more than half, in East Florida only a small fraction of the population.

In December 1821, approximately 180 "former Spanish citizens of West Florida" protested against attempts by Alabama to annex parts of Florida with Pensacola and based their protest on the fact that "the right for self-government is fundamentally respected" (Carter 1956, 312-315). The "provisional city council" of St. Augustine, which was formed in July 1821 and which was almost entirely Spanish, employed its own "public translator" (Carter 1956, 121). At least two Spaniards were included in the first appointed legislative council, and the fact that the first delegate which the territory sent to Washington in 1823 was the Spaniard J. M. Hernandez is in itself already a part of nationality rights. Nevertheless no official Spanish printings are known from Florida, which may perhaps be explained by the absence of an elected representative body (Florida State Library Board and the Library of Congress). The Spanish language survived for a long time, particularly in St. Augustine. It was reported in 1890 (*Report of the United States Commissioner of Education* 1889, 435) that the children of local (i.e., Spanish-speaking) Catholics had attended the public school only after Catholic sisters began to teach there; it is quite possible that Spanish as a subject came to this school together with the sisters.

In recent years Dade County, which includes Miami, has become one of the centers of Spanish-speaking refugees from Cuba. As a result of the FLES movement, Spanish has been taught in the public schools since 1953, beginning with the fifth grade, with 7,500 participants and since 1955, beginning with the first grade, with 93,700 students. In 1961 the Spanish-S "Spanish for Spanish speakers" program started under which these children studied the Spanish language, arts, and certain other subjects through the exclusive medium of Spanish in grades 3 through 12. In September 1963, the Dade County School Board made what has been called an "extraordinarily generous decision, unprecedented in American public schools" (Gaarder) (actually there was a precedent in an 1840 decision of the Cincinnati school officials).

1. The Dade County School Board expanded the Spanish-S program to all public schools in the county with 100 or more Spanish-speaking children (9,000 children were affected, distributed among 55 schools).

2. Also the Dade County School Board initiated a fully bilingual program in the Coral Way elementary school (Gaarder 1967, 110-120) where roughly equal numbers of Spanish-speaking and English-speaking pupils are being taught. In

grades one through four they are being taught separately in such a way that the same subject matter is first presented in the mother tongue in the morning, then reinforced in the second language in the afternoon. From grade five upward, the two groups of pupils are in class together.

The overall situation in Miami was reported in an earlier chapter of this book (Section 4-8).

6-3   STATES WITH SMALL, LONG-ESTABLISHED DUTCH AND GERMAN MINORITIES

New York State

In the year 1614 the Dutch established their first permanent settlement in North America and founded the New Netherlands colony. Its borders were undefined, but it covered primarily the area of present-day New York State. Here New Amsterdam, the present New York, was founded in 1626. In the year 1655 the colony was enlarged by the area of New Sweden, a colony founded in 1638 farther to the south, which primarily covered the area of the present state of Delaware. New Netherlands was conquered by the British in 1664, but was again under Dutch rule for a short time in 1673-1674. In 1660 it had a population of 6,000 as compared with 25,000 in what was then Massachusetts. The Dutch element predominated by far, but there were also French and Walloons—especially in New York—and Germans. In 1657 a High German Lutheran congregation, the first German organization in the New World, was formed in New York. Incidentally the French element is said (Fosdieck 1906, 216) to have been sufficiently numerous under Dutch rule so that "by the year 1656 all government and town proclamations were issued in French as well as in Dutch."

The Dutch element developed vigorously under British rule. As a result of a high birth rate the number of persons of Dutch descent increased from about 6,000 in 1664 to about 105,000 in 1790—55,000 in New York State alone—and this without subsequent immigration from Holland. Outside of New York City, where from 1760 to 1763 a grave internal controversy arose over the question of the language of the sermons, this Dutch population retained its specific characteristics, including its language, up to the time of the War of Independence. In the very heart of the Dutch settlements in New York State, quite a few German and Anglo-Saxon settlers and one French settlement (New Paltz) were even absorbed by the Dutch element and became Dutch speaking.

After the War of Independence an Anglicization process began which, however, was not completed by the first half of the nineteenth century (Wertenbaker 1938, 110-118). It is reported that Dutch was still spoken in many families at the time of the Civil War, and in Bergen County, New Jersey, the Dutch language survived until quite recent years; here in 1910 about 200 people still spoke Dutch (Mencken 1923, 426-428, 460; Prince, 439). According to L. G. van Loon (1938), in the vicinity of Albany some farmers still spoke Dutch in 1938 (Rice 1941, 271-274).

At first the schools remained Dutch throughout New York. After the short-lived second Dutch rule (1673-1674) only private Dutch schools were still tolerated in New York City. In the rural areas, on the other hand, the public Dutch schools continued to exist. These early public schools were remarkable in the North America of that time, as there generally were only private parochial schools (Kilpatrick 1912). This enabled the Dutch element to preserve its substance so well that the New York State legislature in 1788 authorized the edition of a Dutch version of the new United States Constitution (Wertenbaker 1938, 116; Hunt, 22).

In at least a few Dutch communities Dutch language teaching was continued beyond 1776 and thus formed a part not only of the colonial British but also of the United States minority law. This Dutch instruction could be found, for example, in Albany, where English was introduced in the schools only after the Revolution, and even more so in rural areas. In the institutions of municipal self-government Dutch has certainly also been used in certain cases after 1776. In Flatbush the school became bilingual in 1758, the church only in 1792; the records of the township meeting were kept in English after 1776.

Maryland

German immigrants came sporadically during the late seventeenth century and in large numbers after 1732, at first from eastern Pennsylvania and later from Europe (Cunz 1948). A part of western Maryland, particularly the counties of Frederick, Washington, and Carroll, became a compact area of German settlement which formed the southern continuation of the German-speaking area of Pennsylvania. Standard German disappeared in western Maryland before the Civil War; but fragments of the Pennsilfaanisch dialect survived until well into the twentieth century (Eshleman 1938). In addition, Baltimore attracted numerous German immigrants; in 1800 more than half of the population was German, and in 1910, 90,700 persons in the city and county of Baltimore were first or second generation Germans from the German Reich. In the 1940 census, 39,800 German-speaking people were enumerated, among them 4,300 (10.7%) children of parents born in the United States.

The development of the German element in Baltimore is characterized by the fact that here recent immigrants and segments of the older German element cooperated in the same organization to a degree unparalleled in other cities, particularly in the Deutsche Gesellschaft (1783) and the Gesellschaft für die Geschichte der Deutschen in Maryland (1886)—the Society for the History of the Germans in Maryland. This is the only nondenominational institution devoted to research in German-American history which still exists and which deals with the immigrants of the nineteenth and twentieth century as well as with the colonial stock.

During the War of Independence Congress authorized the organization of German troop units in Maryland (Section 2-1). The State Constitution of 1776, which remained in effect until 1851, granted certain indirect privileges to the German element. For instance, Article XXXVI of the Bill of Rights, which preceded the Constitution proper, makes concessions to certain religious sects with respect to oath taking and lists in this connection not only the Anglo-Saxon

Quakers but also the German Mennonite and Dunker sects. Similar provisions may also be found in Articles III and V of the 1798 amendments of the State Constitution.

According to Felix Reichmann (1950, 15) provisions authorizing German editions of government prints were in effect from the War of Independence to the Civil War. Nevertheless only a very few such editions can be found. Hoffman (1911, 18) states that the session records of the legislature have repeatedly been issued in German for the Germans in western Maryland. The legislature, moreover, in 1787 had printed 300 German copies of the deliberations of the Constitutional Convention in Philadelphia (Cunz 1948, 153; Reichmann 1950, 15) while in 1779 a resolution of the State House of Representatives to promulgate certain laws also in German failed to win the approval of the Senate. But it was perhaps put into practice in spite of this (Reichmann 1950, 15-16). According to Cunz (1948, 153), the assembly authorized the German edition of 1779 and according to a letter from Reichmann (1961), each of the two houses could order the printing of a German edition in its own right.

Furthermore, twelve German government prints are preserved from the years 1864-1868, among them six messages or addresses of Governors or Lieutenant Governors but also some official reports; the numerical relation between German and English copies was usually one to five (Reichmann 1950, 16-17).

German editions of municipal publications were also permitted; in Baltimore they were permissible after 1850 and a considerable number of them, mostly messages of the Mayor to the City Council, have been preserved for the years 1875-1898 (Reichmann 1950, 17, 57ff.).

Legal notices in German were rather frequent. A federal law of 1805 about chartering three turnpike companies provided for the publication of notices in bilingual newspapers in Frederickstown and in Hagerstown, among other places (Kloss 1940, 493; *American State Papers* 1834, 901-902).

According to a law of January 26, 1844, it was provided that new state laws should in the future be published in a German newspaper in Baltimore (Reichmann 1950, 16). According to another law of March 30, 1868, new state laws should be printed daily for a week in a German newspaper in Baltimore (text in Kloss 1940, 494; Cunz 1948, 321). Cunz's statement that this law was in effect until World War II is erroneous. Important municipal notices have to be added to this; in 1873 the city council of Baltimore decided that all city ordinances should be published also in a German newspaper. According to Reichmann (1950, 17) they appeared in the *Correspondent* until 1918.

The Germans of Maryland achieved their most substantial successes in the field of education. In Baltimore following a suggestion of the City Council of 1873, several bilingual public schools were established in 1874, in which one-third of the class hours was devoted to German. In the upper grades German was used as the only language in German, art, and music, and it was used along with English in geography, history, and physics. The number of students taking German lessons was 5,700 in 1886, while in 1900 it was 8,450. These, together with the 7,250 students who learned German in private schools, comprised 16% of the total school population of the city in 1900. Only 3,100 took German in 1913, but the bilingual character of these schools had been preserved, and attempts at expansion were under consideration from 1913 to 1914 (*Monatshefte* 1913, 14: 377 and 1914, 15: 135). The private German schools in Maryland also have a rich tradition, and the oldest German educational magazine in the country, *Allgemeine Schulzeitung*, was published here in 1839-1840.

Virginia and West Virginia

In Virginia the first permanent English settlement on the American continent was established in 1607. In the year 1863 the western half of Virginia split from the rest of Virginia and became a separate state under the name of West Virginia.

In 1783 Virginia had ceded to the Confederation territories in the Midwest to which it had nominal claims and which were inhabited by Frenchmen whose rights Virginia had espoused during this time (Section 6-1).

From as early as 1608 smaller German immigrant groups were occasionally found in Virginia. Around 1720 a mass immigration of Germans began. They came into Virginia via Pennsylvania and Maryland and, until the War of Independence, made large parts of the Shenandoah Valley entirely German. About 1726-1727 they founded Shepherdstown, the first white settlement in what was later to be West Virginia.

The German element retained its language until about 1850, but during the period 1829-1835 the parochial schools became English (Wust 1967, 161-162). There had been a short time when some German or bilingual schools received state tuition grants, i.e., state aid for the pupils who came from poor families. In the years after 1850, standard German and slowly afterward also the Pennsilfaanisch dialect were lost (Wayland 1907). Pennsilfaanisch has survived until today, however, in the western parts of Shenandoah County (Jerome) and of Rockingham County (Criders and Dayton) and in Pendleton County, West Virginia (Sugar Grove and Propst Gap) (Wust 1953, 57; Wayland 1907, 95, 102).

In 1792 the House turned down a petition from Augusta County for a German edition of the state laws. Still, on December 23, 1894, the State House of Representatives decided to have important state laws published in a German edition, which appeared the following year in Philadelphia (Smity, Stewart, Kyger, 1964; Cist 1795; Wust 1969, 113-114). The decision coincides, not entirely by accident, with the 1794-1795 attempts to secure in the United States Congress the publication of federal laws in German, attempts which had been initiated by a Virginia proposal (Section 2-1). Beyond this, we have knowledge of only one edition which possibly had official character, a German edition of 1812 of little importance (Wust 1953, 61).

During the nineteenth century numerous Germans settled primarily in the cities. By 1910 there were 9,700 people in Virginia and 17,600 people in West Virginia who were first or second generation Germans from the German Reich.

These later immigrants worked for the introduction of German in the public elementary schools. They had almost no success in Virginia, where such attempts were made in Richmond in 1869, 1886, and 1896 (Schuricht; Wust 1967, 238). However, Richmond is included in a list of places where German was at that time taught in public elementary schools. This list appears in *Amerikanische Schulzeitung* (Sept. 1874, 7). These immigrants had somewhat better results in West Virginia, where in 1860 German was introduced in Wheeling and Parkersburg. In Wheeling German was limited to the upper grades in 1877, but it survived there with certain changes until at least 1909, perhaps even until 1917.

Texas

We have already reported about the Germans in Texas, who here belonged to the old established settlers (Section 6-2).

CHAPTER SEVEN

Nationality Rights in Outlying Areas
Which Became States

7-1 GENERAL REMARKS ABOUT THE OUTLYING AREAS

Common Characteristics

Under outlying areas we group all parts of the American sphere of jurisdiction which do not belong to the area of the 48 states which formed the United States before World War II. (For the distinction between sphere of jurisdiction and sphere of sovereignty, see Section 1-1). These areas are quite different in size, history, population, and legal status, but they share five common characteristics:

Geography: They all are separated by ocean or (Alaska, Canal Zone) by foreign territory from the 48 states.

History: Their annexation began (Alaska 1867) 14 years after the last territorial acquisition in the area of the 48 states (Gadsden Purchase 1853), and their advancement toward statehood (Philippines 1935, see Table 7-7) came 23 years after the last such development within the area of the 48 states (1912 Arizona and New Mexico).

Ethnicity: They had been under American rule for a long time, and were inhabited by a majority that was not Anglo-Saxon and, with the exception of Puerto Rico, nonwhite. An exception was the Bonin Islands, simply because their inhabitants were not permitted to return (Section 8-5).

Psychology: The acquisition of each of these areas met with opposition from parts of the nation, beginning with the purchase of Alaska, which was ridiculed as "Seward's folly," and ending with the acquisition of the Ryukyus.

Legal status: Their status of not being part of the fully integrated American territory was either certain or being maintained by important factions and had become a matter of legal disputes. This status is still accepted for most of these outlying areas.

In the organic laws which were given to these outlying areas before they advanced to statehood, we find several peculiarities with no counterpart in the territorial constitutions of the United States proper.

In Alaska the territorial government had fewer rights than were usually granted to territorial governments. In Hawaii only a resident of the territory could be appointed Governor between 1900 and 1959. In the Territory of Puerto Rico the Governor could be elected by the people after 1947; the same holds for Guam and the Virgin Islands after 1968.

The territorial cabinet served at the same time as the upper house in Puerto Rico from 1900 to 1917, in the Philippines from 1907 to 1916. On the other hand, the institution of an upper house was abolished in the Philippines between 1935 and 1940 and was not even established in Guam, the Ryukyus, and Samoa. In the Virgin Islands the two municipal legislatures served at the same time as the territorial legislature between 1936 and 1954.

From a population point of view the territories and outside areas may be divided into three main groups:

1. Established (before English-speaking days) population with a non-English mother tongue: (a) belonging to only one language group—Hawaii, Puerto Rico, Guam, American Samoa, Ryukyu, Bonin Islands; (b) divided into many language groups: Alaska, Philippines, Micronesian Trust Territory.

2. Established population with English mother tongue: American Virgin Islands, intermingled with white non-English (French, Spanish) immigrants.

3. No indigenous population existing, only immigrants, partly of English, partly of Spanish mother tongue: Canal Zone.

Legal Position

According to their present status Alaska, Hawaii, the Philippines, and Puerto Rico are states. Puerto Rico is not, however, undisputedly a state (Section 7-4), and the Philippines are now an independent country. Guam and the Virgin Islands are territories of the fourth category. American Samoa and the Ryukyu Islands became quasi-territories, polities of a special type for which the term "presidential territories" has been suggested (Sections 8-3 and 8-4).

Micronesia, the Ryukyu Islands, and the Canal Zone belonged to the American sphere of jurisdiction but not to the American sphere of sovereignty. Rather, sovereignty for the Ryukyu Islands rested with Japan and for the Canal Zone with Panama (Section 8-1). Micronesia is administered under the auspices of the United Nations.

Alaska and Hawaii form part of the fully integrated United States territory. Puerto Rico, the Virgin Islands, Guam, and American Samoa belong to the sphere of sovereignty, but are not fully integrated.

When the United States acquired a number of Spanish colonies and Hawaii in 1898, the question was raised as to whether the United States Constitution would become fully effective in these areas after sovereignty had changed hands, whether "the Constitution follows the flag." The United States Supreme Court had already given to Congress much larger power over the mainland territories in a decision of 1890 (*Mormon Church* v. *United States*). But by now, in 1900-1901, the Supreme Court went farther by answering the above question with a "No" in a series of decisions (*Downs* v. *Bidwell*; *Dooley* v. *United States*; *Pepke* v. *United States*; *De Lima* v. *Bidwell*. The source of publication is Howe 1901, and further details are to be found in Littler 1929, 38-51; Coudert 1926, 801-864; Pratt 1950, 157-164.)

The United States Constitution is divided into compulsory (fundamental and natural) provisions and flexible (formal, artificial, remedial) provisions. The border between them would have to be determined by court decisions in disputes, and only the compulsory fundamental provisions would be automatically applicable to the new possessions. According to American legal interpretation, it is not the Constitution but the governmental authority of the federal government which rules, therefore, in the outlying areas. Even the elevation of Guam into an organized territory did not make Guam an incorporated part of the Union. The legislative authority of Congress goes so far that it may give them any administrative form it sees fit which is not clearly violating the spirit of the American Constitution. The new nationals have no legal claim to self-government, let alone to self-rule.

The United States Supreme Court has never given a complete list of the inalienable basic rights; named in different cases were: freedom of religion, freedom of speech and press, protection against unreasonable search and confiscation and from cruel or unusual punishment, the right of appeal to the courts, protection against violations against life, liberty, and property without due process of law (*Downs* v. *Bidwell*; *Balzac* v. *People of Puerto Rico*). On the other hand, a claim of the area to be incorporated into the American customs revenue district was expressly denied, just as was the claim to trial by jury (*Downs* v. *Bidwell*; *Dorr* v. *United States*).

The first such decisions of the United States Supreme Court were based on the example of Puerto Rico. In the following years the Supreme Court ruled:

1903: that Hawaii after 1898 was at first not fully incorporated, but had become integrated in 1900 by the provisions of the Organic Act drafted for it by Congress, which expressly extended the provisions of the United States Constitution to the islands (*Hawaii* v. *Mankichi*).

1904: that the Philippines did not belong to the fully incorporated nation (*Dorr* v. *United States*).

1905: that Alaska belonged to the fully incorporated national territory because the cession treaty had guaranteed to the white inhabitants their civil rights because the customs laws and the taxation laws of the United States had since then been extended to Alaska, etc. (*Rasmussen* v. *United States*).

1918 and 1922: that Puerto Rico, even under its Organic Act of 1917 which made its inhabitants American citizens, was still unincorporated territory (*People of Puerto Rico* v. *Tapia*; *People of Puerto Rico* v. *Muratti*; *Balzac* v. *People of Puerto Rico*).

The nonintegrated status of the Virgin Islands has been confirmed by several expert opinions of the Justice Department (Evans 1945, 50; Pratt 1950, 408). For Guam and Samoa this status was not questioned. Congress gave a bill of rights to the Philippines in 1902, to Puerto Rico in 1917, to the Virgin Islands in 1936, and to Guam in 1950. In American Samoa the Governor proclaimed basic rights in 1931, but in the following year they were repealed by the Navy Department.

That the United States Supreme Court declared most of the overseas possessions to be nonintegrated parts of the United States was, legally speaking, an ambivalent action which could be interpreted as being conceived against, as well as in favor of the new subjects. At first the negative aspect predominated: the new nationals did not become citizens as had the people of Louisiana, Texas, New Mexico, etc., and Congress had powers over them which it had had in no part of the mainland. But in the course of time the advantages which this special status afforded became more and more evident. It facilitated special regulations which did more justice to the particular living conditions of these overseas areas than a development would have which strictly followed the norms established on the mainland. Above all, this special status enabled Congress to grant or offer independence to some of these areas, which would have been much more difficult to do in cases of territories not subject to Congressional rule but under the Constitution of the United States.

Outlying Areas and International Organizations

The United States submits annual reports about the Virgin Islands, Guam, American Samoa, and the Micronesian Trust Territory to the United Nations. Initially, reports were also submitted about Alaska, Hawaii, and Puerto Rico. The reports were, however, discontinued as soon as these areas had become states with complete self-government (Puerto Rico is a Commonwealth rather than one of the regular 50 states). Only one report was submitted about the Canal Zone (1946), an act which was protested by Panama (*Non-Self-Governing Territories* 1951). It has been repeatedly maintained, for instance, in a letter from the United States State Department to me, that the United States never did report to the United Nations about the Canal Zone. There were indeed no reports about the Ryukyu and Bonin Islands.

In 1946 the United States, Great Britain, the Netherlands, and France formed the Caribbean Commission with its seat until 1960 in Trinidad and after that in Puerto Rico. Puerto Rico and the Virgin Islands were partially taken care of by this commission. The Commission was active in social and economic questions. On September 6, 1961, on the basis of a treaty of June 21, 1960, by the same four powers, the Commission was replaced by the Caribbean Organization with its seat in San Juan, Puerto Rico. It differs from its predecessor primarily in two points: (1) cultural questions are also included in its activities, and (2) members of the Caribbean Organization are, with the exception of France, not the founder states but the Caribbean states or autonomous areas associated with them, i.e., in the case of the United States, Puerto Rico and the Virgin Islands. From the Netherlands, Surinam and the Netherlands Antilles became members, from Great Britain, British Guiana and the West Indian Federation (since then dissolved). Every member sent one representative to the Caribbean Council, which guided the Caribbean Organization. Official languages are English and French, but the founding documents were published also in an official Dutch version and (because of Puerto Rico) in a Spanish version (*Treaties and Other International Acts* 1961).

By a treaty of February 6, 1947, effective after July 29, 1948, the United States became also a founding member (along with Australia, France, Great Britain, the Netherlands—for West New Guinea—and New Zealand) of the South Pacific Commission (1948), which was patterned after the Caribbean Commission and which includes in its activities American Samoa, Guam, and the Micronesian Trust Territory. The latter, however, are not members themselves. One of the first tasks which the commission undertook was of importance to the nationality policy: studies concerning the most suitable method of teaching illiterate persons how to read and write in their mother tongue. This was laid down by the resolution concerning immediate projects which was attached to the founding treaty.

Central Administration

The Washington offices responsible for the outside areas have never been merged into one central office. There were two offices which somehow came close to being a Colonial Office: the Bureau of Insular Affairs and the Office of Territories. The Bureau of Insular Affairs was founded on December 13, 1898, as a Division of Customs and Insular Affairs. On December 10, 1900, it was renamed Division of Insular Affairs and in 1903, by 32 Statute 712, it became Bureau of Insular Affairs.

The Bureau of Insular Affairs of the Department of Defense was responsible for the Philippines from the very beginning and after 1909 also for Puerto Rico, while Hawaii was entirely and Alaska was predominantly under the control of the Department of the Interior (Pomeroy 1944, 521-532; Forbes 1928, 136-138; *Preliminary Inventory of the . . . Insular Affairs* 1960).

The Division of Territories and Island Possessions was established in the Department of the Interior on July 29, 1934, pursuant to Executive Order No. 6726 signed by President Franklin D. Roosevelt on May 29, 1934. On July 28, 1950, by the order of the Secretary of the Interior, the Division of Territories was reorganized and renamed the Office of Territories (Pratt 1950, 155-157). It had immediately been given control over Hawaii, Alaska, Puerto Rico, and the Virgin Islands. The Philippines, where the authority of the United States had already been limited topically and temporally during the previous years, were added in 1939, in 1950 Guam, and in 1951 American Samoa and the Micronesian Trust Territory. Parts of the Micronesian Trust Territory were returned to the Navy

Department from 1952-1953 until 1962 (Section 8-6). In the meantime, Alaska, Hawaii, and Puerto Rico have, in addition to the Philippines, outgrown the control of the federal government. The compilation of the annual report to the United Nations for these three areas was the responsibility (and still is for dependent areas) of the Office of Territories. The Office is responsible for all dependent areas belonging to the American sphere of jurisdiction and in the case of Micronesia also for a mere Trust Territory of the United States. The Canal Zone and the Ryukyus remained under the control of the Department of Defense. These areas were under American jurisdiction, not under American sovereignty.

7-2 ALASKA

Alaska was discovered in 1714 by the Dane, Vitus Bering, who was in the service of Peter the Great. A certain planned opening began with the founding of the Russian-American Trade Company (1799). Russians also immigrated in small numbers. They were mostly traders and hunters and, since they were predominantly men, often took native Eskimo or Indian wives. The children of these marriages were called Creoles; some of them still used the native languages as domestic languages, but all became members of the Greek Orthodox church and had Russian as their church language. There existed a Russian-invented Cyrillic system of writing for Eskimos (Schmitt 1951). According to Tikhmeniev (Kashevaroff 1936) 784 pure-blooded Russians, among them only 208 women, were enumerated in 1860 and in 1867 there were 1,687 so-called Creoles. Among them 825, or almost 50%, were women.

The overwhelming majority of the inhabitants, however, spoke their native languages. In 1930 there were still 19,000 Eskimos and 11,000 Indians enumerated among the 59,700 inhabitants. However, not only the Indians but also the Eskimos can be divided into several language groups. The inhabitants of the Aleutians speak three closely related dialects. The Eskimos of the mainland north of the Yukon speak a language which is essentially identical with that of the Eskimos in Canada and Greenland. They call this language Inupiaq, while in the most important areas where it is spoken it is called Greenlandic. South of the Yukon a separate (even though related to Inupiaq) language is spoken, which the Eskimos call Yupik (Voegelin 1941, 17-18). The most important Indian languages are that of the Athapaskans (1930: 4,900 persons) and the Tlingit (1930: 4,500 persons).

In the year 1867 Alaska was sold by Russia to the United States. After the cession only part of the Russian but probably most of the Creole population remained in the country. The Russian language was retained rather stubbornly. In 1890 Russian was still reported as the mother tongue of 805 persons, English of 7,115, and the Eskimo languages by 10,302 inhabitants. At that time a part of the Creoles who did not use Russian as a mother tongue still retained Russian as the language for church services (*Report of . . . Alaska* 1893, 196, 192). As late as 1954 L. C. Hammerich (1954, 426, 401-428) reported that Russian was still being used in church services, especially on the Alaskan Peninsula (e.g., Chignik, Perryville, etc.) and in some few places, such as Uzinki, there were even some native speakers of the language left. His statement contradicts A. P. Kashevaroff, who said in a letter to me in 1936 that the indigenous Russian and Creole stock had all but disappeared as a result of mixed marriages. Another scholar (Jockelson 1933; cf. Voegelin 1941, 17-18) tells that Russian remained the link language between the speakers of some distinct though closely related Aleut dialects. The number of later immigrants from Russia was negligible; in 1930 only 459 first or second generation Russians were enumerated.

Although the Russian element has become negligible, there is still an indigenous nonwhite—and largely non-English—element to be reckoned with. In 1960 it comprised 38,000 individuals, among 226,200 total inhabitants. Of these 38,000 roughly 16,000 may have spoken Yupik, the Eskimo language of southern Alaska, while 8,000 spoke Inupiaq, the Eskimo language spoken in northern Alaska, Canada, and Greenland. At most 2,000 spoke the Aleut language, while 12,000 spoke Indian languages such as Tlingit, Hyda, and some Athapaskan languages. Remarkably there were also some 7,000 Negroes and 2,000 Asians, raising the nonwhite total to 47,000.

In the years 1868-1869 the Ukrainian priest Andreas (Ahapiy) Honcharenko twice a month in San Francisco published the *Alaska Herald* for the Alaskan Russians. This paper, which was written in English and Russian, was financially supported by the federal government, since it was hoped that this would help to inform the Alaskan Russians about the way of life and the laws of the United States (Brown and Roucek 1937, 211, 207).

When in 1870 the optional period for the Russian population had expired, it was evident that a part of it had remained in the country. But Alaska remained for a long time without any civil self-administration. Until 1877 Alaska was administered by the War Department in Washington and from 1877 to 1884 by the Treasury Department. This situation led the Russians to threaten in 1882 that they would complain to the Tsar since they were deprived of the rights guaranteed to them in 1867 (Underwood 1913, 1397-1398). A provisory solution was therefore adopted in 1884. Alaska became a "civil and juridical district" similar to a territory (Farrand 1900, 680 and Section 1-1 of this book). The laws of Oregon were to be introduced as far as they were applicable to Alaska. The Attorney General was directed to have published an English edition of all the laws that were effective in Alaska (Section 11 of the agreement). The entire regulation was motivated, as Jeannette P. Nichols writes (1924, 72), by "a sense of moral obligation towards the Russians who had remained in Alaska, and towards the Americans who had gone there to make money or convert the Indians."

In no other area which was annexed by the United States has the former government taken such an active interest in the school system after the change of ownership as Russia did in Alaska (Tracy 1919). In the year 1887 a total of 17 schools existed in 7 places which received annually $20,000 from the Russian government, while Washington at that time appropriated only $15,000 annually to 15 schools. In the year 1890 the Russian schools were attended by 256 students, most of them nonwhite, but some of them also children of the local Russian population. Of these students, 94 attended a school maintained by the

Holy Synod; the rest attended schools sponsored by the Russian government (*Report of . . . Alaska* 1893, 192). All schools were church-oriented. The last of these schools to close (in 1916) was a girls' boarding school in Kodiak (Marsh 1967, 9).

For the schools established by the federal government, a regulation for teaching in public schools in the "Territory of Alaska" was issued by the Department of the Interior in 1884. (The use of the term Territory here is interesting!) According to this regulation all instruction in public schools had to be given in English, and no foreign language textbooks were permitted (Kloss 1940, 506). But it is reported at the same time from several places in Alaska (for example, Kodiak) that teachers in public schools learned Russian so as to be able to make themselves understood by their students (*Report of the United States Commissioner of Education* 1887-1888, 98 105).

Not until 1906 did the white population in Alaska have a representative in Congress and not until 1912 was Alaska organized into a Territory with its own representative body. The Russian splinter groups had in the meantime been definitively reduced to a minute minority among the white population. In the year 1959 Alaska became a state of the United States (Wells 1959, 161-162; Gruening 1954, 65-70).

That this advancement to territorial status and later to statehood was delayed by so many decades was, however, not the result of the presence of those few Russians or people of Russian descent but was primarily the result of the conviction that Alaska was considered to be suitable for settlement only to a limited degree. Therefore, some joint stock companies which were not Alaskan based (such as the Alaska Commercial Company in San Francisco and the salmon industry, which were eagerly propagating this prejudice) won an undue influence which proved quite harmful for Alaska (Wells 1959, 161-162; Gruening 1954, 65-70). It is easy to see this development as *exclusively* the influence of big business, which was indeed quite powerful, without paying some attention to problems of a more basic nature. In reality one point played a role which is also of considerable importance for many problems of self-determination in the world: It is far from self-evident that the few inhabitants in areas which are clearly underpopulated decide their country's destiny and dispose of its treasures. This still happens today, for example, in such a case as French Guiana (which is almost unpopulated) and forms an essential justification for the takeover of the land by whites in North America, Australia, and Northern Asia. The federal government expressly took the position that it had to control the riches of Alaska not exclusively in the interest of its few inhabitants but in the interest of the entire American nation.

That the region had a majority of nonwhite people was of very little importance for a long time because the nonwhites could not vote. Only after 1915 could individual natives acquire citizenship, and in 1924 citizenship was given to them, as in the United States proper. Gradually this had the following effect: By 1924 the first Indian representative was elected, but not until 1948 were the first two Eskimos elected. At about the same time the first Indian became speaker of the Alaskan Senate and in 1951 there were 7 nonwhites among the 40 members of the legislature (3 senators, 4 representatives).

It is certainly no accident that statehood was achieved only after the 1950 census had shown a clear majority of white inhabitants. The 1950 census showed 128,100 inhabitants, of whom 20,400 were members of the military; also there were 19,800 Eskimos and natives of the Aleutians as well as 14,100 Indians. Together Eskimos and Indians totaled 33,900, or 31% of the civilian population. In 1930 the nonwhites had still formed a small majority of the inhabitants and also of the voters. The 1930 census showed 59,700 inhabitants, among them 19,000 Eskimos and 11,000 Indians of whom 4,900 were Athapascas and 4,500 were Tlingits.

The territorial government counteracted tendencies toward segregating the races which were not absent in Alaska also. In 1945 an antidiscrimination law was passed which prohibited segregation (for example, in restaurants and movie theaters). Certain tendencies to the contrary were the result of a federal law, the Wheeler-Howard Act, adopted in 1934 and since 1936 also applicable in Alaska, which promoted the creation of self-administering native reservations. In Alaska this led to tensions; the Federal District Court ruled in 1951 that the establishment of the Hydaburg Indian Reservation was invalid, as it would favor racial segregation. On the other hand, Alaska was still unable to integrate into the general school system the separate schools for natives that were maintained by the Alaska Native Service. In 1958 there were still 80 of them. This was of no importance to a discussion of nationality rights because the 4,700 students in 1958 of these separate schools were taught in English. Besides these students there were 34,000 students in public schools and 1,700 in private and parochial schools.

The use of the English language was not a foregone conclusion. Denmark in Greenland, for example, during the nineteenth century had made the Eskimo language the first language of instruction in the schools for Eskimos (Oldendown 1939, 21-53; Gad 1957, 20-24; Gad 1960, 135-137), and thus was the first country in the Western Hemisphere to grant this rank to a native language in the modern public school system. According to information in a letter of the Department of Northern Affairs and National Resources (1961), Canada had so far taught the Eskimos only in English employing white teachers, but planned to have bilingual Eskimo teachers handle instruction in the future, particularly in the first grades. The Soviet Union finally followed a systematic language policy among its few Eskimos in the Chukotka District. Books were printed in the Eskimo language, a special Chukcha Eskimo National District was created, and in 1929 a Congress of Eskimo Soviets was held (Kolarz 1956, 120). The Soviet Union cultivated the language of its one hundred Aleuts with equal intensity so as to impress the five times more numerous Aleuts of Alaska (Kolarz 1956, 102-104). The Americans themselves have encouraged native languages quite extensively in Samoa and even more in Micronesia (Sections 8-3, 8-6). In Hawaii the Hawaiian language was promoted to a limited degree (Section 7-3).

Small wonder that in the late 1960s, partly because of work done privately by members of the Summer Institute of Linguistics among tribal groups, state authorities displayed growing concern regarding the problem of native languages. While a comprehensive program drafted in 1968 at the University of Alaska, in College, Alaska, for the cultivation of a number of indigenous tongues was rejected by the State Department of Education, the same University launched an on-going Alaskan Native Language Project, which was first limited to research and documentation. In October 1969, a grammar of Yupik was nearing completion and already was being used in Eskimo classes offered at the University. On November 18-20, 1969, a BIA-sponsored Conference on Bilingual and Bicultural Education for Alaska Native Youth at the University of Alaska decided to start a bilingual Yupik-English pilot school program in three schools of the Kuskokwin area beginning September 1970. The Yuk dialect of Yupik was to be used; one hour per day out of a total of four would be devoted to the study of English in grade one, the ratio to be changed gradually to four out of six hours in grade eight. In addition, there was considerable support for the employment in many villages of a bilingual resident as a teaching aide to assist teachers and pupils in bridging the language gap. These aides were to be in most cases educated Eskimos or Indians; in some cases, members of the Summer Institute of Linguistics or natives trained by them would be made available.

A law enacted in 1972 (sec. 14.08.160 and 170, am. sec. 2 ch. 172 SLA 1972) made it mandatory for all state-operated schools attended by at least 15 children speaking the same indigenous language to employ at least one teacher familiar with the language, and to supply adequate teaching materials. This excluded the federally funded BIA schools.

7-3 HAWAII

Background

In the eighteenth century, this group of Pacific islands was inhabited only by Polynesians. The language of the original Polynesian inhabitants of Hawaii we may call Old Hawaiian. From 1782 to 1810, King Kamehameha united the islands into a kingdom which after 1820 came under the influence of white missionaries and planters. The attempts of Hawaiian circles to reduce the influence of the whites led in 1893 to a revolution of the whites, who were supported by some of the Hawaiians. Since the desired annexation by the United States did not materialize at that time, an independent Hawaiian Republic was established in 1894, headed by S. B. Dole, the son of a missionary. In the year 1898 at the end of the Spanish-American War, Hawaii was annexed by the Union, became a territory in 1900, and a state in 1959. The state constitution, which had already been drafted in 1950, became effective on August 21, 1959 (*Proceedings of the Constitutional Convention of Hawaii*).

The number of Hawaiians at the time of discovery is estimated at about 300,000, but they declined to about 82,000 by 1850. After 1878 when the Chinese immigration (having feebly begun in 1852) assumed sometimes torrential

Table 7-1   Ethnic Composition of Hawaii

Group	Principal Immigration	1960	Number 1950	1930
Pure Polynesians[a]		11,900	12,100	22,700
Part Polynesians[a]		91,100	73,500	28,200
Whites				
"Haole"	20th century			44,900
Portuguese	1877-1882		95,300	
	and			27,600
	1906-1907	219,800		
Puerto Ricans	Early 20th century		8,900	6,700
Koreans	1901-1910		7,000	6,500
Chinese (mostly				
Cantonese)	1878-1898	38,200	32,200	27,200
Japanese (including				
many Ryukyuans)	1890-1908	203,500	184,100	139,600
Filipinos,				
(90% Ilocanos)	1920s	69,100	60,500	63,600
TOTALS		632,800	499,800	363,400

[a]In 1900 there were 28,700 pure-blooded Polynesians and 9,500 Polynesians of mixed blood.

proportions, a large number of Asians, notably Japanese, came to Hawaii, also Iberians (Portuguese and Puerto Ricans). Almost all of them had been brought to Hawaii as plantation workers. As opposed to the American mainland, from the very beginning, mixed marriages became frequent between Hawaiians and Europeans or Asians and subsequently also between the two latter groups. By the 1930s one-fourth of all children born in Hawaii were of racially mixed marriages. Official statistics normally group these children according to their father's racial background and are, therefore, today only of limited value (Table 7-1).

The actual mingling is illustrated by an example given by E. V. Stonequist (1937, 40-41) of a family in which the mother was a pure-blooded Hawaiian and the father Caucasian. Of the children, one married a Korean, one a Caucasian, one a Chinese-Hawaiian, one a Chinese-Caucasian-Hawaiian, and the fifth child planned to marry a Caucasian-Hawaiian-Filipino. "Miss Hawaii" of 1953 had British (English, Irish, and Scottish), German, Old Hawaiian, Chinese, and Japanese blood (Day 1960, 236). The German admixture was not trivial. For example, 3,200 Germans of the first or second generation were in Hawaii in 1930.

Even more rapid than the racial mingling was the lingual assimilation which today is considered completed in the case of the Chinese and Portuguese but which has also affected large segments of the other racial groups. Since there were only a few persons of English mother tongue in Hawaii during the last third of the nineteenth century, several forms of pidgin English developed as a means of communication between the non-English groups. Today these varieties of pidgin English have given way to a new, specifically Hawaiian variety of creolized English. It uses about 1,000 borrowed words (among them about 250 in general use) of the Hawaiian language and also shows certain influences from Chinese and Japanese on the vocabulary and from Portuguese on the syntax (Reinecke and Tokimasa 1934, 48-58). Pidgin English, which has become more and more uniform, has of course survived (Aspinwall 1960, 7-8). Moreover, considerable segments of the Haole and Japanese population have not yet been affected by this process of general assimilation. Among the Japanese—just for quantitative reasons alone—the old language has been retained longer than among the other groups.

The Hawaiians as an Ethnic Group

The Hawaiians and the earliest white missionaries after the first contact between Hawaiian and Western culture attempted at first to adapt the native language to the modern culture (Section 7-3).

The first printed law and textbooks in the Hawaiian language were published in 1822; they were followed by other publications such as the New Testament in 1832, the Bible in 1839, a dictionary and a complete collection of laws in 1842. There were two Hawaiian-language newspapers as early as 1834. And from 1831 on the Lahainaluna Teachers' Seminary was in operation where until the 1870s instruction was given in Hawaiian. A compulsory school law was passed in 1840. Ten years later the entire population was able to read and write in their mother tongue.

But during the second half of the nineteenth century the Hawaiians began to adopt the English language in education. After 1853 English-language schools were established for the native population, and in 1882 only about one-third of the approximately 8,200 students were still taught in the Hawaiian language. In 1892 Polynesian was the language of instruction for only 552 (5%) of the students, but 10,200 (95%) were instructed in English (Kloss 1940, 592; Kuykendall and Day 1949, 81 passim). The private schools also were entirely English. They were particularly numerous in Hawaii, the oldest being a Catholic school (1846) on Oahu. The most important of the private schools were the well-endowed Kamehameha Schools (1884), which were open only to students with Old Hawaiian background.

After World War I, several attempts were made to give the Hawaiian language again a permanent and important place in the school system. Also attempts were made to establish compact Hawaiian settlements which would create more favorable conditions for survival of the language. For this purpose a federal law was adopted in 1921 which established a Hawaiian Homes Commission and entrusted it with leasing federally owned land to Hawaiians (Kloss 1940, 596-597). Originally the plan was primarily to promote agricultural activities of the Hawaiians, a program which was started particularly on Molokai. A more important result of these attempts was the creation of suburban settlements, mostly around Honolulu, where the Hawaiians besides cultivating their plats could find additional occupation. By 1946 a total of 4,000 such homesteads had been created. Of this number 1,500 were located on Molokai (Weaver 1959, 124-125; Webb and Webb 1959, 200-203).

Generally speaking, the Hawaiians maintained their position as officials on the one hand and on the other hand in a variety of manual jobs (for example, as fishermen or city workers) while they have been practically eliminated from agriculture and commercial activities. There exists a strong tendency among the Hawaiian group to withdraw in semiresignation, and a kind of negative, defensive group or even ethnic solidarity has developed (Elkin 1957, 285). But it seems doubtful that these resentments will again lead to attempts at a revival of the language. Beaglehole (1937, 105) quotes Hawaiians who favored language schools patterned after those of the Japanese (because the public schools had no suitable teachers) or else a cultural association for the encouragement of the use of the language.

The language of the Hawaiians, once far ahead of its sister languages on New Zealand and Samoa, is now far surpassed by them. A considerable percentage of the Hawaiian youth speak only English; among the others the vocabulary has often so degenerated that they are hardly able to understand "classical" Old Hawaiian (Beaglehole 1937, 102-106). But there exists still a strong group solidarity which includes many of mixed lineage (part Hawaiians). The Polynesian language, however, seems to be doomed. Professor S. H. Elbert (1966) of the University of Hawaii estimated the number of native speakers to be just 1,000, adding that the language is sure to be extinct 100 years from now.

Struggle for Self-Government

It should by no means be considered natural that Hawaii was to remain a territory for such a long time. Hawaii had a long state tradition of its own. It had become, in contrast to Puerto Rico, part of the American sphere of sovereignty by voluntary incorporation in the manner of Texas and was in economic terms not in need of federal subsidies but rather contributed money to the federal government. The delay in the achievement of statehood was therefore primarily caused by the ethnic composition of the population.

The Organic Act of 1900 had enfranchised a large, relatively poor, and predominantly Hawaiian part of the population which in the 1894 Constitution had been deprived of the right to vote. Consequently, the Territory had until about 1920 a clear Hawaiian majority among the voters. This majority was reduced very slowly because, according to a 1922 Supreme Court decision (*Takao Ozawa* v. *United States*), foreign-born Asians could not become citizens. Only their Hawaiian-born children upon coming of age would be able to vote (Section 1-3). Until about 1950 the Hawaiians remained the largest ethnic voter bloc; in 1947, of all state representatives, 40% were Hawaiian.

Around 1910 a rather unique balance between three coexisting majorities had come into existence: (1) the Hawaiians who had a majority at the polls; (2) the Haoles with a majority of economic and cultural influences; and (3) the

Table 7-2 Nationality Groups in Hawaiian Politics According to Names of Legislators

Legislators	Asian	Old Hawaiian	Iberian	Others
15 Senators	8	0	2	5
30 Representatives	14	3[a]	5	8

[a]Including the Speaker.

Asians with a majority of the population. Initial attempts of the Hawaiians to pursue a political course of their own with the help of a Home Rule Party failed because of the lack of skilled leaders. The party, which had been led by the white monarchist Wilcox, was dissolved in 1912. The majority in the legislature which it had achieved in 1900 and which, for example, intended to give the Hawaiian medicine men (kahunas) equal status with western-style doctors, did considerable harm to Hawaii's prestige on the mainland and Hawaii's hopes for speedy statehood.

It should be noted that from 1903 on, practically every legislature in Hawaii adopted a resolution demanding statehood and that from 1919 on Congress was presented at short intervals with new bills to this effect. The territorial legislature issued on April 26, 1923, a bill of rights, which was termed unique in its preamble. It proclaimed no individual rights but the claim of Hawaii to be recognized and treated as an integral part of the United States (*Administration of Hawaii* 1933, 133-141). However, the Hawaiians themselves were initially suspicious about statehood, since they feared the coming Asian majority among the voters (*Statehood for Hawaii* 1950, 24, 34, 36). In their apprehension the Hawaiians found allies in the most influential Haole element, notably the Big Five, the five largest sugar-producing firms. The latter, however, changed their attitude when Hawaii in 1934 was grouped by Congress among foreign areas (for example, Cuba) with respect to the sugar quota. The advance of the Asian voters could of course not be stopped. In 1949 Fong, a man of Chinese descent, became Speaker of the House, and Tsukiyama, a man of Japanese descent, became President of the Senate. The apprehension that the Asians would vote along ethnic lines proved correct only in a few instances; generally speaking ethnic and party lines overlap. The Hawaiian political influence is rather unimportant today.

In 1955 the name count revealed the picture shown in Table 7-2. In contrast, of the 30 leading governmental officials, only 3 had an Asian and one each an Iberian and Hawaiian name (Epstein 1956).

On the mainland, objections to statehood were even stronger than in Hawaii itself. They also were primarily founded on the alien ethnic character of the majority of the population, less because of the foreign languages spoken but more because of the different racial background.

When in 1932 an investigation initiated by the Attorney General discovered irregularities in the police system of the territory, plans were discussed in

Washington to put the Islands under tutelage, i.e., either take away substantial parts of law enforcement control or even take away the territorial status and put Hawaii under military rule (Webb and Webb 1959, 209-211).

That Hawaii finally became a state was far from a matter of course. For the first time an area which did not belong to the American continent became a component state of the Union. Prior to 1959 it had been seriously debated whether it would be constitutional to make an area which belonged to another continent part of the United States of *America.* Also for the first time a Territory with a nonwhite majority of citizens (not only inhabitants) became a state. Both factors seem to have contributed to a movement in Hawaii during the 1940s and 1950s which aspired that Hawaii should have the Puerto Rican solution of an Associated Commonwealth (*Statehood for Hawaii* 1950, 12; Webb and Webb 1959, 241-242). It may be said with some degree of certainty that Hawaii would not have been granted statehood if its inhabitants had not given up their old languages to a large degree, i.e., if they had remained alien not only in their race but also in their language. That Hawaii, which was alien only in race, became a state but Puerto Rico, which was alien only in language, became an associated state could easily stimulate speculations about the relative importance of racial and language factors in the subconscious of the Americans.

Language Provisions in the Constitutions

The Constitutions of 1840 and 1852 do not contain language provisions; that of 1864 provided in Article 44 that the Minister of Finances should present the annual budget in the Hawaiian and in the English languages. The Constitution of 1887 makes the right to vote for the Upper (Article 59, Section 3) and the Lower House (Article 62) dependent upon the knowledge of Hawaiian, English, "or any other European language," a provision presumably designed to exclude Asians. The republican Constitution of July 3, 1894, stated in Articles 56 and 58 that Senators and Representatives had to have an oral and written command of either English or Hawaiian and in Articles 74 and 76 the same with respect to the voting right. Article 77 (7) provided for language tests for voters, Article 103 (4) for the publication of amendments and new versions of the constitution in English and Hawaiian newspapers of Honolulu.

In the Organic Act of 1900 Section 44 stated that the debates of the legislature should be held in the English language, and Section 60 stated that the right to vote in territorial election was, among other things, dependent upon a command of either English or Hawaiian. Furthermore, Article II (91) of the State Constitution of July 22, 1950, stated with respect to all state and county elections: "Nobody shall be eligible to vote who cannot speak, read, and write the English or Hawaiian language." During the drafting of the Constitution, white representative Heen questioned the privileged position of the Hawaiian language, and representative Mizuha endorsed it (*Proceedings of the Constitutional Convention* 1961, II, 52). Article XI of the 1950 Constitution incorporates the Hawaiian Homes Commission Act (passed by Congress in 1920) into the Hawaii

State Constitution, makes future changes difficult (they can be made only with the consent of Congress), and obligates the state to continue to work earnestly "for the rehabilitation of the Hawaiian race." An amendment was adopted on June 27, 1959, which distinguished between provisions of the 1920 act which could be changed in a normal fashion and those which are considered essential and could be changed only with the consent of Congress.

Other Language Laws, Excluding School Laws

The State of Hawaii does not have an official anthem. "Hawaii Ponoi," which was the official anthem of the Hawaiian kingdom, is used as an unofficial anthem and is always sung in Hawaiian. There have been suggestions to make the anthem official, but as it is a pledge of loyalty to the king and the kingdom, it does not make a very good official song.

Ever since printed versions of the Island laws have existed, they have been published in English and Hawaiian, not on the basis of a statutory regulation but as a result of a continued practice by the legislature. At first in cases of dispute the Hawaiian version reigned (Laws 1864, Sec. 68, 1 H 402, 1 H 457). It seems that in 1924 the precedence of the English version was finally secured (Revised Laws 1925, Sec. 26; Revised Laws 1955, 71, Sec. 1-6).

According to a 1901 law (Kloss 1940, 590-591) all laws had to be published in English in a daily newspaper and in Hawaiian in a Hawaiian weekly; only with publication did they become legally binding. This provision is meaningless today, since no periodicals in the Hawaiian language exist any more, only a Sunday school quarterly *The Friend* edited in Honolulu by the Reverend E. Kahale of the United Church of Christ. In 1930 two weeklies were still published, the *Nupepa Kuokoa* (founded in 1863) and a Sunday school paper.

Of other laws concerning the use of the Hawaiian language which were adopted during the territorial phase or were effective during the same time, the following have since been repealed or invalidated: In 1933 an 1894 law concerning the official announcement of impending elections [Revised Laws 1925, Sec. 57; Act 96 (2) Session Laws 1933; Orig. Sec. 69 Rules and Regulations of 7/17/1894, amended on 3/11/1907, L. 6 (1)].

In 1929 a 1913 law concerning the announcement of primaries (R.L. 1925, Sec. 35; amend. 1929 c. 177 and 1933 c. 97; recent version R.L. 1955, 11-93).

Still in effect in 1970 were provisions from 1894, concerning bilingual ballots [R.L. 1955, Sec. 11-38 of 7/17/1894, amended on 4/30/1900 Organic Act 67; 4/6/1911, L. 67 (1); 5/13/1943, L. 192 (2)]; from 1876, concerning announcements relative to the disposal of government land (R.L. 1955, Sec. 99-44 of 9/25/1876); from 1913, concerning announcements relative to the sale of government land (R.L. 1955, Sec. 99-41, with the addition "not ratified by Congress," which makes it questionable whether the provision ever became effective); also from 1913, concerning the distribution of homestead land (R.L. 1955, Sec. 99-75, with the addition "not ratified by Congress," which makes it likewise questionable).

Very impressive is a 1921 law concerning the "foreign-language" press (R.L. 1955, Sec. 167-20). It prescribes that the editors of non-English newspapers and related information sheets must submit immediately upon publication a copy to the state archive and adds: "Every language except the English and Hawaiian languages shall be considered a foreign language." In the spirit of this law the legislature repeatedly appropriated funds for the cultivation of Hawaiian: $10,000 for the publication of a dictionary in 1913; $20,000 for the same purpose in 1957; $25,000 in 1959 (at the time of statehood) for the general purpose of the "preservation of the Hawaiian language, art, and culture." The state university was entrusted with the handling of the last sum. The University then appointed a Committee for the Preservation of Hawaiian Language and Culture. Acting in this capacity, the University did, among other things, finance a textbook of Hawaiian (Elbert and Keala 1961) and introduced language courses for the faculty of the university.

Contrary to a popularly held view, no law or decree was ever issued requiring that street signs must be in both English and Hawaiian. There is, however, a policy in the city of Honolulu to give Hawaiian names to streets. The signs with the names of the streets have only the Hawaiian name, as there is no need to translate this type of sign which, in many cases, may be a proper name that does not lend itself to translation.

School Language Laws

As shown in Section 7-3, English had already become the language of the schools during the time of the Hawaiian kingdom. A school law (1896) during the Republic (Kloss 1940, 593) prescribed English as the language of instruction for all public and private elementary schools. The introduction of non-English languages was possible only with the specific permission of the school authorities, each case requiring separate permission. No exceptions were made for the Hawaiian language. At the time of annexation the Hawaiians had thus already abandoned a systematic cultivation of their language.

Under American rule measures were once more taken in favor of the Hawaiian language. The 1896 school law was amended in 1919 and provided that Hawaiian should be taught as a subject in all high schools and teachers' colleges. For high schools this provision was in effect until 1965 (R.L. 1955, 40-43; Kloss 1940, 594; Adam 1959, 166). On May 2, 1923, the legislature appropriated $2,000 for the writing and publication of textbooks in Hawaiian. Hawaiian was actually taught for some time not only as an elective in many high schools but, according to 1931 information from the Superintendent of Public Instruction (Kloss 1940, 594), also in some elementary schools with a large proportion of Hawaiian students.

In 1965 the State Legislature deleted that portion of the statute which made it mandatory to provide instruction in the Hawaiian language for all those wanting to learn Hawaiian. Hawaiian continued to be offered as an elective where a sufficient number of students elected it and a qualified teacher was available to teach it. The latter condition, however, was growing increasingly difficult to meet, and the time seems not far off when the teaching of Hawaiian will be restricted to college and university level.

In the same year the legislature struck out the provision in the Revised Laws that (apart from the privilege granted to the Hawaiian language) all instruction would be in English. This step was based on the expressed belief that, because English was the undisputed language of the nation, it was redundant to state the obvious (State Department of Education 1969).

According to a 1935 law, in the elementary schools of the settlements of homesteaders under the Hawaiian Home Commission (1921, see above), daily instruction of at least ten minutes in Hawaiian conversation or writing was to be given (Kloss 1940, 595). The modesty of this concession prompted some ironical remarks by H. L. Mencken (1948, 241). In the private Kamehameha Schools, which admitted only students of at least one-eighth Hawaiian blood, the language was an elective from 1924 to 1931 (Beaglehole, p. 103) but seems to have been introduced again at a later time, since according to Adam (1959, 166) it was then a subject of instruction in the Kamehameha schools. For 1960, there were 263 students who were listed as enrolled in Hawaiian classes below the seventh grade in regular public schools in Hilo (Breunig 1961, 6, 24). In 1965 there were three public elementary schools teaching Hawaiian to 867 pupils, and three public high schools teaching Hawaiian to 127 students (*The Status of the Foreign Language Program in Hawaii's Public Schools* 1965, 12, 15, 27).

This promotion of the Hawaiian language, though modest, was for a long time in sharp contrast to the treatment of other non-English, especially Asian, languages. Since they were practically excluded from the regular schools after 1896 (see above), the Asians established many supplementary schools, so-called language schools. At the end of World War I there were 163 (of which 7 were Chinese, 9 Korean, and the rest Japanese) of these schools, with 300 teachers and 20,000 students. These schools were restricted by a 1920 law which stated at the beginning (Kloss 1942, 786-789): "The term 'Foreign Language School' as used in this chapter shall be construed to mean any school which is conducted in any language other than the English language or the Hawaiian language except Sabbath schools." It continued by saying that teachers in these schools were not permitted to work without a teacher's license. This license, however, would be granted to them only if they were good followers of democracy and had a knowledge of English; they were not permitted to teach longer than 1 hour per day, 6 hours per week, and 38 weeks per year; and they had to use textbooks which presupposed a command of conversational English on the part of the students.

The Japanese began fighting these restrictions, and the United States Supreme Court ruled in 1927 in *Farrington* v. *Tokushige* (see also Section 3-4) that the law was in violation of the Fifth Amendment of the United States Constitution. The language schools again began to flourish; in 1936 there existed 178 Japanese, 12 Chinese, and 9 Korean schools. During World War II the Japanese schools were immediately closed, the textbooks burned, and the teachers

Table 7-3   Public School Students of Foreign Languages in
             Hawaii in 1965

Public School	Japanese	Chinese	Spanish	French
Elementary	2,330	841		
High School	1,463	113	3,932	3,012

sent to the relocation camps for the mainland Japanese (Aspinwall 1960, 8; see also Section 3-1). Also during World War II a law restricting language schools was again passed in 1943 according to which foreign language instruction of any kind (1) could be given only to students who had completed the third grade and (2) in cases of students under fifteen years of age, could be given only by teachers who had a good command of English (Law 104 of 1943 = R.L. 1945 c. 31; text also 336 U.S. 372).

In this case the Chinese went to court and were upheld by the Federal District Court in San Francisco in 1947 (Kuykendall and Day 1949, 244-245; 11 F 2d 710). The Supreme Court reversed the decision on a procedural ground. In 1949 the law was greatly tempered, and after statehood it was dropped altogether. In 1966 there were still 88 Japanese language schools, attended by 12,600 students, and three Chinese language schools [775 *Stainback* v. *M. O. Hook*, 336 U.S. 369 (1949); R.L. 1955, 41-1 to 41-4; Leibowitz 1969, 18-19].

During the 1950s the climate changed; anti-Japanese feelings declined and the FLES movement (Section 2-2) had its effects in the Islands. In the year 1960, there were 673 students who took Japanese in regular public schoools of 10 communities, and in the schools of Honolulu, 214 were taking Chinese (Breunig 1961, 6). Table 7-3 shows the numbers of students studying Japanese and Chinese in the public schools and shows that these were rather small groups compared with the students of Spanish and French (*The Status of the Foreign Language Program in Hawaii's Public Schools* 1965, 12, 15, 27).

At the state university the numerous students of Japanese and Chinese descent (57% and 17% of all students in 1960) and the few (2%) of Hawaiian descent are systematically encouraged to study the language of their ancestors. This holds true also for non-Asian languages. Until 1956, for example, Portuguese was taught at the University because the territorial legislature had ordered it in order to accommodate the descendants of the Portuguese immigrants (Aspinwall 1960, 9). A special Hawaiian Association of Language Teachers (1957) devotes considerable efforts to spreading this teaching, which lies halfway between nationality rights and cultural exchange. According to a letter from Mrs. E. Freitas of Honolulu, the Hawaiian Association of Language Teachers does not include teachers of the private Japanese and Chinese language schools (Aspinwall 1960, 11-12). However, private colleges of the Islands participate in the Association of Language Teachers. In addition to German, Church College offers Hawaiian,

Chinese, Japanese, and Samoan; Jackson College, in addition to regular offerings in French and Spanish, also teaches Chinese, Japanese, Korean, Tagalog, and German as electives (Aspinwall 1960, 10).

Language laws of Hawaii have a double nature. If one compares the position of the Hawaiian language with that of its sister languages in both parts of Samoa and in New Zealand or with that of the Eskimos on Greenland, one has to say that a development which was very promising until 1850 has fizzled. But if one is to compare the position of Hawaiian to that of Japanese and other immigrant languages of Hawaii, the situation is quite different. Hawaiian was clearly put in a privileged position as compared to these languages, and there are hardly similar laws in the legal systems of other states which express the difference between later immigrants and established settlers as clearly as those 1920-1921 laws (listed above) according to which only those schools and newspapers are considered "foreign-language" which are neither in English nor in the Hawaiian language.

7-4   THE FREE ASSOCIATED STATE OF PUERTO RICO

Background

In 1508 the Spaniards began their exploration and settlement of the Island of Puerto Rico. Around 1620 the present capital of San Juan was founded. The English form of the name for the Island, Porto Rico, was officially used until 1932. Since then the Spanish form, Puerto Rico, has been used. The Island of Puerto Rico has an area of 3,450 square miles (8,900 square kilometers).

By the end of the sixteenth century the indigenous Indian population had become partially extinct and had been absorbed by the white population. The island did not participate in the Ibero-American independence movements at the beginning of the nineteenth century. On the contrary, after 1810 the island admitted about 7,000 loyalists from the mainland, mostly from Venezuela, who came to dominate the intellectual life of the island and who cultivated close contact with Spain. Trade with non-Spanish countries and immigration from these countries was liberalized in 1815.

Table 7-4   Increasing Population of Puerto Rico

	1815	1899	1960	1970
Population	221,000	885,900	2,349,500	2,712,000

On December 10, 1898, the island was ceded by Spain to the United States. The increasing population of the Island is shown in Table 7-4. Puerto Rico has had a high birth rate and, during the twentieth century, a decreasing mortality rate so that the population has increased very rapidly. During the 1950s a mass emigration to the United States eased the pressure to a certain degree: In 1960 the Puerto Rican population on the mainland of the United States was estimated at 850,000.

Between the years 1510 and 1820 black slaves were imported. As a result, an Afro-Puerto Rican racial group of Spanish tongue came into existence which was concentrated in the coastal districts, primarily those of the northeast. That the percentage of colored persons decreased from 56% in 1820 to 36% in 1897 and to 20% in 1950 is not the result of a white immigration or a lower birth rate among the colored population but rather the result of the fact that hundreds of thousands had crossed the color bar and had been absorbed into the white population. In 1960 there was no count of the colored population. Most of the colored people have some white blood anyway; as early as 1910 only 50,200 pure-blooded Negroes were reported in addition to the 335,000 mulattoes.

The border between the white and colored population is not so clearly one of different skins, as on the North American mainland, but rather one of social differences, as on the Spanish American mainland. This indeed provides no protection against social decline for whites, and it also provides an obstacle to rising in the social scale for colored people. Nevertheless the situation quite often permits individual nonwhites to become part of the white world as a result of personal initiative and achievement, a process which constantly drains much talent from the colored population.

In the vernacular of the Puerto Ricans, the Andalusian and Estremaduran characteristics predominate (Malaret 1937; Tomas 1948). In the cities the influence of English is noticeable, particularly among the younger generation.

The first newspaper was established around 1806, the first periodical, *Boletin Mercantil,* in 1839. As a result of the strong process of consolidation, the newspapers are all located in San Juan today. In connection with the University alone, 20 periodicals are published, of which 3 are in English. The University publishes also 5 study series. Ayer's otherwise highly useful *Directory of Newspapers and Periodicals* is completely useless for Puerto Rico, since it lists no periodicals and perhaps not even all the newspapers.

In contrast to the case in New Mexico, literature in the Spanish language developed relatively early and extensively. The first anthology, *Aguinaldo Puerto Riqueno,* appeared as early as 1843. A Royal Academy, founded in 1851, promoted this development. The importance of the literature for the ethnic solidarity of the Puerto Ricans is shown by the fact that the island legislature in 1905 ordered for the use of the schools the compilation of an anthology of the best native literature (Osuña 1949, 204). On the basis of this resolution by the legislature, M. F. Jancos edited *Antologia Puertoriquena* (see also Cabrera 1956). More recently there have appeared two volumes, *Poesia Puertoriquena,* one for secondary schools (1955), the other for elementary schools (1958).

Problems of Self-Government until 1952

During Spanish times there were attempts at home rules and beginnings of self-government (Quinones 1957). In 1868 a rebellion to achieve the goal of independence failed because it did not have any noticeable response among the masses. In the following year the island was granted the establishment of the

Disputacion Provincial, a provincial legislative body, which convened for the first time in 1871.

Puerto Rican delegates participated also in drafting the Spanish constitution of 1876 which was not to become effective in the island until 1881 and which was never implemented. A movement for autonomy, gaining in strength after 1887, succeeded in obtaining far-reaching autonomy for the island in 1897. (The program for this movement is given in Quinoñes 1957.) In addition to the Governor General, who was appointed by the King, there was an elected house of representatives and a so-called Administrative Council, 8 of whose members were elected and 7 appointed by the Governor General. The House was permitted to send a delegate to all negotiations which Spain undertook with third powers for the purpose of reaching a trade agreement which would affect Puerto Rico and was authorized to establish its own tariff rates. All institutions of self-government provided for in this charter were established but could not become active because of the Spanish-American War.

The United States took the position that Puerto Rico had not become an integrated part of the United States (Section 7-1). The Peace Treaty of 1898 (Article IX, 2; text in Kloss 1940, 540) left expressly to Congress the regulation of civil rights and the legal status of the inhabitants, while the inhabitants of Louisiana and New Mexico had been promised equal political rights in the cession treaties. The right for an option was also granted only to those few inhabitants who had been born in Spain.

In the Foraker Act (April 12, 1900, section 734) Congress granted the Island an elected legislature. The Governor, however, was appointed by the United States President as were the six members of the Cabinet who, together with five other persons (appointed by the President with the advice of the Senate), formed the Executive Council. This council together with the House of Representatives formed the legislative assembly, hardly a liberal amalgamation of executive and legislative power. The authority of the Legislative Council was, according to Section 32, unlimited within the framework of the United States Constitution, i.e., it went as far as in a State or in an incorporated Territory (*Puerto Rico* v. *Shell Co.*; *Ponce* v. *Roman Catholic Apostolic Church*; *Grommer* v. *Standard Dredging Co.*; *Puerto Rico* v. *Rosalio y Castillo*).

A symptom of the spirit of the Foraker Act is that in Article 7 the Puerto Ricans were not given United States citizenship but a separate Puerto Rican citizenship. This was primarily intended as a negative move.

But even though the Puerto Ricans were denied American citizenship, the fact that "The People of Porto Rico" collectively was declared a legal person according to public law could be interpreted as granting the status of a legal person to an ethnic minority. At that time it would have been difficult to determine the value of this action so far as nationality rights were concerned, but objectively speaking, it was nevertheless important (see Section 9-1). Within the new economic policy adopted by Congress, a resolution (31 Stat. at L. 716) of May 1, 1900, was especially significant; this resolution limited the real estate holdings of individuals and joint stock companies to 500 acres. For a long time this resolution was largely ignored by the Anglo-American commercial groups so that the mass of rural population was transformed into workers; in 1935 we find 180,800 agricultural workers as compared with only 45,900 independent farmers and tenants.

The political parties of the Island rallied almost exclusively around the question of the political status of the Island and the relationship to the mainland parties. A party of the Republicans, which came into existence in 1899, aspired to gradually achieving statehood. The party of the Unionists (from 1900 to 1904 still called Federalists) came into existence in 1900 as a reaction to the Foraker Act. The Unionists aspired to gradually advancing to the standing of an autonomous country after the then Cuban model, i.e., a kind of protectorate with only slightly restricted independence. Most debates between the two parties continued to center around the distant objectives of statehood or independence, even though the plight of the rural workers after World War I gave rise to a Socialist Party which was quite strong at times.

In 1922 the radical Nationalist Party was formed. At first it was rather small. From 1936 to 1945, under the leadership of the belligerent Pedro Albizu Campos (imprisoned after 1937), the Nationalist Party attracted considerable attention through its terrorist methods. Thus the conviction was deepened that the previous status was untenable. The Nacionalistas received 5,032 votes of a 278,000 total in 1932. They boycotted the 1936 elections and in 1937 and 1950 bloody local clashes occurred between Nacionalistas and American troops.

The Organic Act of 1900 was scheduled to be succeeded in 1910 by the more liberal Olmstead Act, but it failed in the Senate after it had been passed by the House. In 1914 a new proposal was put before Congress but was not voted on as a result of the beginning of World War I. But on March 2, 1917, a new Organic Act, the Jones Act (39 Stat. at L. 951), became effective. Among other things, it brought four important improvements: the Puerto Ricans became American citizens, they obtained a bill of rights and an elected senate, and the President appointed in addition to the Governor only two members of the executive council while the other five were appointed by the Governor with the advice and consent of the Island Senate. While in 1900 five of the eleven members of the executive council had to be born in Puerto Rico, five of the seven members now had to have been Island residents for at least one year. In practice this led to a strong Spanish majority in the island cabinet.

The granting of American citizenship led the Puerto Ricans to assume that their island was from now on an incorporated territory. The Federal District Court for Puerto Rico decided also along these lines (Puerto Rican Federal Reports 1917, 452, 527), especially since the United States Supreme Court had justified a similar ruling for Alaska in 1904 by an analogous situation (*Rasmussen* v. *United States*). But with respect to Puerto Rico the United States Supreme Court ruled in 1922 in *Balzac* v. *People of Puerto Rico* that the Island was still an unincorporated territory.

Judging by absolute standards, after 1917 Puerto Rico enjoyed a considerable degree of self-government. But, within the framework of a basically free and federal country like the United States, the position of Puerto Rico remained unsatisfactory. The 1917 solution was much behind even the Spanish solution of 1897. Consequently the people of the island remained dissatisfied. When the Republican Governor from the mainland, E. M. Reilly, attempted to govern against a Union Party majority, he was forced to resign in 1923. During the following years almost all governors showed a great deal of understanding for Puerto Rico.

After 1922, the Union Party advocated the status of a "free associated state" for Puerto Rico. Thus they favored a middle of the road position between independence and statehood. A proposal to this effect, which was drafted by the Puerto Rican Mondragon, was put before the United States Congress in 1922. This concept of the "free associated state" was approximately that of dominion or commonwealth status. The commonwealth platform of the Unionists is reprinted in the *Blue Book of Puerto Rico* (1923). Theodore Roosevelt, Jr., the most popular of the Anglo-American Governors (1929-1931), belonged to the advocates of commonwealth status. After 1931, however, the Union Party returned to their demand for independence.

It is interesting that Congress, by an Act of May 29, 1928 (Section 128), renounced its right to annul any new law adopted by the Island legislature but a few months later restored the former situation by Section 1 of an Act of February 28, 1929 (*Documents on the Constitutional History of Puerto Rico* 1964, 289).

While during the election campaigns of the 1930s the question of "component state or independent state" remained in the forefront, the economic situation of the Island became increasingly intolerable. In 1930 unemployed and part-time workers constituted 60% of the wage earners. Four years later Congress fixed the import quota for Puerto Rican sugar at four-fifths of the one-million-ton capacity of the Island sugar industry. But sugar accounted in value for two-thirds of the exports to the United States; in 1936-1937 the Island sold to the United States sugar worth $112.9 million as compared to only $2.1 million to the rest of the world.

The sugar, coffee, and tobacco plantations were predominantly owned by mainland companies; in spite of the 500 acre clause of 1900, 27 "farms" (less than 0.1% of all agricultural enterprises), for example, owned in 1940 more than 12.5% of the agriculturally used area and 46% of all agricultural tools and machines. All this led to sustained loss in dividends; in 1928 a $14 million surplus in exports was more than offset by a $25 million deficit in the balance of payments. The average income was so low that the larger part of the population was chronically undernourished.

Into this situation came Muñoz Marín (born 1898), the great son of an important father. His father, Muñoz Rivera (1859-1916), had headed the autonomous Island Government of 1897. In 1900 he founded the party of the

Federalists, later called Unionists. Between 1911 and 1916, he represented the Island as Resident Commissioner in Washington, D. C.

Like his father, Muñoz Marín was a statesman and poet. In 1938 he founded the Democratic Peoples Party (Partido Popular Democratico), which proclaimed the priority of economic and social questions. In the elections of 1940, the party scored 38% of the votes and became a partner of the coalition government. After 1944, the party ruled alone until 1968, when it increased its share of the votes to 64%—383,600 votes against 101,800 votes for the Union Republicans and 68,100 for the Socialists (Table 7-5).

The Democratic Peoples Party under Muñoz Marín initiated under the name "operation bootstrap" a large-scale program for the economic strengthening of the Island. The Puerto Rican Industrial Development Company, PRIDCO (Administración de Fomento Económico, 1942), which was established for this purpose under the energetic Teodoro Moscoso, made some state socialist attempts during the first years, but very soon turned to an intensive promotion of private initiative by using a ten-year tax holiday and the low wage level of the Island as major incentives. By about 1960 almost 800 industrial plants had been newly constructed, of which three-fourths maintained themselves. Based on a 1940 Supreme Court decision (*People of Puerto Rico* v. *Rupert Hermanos*) which reaffirmed the right of Puerto Rico to enforce the 500 acre limit for real estate owners, the government began to attack the latifundia of the commercial companies and attempted to supplement the sugar industry by the introduction of new cultures (pineapple) or the reintroduction of almost extinct cultures (coffee) and by the modernization of the cattle and dairy industry.

Promotion of social housing, highway systems, hotels, and tourism are other important sectors of this economic development. Especially urgent was the expansion of the school system. During the period from 1940 to 1958, expenses for education increased more than eightfold while the net income of the entire population increased almost fivefold and the per capita income increased almost fourfold (Table 7-6).

Progress was clearly evident, even though all poverty could not be eliminated. Muñoz Marín proclaimed that the 1950 standard of living in the continental United States would be the goal to be reached by 1975 in Puerto Rico. Especially because of its economic and social policy, but not merely because of it, Puerto Rico has become the destination of countless visits from other developing countries; Jamaica, Surinam, and Trinidad were inspired in their own development programs by the Puerto Rican model.

The Commonwealth Constitution of 1952

Only after the economic rejuvenation of the island had been successfully initiated did Muñoz and his Peoples Party attempt to bring about fundamental changes in the political field also by adding the policy of "operation Commonwealth" to the economic policy of "operation bootstrap." It is proof of Muñoz Marín's political

Table 7-5   Number of Votes in Thousands Received by Puerto Rican Parties

Party	Goal	1944	1948	1952	1956	1960	1964	1968
Partido Popular Democrático	Commonwealth	383	392	429	433	458	487	368
People's Party	Commonwealth							88
Unión Republican Estadista	Statehood	102	88	85	173	252	285	4
Partido Nuevo Progresista founded in 1967	Statehood							391
Indepentistas	Independence		66	126	86	24	22	25
Socialists	Statehood	68	64	22				
Liberals (Reformista)	Independence	39	28					

Table 7-6   Some Socioeconomic Data for Puerto Rico

Socioeconomic Factor	1940	1958
Net per capita income	$122	$469
Net income of population		
75% from business	$228,000,000	$1,148,000,000
Value of agricultural production	$84,000,000	$228,000,000
Number of motor vehicles	$27,000	$140,000
Expenditures for education	$7,300,000	$63,000,000
Illiterates	32%	16%

genius that he later added to the economic program a cultural rejuvenation movement, "operation serenity" (Hancock 1960, 113-115). He is also credited with having coined the phrase "to govern means to invent."

One of his first preliminary political accomplishments had been to have the Governor be elected by the people. This was achieved by a federal law of 1947, the Elective Governor Act, which stated moreover that the elected governor in turn would appoint all leading officials with the exception of the Auditor but including the Judges of the Supreme Court of the island. This regulation was unique in the history of American territories. And of course Muñoz was elected. In 1946 a Puerto Rican, Jesus Pinero, had for the first time been appointed the governor.

After this a comprehensive political rearrangement was desired. This new attempt differed from similar plans of the 1920s primarily in that it was accomplished not by a unilateral act of Congress but rather as the result of a bilateral treaty. Federal Law No. 600 of 1950, drafted "in the nature of a compact," empowered the people of Puerto Rico to write a new constitution for themselves through a constitutional convention as specified in the law; this constitution would at first have to be approved by the Island population and then by Congress and would finally be ratified by the Island legislature and proclaimed by the President. Certain parts of the 1917 Organic Act which regulated the relations between the Island and the Union and which are listed verbatim in Public Law 600 under the title "Federal Relations Act" were to remain in effect.

An island-wide referendum of July 4, 1951, approved Law No. 600 including the procedure outlined in it and the Federal Relations Act, a decision which may well be interpreted as a kind of approval given by those who were governed to the form they were governed by.

The constitution, drafted by a constitutional convention, was adopted by the people on March 3, 1952, with 374,600 votes for and 82,900 votes against. Even the advocates of statehood for the larger part voted "Yes." The United States House of Representatives approved the Constitution en bloc while the Senate eliminated some essential provisions, partially because they appeared to be too leftist (for example, the basic right to work and the right to strike). While Article II (20) was deleted, Article II (5) and Article VII (3) were altered. The original wording of the Constitution may be found in *Notes and Comments on the Constitution of the Commonwealth of Puerto Rico* (1952).

Thus a unilateral act was taken by which the character of this constitution as a quasi-treaty was certainly watered down even though it was not changed in form. Fortunately, firm Puerto Rican opposition caused Congress to reject a proposal that all future amendments to the Constitution must be approved by Congress (*Documents on the Constitutional History of Puerto Rico* 1964, 269). On July 25, 1952, Governor Muñoz promulgated the constitution; it was approved in its slightly altered wording by a plebiscite on November 4, 1952.

On November 27, 1953, the General Assembly of the United Nations, with votes of 26 for, 16 against, and 18 abstaining, agreed that the United States should discontinue its annual report on Puerto Rico since the latter could no longer be considered a dependency. For details about the debate in the United Nations, see the session records and also the *Yearbook of the United Nations,* 1953 (1954, 535-539) and Sady (1957, 98-102). The resolution mentioned the ethnolinguistic aspects of Puerto Rico's new status: "The agreement . . . , in forming a political association which respects the individuality and the cultural characteristics of Puerto Rico, maintains the spiritual bonds between Puerto Rico and Latin America."

However, in general it was the weaker nations who voted for the American proposal. In addition to the United States itself, 16 Latin American countries voted for the United States proposal plus Ethiopia, China (Formosa), Iran, Israel, Liberia, the Philippines, Thailand, and Turkey. Against it were, in addition to 6 Communist votes (including Yugoslavia), 3 American countries (Guatemala, Canada, Mexico), Australia, Belgium, Burma, India, Indonesia, Iraq, and South Africa. Abstaining were, in addition to 2 Latin American countries (Argentina and Venezuela), the great powers France and Great Britain, also Egypt, Afghanistan, Denmark, Iceland, Yemen, Lebanon, Luxemburg, New Zealand, the Netherlands, Norway, Pakistan, Saudi Arabia, Sweden, and Syria. In the preceding debate representatives of the Eastern block as well as those from Burma, Guatemala, Honduras, India, Indonesia, and Mexico had questioned the contention that Puerto Rico enjoyed complete self-government. The representative of Mexico had declared that Puerto Rico enjoyed fewer rights as a Commonwealth than under the 1897 constitution granted by the Spaniards.

Certainly an important factor in the voting was the tendency of many nonbloc nations to consider inadequate any solution short of independence or integration. Some member nations "seemed to be willing to put their own judgment or that of the General Assembly over the freely expressed desire of the affected population" (Sady 1957, 102).

But it was clearly pointed out by the French expert, Professor Georges Fischer (1954, 169-199), that the regulation of 1950-1952 did not quite live up to the list of features compiled by the United Nations in 1953 to gain a better frame of reference for determining when the claim to self-determination could be considered fulfilled (United Nations Doc. A/2630; Kloss 1962, 75-78; 93-94;

Fahrni 1967, 44-50). The compilation of this list, which does not consider independence as the only possible solution, was closely connected with the United Nations debate about the Puerto Rican question, as shown by the date of the respective United Nations resolutions, both of November 27, 1953, and also with the new status arrangement of the Netherlands Antilles and Surinam within the framework of the Kingdom of the Netherlands (1954).

The contention that self-determination could be achieved only by independence or integration had at that time been abandoned by the United Nations Organization (Section 9-1). Association as a third solution in addition to independence and "integration" (incorporation) has been considered by Muñoz Marín himself as the best answer to the particular problems of smaller ethnic groups. He called it "a brand new device to save relatively small segments of cultural groups from the agonies of strident nationalism or the indignities of continued colonialism" (Hunter 1959, 50).

More recently a majority of United Nations member states has swung back to the position that, even for very small nations, independence should be the only desirable and acceptable goal, an attitude which runs counter to common sense (Fahrni 1967, 60-62). The Soviet Union, while holding, not entirely without reason, that in our supranational age independence is an outmoded goal for 50 million Ukrainians, has never ceased to demand independence for the 5,000 inhabitants of the Island of Nauru. A reappraisal of the whole issue has been overdue in the light of the solutions found for such places as Puerto Rico, the Faroe Islands, Surinam, and the Cook Islands.

The official English term for the Island is *Commonwealth*, i.e., the designation given to the Philippines from 1935 to 1946 and equivalent to the Spanish *"estado libro asociado."* The term *Commonwealth* as used by the states of Kentucky, Massachusetts, Pennsylvania, and Virginia has only decorative significance and does not constitute a distinct legal status. The English word has been preempted in American political terminology to refer to member states of the Union. In German the term "Commonwealth" can perhaps be best represented by *Beistaat*. The term *zugewandte Orte* was used in Switzerland before 1798 for associated polities whose legal basis was not completely equal with that of the older cantons.

The Puerto Rican constitution begins with a long preamble which states (in Section 5): "We consider as determining factors in our life (1) our citizenship of the United States of America and our aspiration continually to enrich our democratic heritage in the individual and collective enjoyment of its rights and privileges; (2) our loyalty to the principles of the federal Constitution; (3) the coexistence in Puerto Rico of the two great cultures of the American Hemisphere."

The third point refers to the special position of the Puerto Rican people as an ethnic group.

The Constitution, which we are of course unable to present here with any degree of completeness, is typical for that of a state, not of a province. The areas of authority of the commonwealth are basically the same as those of a state of the Union with only a few negative exceptions (for example, naturalization and debt of the Commonwealth). Congress has waived its right to annul Puerto Rican laws during the time that the Constitution remains in effect. The Island continues to belong to the American tariff area, and the Union retains a monopoly in foreign policy and military matters. In contrast to a state, Puerto Rico does not participate in the congressional or presidential elections. As it had done before 1952, Puerto Rico can influence policy and legislation of the Union only through its popularly elected Resident Commissioner, who can participate in Congressional debates but cannot vote. The compensation for this serious shortcoming consists not in the fact that the Union in turn does not send a representative of its own to the Island (there exists not even a counterpart of the Governor General who serves as a mere symbol of the crown in the non-European states of the once British Commonwealth), but rather in the fact that the Union does not levy any taxes on the Island. This is according to the principle of "no taxation without representation."

The Constitution of 1952 is considered very progressive. In several points it realizes the pet demands made by leading North American political scientists and administrative experts. Friedrich (1959, p. 42) says, "It corresponds to the blueprints of public administrative theorists." The position of the Governor is extremely strong; the members of the island cabinet are appointed by him, not elected. Should a weak person become governor, his powerful position has built-in dangers. In the provisions of the Constitution concerning the legislature, the special protection granted in Article III (7) to the minority parties deserves attention. In the provisions concerning the judiciary branch of government the organization of all Island courts is concentrated into one single court. One weakness of the Constitution is the absence of an elected Lieutenant Governor. The Secretary of State, who is also appointed by the Governor, serves as his deputy in case of death, sickness, or resignation of the Governor. Another and far more important shortcoming is the absence of genuine municipal self-government (Friedrich 1959, 42-43). This strikes one as particularly odd in a country which was so unified in its passionate insistence upon self-administration, but this shortcoming is partially offset by the vigorous development of elementary education and community development (Friedrich 1959, 12, 44; Kloss 1960).

Attempts at Improvement of Commonwealth Status

The present status of Puerto Rico shows some obvious weakness (Freidrich 1959, 32; Hunter 1959, 51, 85; Wells 1955, 215-218). The Island can participate in Congressional debates only (through its Resident Commissioner) but not in the voting about federal laws which affect the Island directly. The same goes for questions of foreign policy or international trade measures and treaties which affect the Island indirectly and for matters of defense, even though the youth of the Island serve in the armed forces. Difficulties arose in connection with the applicability of new federal laws in Puerto Rico. In some matters the Island has less authority than the states of the Union (see above). It is clear that the Island is still too poor to make a contribution to the federal treasury, but even for the future, there is foreseen no such contribution and corresponding right of co-determination, but rather a sort of permanent half-coming-of-age. Up to the present the Island has not joined any of the subsidiary agencies of the United Nations.

Numerous proposals have been made outlining what changes should be introduced to improve the status of the Island. A permanent participation of the Island has been suggested in connection with determining, among other things, which new federal laws should be considered as being not locally applicable. Thought has been given to the possibility of replacing many federal offices on the Island by commonwealth offices which would serve the particular function on behalf of the Federal Government, which would be a rare solution in the United States. Regular conferences have been suggested between the State Department or even the President and the Island government concerning United States policy in the West Indies and Latin America. Another proposal was made for the provident establishment of a regular, even if merely symbolic, contribution of the Island to the federal treasury which would be due as soon as the Island should reach a certain level of prosperity.

Even more important than such individual proposals is the basic question by which method Law No. 600 of 1950 and the Constitution of 1952 can be changed at all. There exist two opposing points of view.

On one hand, we find numerous Anglo-Americans who say that Puerto Rico is basically still a territory and that Congress still has ultimate authority over the Island (Helfeld 1952, 225ff.; Gordon 1953, 42ff.). Although Congress under the regulation of 1950/52 cannot annul an island law, it can annul this very regulation at any time and at its own discretion and thus regain full freedom of action and full authority. The fact that Law No. 600 acquired the character of a treaty was entirely the result of Congressional preference; Congress is therefore at liberty to replace this regulation unilaterally by another regulation. Says Helfeld (1952, 225ff.), "The compact is not a contract in a commercial sense. It expresses a method Congress chose to use in place of direct legislation."

On the other hand, many Anglo-Americans and of course most of the Puerto Ricans maintain that a contract has been made which equally binds Congress and the Island regarding the 1952 Constitution. Some people such as Henry Wells and Petro Muñoz Amato (Friedrich 1959, 80) even claim that Puerto Rico could unilaterally change this constitution. C. J. Friedrich (pp. 79-80) rejects this thesis as well as the claim of undiluted Congressional authority. The United States Supreme Court would have to decide whether or not the Island could still be considered unincorporated. As Friedrich (p. 79) says, "Does *Downes* v. *Bidwell* still apply? I should say no." In this question every Congress is bound by the word of its predecessor as of 1950.

A third group of authors finds that both views are accurate. McIntosh (1955, 205, 214) concludes in the same article that "The island remains an unincorporated territory" and that "Puerto Rico might justly be called a new kind of state." Writing as a man with a practical bent, Hunter (1959, 24-25) thinks it

Table 7-7   Status of Puerto Rico as Territory or State as Indicated by Decisions of the U. S. Courts

Court	Case	Date	Statement Concerning Status
United States Supreme Court	Koppel v Bingham	1909	Puerto Rico a territory within the meaning of Sec. 5278 of the Revised Statutes.
United States Supreme Court	People of Puerto Rico v Shell	1937	Puerto Rico not a territory within the reach of the Sixth and Seventh Amendments.
United States District Court San Juan	Mora v Torres	1953 June 19	Puerto Rico not a federated state; the Fourteenth Amendment and the Interstate Commerce Clause are not applicable.
United States Court of Appeals First Circuit	Mora v Mejias	1953 July 24	"Puerto Rico has . . . not become a State in the Federal Union like the 48 States but it would seem to have become a State within a common and accepted meaning of the word."
United States District Court San Juan	Mora v Mejias	1953 Nov. 3	"Within the intendment and policy of Sec. 2281, Title 28 U.S.C.A., the Commonwealth of Puerto Rico must be considered a State."
United States District Court San Juan	Consentino v Longshoremen's Association	1954	"Puerto Rico is no longer a Territory in the sense that the term is used in the constitution."
United States District Court San Juan	United States v Figueros Rios	1956	Puerto Rico no longer a "Territory or possession" within the meaning of 15. U.S.C.A., Ch. 18, Secs. 201-909.
United States District Court N.D., Illinois	Detres v Lions	1955	Puerto Rico not a Territory as the term is used in Sec. 1332(b) Judicial Code.
United States Court of Appeals	Detres v Lions	1956	Judgment of District Court reversed.

possible that those who favor unrestricted Congressional authority may be theoretically accurate but thinks it completely inconceivable that Congress would ever use it. It has also been maintained in this connection that Congress has never made use of its right to annul a territorial law and also that Congress has never demoted a territory to a status inferior to the one already achieved. But both contentions are inaccurate; territorial laws have repeatedly been annulled (Section 5-2). In 1954 Congress dictated a territorial constitution for the Virgin Islands which was considerably less favorable than that of 1938 (Section 8-7). For Hawaii a similar restriction of rights was seriously considered around 1932 (Section 7-3).

The clarification of this issue becomes more difficult because of the vagueness of the focal terms state and territory. As the United States Supreme Court stated (*People of Puerto Rico* v. *Shell*) earlier in 1937, "Words generally have different shades of meaning, and . . . this meaning in particular instances is to be arrived at only by a consideration, as well, of the context, the purposes of the law, and the circumstances under which the words were employed." Table 7-7 gives a few examples of decisions by United States courts regarding Puerto Rico. In *Moreno Rios* v. *United States* a federal court even pointed out, "When Congress uses the term 'territory' this may be meant to be synonymous only with 'place' or 'area,' and not necessarily to indicate that Congress has in mind the niceties of language of a political scientist." (*Documents on the Constitutional History of Puerto Rico* 1964, 320).

The most important argument against a continuation of unrestricted congressional authority is C. J. Friedrich's statement that each Congress is bound to respect international agreements entered into by its predecessors. To me, however, this agreement seems to consist less in the fact that, as Friedrich believes, the granting of Commonwealth status had to be considered analogous to granting independence, which would *eo ipso* constitute an international commitment.

Even less valid seems to be Friedrich's argument that the establishment of the Commonwealth had to be treated like the advancement of a territory to statehood, which would likewise bind all future Congresses. This comparison is logically not permissible, since it presupposes something which would have to first be proved, that the Island is indeed a state today.

The agreement seems rather to lie directly in the consent on the part of the United States to the resolution of November 27, 1953, by the United Nations. In this resolution the United Nations recognized that Puerto Rico had enjoyed self-government since 1952 and it had ceased to be a dependency about which, according to Article 73e of the United Nations Charter, the United States would have to give annual reports. This agreement does not need to be justified by analogous acts.

In this resolution (United Nations Documents, 25-26), which had the approval of the United States, it is stated that the General Assembly expressed its assurance "that, . . . in accordance with the spirit of this resolution, the ideals

Table 7-8   Votes Received by the
                   Independence Party

Date	Votes	Percent of Total
1948	66,100	
1952	125,700	
1956	86,400	
1960	24,000	3.07
1964	22,200	2.7

embodied in the United Nations Charter, the traditions of the people of the United States and the political advancement attained by the people of Puerto Rico, due regard would be paid to the will of both the Puerto Rican and American peoples in the conduct of their relations under their present legal statute, and also in the eventuality that either of the parties to the mutually agreed association might desire any change in the terms of the association."

In the discussion of the case of Puerto Rico at the United Nations Committee on Non-Self-Governing Territories, the United States representative, Mason Sears, declared on August 28, 1953, "A compact is far stronger than a treaty. A treaty usually can be denounced by either side, whereas a compact cannot be denounced by either party unless it has the permission of the other" (*Documents on the Constitutional History of Puerto Rico* 1964, 253).

Several attempts have already been made in Congress to improve the status of the Island; especially important was House Bill 9234 of September 12, 1959, a proposal by Resident Commissioner Fernos Isern intended to replace Section 4 of Public Law 600 of 1959 by sixteen "Articles of Permanent Association." Nothing has changed so far, but a stubborn insistence on the part of Congress on the 1950 provisions could well strengthen a radical nationalism as well as the independence movement, which is quite weak today. This would endanger an achievement which, with all its shortcomings in details, is nevertheless very stimulating as a whole and which may even be regarded as a model for the rest of the world.

It is quite remarkable that in Puerto Rico the independence movement has been reduced to a point of utter feebleness. The votes received by the Independence Party are shown in Table 7-8.

In Puerto Rico, a party can participate in the elections only if it either received 10% of the votes during the preceding election or if it submits a petition prior to the new election which is signed by a number of people equal to 10% of the votes cast in the preceding election. The Independence Party is therefore out of the political race for the time being, even though they can again gain influence in case of possible economic setbacks or possible Anglo-American mistakes in their handling of relations between the United States and Puerto Rico.

The Socialists had already dropped out of the race in 1952 when they received only 3% of all votes. The partisans of statehood, on the other hand,

Table 7-9   Tally of Votes, 1944-1960

Party	Goal	1944	1948	1952	1956	1960
Partido Popular Democratio	Associated State Component	383	392	429	433	456
Statehood Republican	State of the U.S.A.	102	88	85	173	251
Independentistas	Independent State		66	126	86	24

gained 32% of the votes in 1960 (Table 7-9). They constitute a right-leaning bourgeois party which today is in many respects similar to the mainland Republicans, while the Muñoz Marín party can be likened to the mainland Democrats. A prochurch Christian Action Party, which participated in the 1960 election, failed to gain any substantial number of votes. This party was started by the clergy to combat the liberal policy of Muñoz Marín. Subsequently its votes were declared invalid because of alleged serious omissions in the application of the party for admission to the election. In 1964 the Christian Action Party received 26,900 votes.

In addition there still exists the movement of the Nacionalistas, which goes back to Campos and which originally leaned more to the radical right but today is close to the most radical left. According to a letter received in 1962 from Hernando Narciso Rabell of the IUS in Prague, the Federation of University Students, which is closely associated with the Nacionalistas, leans toward the Communist IUS (with its seat in Prague). The Nacionalistas proclaim an election boycott, but the turnout for elections in Puerto Rico is unusually heavy and was heavier in 1960 than in 1956. The number of those who boycotted the election was estimated at 177,300 or 21% in 1956, and at only 151,500 or 17% in 1960. But the latter figure contains 51,100 votes for the Christian Action Party, which were subsequently declared invalid, so that in reality only 11% of the qualified voters stayed away from the polls. In 1964, however, there were 181,000 abstentions (18%). This figure does not include votes for the Christian Action Party. The number of members of the Communist Party in 1962 was estimated at only 300.

In a resolution of December 3, 1962, the legislature in San Juan expressed its desire that Puerto Rico's Commonwealth status be reexamined and brought up to a plane which would preclude any doubt of the noncolonial nature of this status. In particular it demanded:

1. Recognition of the sovereignty of the Puerto Rican people so that the compact should be concluded on the basis of full legal equality.

2. Assurance of a lasting and indissoluble union between the United States and Puerto Rico on the basis that citizenship, defense, currency, and the home market should remain common to both.

Table 7-10   Results of 1967 Plebiscite on Status of
                    Puerto Rico

Status Voted for	Number of Votes	Percent of Total
Commonwealth	425,100	60.4
Statehood	274,300	39.0
Independence	4,200	0.6

3. With reference to the Island, Washington should retain only such areas of authority as are indispensable for the continuance of the association.

4. All other powers should be exercised by Puerto Rico exclusively.

5. The Puerto Rican right of codecision in the exercise of the powers remaining with the United States insofar as the interests of Puerto Rico are affected thereby; possibly participation in the election of the President.

6. As soon as the Congress has clarified the statute of the coming association in the sense of these six points, it may have the people of Puerto Rico vote once more on the three possibilities of association, statehood, and independence.

Congress, however, instead of trying to draw up an improved draft constitution, invited the legislative assembly of the Commonwealth to establish the "United States-Puerto Rico Commission on the Status of Puerto Rico," which was to be composed of both Puerto Ricans and mainlanders to "study all factors ... which may have a bearing on the present and future relationship between the United States and Puerto Rico." This commission submitted to the general public, on more than 2,100 printed pages, an incredible wealth of printed information (Status of Puerto Rico 1966).

In the late sixties two important referendums yielded results which at first sight look very much contradictory. On July 23, 1967, the problem of Puerto Rico's status was subjected to a new plebiscite in which, however, only 66.3% of all registered voters took part. The results of the vote are shown in Table 7-10.

From the standpoint of international law, this plebiscite was more significant than the one held in 1952 because this time the voters were offered a free choice among independence, integration (statehood), and association; in 1953 the question was simply: "Association: yes or no?"

In 1968, however, a newly formed statehood party, the New Progressives (which reduced to almost zero the statehood Republicans), gained the upper hand, receiving 45% of the votes as compared with 42% for the party of Muñoz Marín, which still retained 16 out of 27 seats in the Senate but in the House merely 5 out of 31 seats. At the 1968 gubernatorial elections the same wave swept into office the leader of the New Progressives, L. A. Ferré. During his campaign, political status did not receive emphasis as an immediate issue; Ferré campaigned rather on the basis of a need for internal change and more effective government. At the same time he promised that he would not press for statehood without an express mandate from the people.

The 1972 election reversed the situation, producing the following returns:

Popular Democratic Party (for Commonwealth)	609,700
New Progressive Party (for Statehood)	524,000
Independence Party	52,100

This indicated a sizable increase in pro-independence sentiment.

In the 1968-1974 period there was no major change in the status of Puerto Rico. However, according to a letter from Mr. Jaime Benitez, the island's Resident Commissioner in Washington, dated July 14, 1975, a bill was about to be introduced in the House of Representatives the 21 articles of which were meant to adapt the principles of 1952 to the realities of 1975 and to give juridical expression to a growth in political maturity. Important changes were foreseen in article 9 broadening Puerto Rico's commercial and trade activities; article 10 pertained to the entry of aliens; article 11 dealt with the representation of Puerto Rico; article 12 related to the applicability of federal laws; article 13 dealt with the assignment of federal functions to the Free Associated State; article 14 pertained to the creation of a joint commission responsible for the examination and recommendation of solutions to several operational problems.

Puerto Ricans wanted to see, in English legal language, the term *Commonwealth* replaced by *Free Associated State*, the literal translation of the current Spanish designation.

Language Provisions in the Constitutions

Since Puerto Rico never absorbed a substantial English-speaking immigration but for the everyday speech of its population always remained a monolingual Spanish-speaking island, the language provisions differ from those of all mainland states and of all United States territories. That Spanish was at least the second official language was taken for granted to such a degree that only relatively few express provisions exist. Controversies over the admission of Spanish into any more narrowly defined sectors of the polity, which were so frequent in other places, are almost completely nonexistent. Furthermore Puerto Rico is the only territory where Congress ordered the equal status of a non-English language. The Organic Act of 1900 began in Section 30: "No person shall be eligible to membership in the house of delegates who is not twenty-five years of age and able to read and write either the Spanish or the English language," and Section 40 ordered the compilation and publication of a bilingual collection of all the laws in force, which should also include recommendations for new laws (Kloss 1940, 551). Only the provisions about the United States District Court (Article 34) and the United States Supreme Court as the last court of appeal (Article 35) prescribed English as the only language.

The 1917 Organic Act reaffirmed the equal status of both languages in the House of Representatives (Article 27) and added a similar provision with respect to the new Senate (Section 26). Section 42 repeated the provisions about the use of English in the United States District Court; according to Section 44 the jurors elected to serve in the District Court had to have a sufficient knowledge of English.

Other Language Laws Excepting School Language Laws

Outside of the Organic Act the position of the Spanish language was made safe in 1902 by two laws. The first, of February 21, 1902, referred to the executive and judiciary branches of government: "Section 1: In all the departments of the insular government and all the courts of this island and in all public offices, the English language and the Spanish language shall be used indiscriminately; ... Section 3: No public or private document written in either of the languages herein named shall be held void on account of the language in which it is expressed."

That Section 5 of the law (Kloss 1940, 555) excluded its application in municipal government could mean only that here Spanish was permitted to be used exclusively.

A large number of additional provisions are contained in the Political Code of March 1, 1902. Here we read with respect to the legislative branch in Section 45: "The Secretary of Porto Rico shall at the close of each session of the Legislative Assembly collate and cause to be printed in Spanish and English all the acts and resolutions passed during the session, together with the Organic Act and the acts and resolutions of Congress amendatory thereof, and such other public laws and documents as he may deem appropriate."

Section 185 of the Code referred again to the executive branch: "All general reports, whether annual or otherwise, of the Governor or heads of departments of government, or of any bureau or division thereof, which are published in English, shall be published also in Spanish." Section 77 of the same code (Kloss 1940, 574) ordered that the written opinions delivered by the Attorney General be published in both languages.

The same regulation was provided for in a 1908 law for the decisions of the Supreme Court of Puerto Rico and in another of the same year for the *Official Gazette* (Kloss 1940, 573, 556, 557). A similar law of 1917 provides that, in case of a discrepancy between the English and Spanish texts of a statute passed by the Legislative Assembly of Puerto Rico, the text in which the statute originated in either house shall prevail in the construction of said statute except in the following cases: (a) If the statute is a translation or adaptation of a statute of the United States or of any State or Territory thereof, the English text shall be given preference over the Spanish. (b) If the statute is of Spanish origin, the Spanish text shall be preferred to the English. (c) If the matter of preference cannot be decided under the foregoing rules, the Spanish text shall prevail. The factual ascendency of the Spanish version was thus established because most of the laws passed before 1917 were presumably drafted in the mother tongue of the representatives. This preeminence of Spanish was now enlarged in principle by the provision that in case of discrepancy the Spanish version always would prevail.

The law consequently went farther than the corresponding law which was in force in New Mexico from 1874 to 1915 (Section 5-2).

Since the establishment of the Commonwealth, the session records of the legisature and the annual messages of the Governor have appeared only in Spanish. The policy of the Commonwealth has been to deemphasize English. A Spanish literacy test is required of members of the parliament, and even jurors in the criminal courts must read and write Spanish. Executive reports in English must be translated into Spanish, while the converse is not required. The Commonwealth's judiciary has ruled that English pleadings must be accompanied by a Spanish translation.

From a practical standpoint, today a language problem exists for the small but economically, culturally, and politically influential English-speaking minority rather than for the Hispanic inhabitants of the Island (Section 5-2).

The supremacy of Spanish makes it superfluous to relate in detail in what areas of government, administration, and court system Spanish is in official use today. We may assume an equal status in theory for practically all areas and for most of them an exclusive use in practice, even though a knowledge of English without a knowledge of Spanish is theoreticaly still recognized as sufficient language qualification for the right to vote, according to Article III (5) of the Commonwealth Constitution. The most important exception exists in the case of the Federal District Court for Puerto Rico for which Federal Law No. 600 of 1950 provides (in Articles 42 and 44) that its proceedings have to be conducted in English and that jurors serving in the court have to have a knowledge of English, a provision which Fernos Isern's draft House Bill 9234 (in Article XIII) attempted to restrict.

School Language Laws

A highly developed school system existed for a small part of the Puerto Ricans even before 1898: In 1832 a seminary was established for priests. This still exists today. In 1880 the Civil College and in 1883 an advanced technical school were established. In the year 1898 the 25,600 students constituted 10% of the total number of children of compulsory school age, but 90% of the population was illiterate. Further information on the language question in the schools may be found in Osuña (1949), Souffront (1950), and Bou (1966).

The first American commissioner of education, V. S. Clark (1899-1900), tried to establish English as the sole medium of instruction. The first commissioner under the 1900 Organic Act, M. G. Brumbaugh (1900-1902), his chief aide Henry Houck, both Pennsylvania "Dutchmen," and his successor, Commissioner Lindsay (1902-1904), adopted a policy of bilingualism aiming at the conservation of Spanish, the teaching tool in the elementary grades and the acquisition of English, which was used in grades 9-12. This was changed by their successors in the period from 1904 to 1916, who used English in all grades of the school system; Commissioner Dexter (1907-1912) decreed that only English should be taught in grade 1 and that the teaching of Spanish should be relegated

Table 7-11   English and Spanish in Puerto Rican Schools

Language Status	Urban Schools 1908		Urban Schools 1911		Rural Schools 1911	
	No.	%	No.	%	No.	%
All English	442	67	759	98.4	188	17
Bilingual	64	10	11	1.6	238	22
English as subject only	157	23	1	0.01	665	60.5
No English					6	0.5

to grade 2. In 1903 the first urban all-English elementary school was established and in 1909 the first rural all-English school. A law of March 10, 1904 (Kloss 1940, 558-560) required of all school principals a good knowledge of both languages, but of other teachers only an elementary knowledge.

Some figures are given in Table 7-11 which may be compared with the figures for New Mexico in Table 5-2. In the all-English schools Spanish was generally taught as a subject; from about 1910 on, however, it was taught only from the second grade on. A picture quite different from Osuña's is given by Padín (1916; see also Kloss 1940, 562). According to him the schools were bilingual throughout but the number of hours devoted to English increased gradually from the second to the seventh grade by in all about 20%.

The system as described by Osuña was applied by France in Alsace before 1940. While France since then has gone to the extreme of banning the mother tongue below the sixth grade and while the timid present-day champions of bilingualism in Alsace are striving for the restoration of at least the shabby prewar arrangement, the United States soon turned liberal again. Paul G. Miller was the first Secretary of Education (after 1915) to have had local experience; he had been director of the teachers' college. In 1917 Secretary Miller reintroduced bilingual instruction in the elementary schools. Different versions are found in the literature about the method adopted. All authors speak of an all-Spanish lower division with English as a subject of instruction and an all-English upper division with Spanish as a subject. The Columbia Report (1926) states: grades one to four Spanish; English is a subject beginning with grade one in the urban schools, beginning with grade two in the rural; classes five to eight are English with Spanish as a subject. A report of the Department of Education in San Juan in 1931 (Kloss 1940, 556) and also Osuña's *History of Education* (1949) state: grades one through four Spanish with English as a subject; grades five and six (Osuña: only grade five) bilingual (half and half); grades seven and eight (Osuña: six through eight) English with Spanish as a subject.

In 1926 a voluminous report on the Puerto Rican school system issued by Teachers' College of Columbia University, New York City, advocated that English be completely dropped in grades one through three because teaching it at that level meant a wasting of time at the expense of content teaching (*The Columbia Report* 1926). This suggestion was not heeded at that time. Jose Padin, the first native Puerto Rican to become (in 1934) Secretary of Education, tried to make Spanish the only teaching tool in all elementary grades; he was, however, forced to resign. Not until 1937 was a successor found in J. M. Gallardo, who had long been a college instructor in the United States. Gallardo was given the task of strongly building up the position of English. President Roosevelt in a letter of April 8, 1937, urged him to make it his main task to establish bilingualism (Kloss 1940, 569-570; Osuña 1949, 376-377; Souffront 1950, 65-67; Bou 1966, 162-163). Gallardo consequently first introduced a system in which English was a subject in the first and second grades and Spanish was a subject in the seventh and eighth grades. In grades three through six instruction was given half a day in one language and the remaining half in the other. But from 1942 on, still under Gallardo, Spanish again became the only means of instruction for grades one through six (except for the study of English); only grades seven and eight remained all English. This led to bitter controversies with the federal government, especially in 1943 with Secretary of the Interior Ickes; finally Gallardo gave way (1946). In that year the legislature overrode the veto of Governor Piñero—a Puerto Rican—against a bill making Spanish the sole medium of instruction, only to have it vetoed by President Truman (October 27, 1946). Thereupon a storm arose in the Spanish-American press, and teachers' associations of Brazil, Mexico, and Uruguay cabled protests (Souffront 1950, 138-144). After a long interim without an officially confirmed Secretary, Muñoz Marín in 1949 appointed Professor Villaronga, who at once set out to make Spanish the only language of instruction not only in the elementary but even in the high schools.

The school law now in force was adopted on June 29, 1969, and provides: "Instruction in Spanish and the intensification of the teaching of English as an additional language shall be unalterable standards." Even the University of Puerto Rico in Rio Pedras, which was founded in 1904 as an all-English institution but which had long given Spanish a considerable part in its curriculum (a landmark was the establishment of a large Spanish Department in 1927), has since switched entirely to Spanish but many English textbooks are still used, and some teachers from the mainland may still lecture in English.

The Position of the Anglo-Puerto Rican Minority

A genuine minority problem exists for the Anglo-Americans in Puerto Rico, who live mostly in San Juan. Their number is estimated by the island authorities at about 30,000 to 50,000, but it seems that the higher figure, which would correspond to 2% of the population, is perhaps more reliable. In 1965, 18,000 persons lived in Puerto Rico who were born in the United States, not of first generation Puerto Rican parents. Together with second to fourth generation Anglos, the total may well add up to 50,000. Besides there were 52,000 born in the United States of Puerto Rican parents, 20,000 immigrants from Cuba, and

7,000 from the Dominican Republic; the small inflow of English speakers was thus more than offset by incoming Spanish speakers.

In 1963, I described the situation of the Anglo-Puerto Ricans as follows: they possess of course the active and passive voting right, enjoy full freedom of language in their organizations and churches, and profit in practical life from the fact that a good many public documents have to be printed in English also as the result of the special status of the Island. Moreover, many Puerto Ricans have learned to express themselves in English. The Anglo-Americans have a daily newspaper, the *San Juan Star*, which carries the official notices of the Island government as well as of the city administration. They also have 3 all-English radio stations, among them one of the armed forces, and some of the approximately 30 Spanish-language stations have reserved several hours per week for English-language broadcasts.

But the Anglo-Americans are at a disadvantage in two respects to an extent which is quite surprising. If they have to settle a dispute before the courts, they have to appear before a Spanish-speaking court; even if the mother tongue of both parties is English, the court helps them only by calling in an interpreter.

There are no English-language lower courts and no public English-language schools. If some English-speaking children are to be educated bilingually, they must either attend one of the private parochial schools with bilingual instruction or one of the few and very expensive secular private schools (such as the Commonwealth School or St. John's School) which have English as the only language of instruction. One Puerto Rican, a resident of San Juan, in a letter to me in 1961 expressed the opinion that he regards the confinement of English as the language of instruction to a few private schools as discriminatory against the Puerto Ricans. In 1969, according to a letter from the Puerto Rico Department of Education, the majority of the nonpublic schools used both English and Spanish. Many used Spanish only, and a few used English as the medium of instruction.

The effort on the part of the Anglo-Saxons to avoid any resemblance of dominance here has led in Puerto Rico to a clear disadvantage as compared with the dominant Spanish-speaking ethnic group. That the Anglos are economically very influential—it is said that the Anglo-Americans control up to 85% of the Puerto Rican industry—makes their restraint in the field of language policy all the more impressive.

It is with surprise that we meet here in the sphere of jurisdiction of the United States a regulation for a national minority which is based on the so-called territorial principle. This principle is applied in Switzerland in a similar, though more resolute, fashion and has contributed to the fame that country enjoys as a model multinational state. The territorial principle fixes for all inhabitants of the speech area of a linguistic minority the legal precedence of the regional language over the language of the ethnic group which forms the majority in the state at large.

In other chapters of this book we report about those Puerto Ricans who immigrated to New York (Sections 4-4 and 4-7) or the Virgin Islands (Section 8-7).

7-5   THE PHILIPPINES UNDER AMERICAN RULE

General Remarks

The Philippines at the time of their independence in 1946 had almost 19 million people—four times more than the inhabitants of all other American overseas possessions together and more than any individual non-English group on the United States mainland at any given time. Strictly speaking, of course, it would be more correct to divide the Filipinos into language groups. Then, among the non-English speaking groups under the American flag, we find the German Americans in first place with approximately 9 million persons in 1910. In second place were the speakers of the Visayan language numbering 7.3 million persons in the year prior to the attainment of independence for the country. Consequently, the description of the nationality problems in the Philippines has to be much more sketchy than that of the other overseas possessions.

The Philippines comprise 114,830 square miles with 21.4 million inhabitants in 1954. There were 7.6 million in 1903, 10.3 million in 1918, and 12.6 million in 1928. At the beginning of the Spanish rule their total number is said to have been only 0.5 million. Their conquest by the Spaniards began in 1665, they were ceded to the United States in the Treaty of Paris on December 10, 1898, and they gained independence on July 4, 1946.

Table 7-12   Language Groups of the Philippine Islands

Language	1916	1946	Number of Books in This Language
Visayan (Bisaya)	3,997,000	7,300,000	700
Tagalog	1,789,000	3,330,000	1,500
Ilocano	989,000	2,000,000	500
Bicol	685,000	1,200,000	300
Pangasinan	381,000	665,000	100
Pampanan	337,000	600,000	270

We shall speak of the Philippines with respect to the geographical terms and of the Filipino with respect to the population, i.e., for example, of the "Philippine flora," but of the "Filipino peasant." The native inhabitants, the Filipinos, belong in the overwhelming majority to the Malayan race and speak languages of the Indonesian subgroup of the Austronesian language family. (In linguistics the term "Indonesian" comprises a larger area than the present political unit.) The linguistic fragmentation is considerable, but the eight major languages are spoken by approximately 90% of the population. The six largest language groups are listed in Table 7-12, figures for which are taken from the *Encyclopedia of the Philippines*, XVI, pp. 82-85. This information on book production is found in articles about the individual languages (for example, Tagalog on p. 76), but the encyclopedia does not reveal the year for which these figures have been compiled or whether they comprise all books ever printed or only those titles which were still available at that time; nevertheless they permit conclusions about the volume of literature in these languages. All native languages are closely related to each other, not closely enough to enable their speakers to communicate with each other without difficulties, but sufficiently close to enable people to learn the language within a very short time in case they move into another language area (Hayden 1942, 587-881). This reduces the inevitable petty jealousies between the language groups and gives the entire population a feeling of solidarity.

The approximately 40,000 Negritos and the commercially important Chinese form separate ethnic groups. The Negritos are mostly of small stature and are considered to be the indigenous population of the islands, but have given up their own language. Among the Negritos we have to distinguish between the Negritoids proper, the proto-Malayan, and the Australoid-Ainu types (Krieger 1942, 39-45; *Encyclopedia of the Philippines*, XVI, 58-63 and X, 3-13).

With respect to religion, 83% of the inhabitants are Catholic, 4% are Moslem, 10% belong to other non-Christian religions, and 2% are still animists ("heathens"). The Philippines are the easternmost country in the world which contains "nationalities by faith," i.e., groups for which the community of the faithful (particularly among the Moslems) is more important than the community of speakers of the same language.

Disregarding the practically unimportant but theoretically interesting special problem of the Negritos who are, according to H. B. Hawes (1932, 63), "probably the only class of Filipinos who do not understand what independence means," we have to distinguish among four problems during the American time with respect to nationality laws: (1) the problem of self-government, (2) the problem of America's language policy, (3) the problem of the religious minorities, and (4) the problem of the Chinese.

Question of Self-Government and Self-Determination

The Spaniards christianized the larger part of the population but did not grant them—in contrast to Puerto Rico—any significant voice in the strongly centralized administration. Not until 1893 did a powerless advisory council, called the "Administrative Council," with mostly appointed members, come into existence. In August 1896, a rebellion against Spain, mostly prepared by intellectuals leaning toward freemasonry, broke out; the rebels made common cause with the Americans during the Spanish-American War (April 21 to December 10, 1898), proclaimed formally the independence of their country on June 12, 1898, but fought against the Americans beginning February 4, 1899, when America proceeded to annex the Philippines instead of setting them free. Of the different draft constitutions produced by the rebels, the "Constitution of Malolos" (January 21, 1899) is important (in Spanish, Kalaw, part II, App. 262 f.; in English, Senate Documents, 56th Congress, 1st Session, 208, part I, 107-119; *Report of the Philippines Commission 1900*, vol. L, app. IV; *Encyclopedia of the Philippines*, XI, 47-69).

The constitution was adopted by a kind of representative body and provided for a parliamentary republic; the legislature elected the President of the Republic, who was also Prime Minister. The delegates of Malolos were chosen as follows: one third of the members were elected by the local authorities of the free parts of the country and two thirds of the members were appointed. It took until May 1902 to suppress the rebellion.

An excellent source for the American period is a study by Georges Fischer (1960), even though he is not entirely free from anti-American bias. In addition, I used primarily Hayden (1942). A good popular summary is Alip (1958).

America governed the country from September 1900, until October 1907, by a five-member collegiate body, the Philippine Commission, which held the combined executive and legislative power. To this Commission belonged, after 1903, three and, after 1908, four Filipinos without portfolio. An Organic Act, passed by the United States Congress on July 1, 1902, granted a bill of rights and regulated the future elections for a representative body (*Encyclopedia of the Philippines*, XI, 87-126). From October 1907, there existed an elected lower house which was composed entirely of Filipinos and which, together with the Philippine Commission (now serving as upper house), formed the legislature—quite similar to the 1900 situation in Puerto Rico (see Section 7-4).

Under the rule of the Wilson Democrats and their representative in the Philippines, Governor Harrison (1913-1921), the influence of the Filipinos increased rapidly. The number of American officials decreased from 2,612 (29%) to 614 (4%), and in 1913 we find a Filipino majority in the ruling Philippine Commission. The new Organic Act of August 29, 1916, the so-called Jones Act (*Encyclopedia of the Philippines*, XI, 127-148), abolished the Commission and put into practice *de jure* the separation of powers by creating a popularly elected Senate. However, this division of power was *de facto* immediately abolished by the creation, at first unofficially, and later by Executive Order No. 37 of October 16, 1918, of a Council of State consisting of the Governor, the members of his Cabinet, the Speaker of the House, and the President of the Senate. This Council actually stood above the legislature and the government, but since Harrison remained entirely in the background, the two speakers exerted considerable influence. The Filipinos had thus attained a high degree of self-government.

As early as 1916 Wilson justified the claim to moral leadership in the world on the part of the United States on the basis of its nationality policy in the Philippines (Fischer 1960, 102). And in 1920 Wilson declared in a message to Congress that with a stable island government safely in the saddle the United States was morally obligated to grant independence immediately (Kirk 1936, 48). But severe setbacks and bitter disputes occurred under the Republican Governor General L. Wood (1921-1927), who again attempted to reduce the political influence of the Filipinos and who was backed up by a 1928 decision of the United States Supreme Court which declared that the establishment of the Council of State violated the principle of the separation of powers (*Springer* v. *Philippine Islands*, 277 U.S. 189). After December 1920, the Philippine legislature appropriated annually $0.5 million for activities promoting independence. This appropriation was canceled in 1924 by the Auditor General (Kirk 1936, 51), but one wonders whether any other colonial power would have been liberal enough not to interdict the appropriation the moment it had first been resolved. A bill adopted by the legislature in 1928 providing for a plebiscite on the question of independence was indeed vetoed by Governor Wood. Under Wood's successor, Stimson, the Council of State was revived by Executive Order of August 30, 1932, but now it served as a mere advisory body.

The Federalistas, who advocated statehood, were the leading political party in the Philippines for a long time, i.e., as long as no campaigns in favor of independence were permitted. But from 1907 on, without any interruption, the leading political party was the Nationalistas, who demanded independence. The United States government had declared from the very beginning that it would attempt to make the Filipinos ready for independence. As early as 1900 the President of the Philippine Commission, Schurman, declared the islands were destined to become a "sister republic" of the United States. Similar statements were made by Secretary of War Taft in his report to President Theodore Roosevelt and by the latter in turn in his message to Congress (Kalaw 1948, 213ff.). The Democrats had included the future independence of the islands in their 1904 platform; the Republicans hesitated longer in this respect. The United States went to great lengths to promote and strengthen the spread of national consciousness, which at first was limited to a small upper class; the United States realized that the country faced the danger of falling apart if it should be granted independence before a popular will for unity had been generated.

At the beginning of the 1930s the following situation, with weighty grounds favoring early independence, developed:

1. The Filipinos governed and administered themselves to an extensive degree—and were not bad at it either.

2. The only strong political party of the islands demanded independence.

3. The Americans had long been willing in principle to set the islands free. This basic attitude of the Americans, which was no doubt altruistic in its essential features but implied hopes for gains in moral prestige, was also prompted by weighty egotistical motives, above all:

4. Complaints of the American business community about the competition of Filipino-produced goods—mostly vegetable oils and sugar, but also tobacco.

5. Objections against immigration from the Philippines—from 1920 to 1929 an average of 8,100 Filipinos immigrated annually to the United States and Hawaii.

6. The fact that the Philippines began to turn from being a military asset into being a military burden. The United States had agreed in 1922 not to fortify the islands, while Japan began to rearm in 1931.

But there were also counterarguments, such as:

1. The great economic dependence of the Philippines upon the United States.

2. The fact that the United States, despite the systematic training of the Filipinos in democratic ideals and democratic practice, had failed to establish one of the essential preconditions for a functioning democracy—a just social order which would eliminate the dependence of the huge agrarian proletariat on the upper class. (Fischer 1960, 8-41, has a masterful treatment of this subject.) An uprising of a peasant organization, the Colorums, occurred on Mindanao (1923-1924), and another, that of the Tangulans on Luzon, took place in 1931. The reasons for both uprisings were intermingled with religious ideas. Certain other local uprisings occurred; that of the Sakdal (Tagalog for accuser) Party in 1935 was the most important. In 1934 the Sakdal Party had participated in the election and received three seats in the House (Hayden 1942, 382-400).

The second of these factors was hardly recognized and discussed at that time, while the first received more attention.

In addition to using well-founded arguments, the opponents to independence made use of pure propaganda, such as the statement that the Filipinos themselves did not desire independence. For example, R. W. Hart stated, "Of twelve million Filipinos, only 5,000, led by five politicking half-breeds, desire independence earnestly" (1928, 161).

Not without danger was the legal argument that Congress could not relinquish United States claims to parts of the American sphere of jurisdiction—a contention which was rejected by the Attorney General on April 30, 1924, and by the Legislative Counsel of the United States Senate on January 29, 1930 (Congressional Record, January 29, 1930; Hayden 1942, 292-296, especially 294).

In America the proindependence view prevailed. On December 21, 1932, Congress approved a bill concerning the independence of the Philippines, the Hare-Hawes-Cutting Act. Although vetoed by Hoover on January 17, 1933, it received a sufficient majority in Congress; but it was rejected by the Philippine Congress on October 17, 1933.

There were many unusually complicated negotiations to which foreign countries contributed, with England, France, Holland, and Australia communicating their objections to the independence plans (Fischer 1960, 100). Eventually the Tydings-McDuffie Act was adopted on March 4, 1934, by the United States Congress and two months later by the Philippine Congress (Hayden 1942, 807-821; Commager II, 467-471).

The Tydings-McDuffie Act, however, contained only one improvement over its predecessor: that American troops would soon leave the Commonwealth. The essence of the Act was that the Philippines should remain for ten years tied to America as a "Commonwealth" with a constitution which the Philippines would work out themselves, and that they would become independent on July 4 of the tenth year after the first Commonwealth government took office. During the Commonwealth period decisions about certain important measures should continue to be dependent upon the approval of the United States President. All changes in the Constitution (and here the Commonwealth was at a disadvantage as compared to regular states), furthermore, all laws concerning immigration, commercial relations with foreign countries, foreign loans, and currency required the approval of the United States President. The United States Supreme Court remained the last court of appeal in a series of cases, i.e., such cases as affected the interpretation of the Constitution, laws and treaties of the United States, and the Commonwealth Constitution. America retained, furthermore, the right of intervention and, of course, the control over foreign policy. The right of intervention remained more limited, however, than the right the United States had secured in Cuba through the Platt Amendment (Fischer 1960, 113).

The Commonwealth Constitution of February 8, 1935 (text in Hayden 1942, 822-859, and *Encyclopedia of the Philippines*, XII, 9-36), which the Philippines adopted and which was approved by the Filipino voters (May 14, 1935) and President Roosevelt, was a presidential constitution patterned after the American model; the Philippines became, together with South Vietnam, the only country in South Asia with such a constitution. Following a Nebraska innovation of 1934 a one-chamber legislature was established, but the Philippines soon returned to a bicameral legislature in 1940. The then Commonwealth can best be considered an associated state similar to present-day Puerto Rico.

According to Kirk (1936, 221-224), "wherever and whenever the Philippino government should so request, American foreign representatives could act for it," just as today those of New Zealand can for Western Samoa. Kirk called the Philippines "a semiprotectorate of some kind"—not a bad definition at a time when the concept of association was still unborn.

The Commonwealth was a creation which combined features of a territory, of a nonsovereign state, and—in contrast to Puerto Rico—those of a semi-sovereign state wherein the Filipino and American interpretations of the legal situation did of course differ. The United States Supreme Court ruled in 1937 that the power of the federal government continued unrestricted in principle, a ruling which suggests a quasi-territorial status. This opinion was stated in the case of *Cincinnati Soap Co.* v. *United States* in these words: "Over such a dependency the nation possesses the sovereign powers of the general government plus powers of a local and a state government in all cases where legislation is possible" (p. 317).

On April 9, 1945, the Supreme Court expressed still similar views: "Congress retains plenary powers over the *territorial* (!) government until such times as the Philippines are made independent" (*Hoover* v. *Evatt*, 675).

In reality America respected the internal autonomy of the Philippines quite carefully. In Article II (1) of the 1935 Constitution, which had after all been approved by the federal government, the country was called "a republican state." In the course of time the Commonwealth was even repeatedly permitted to act in the role of a subject in international law; it signed on June 10, 1942, for example, the Washington United Nations declaration of January 1, 1942, and the United Nations Relief Association (UNNRA) agreement of November 9, 1943. It was represented at the Bretton Woods Conference in 1944, and was admitted to the United Nations on October 11, 1945.

The occupation of the country by the Japanese during World War II, which lasted from April 1942 until October 1944, created some new situations. On October 14, 1943, the Japanese established a puppet government under President J. P. Laurel, which was recognized by the Axis powers and by Spain. In America an exile government was established which returned to its native soil on October 23, 1944.

The most important state documents of the Laurel government, especially its constitution, are printed in *Encyclopedia of the Philippines* (XII, 131-168). There is a summarizing treatment of the Laurel government from a Filipino point of view in Alip (1958, 414-423), and from an American point of view by Linebarger (1958, 216-221).

The Philippines finally became independent on July 4, 1946. The last High Commissioner, McNutt, compared this day with the American A-bomb: as the latter was an expression of the unlimited power of the United States, the events of this day were an expression of its unlimited generosity (*Encyclopedia of the Philippines* XII, 199-208; Fischer 1960, 101). But the actual decision had already been made in 1932/34. The Philippines were at that time the first country of the nonwhite world which had been granted (if only under inclusion of a transitional period) complete independence by its "white" colonial power. The only forerunner was Iraq which, however, was not a colony but only a mandated territory. The Philippines were at the same time the first independent state of the Malayan world (they have been followed since by Indonesia, Malaya, and Madagascar). The Americans very consciously applied in 1934 the idea of self-determination (cf. President Roosevelt's message of November 15, 1935). Even American authors (Pratt 1950) have attempted to deny that this procedure had any ethical value because the United States had been guided by economic interests and had put up some petty demands between 1932 and 1934. But is the mere fact that the action of a nation corresponds to its economic interests proof enough that it is amoral or even immoral? Would America have acted more morally if she, like several Romance colonial powers, had put her economic interests below her desire for power and prestige and denied independence to the islands? That this desire for prestige was almost completely alien to the Americans, that it was therefore relatively easy for them to ignore this aspect, does not depreciate the objective value of their action any more than in the case of those rare soldiers who happen not to have to suppress an internal cowardice in battle because they know no fear but are not denied a medal for this reason.

The way in which the Philippines were prepared for independence has to be evaluated positively. From 1900 they were introduced to local self-government and from 1907 to parliamentary self-government; since 1935 they had again to undergo a ten-year period to get practice in even higher forms of responsibility. Such a ten-year term would have made it much easier for many of the states which have come into existence since 1945. Unfortunately, only one single counterpart exists: the way Somalia was prepared for independence during the 1951-1960 decade.

The Language Policy of the Americans and
the Question of the Languages of the Minorities

As great as the accomplishment of the Americans was in the realm of self-government, at first glance the balance in the realm of language rights appears just as negative. For after a short time they made English the only language of instruction in the public schools, without allowing any place for the Philippine languages.

Thus in the Philippines—in contrast to Louisiana, New Mexico, Pennsylvania, Puerto Rico—from the very beginning they proceeded with methods designed to produce assimilation. This is the only case where the United States deprived a large indigenous ethnic group of instruction in its mother tongue from the very beginning. It was only in 1939 that Jorge Bocobo, the Secretary of Public Instruction, permitted the auxiliary use of the vernaculars; from now on public school teachers were free to use the local dialect wherever they found that their pupils were unable to understand their question, direction, or explanation (Sibayan, 180).

It has to be said in justification of the measure that the Americans encountered an unusually complicated situation. There was no uniform colloquial language in the Philippines, but a variety of speech communities of which none formed a majority. Among the eight leading speech communities, that of the Visayans comprised the largest numbers, but that of the Tagalogs was the most vigorous with the best developed literature. Of the several draft constitutions which originated during the war of independence between 1896 and 1902, two envisioned Tagalog as the official language of the country. The Constitution of Malolos left the language question unanswered (compare also the table of books in Section 7-5).

European languages predominated so strongly during the Spanish and the territorial period that the ranking order of the native languages was considered entirely unimportant.

The Filipino languages, however, had for centuries served as languages of instruction in the lower grades of the parochial elementary schools; but after the state took over the school system in 1863, Spanish became the only school language (Alip 1958, 95, 104-105). And to replace Spanish with the native languages would have been the more difficult, since it would have immediately presented the task of writing textbooks and training teachers for at least eight language groups at once. The insight that instruction in the mother tongue is educationally more appropriate, and therefore ethically more just, was at that time not as widely accepted as it is today when UNESCO has come to promote the vernacular languages (*The Use of the Vernacular Languages in Education*, 1953). It should also be mentioned that the Filipinos themselves did not demand schooling in their mother tongue at that time. Still the fact that in 1935 even the Commonwealth retained English as the major language of instruction should not be taken as basis for generalizing conclusions, for this provision had been made mandatory by Section 2 (8a) of the Tydings-McDuffie Act. But the Independence

Missions which the Filipinos sent to Washington in the years after 1918 expressly asked that English be retained (*Encyclopedia of the Philippines* XI, 368-369). The revolutionary Sakdal Party demanded instruction in the vernacular languages and even established some schools where instruction was given in Tagalog (Hayden 1942, 916).

The Americans therefore had only the alternatives of either retaining Spanish or introducing English. They were guided in their choice by the conviction that in the rest of Asia the Spanish language enjoyed practically no currency but the English language a very high practical esteem, so that America could actually hope, based on the prevailing convictions of that time, to perform a service to the Filipinos by changing the language instruction. Only a very few extremists had in view a replacement of the native languages in the sense that English would become the everyday language of communication among all Filipinos.

We also have to consider that the Americans, by making one single language the language of education, made an effective and conscious contribution to generating a uniform national consciousness among the various language groups. This spirit existed only in its beginning during the years 1896 to 1902; the speakers of Visayan at that time hardly participated in the war for independence, and distinct jealousies existed between the Ilocanos and Tagalogs.

Furthermore, the Americans hardly restricted the position of Spanish in private educational institutions. Spanish remained the language of instruction at the Catholic University of Santo Tomas (founded in 1611) until at least the 1920s.

There were always individual Americans, as, for example, Vice-Governor George C. Butte in 1931, who spoke out in favor of instruction in the vernacular languages. And it was in the Philippines, among the Maros, where the American Frank L. Laubach first launched in 1929 his campaign against illiteracy, "Each one teach one." He made, of course, exclusive use of the illiterate person's mother tongue in his campaign.

But even if America's attitude in the question of school languages may not be viewed with undivided enthusiasm, America's attitude toward the question of official languages can clearly be evaluated as positive. Spanish was retained as official language not only for a limited transitional period but with no time restrictions while English was, of course, added. Spanish was permitted side by side with English in the Philippine Congress; English was spoken for the first time in the House of Representatives in 1922. Only during the Commonwealth period did English become the most widely used language in Congress (Hayden 1942, 602-603). The civil service tests could be taken in English or Spanish at the choice of the applicants; in 1905, 80% selected Spanish, in 1925 only 1%. During the first year of the Commonwealth only 80 (0.2%) of 44,213 applicants were still tested in Spanish (Hayden 1942, 117-118). English came to be used quite exclusively in the central administration in Manila, while throughout the provinces Spanish and the Filipino languages held their position much longer. Officially no

Filipino language was permitted in the civil service until 1940. This led to a monopoly of English at the national level, since Spanish was no longer understood by the younger generation (Hayden 1942, 601, 937).

If it is pointed out to an American how generous his country was in the question of official languages, he will presumably shake his head and ask, "What do you mean by generous? After all, the people had no knowledge of English so that for practical reasons we had no choice." In this answer America's limited knowledge about the mentality of foreign countries again becomes evident. To a nation which conquers and retains a colony primarily for the sake of national prestige and for the sake of spreading its own language, practical difficulties resulting from an overhasty replacement of previously used languages are of no concern. In multi-lingual Togo, for example, the German language had become prior to 1914—more than in any other German colony—quite current among the educated Negroes; yet one can hardly imagine that the French would have retained German as a second official language after the conquest even for only a transitional period of five years. But the Spaniards had long used Quechua as the administrative language during the sixteenth and seventeenth centuries in those parts of South America which belonged to the Inca empire but which were not Quechua-speaking.

After the Philippines had become a Commonwealth, the government could begin preparations for a solution of the language problem. The Commonwealth Constitution itself, according to Article XIII (10), was promulgated in English and Spanish, whereby, however, in case of controversy the English version would govern. At the same time Article XIII (3) expressly prescribed that a native language should also become an official language without, however, naming any particular language.

By a law of November 13, 1936, a National Language Institute, whose eight members represented all the important speech communities, was established, not with the aim of having it suggest which of the existing languages should become the official language of the country, but rather upon which of the existing languages the future national language should be based—psychologically a very clever detour. In September 1937, the Institute suggested Tagalog as such a basis, and on December 30, 1937, President Quezon proclaimed Tagalog "as the basis of the national language." In April 1940 he ordered the future national language as based on the Tagalog dialect to be taught in all schools, beginning June 1940, and by a law enacted June 7, 1940, Tagalog was to become an (not "the") official language on July 4, 1940—the mother tongue of an ethnic group constituting a minority not only in absolute numbers but even relatively, i.e., held against Visayan (Hayden 1942, 583-588; Sibayan, 178). In 1959 the official language was given the name "Pilipino."

Religious Minorities (Non-Christians)

The Moslems, called Moros, constitute the most important separate nationality in the Philippines. That they also speak their own languages is important because these languages—the most important being Sulu and Samal—are also spoken outside the Philippines, notably on Borneo; the Moros therefore speak no specifically "Pilipino" languages as do the rest of the Filipinos. At the same time there always exists the possibility that either the Philippines will claim foreign Sulu or Samal language areas or that foreign countries will claim the area inhabited by the Moros. In 1962 the Philippines indeed claimed parts of North Borneo which had previously belonged to the Sultan of Sulu; the claim was advanced, however, only in historical terms and not in terms of language affiliations. In the future we may well see Indonesian claims to the area of their fellow Moslems; the language question will presumably play a secondary role in this connection. The languages of the Moros, especially Sulu, were written in the Arabic script, which was also taught in their few public schools during the American period.

The Moros constitute, with 800,000 persons (in 1900 about 300,000), only 4% of the population but inhabit a much larger part of the Philippine territory. The statement by Fischer that these 4% inhabit 40% of the land area is almost certainly exaggerated. He presumably considers all of Mindanao a part of the *Moro* area of settlement (Fischer 1960, 70). The Spaniards forced them into submission in 1850 and even then only very superficially in the form of a protectorate, while the Americans were forced to fight them from 1902 to 1914, i.e., for twelve more years after the suppression of the national independence movement proper. (On the Moros, see Hayden 1928; Worcester and Hayden 1930, chaps. 20-23; Kuder 1945; Hunt 1953).

Even though they have been left far behind the Christian Filipinos in most recent times, the Moros belong to a culture which is able and willing to remain on equal terms with the Christian culture and compete with it. The attitude of the pagans is purely defensive, since they are also geographically far more scattered. Of the 626,000 pagans counted in 1939, approximately 250,000 lived in the "mountain province" of North-Central Luzon; the rest were scattered, particularly on Mindanao.

All non-Christians were put under a military governor until 1913. From 1913 to 1920 the "Department of Mindanao and Sulu" with its seat in Zamboanga was at first headed by a civilian governor who was not responsible to the legislature but only to the Philippine Commission. Only the 1916 Organic Act put the non-Christians under the authority of the Philippine legislature; but the representatives of the non-Christians in the legislature were appointed by the Governor General. In the year 1920 the non-Christians were put under a special office in the Philippine Ministry of the Interior, the Bureau of Non-Christian Tribes, with its seat in Manila. After 1913, the more Christian Filipinos came to occupy official positions side by side with the Americans or replacing them, the more frequently friction occurred between them and the Moslem population. After 1922 some non-Christian provinces were permitted to elect their own governors; other provinces were not granted this right until after World War II.

One example for the gradual expansion of the right to vote among non-Christians was the province of Cotabato, which was permitted from 1935 on to elect its representatives to the legislature; after 1945 a Moslem was for the first time appointed governor. Since 1948, members of the provincial council have been elected instead of being appointed, and in 1955 the governor was elected for the first time.

That the Americans established a kind of special government for non-Christians aroused the suspicion of many Filipinos that America was to follow a policy of "divide and rule." This suspicion increased when in 1926 the Bacon Act was twice put before the United States Congress in Washington; this proposed bill would have separated Mindanao and the Sulu islands from the Philippines and put them under permanent American rule (H.R. 12,722 May 6, 1926; H.R. 15,479 Dec. 20, 1926; Bacon, *Congressional Record*, June 24, 1926; Hayden 1942, 863). In President Coolidge's message of April 6, 1927, and President Hoover's veto of January 13, 1933, against the Hare-Hawes-Cutting Act, the still unsolved problem of the non-Christians was listed among the arguments against early independence.

Under these circumstances it is justified that Georges Fischer should raise the question why the Americans did not include provisions for the protection of minorities in the Commonwealth and independence laws of 1932-1934, while such provisions were imposed on Iraq, which was given its independence at the same time (Fischer 1960, 140-143; Conseil de la S.D.N. 1932, 1342ff.). The Americans were presumably not sure whether they would do more harm than good to the forming of the Philippine nation, which was desired as much by Washington as by Manila, and with it at the same time also to the minorities themselves; such a provision would probably have been considered by the Christians as a permanent interference by foreign countries in internal Philippine affairs, while the non-Christians could perhaps consider it an encouragement for engaging in conspiratorial activities. The Americans consequently confined themselves to a provision in very general terms about freedom of religion of an entirely individual nature. The Tydings-McDuffie Act provided, for the duration of the Commonwealth, a constitutional guarantee of religious freedom (fulfilled in Article IIIc of the 1934 Constitution) and, for the period of independence, the acceptance of the respective obligation which the United States entered into in Article X of the 1898 Paris Peace Treaty. This provision did not give an effective protection against a possible abolition of religious educational institutions or discrimination in public life, such as in official positions or the division of the election districts.

After the establishment of the Commonwealth, the government attempted to gradually abolish all special regulations for non-Christians; the Bureau of Non-Christian Tribes was abolished by a law of October 24, 1936, and replaced by the office of a Commissioner for Mindanao and Sulu (Hayden 1942, 863). Formally the non-Christians enjoyed equal rights. For example, they frequently became governors or representatives of their home provinces, but were shut out from administrative key positions by the Christians, who were much better trained.

The Chinese

The history of the Chinese in the Philippines goes back far before the conquest of the Philippines by the Spaniards. Their dual position, notably in the commercial field, as an indispensable group which is at the same time alien in its religion, descent, and language, and is the object of envy or even hatred because of its economic position, is similar to the former position of the Jews in many parts of Europe—even ghettos, bloody massacres, and expulsions were not missing. The first Chinese ghetto ("parian") was established in 1581; in 1596, 12,000 Chinese were expelled; in 1603, 23,000 to 30,000 Chinese were reported to have been killed during a riot; in 1639, 30,000 to 38,000; in 1762 during a British invasion of the islands, 6,000. A decree of 1804 permitted only those working in agriculture to stay in the Philippines (Liao 1958).

On the other hand, many Chinese married into native families and many of them became Christians; at least 800,000 Filipinos are part Chinese. The first book printed in the Philippines, the *Doctrina Cristiana* (1598), appeared in a Spanish-Tagalog and a Chinese edition. The number of Chinese residents was 41,000 in 1903, 43,800 in 1918, and 117,500 in 1939. The Chinese were well organized, with their chambers of commerce being the most important individual organizations; they had a good Chinese-language press (1938, 33,000 copies), and their own schools, which usually were divided into two sections, one all-Chinese, one English.

Remarkable for ethnic groups anywhere in the world, the Chinese performed a miracle by keeping their schools free of tuition charges; they covered their costs by means of a system of voluntary self-taxation of the group. Another tricky problem was the particular Chinese dialect taught in these schools; most schools taught Amoy Chinese (Fukienese), but some Cantonese (Weightman 1954).

Concerning the history of the Chinese under American rule, it is especially important to mention that the United States Supreme Court in Washington in 1926 invalidated a territorial law of 1921 which demanded that business firms keep their books in English, Spanish, or a native language (*Yu Con Eng* v. *Trinidad*; cf. Section 3-2).

Two later laws of 1926 and 1934, which attempted the same in a somewhat milder form, were not enforced because of the resistance of the Chinese residents (No. 3292 Dec. 2, 1926; No. 4176, Dec. 5, 1934). Commonwealth Law No. 113 of November 1, 1936, prescribed that the books could be kept in any language, but that they had to contain an English, Spanish, or Filipino translation. Under the Commonwealth government active attempts were made to increase Filipino participation in wholesale and particularly in retail trade, which the American authorities tried to brake. For example, the American High Commissioner intervened against a city ordinance of Manila in 1941 stating that in the future only Philippine and American citizens would be permitted to sell in the markets of the city (Hayden 1942, 724-729).

The immigration and naturalization policy of the Commonwealth government was likewise strongly influenced by its anti-Chinese bias. The naturalization law of 1939 permitted the naturalization of foreign born Chinese—which at that time was not yet possible in the United States proper—in cases where these Chinese had demonstrated their willingness to become culturally assimilated by fulfilling very difficult conditions: they had to have a ten years' residence in the country, had to be able to speak and write English (or Spanish) and one of the Filipino languages, had to have had social intercourse with the Filipinos, and had to have sent their school-age children from the time of immigration to schools which prepared for a life in the Philippines and not in China; if the latter provision was violated after naturalization had been accomplished, it could be revoked (Hayden 1942, 724-729).

The immigration law of 1940 fixed the Chinese quota at five hundred persons annually. It is demonstrated again that in the Philippines, as well as in British North Borneo until very recent times, the "white" colonial powers granted more protection to the Chinese minorities in Southeast Asia than did the native governments.

The areas of contact and conflict with the Japanese people were by far less numerous throughout these years. Since 1904 a rather large Japanese community had developed slowly in the city and province of Davao on Mindanao; this Japanese community grew more quickly after 1920. Around 1940 the number of Japanese was estimated at approximately 19,000; of this number more than three-quarters lived in Davao. With the exception of a very few naturalized Japanese, all Japanese residents were repatriated at the end of World War II (Quiason 1958).

CHAPTER EIGHT

Nationality Law in Overseas Possessions
Which Did Not Become States

8-1 INTRODUCTORY REMARKS

The general remarks about the overseas possessions dealt with in this chapter may be found in the introduction to the preceding chapter. Guam, American Samoa, and the Virgin Islands belong to the American sphere of sovereignty. But here some additional remarks are necessary about some of the possessions which constituted part of the American sphere of jurisdiction but not of the American sphere of sovereignty, i.e., the Ryukyu and Bonin Islands and the Canal Zone.

For the first two, the 1952 Peace Treaty of San Francisco (Article 3) expressly reserved Japanese residual sovereignty—a *nudum jus* of not clearly definable proportions.

Concerning the Canal Zone, the U. S. Supreme Court expressly stated in 1930 that it constituted foreign territory (*Luckenback* v. *U. S.*). This decision does not conflict with the 1907 decision (*Wilson* v. *Shaw*) that any doubts concerning the legality of the United States claims to the Canal Zone were "hypercritical." The Superior Court of the Zone itself said, "There remains a scintilla of sovereignty—a reversionary sovereignty still in the Republic of Panama" (Canal Zone Superior Court Reports I, 3-4, 54-55; III, 23, 465).

As late as 1940 N. J. Paddelford wrote of an undisputed continuing nominal Panamanian sovereignty. He points out that titular and fictional sovereignty continues to reside in the Republic of Panama. He quotes a statement by the Secretary of War, Taft, of 1906, that such merely titular sovereignty is meaningless to Anglo-Saxons, but quite important to the more poetic and sentimental Latin peoples, who stress titles and forms (American Journal of International Law 1940, 34: 416-442; see also Frangulis 1957, 877-878).

In view of this similarity, if not equality, in the status of the Ryukyu and Bonin Islands on the one side and the Canal Zone on the other side, it is remarkable that as a rule in American official and private publications only the Canal Zone is mentioned and treated as part of the American possessions. The reason for this may be found less in any different legal properties of the respective areas but more in the different ideas existing in America about the duration of the present situation; the possession of the Canal Zone was considered perpetual, that of the Ruykyus only temporary.

None of the overseas possessions dealt with in this chapter can clearly be considered a state, even though the status of the Ryukyus came very close to that of a state. The majority of these territories—clearly in the case of Guam, Eastern Samoa, the Virgin Islands, but in principle also in the case of the Micronesian Trust Territory—have too small a population ever to make it appear meaningful to grant them the status of independent states. If this should occur, however, it would be feasible to have them cooperate in the form of an "external association" with a larger state to which they would entrust the conduct of their foreign policy, especially diplomatic tasks (see Section 9-1). This would be similar to the arrangements under which West Samoa and New Zealand in 1962 were at least temporarily associated. Even more practical, however, would seem to be an internal association patterned after that existing in the case of Puerto Rico. Association protects these territories from the danger of having their already very small elite absorbed by representative foreign service positions (ambassadors, consuls, United Nations delegates, etc.).

On December 10, 1962, the American representative, J. B. Bingham, declared in the Trusteeship Council of the United Nations that his government had sounded out the representative bodies in American Samoa, Guam, and the Virgin Islands and learned that they were in no way inclined to sever their ties with the United States. Each of the three territories had fewer inhabitants than an average county in the United States, but enjoyed a far higher degree of self-government. Furthermore, of those employed in the civil service, 82% were local people in Guam, 95% in Samoa, and 99% in the Virgin Islands.

Another open question with respect to the future of the smaller overseas possessions is whether or not they will continue as political entities in their present—often more historically than ethnically determined—boundaries or whether they will be changed on the basis of ethnolingual relationships. Two outstanding problems in this respect are the ethnic relationship of the Samoans of American Samoa with those of West Samoa, and that of the Chamorro of Guam with those of the Micronesian Trust Territory (see Section 8-6).

8-2   GUAM

Guam is a Pacific island with an area of 209 square miles. It was conquered by Spain in the seventeenth century, administered until 1815 from Mexico and later from Manila, and ceded to the United States in 1898. The capital, Agana, was also the seat of the administration of the Trust Territory until 1962 and of the Bonin Islands until 1968 (see Sections 8-6, 8-5). Between 1901 and 1960, the native Chamorros increased in numbers from 9,600 to 34,800 persons; in addition we find in 1960, 20,700 whites (1,000 born on Guam, 18,880 born on the United States mainland), 7,500 Filipinos (who for the most part immigrated during the 1940s), and 3,000 others. In 1970 the number of inhabitants was 84,996. The whites are mostly fluctuating members or employees of the Navy.

The Chamorros are a racially mixed people, the result of the eighteenth century mixture with many Filipinos and Spaniards. Their language is Chamorro, a language of the "Austronesian" language family, which possesses a vast amount of borrowed words from many other languages, especially from the related Philippine Tagalog and even more from the unrelated Spanish (for example, all numerals. Compare with Hubbe 1959). In 1903 Georg Fritz published the first grammar; in 1904 the first dictionary appeared.

Under Spanish rule a system of co- and self-administration had developed in Guam which was very progressive for that time. The natives were Spanish citizens and occupied almost all leading posts. The system of appointments consisted of a complicated blend of appointment by higher authorities and election by a broad group of notables, which was by no means identical with the traditional group of chieftains (Thompson 1947, 58-64). It has been claimed that at that time 50% of the over seven-year-old inhabitants were literate in Spanish and 75% in Chamorro (Carano and Sanchez 1964, 405).

Their long training in self-government enabled the people of Guam to establish a provisional government under a governor and an advisory body of notables during the time between the departure of the Spaniards and the final occupation by the United States; their attempt to establish a regular legislature (July 1899) failed because it was opposed by a Navy lieutenant.

Guam was put under a Navy governor who governed the island with dictatorial powers in the manner of a battleship or a naval base. Since no court of appeal was available outside of the island—and no trial by jury—the powers of the governor on the island exceeded those of the President; he was practically ruler over life and death and decided in his own right over deportation or admission of groups of people and individuals. Among others, all Spanish priests (i.e., practically all but one Catholic priest), all natives of the Caroline Islands, and all Filipinos were deported during the first years.

The native police force was initially replaced by one from the United States mainland; all elections were abolished; all civil servants appointed; the clock of self-government was set back 100 years. From 1910 on, the people of Guam repeatedly appealed to Congress for self-government. They found at first a positive echo in the Senate but were turned down in the House at the intervention of the Department of the Navy. Even though the governor was joined in 1917 by an appointed bicameral council, and after 1931 even by an elected one, both bodies had no legislative functions for a long time, in spite of their proud name

"Congress." The only real concession, the election of local top officials, was repealed in 1936 by the governor. In 1968 Congress passed a law making the governor elective.

Since the schools continuously impressed upon the youth of Guam the American ideals of freedom and self-responsibility, an unbearable tension was generated between ideal and reality. The most important argument against self-government used during the last years was that Americans from the mainland would gain a majority and rule over the natives. From 1940 on, the people of Guam could become United States citizens on an individual basis (Law of Oct. 14, 1940; Law of Aug. 1, 1950). Not until 1949 did the President place Guam under the administration of the Department of the Interior, effective June 30, 1950; but a civil governor, appointed by the Department of the Interior, officiated as of August 1949.

On August 1, 1950, Congress elevated Guam by an Organic Act to the status of "organized territory" of the fourth category with a genuine, elected unicameral representative body; only now did the natives become citizens instead of mere nationals. Eligibility for the representative body was made dependent upon a five-year uninterrupted residence in Guam. This excluded the large number of white persons who lived only temporarily on Guam. In the Virgin Islands and Hawaii eligibility is made dependent upon three years of residence; in American Samoa, on five years, of which only one has to directly precede the elections. On the other hand, Congress struck out those provisions from the draft which protected practices of native customary law.

In contrast to the question of self-government, that of language took a long while to be solved satisfactorily. Chamorro has long been the language used in preaching the sermons for the Catholics, who include up to 95% of the inhabitants. Monsignor F. C. Flores of Agana, as revealed in a letter to the author, has translated the four Gospels, liturgical texts, and the Imitation of Christ (Thomas a Kempis) into Chamorro. It was also widely used in the sessions of the representative body; it was occasionally used on radio and television, particularly during election campaigns. The Catholic weekly, Umatuna Si Yuus, regularly contains one page in Chamorro. In 1918 the Government Printing Office in Washington published the "Dictionary and Grammar of the Chamorro Language" by Edward Ritter von Preyssing.

Yet Chamorro had no status whatsoever. Until 1974 section 3,000 of the Guam statutes declared English to be the official language of Guam and required all persons employed by the government to "speak only English during working hours. Other languages must not be spoken except for official interpreting." A similar provision would be unthinkable in American Samoa.

All official documents, including the records of the Guam Congress, were kept only in English. In the schools—a fact lamented by an expert like L. Thompson (1947, 233)—Chamorro was admitted neither as a language of instruction nor as a mere subject, and the same holds true for the two normal schools. Still the Annual Report of the Governor for 1960 at least mentioned specific in-service training for the teaching of English as a second language (1960 Annual Report of the Governor, 83). In the beginning, however, native teachers seem to have used Chamorro often as a teaching aid for the first instruction in English; this practice was ended in 1922, when all Chamorro dictionaries were gathered and burned. There was missing, along with the teaching of the language, the most important prerequisite for an eventual use of the language in the records and documents of the territorial and local administration.

Three reasons may be cited for this long-lasting neglect of Chamorro: the tradition of Spanish administrative practices, which established it as a familiar pattern for the people of Guam to see their language excluded from written usage; the fact that Chamorro is a mixed language and as such found less esteem among the Americans than did "undiluted" languages, a reaction which is by no means without precedent in other countries; and above all the continuous presence of a large number of American military and civilian personnel who at the same time exercised sole political power on the island. They took the sole recognition of their language for granted, even though most of them stayed only temporarily in Guam.

In 1964 the territorial legislature indicated its interest in the local vernacular by Law No. 1630, which provided for the creation of a "Commission on the Chamorro Language."

Since about 1972, Chamorro has been taught and used at one public school under a BEA grant (cf. Section 2-2) and P.L. 12-31 dated June 22, 1973, authorized and exhorted the Department of Education to prepare and introduce a system-wide Chamorro Language and Culture curriculum.

In 1973, legislation was introduced by the 12th Guam Legislature to amend the Government Code of Guam to provide that English and Chamorro be the official languages of Guam; provided, however, that the Chamorro language shall not be required for official recording of public acts and translations. This amendment, which became Public Law 12-132 on May 23, 1974, constitutes a landmark in the history of America's "bilingual tradition," since it did away with the last instance of suppression by the American authorities, both federal and local, of the indigenous language in an outlying area under the American flag.

The 35,000 Chamorro of Guam form the major group of a small ethnic group whose remaining 9,000 members on the Northern Marianas live under American rule in the Micronesian Trust Territory; this fact has led to attempts to unite all Chamorro into one single territory or state (see Section 8-6). For the time being there is a strong sentiment to have the Chamorros living on the Marianas incorporated with Guam as a United States Territory. There is also much movement of the islanders to and from Guam.

In 1967 members of the Marianas Islands District Legislature visited Guam and met with representatives of the Guam legislature with whom the question of unification was discussed. The Territorial Legislature had adopted a resolution in support of the reintegration of Guam and the Northern Marianas.

In 1963 for the first time a native Guamese, Manuel Guerrero, was appointed governor. Five years later a federal law (Public Law 90-497) provided for the popular election of the governor. Section 5 of this law created the office of a "government comptroller" to be appointed by the United States Secretary of the Interior, a provision which was strongly resented by many Guamanians. Section 8 of the same Act, effective January 4, 1971, eliminates the authority of the President to act on territorial legislation; furthermore, there is the provision of the 1950 Organic Act (Section 19) that "if such (territorial) law is not annulled by the Congress of the United States within one year . . . it shall be deemed to have been approved." That section, however, does not affect adversely the existing, constitutionally derived plenary power of the Congress with respect to the territories.

With respect to the political future, the long-range thrust of the Guamese has been toward eventual statehood rather than full-fledged independence. Occasionally even the possibility of a special "commonwealth" status à la Puerto Rico has been under discussion. The more immediate goal of many Guamese is to become an incorporated territory of the United States with the Northern Marianas included, if possible.

The 13th Guam Legislature in 1975 adopted a law (P.L. 13-24) setting up a new political status commission. On May 6, 1975, Congressman Antonio B. Won Pat, Guam's nonvoting delegate to the U. S. House of Representatives, reintroduced a former bill of his in the House to extend to the Territories of Guam and the Virgin Islands the right to vote in the U. S. presidential elections. This legislation would require an amendment to the U. S. Constitution.

According to some competent observers the mood of most Guamese was not one of major change. They have been fairly content with the Guam-federal government relationship, except in certain areas where they could be allowed more freedom and autonomy.

8-3 AMERICAN SAMOA

From 1899 to 1911 this area was officially known as United States Naval Station Tutuila, since 1911 as American Samoa. It comprises the smaller (76.1 square miles) eastern part of the Samoan archipelago with 20,100 inhabitants in 1960 who speak almost exclusively the Samoan language (a member of the Polynesian language family) and who are for the most part not racially mixed with whites. The number of inhabitants as of 1970 was 27,200. The islands were occasionally visited by European ships after 1722.

The self-government of the individual islands was once based on the matais (sib chieftains), who were elected in open meetings, and the major chieftains who stood above them. In 1975, under cooperation with whites, a loose all-Samoan government under a king was established. Steinberger, an American, became the first prime minister. In 1887 the king of Hawaii, Kalakaua, harbored vague plans of annexing the islands into a United Polynesia (Grey 1960, 76).

From 1889 to 1899 a four-power rule, theoretically exercised by the United States, the German Empire, Great Britain, and the native government, existed over the archipelago. But in reality this form of government constituted a protectorate of the three great powers over the native government. In 1899 the king was deposed and a treaty of November 7 divided the archipelago, with the larger western part going to Germany and the smaller eastern part (with only 5,500 inhabitants) going to the United States. Great Britain was compensated someplace else. After 1920 Western Samoa was put under the Mandate (later Trusteeship) administration of New Zealand and became independent in 1962. The capital of American Samoa is Pago Pago. The far-off Swain's Island (about 100 Tokelauan-speaking inhabitants) was incorporated in 1925.

American Samoa was put under the Department of the Navy; the officer who heads the administration has been given the title of governor since 1903. Similar to Guam, the administration was at first one-sidedly determined by the style and the needs of a military government. Thanks partially to the example of German Samoa, a quicker way of ensuring native participation was found than in Guam (Grey 1960, 158ff.). A representative body, called "fono," met as early as 1905; its members were the matais (sib chieftains, see above) and not representatives of the people elected by secret ballot, as the Americans had wished. The fono remained the advisory body.

In 1920 an opposition movement, called Mau, developed which resented, among other things, that the laws were made public only in English and not also in the Samoan Language, and which also criticized a variety of other conditions. This movement broke up, however, in the 1930s. Repercussions came from young Samoans who had studied in Hawaii and had seen how their blood relatives were overwhelmed by foreigners.

The Naval Administration in 1948 by Executive Order 10264 established an advisory bicameral representative body; the 12 major chieftains constituted the upper house, the 52 matais of the 52 villages the lower house. Since July 1, 1951, the territory has been under the jurisdiction of the Department of the Interior with a civil governor appointed by the Department. Perhaps for the first time in the history of the United States the transition from military to civil administration was not accompanied by replacing the President with Congress as the highest authority. In 1952 a new advisory representative body was elected by secret ballot. Of the 18 original members, 12 (among them 2 women) were not major chieftains.

Efforts to get Congress to pass an Organic Act for Samoa, which would elevate the islands to the status of a regular territory, go back as far as 1930, when a Congressional committee, the Bingham Committee, visited Samoa. The Bingham Report of 1931 calls the Naval Administration on Samoa, in rather exaggerated terms, "the most unlimited autocracy the world has ever seen"; it proposed a more elastic form of administration which should enable the Samoans to abolish, if they wished, their previous customary law which had the sib as its basis. There were several bills. In 1931 and 1932 bills were adopted by the Senate but rejected by the House.

The obstacles were initially found in Washington, but later increasingly in Samoa itself, when it was concluded from the example of Guam that Congress was not willing to include the customary law of the natives in the Organic Act. For example, the prohibition to sell Samoan real estate property to whites could easily be interpreted as "segregation," and several traditional forms of services to chieftains as "peonage" (Coulter 1957, 104-105). On the other hand, in June 1951 the fono demanded its transformation from an advisory into a decision-making body.

A peculiar compromise was found: a committee, meeting since 1954 under the chairmanship of the governor, drafted a constitution which was approved by the Secretary of the Interior and which became effective on October 17, 1960. For the first time a possession belonging to the United States sphere of sovereignty was given a representative body, having decision-making power, without officially advancing to the status of a territory. This status, according to previous theory and practice, could be achieved only by a legislative act of Congress ("Organic Act"). But it would be worth pondering whether or not Samoa (and similarly the Ryukyus) can be considered as constituting a new type of territory, i.e., a "Presidential territory" created by the Executive. The Samoans continued to be just nationals and not citizens of the United States.

Under the 1960 ruling only those who had lived at least five years on Samoa could be elected to the representative body; only registered family heads who still lived according to Samoan customary law could be elected to the Senate. The election for the House was by secret ballot, that for the Senate "in accordance with Samoan custom by the council of the county he is to represent." Swain's Island possessed an untraditional representation in that the approximately 100 inhabitants were permitted to send one "delegate" who could not vote to the lower house. Every law could be vetoed by the governor, and, if adopted over the veto by a two-thirds majority, by the Secretary of the Interior (Article II, 9). The declared goal of the constitution was (Article I, 3) the protection of the "Samoan way of life and language"; possession of land, customs, and family organization should be protected by law. The governor appointed to the department of local government a major chieftain who, as Secretary of Samoan Affairs, supervised and protected the traditional communal administration (Article IV, 4).

The revised constitution as of 1966 retained most of the provisions of the 1960 version, but strengthened the position of the legislature against the governor by transferring some authority to the former, for example, in the preparation of the budget. Article 1, Section 3, of the constitution still reads (the italics are mine): "It shall be the policy of the Government of American Samoa to protect persons of Samoan ancestry against alienation of their lands and the destruction of the Samoan way of life *and language,* contrary to their best interests. Such legislation as may be necessary may be enacted to protect the lands, customs, culture, and traditional Samoan family organization of persons of Samoan ancestry, and to encourage business enterprises by such persons." This is a rather unique declaration of a polity under the American flag to protect—among other things—a non-English mother tongue and thus to perpetuate the bilingual situation.

Year by year members of the Congress of American Samoa participate in the National Legislative Conference of States and visit the Legislative Reference Bureau in Hawaii to obtain expert advice for the preparation of their own laws.

According to the spirit of the 1960 constitution, Samoan was recognized and promoted as the second official language. Most of the more important official publications appear in both languages; the deliberations of the representative body are conducted in Samoan and translated into English. Since there is no Samoan shorthand, the deliberations are taped. In 1956 P. F. Coleman, a half-Samoan, became governor. The government has published several newspapers in the Samoan language, for example, O Le Fa'atonu (1903-1953); the only radio station in the islands grants considerable time to the native language.

The school system was at first completely in the hands of missionaries who had developed Samoan into suitable forms for school instruction, written expression, and use in church sermons. An institution of higher learning designed to train young Samoans for the clergy was established in Upolu as early as the 1840s. By 1902 fifty-seven church congregations had their own schools, among them forty Methodist and thirteen Catholic. But because from 1903 on public schools which operated entirely in English were gradually established, the cultivation of the Samoan language was left as a task for the parochial "pastors' schools."

From about 1949 on, Samoan was given greater attention in the public schools, but only as a teaching aid, not as subject matter. The textbooks were entirely in English from the first grade on; for oral instruction, however, Samoan was also used. Samoan was used during the 1950s for 75% of class time in grades one through three, 50% of the time in grades four through six. After 1956 Samoan was used for 25% of class time in grades seven through nine, which had previously been taught entirely in English (Annual Report of the Governor, 1955, 20; 1956, 43).

During the school year 1960-1961, Samoan was used 40% of class time in grades one through three, 25% of the time in grades four through six, and 5% in grades seven through nine. Within each group the share of Samoan decreased somewhat with each higher grade (Report of the Department of Education 1961). The courses in the senior high school were conducted entirely in English. The public schools left instruction in the Samoan language entirely to the denominational pastors' schools.

More recently, however, the public schools have become more truly bilingual. The Department of Education, in a letter to me, states: "Our purpose is to make the Samoan truly bilingual. Because of the impact of teaching English, the deterioration of the Samoan language (especially because of its strongly oral tradition) is an everpresent danger which we must guard against daily." This consideration for the fate of the indigenous language is a factor which, as we have seen, was largely absent in American language policy on Guam.

The system of instruction is based upon the necessity of teaching English to be used as a language of instruction for needed concepts and subjects found in the twentieth-century western world that the Samoan has chosen to become a part of.

There is no Samoan literature, and the language is not suited for any kind of technical or abstract learning. Acquiring this "second language" is the chief goal of the elementary years. This approach is based upon the premise that literacy in Samoan must precede literacy in English, and for that reason the total preschool program, the first grade, and the second grade are taught wholly in the Samoan language. Beginning to a limited extent in the second grade and to a considerable extent in the third grade and beyond, English is introduced in its written form.

Oral English is begun in grade one, taught by native-English speakers supported by Samoan teachers. Instruction in Samoan virtually disappears in the upper elementary grades and high school, except that a number of courses dealing with the Samoan language and culture are continued throughout the system.

Televised instruction in the Samoan language is provided to students in lower levels on the principle that "a youngster must become proficient in his own language before learning another" (Annual Report American Samoa 1967, 17).

It is the declared policy of the Department of Education to preserve the still meaningful characteristics of "The Samoan Way of Life" (fa'a-Samoa) and to prevent the alienation of the Samoan youth from their own culture. Language is considered to be not merely an end in itself but to be bound up with a well-definable cultural inheritance. Therefore, a special course describing—in Samoan!—the history and customs of Samoa is presented to all students in level five, which consists of grades eight and nine (Annual Report American Samoa 1967, 17).

There are strong indications that some Samoans will strive for reunification with the former New Zealand Trust Territory, which became independent on January 1, 1962. But there are a number of powerful arguments against this objective, as, for example, the fear that the inhabitants of American Samoa run the risk of being outvoted within the framework of an all-Samoan state by the more than three times as numerous population of West Samoa and, above all, the sentiments created by the considerable ties established since East Samoa became part of the American sphere of sovereignty.

In this context, we have to consider the impact on the Samoan way of life as well as the emigration to Hawaii from overpopulated Samoa, which is quite considerable in relation to the small total population. In California, we also find associations of Samoans. The prevailing tendency has been to strengthen the ties with Western Samoa, short of political linkage. The establishment of an independent Eastern Samoa seemed entirely impractical. Instead, solutions patterned after the examples of Guam (territory) or even Puerto Rico (associated state) seemed to be more feasible. Political status of American Samoa as an unincorporated or unorganized quasi-territory was expected in mid-1975.

The fate of American Samoa and its language is best understood if held against a threefold background:

1. The fate of Hawaii, where the sister tongue of the Samoan language is dying out because there the Polynesians have drowned in a flood of Occidental and Oriental immigrants.

2. The modest role of the Chamorro language on Guam, where the indigenous population, while by no means inundated by "other-ethnics," is living side by side with a substantial (though fluctuating) English-speaking element.

3. Puerto Rico, which, like American Samoa, is a full-fledged bilingual polity.

8-4 THE RYUKYU

We have discussed earlier what the Ruykyu Islands (Japanese, Nansei Shoto— explained later in this section) had in common with the Bonin Islands. Both had belonged, since the second half of the last century, to Japan and were occupied by American troops in 1945. Commodore Perry, who opened Japan, had already suggested the annexation of both island groups as well as of Formosa (Pratt 1950, 5).

In Article 3 of the American-Japanese peace treaty of April 28, 1952, Japan surrendered the right of exercising all rights of sovereignty, but expressly retained "residual sovereignty" (see Section 8-1). In case America should move to place the islands under the United Nations with itself appointed as their trustee—a solution already realized for Micronesia—Japan obligates herself not to oppose this move. But the United States has never moved in this direction. On March 20, 1962, President Kennedy declared in Washington with respect to the Ryukyu Islands (not with respect to the Bonin Islands): "I recognize the Ryukyus to be a part of the Japanese homeland and look forward to the day when the security interests of the free world will permit their restoration to full Japanese sovereignty."

The Ryukyu and Bonin Islands once had a similar legal status, and on the basis of this similar status they would occasionally be found in reference works listed together under the general term "Pacific Islands under United States Control." But such similar status did not lead to common administrative ties for both island groups.

The inhabitants were considered Japanese citizens and wards of the United States.

The Ryukyu Islands are located between Japan and Formosa. The political realm comprised 2,205 square kilometers housing 945,000 inhabitants in 1970. This political unit differed from the geographical realm of the "Ryukyu Islands" insofar as on the one hand, the Daito Islands were included, while on the other hand, the northernmost Amami Gunto islands were restored to Japan in 1953.

The Daito Islands, located 340 miles east of Okinawa, are 41 square kilometers in size, and in 1960 were inhabited by 4,400 people. They were occupied by Japan in 1885 and settled from 1891 on for the purpose of raising sugar cane. No American forces were stationed there.

The Amami Gunto Islands, according to European-American usage, constitute part of the Ryukyus. Western and Japanese usage differ essentially on this question. In Japan the Nansei Shoto (Nansei Islands) are divided into the northern Satsunan group and the southern Ryukyu group (in Japanese Okinawa Gunto). The Satsunan group is divided into the smaller groups (north to south) of the

Osumi, Tokara, and Amami Islands. On the first two a dialect of the Japanese language is spoken; on the third, however, a dialect of the Ryukyuan language is used. The major island, Okinawa, includes 85% of the population and the capital of Naha.

The Ryukyuan vernacular is a sister tongue of Japanese, a linguistically autonomous language which has been dialectized (Hattori 1948, 101-133; Kloss 1967b, 29-41). According to Hattori (1948, 102), "Japanese and Ryukyuan are independent languages . . . and . . . not mutually intelligible." Its speakers have adopted the closely related Japanese language as their sole medium for purposes of writing and publishing and feel the mother tongue to be a mere dialect of the standard language, opposing statements on the part of linguists notwithstanding. However, there have been instances when attempts by the prefectural government to make the Ryukyuan abandon their native speech have led to considerable unrest. Sakamaki (1963, 249-268) mentions a "language controversy," concerning which information can be found in the first three issues of volume 2 (1940) of the magazine *Gekkan Mingei.* In the nineteenth century, incidentally, a European missionary, Bernard J. Bettelheim, translated parts of the New Testament into Ryukyuan, which was published in Hong Kong in 1852 and 1855.

Still the question whether or not the everyday Ryukyuan language, which itself is divided into many subdialects, can be considered a dialect of the Japanese language or a language remains disputed. As a language Ryukyuan is listed, among other places, in the Languages of the World Archives in Bloomington, Indiana. M. T. Newman and R. L. Eng (1948, 382) speak of "the Ryukyuan language, a sister tongue to Japanese." As expressed in a letter to the author, Dr. Loveless, a specialist in Japanese, also considers Ryukyuan a language.

For centuries the Ryukyu Islands constituted a kingdom which maintained loose political relations with Japan and China (Haenich 1937). Not until 1871 was Okinawa incorporated into the Japanese Empire. In subsequent years the king was deposed and taken to Japan; from 1879 on Okinawa was a separate prefecture. The older generation for a long time deplored the loss of independence (Kerr 1953, 205-206).

This overpopulated area sent out many emigrants, predominantly to Japan proper, to the Micronesian Trust Territory (then a Japanese mandated territory), and to Hawaii. In 1945, 285,000 Ryukyuans lived on the Japanese home islands, of whom 90,000 were evacuated there during World War II. The Ryukyus were occupied together with the rest of Japan from 1945 on by the Americans.

The most helpful references for the material that follows are Braibanti (1954, 472-498); Higa (1963), with an important bibliography; *Ryukyu Islands Facts Book*; much information from offices in Washington and Naha; and Ballantine (1953, 663-674). Further references may be found through the bibliographies by Sakamati (1963) and Kerr (1954).

It was far from self-evident that the United States should separate the Ryukyu Islands from Japan. The islands fell under none of the categories established by the Allies during the war for territories to be ceded by Japan in the future. The formula arrived at in Cairo on December 1, 1943, stated that Japan should cede territories conquered after 1914 and territories annexed by force and robbery (Commager vol. II, 660, 672; *A Decade of American Foreign Policy* 1950, 45-50).

The United States did, however, refer to the Potsdam Proclamation of July 1945, which stated that "Japanese sovereignty should be limited to the four home islands and to such minor islands as the parties to the surrender proclamation might determine." The Ryukyus question, among other things, contributed to India's refusal to participate in the peace conference at San Francisco. At the conference, Egypt demanded that the will of the Ryukyuans be respected on the basis of the right of self-determination.

The Soviet and Polish demands for a return of the islands to Japan were answered by the representative of Ceylon with the question why the same principle should not also be applied for the Kurile Islands and Southern Sakhalin, which the Soviet Union had immediately fully annexed. No historical, ethical, or ethnic reasons could be cited. It is revealing that during the debates about the peace treaty in the Senate the legitimacy of the cession was not discussed (Braibanti 1954, 475).

A glance at the map reveals that the Ryukyu Islands form a kind of natural protective belt between Japan and Formosa. The military-strategic importance of the islands in 1951 is a question, but certainly it accounted for the fact that the United States neither returned the administration to Japan nor asked that it be formally turned over to the United States by the United Nations. Ralph Braibanti concluded that the United States by abstaining from seeking United Nations Trusteeship showed its intention of returning the islands to Japan in the not too distant future, while an Indian author, R. N. Chowduri, considered it a moral obligation of the United States to accept such a trusteeship (Braibanti 1954, 983; Chowduri 1955, 125).

From the beginning of the occupation in June 1945, until July 1, 1946, the Navy was in charge of the Ryukyus; since then it has been the Army; the affairs were locally administered by a Military Governor. In 1945 the reestablishment of a native local administration was begun; and in April 1946, a native central administration for Okinawa was established.

On December 5, 1950, the United States Civil Administration of the Ryukyu Islands (USCAR)—to be distinguished from the purely military Ryukyus Command (RYCOM) was formed, but for all practical purposes it continued to have purely military top officials. The Military Governor by virtue of his post was the Supreme Commander Far East; the Deputy Governor was the Commander General for the Ryukyu Islands and was assisted by an administration expert in the person of the Civil Administrator.

When it became evident that America intended to hold onto the islands for an indefinite time, a reversion movement began to engulf the islands demanding the reversion of the islands to Japan; petitions to this effect were signed within three weeks by 199,000 persons (72% of the voting population) in the Okinawa

Island group, and within five days by 33,000 (89% of the voting population) of the Miyako Island group.

On December 25, 1953, the northernmost islands "Amami Gunto" with 21% of the population (in 1950, 148,500) were returned to Japan. Amami Gunto contains the islands between the 27th and 29th parallels. Some islands north of the 29th parallel (Jitto-son) had already been returned in December 1951. (For the text of the reversion treaty see *Ryukyu Islands Facts Book* 1961, 4.)

The gesture in 1953 relieved not only the tensions between America and Japan but also those within the Ryukyu Islands. The Amami group had to be subsidized; its historical connection with Okinawa was loose; prior to 1945 it belonged to Kagoshima Prefecture. On the same day the Secretary of State, John Foster Dulles, declared that the occupation of the remainder of the Ryukyu Islands was to continue "so long as there exist threats and tensions in the Far East"; the occupation was "essential for the success of the common efforts of the free nations of Asia and the world for peace and security" (*Civil Affairs Activities in the Ryukyuan Islands* II, 3: 76; Braibanti 1954, 986). During a short visit to Okinawa on June 19, 1960, President Eisenhower addressed the Ryukyuans more as allies rather than as conquered people, "Together we of the Ruykyus and America present to the world a splendid example. . . ." (*Civil Affairs Activities in the Ryukyuan Islands* VIII, No. 2, p. 10).

Between 1945 and 1951 an ill-defined transitory state existed in the islands. The administration slowly began to function; America sent her best occupation personnel to Japan proper. The Ryukyuans themselves had lost their skill in self-administration during the time between 1871 and 1945 when the islands formed only one of the 47 prefectures in the centralized Japanese state. The Ryukyuans were initially granted only a degree of self-administration within the framework of municipal government and the four island groups (gunto) of, from north to south, Amami, Okinawa, Miyako, and Yaeyama.

In 1947, in Okinawa gunto, which comprises the vast majority of all the inhabitants, the Okinawa Democratic Alliance (advocating independence), the Ruykyu Socialist Party (advocating United States Trusteeship), and the Okinawa People's Party (see below), which at that time did not yet take a position on the status question, were formed.

In 1950 each of the "gunto" was permitted to elect a governor; in Okinawa gunto the joint candidate of the Alliance and the Socialist Party, Matsuoka, who favored independence, received 69,900 votes; the bourgeois Taira, favoring reversion, was victorious over both Matsuoka and Senaga, the left-leaning pro-reversion candidate, with a total of 158,000 votes. Senaga received 14,100 votes.

Since 1952 there have been parties for the entire Ryukyus. In 1963 the three most important parties, which scored 86.2% of all votes in 1962, were:

1. Liberal Democratic Party (OLDP), founded in 1959, conservative, officially in favor of reversion, but relatively lukewarm; contains also some

Table 8-1   Votes in Thousands for Parties in Okinawa

Parties	1954	1958	1962
Ryukyu Democratic Party RDP	142 = 46%	78 = 22%	
Liberal Democratic Party OLDP			193 = 49%
Socialist Masses Party OSMP	130 = 41%	74 = 21%	107 = 27%
Okinawa People's Party OPP	18 = 6%		40 = 10%
Minren		94 = 27%	
Okinawa Socialist Party OSP			8 = 2%
Independents	23 = 7%	107 = 31%	47 = 12%

members who favor independence. The older Ryukyu Democratic Party (RDP), 1952-1959, was absorbed into the OLDP.

2. Socialist Masses Party (OSMP), founded in 1950 by Taira, not socialist in the Western sense, but rather left-bourgeois, clearly but not violently in favor of reversion, not opposed to the continued existence of American military bases.

3. Okinawa People's Party (OPP), founded in 1947, rather leftist, "pink," anti-American, violently for reversion, not Communist itself, but pro-Communist.

In addition there existed an Okinawa Socialist Party (OSP), which was founded around 1956 but remained relatively weak. The OSP was clearly Socialist and favorably inclined toward reversion. The party is not to be confused with the Ruykyu Socialist Party, founded in 1947, which advocated a trust territory. The OPP and OSP in 1957 formed a rather loose roof organization, "Minren," for election purposes. The name consists of the first letters of the Japanese name for Liaison Council for the Protection of Democracy. The two Minren parties demanded "immediate reversion," the OSMP, on the other hand, only "early reversion," and the pro-American OLDP, only very generally, "unification with Japan" (Higa 1963, 38). Independence was favored by the Ryukyu Nationalist Party, founded in 1958 by Ogimi Chotoku, who in 1947 had also founded the Ryukyu Socialist Party, which advocated a trust territory. The Ryukyu Nationalist Party in 1960 received only 4,500 votes and did not participate in the 1962 election.

Voting for parties is shown in Table 8-1, and the number of seats obtained by the various parties is shown in Table 8-2. The strong position of the conservative RDP (1956, 52%) and OLDP (1960, 48%) is remarkable, as is the relatively important role of the Independents, of whom many joined one of the party factions after the election.

On April 1, 1951, a provisional central government, consisting of natives, was installed; it was succeeded on April 1, 1952, by a permanent government. The official abbreviation of the Government of the Ryukyu Island was GRI. It consisted of an elected unicameral representative body and a "Chief Executive"

Table 8-2   Number of Seats Won Recently by Parties in Okinawa

Parties	1962	1964	1968
Liberal Democratic Party OLDP	18	19	20
United Opposition Bloc			15
Socialist Masses Party OSMP	7	7	
Okinawa Socialist Party OSP	1	2	
Okinawa People's Party OPP	1	1	
Independents	2	3	

who was appointed by the Americans after consultation with the Ryukyuans, and who in turn organized his own cabinet. The island parties insisted soon on two changes: the election of the Chief Executive by the parliament, and the transformation of the American authorities into genuinely civil authorities. Many steps have been taken in both directions: Executive Order No. 10,713 of June 5, 1957, replaced the American Governor by a High Commissioner who announced on June 14, 1960, that in the future he would appoint the Chief Executive from the majority party. He did, however, reserve the right to select the persons, and was himself subordinate to the Secretary of Defense rather than the Secretary of the Interior, as in Samoa an unorthodox compromise.

The High Commissioner, like the governors preceding him, had to be an active member of the armed forces (Paragraph 4). From now on the American Secretary of State was responsible for the relations between the Ryukyus and foreign countries and international organizations, such as the United Nations (Paragraph 3).

The Order defined the powers of the High Commissioner and of the local authorities. If the Chief Executive vetoes a bill passed by the chamber, the latter has the right to have it approved by the High Commissioner (Paragraph 9).

In addition to the network of native courts, a corresponding network of American courts was established. These courts were, therefore, for the first time separate from the executive power. They had long formed a part of the Government and Legal Department of USCAR; only from February 27, 1957, on there existed at least a separate Judicial Department. The American courts could at any time take over pending cases from the Ryukyuan courts when the case, in the opinion of the High Commissioner, "affects the security, property, or interests of the United States" (Paragraph 9b).

The High Commissioner was entitled to enact, within the framework of his function, laws, regulations, or guidelines; he could also veto any proposed bill, annul any law, and dismiss any official when, in his opinion, the security of the islands, their relationship to foreign countries or international organizations, or the foreign relations of the United States are affected (Paragraph 11). The power of intervention thus granted was therefore very extensive. Even though it does nor formally go as far as the power given to federal authorities with respect to territories (which goes *theoretically* so far as to empower the federal authorities to annul *any* law without the need to justify this annulment), for *practical* purposes such security clauses can be so stretched that, given the intention, every Ryukyuan law could be annulled.

But the High Commissioner saw his role more as a supervising and advising one rather than, as did the earlier governors, as an administrative function. His position seemed to be similar to that of the American civil occupation authorities in West Germany during the time preceding the founding of the Federal Republic. Under these circumstances it was possible to define the status of the Ryukyus as resembling that of a state more than that of a territory. For example, the Ryukyus were called an "autonomous state" in the Grosse Brockhaus (1956). But the High Commissioner's powers of intervention went so far as to make the status of Ryukyu more like that of the "Presidential territory" of American Samoa.

Distinct similarities can also be found in the legal status of the Saar region between 1947 and 1957, while the Saar region between 1920 and 1935 was substantially more dependent, because it did not have an elected legislature or a government composed of local people. An Executive Order of March 19, 1962, changed the Order of June 5, 1957, in several places: The High Commissioner was to be joined by a "Civil Administrator," appointed by the Secretary of Defense, as the highest civilian official; the Chief Executive was from now on to be nominated by the representative body, but continues to be appointed by the High Commissioner, to whom he must be acceptable; the High Commissioner was instructed to "give due consideration to the rights of the Ryukyuans" in exercising his power of issuing, vetoing, or annulling laws granted him under Paragraph 11. But all this did not restrict his authority in principle. The character of the Ryukyus as one similar to the status of a territory was therefore not formally abolished.

Higa (1963, 58) states as late as 1963, "In short, the High Commissioner has well-nigh absolute powers in the Ryukyus." Chief Executive Thoma defined GRI in 1957 as "an agency of USCAR"; this theory was severely criticized both in and out of the Legislature (Higa 1963, 61-62). All political parties demanded popular election of the Chief Executive.

On December 20, 1965, the President signed an amendment according to which the Chief Executive henceforth would not be appointed by Washington but elected by the legislative body of the Ryukyus. A later amendment provided for popular election of the Chief Executive. In the first popular election (November 1968) 237,600 votes were cast for Chobyo Yara, who favored immediate reunification with Japan and a gradual removal of American military bases, while his moderate opponent Junji Nishime (OLDP), who for economic reasons advocated a more gradual reversion, got only 206,200 votes. At the simultaneous election to the legislature the OLDP retained a majority of the seats (see above) though not of the votes. This constitutes a curious parallel to the November 1968 elections in Puerto Rico, where the newly elected chief executive also represented a new and less moderate trend in insular polities and where also the moderates fared slightly better in the elections to the legislature.

The Japanese public lamented and criticized the separation of the Ryukyus. This held particularly true for the political Left and the students. Attorney General Robert F. Kennedy was exposed to these sentiments during his visit to Tokyo in February 1962. First steps preparing the future return of the Ryukyus to Japan have already been made. In 1964 two important agencies were set up to ensure permanent cooperation between the governments of Japan and the United States in providing assistance to promote the economic development of the Ryukyu Islands: the "United States-Japan Consultative Committee" and the "United States-Japan-Ryukyu Technical Committee." Both were formally inaugurated by an exchange of notes between the two governments on April 25 (Civil Administration of the Ryukyu Islands, 20, 269-274). The Consultative Committee met in Tokyo, the Technical Committee in Naha, Okinawa. In this way Japanese technical assistance was being channeled into the Ryukyus.

In Tokyo the House of Representatives in 1956 and 1961 and the House of Councilors on March 14, 1962, both unanimously asked the government to start negotiations for a return of the Ryukyus. Similarly, a unanimous resolution of the legislature of the Ryukyus of February 1, 1962, urged both American and Japanese authorities as well as all United Nations members to restore promptly Japanese administrative authority over the Ryukyus. The resolution even implied that the United States was operating a colonial-style administration within Japanese territory and quoted from the United Nations General Assembly declaration of December 14, 1960, on "the necessity of bringing to a speedy . . . end colonialism in all its forms" (Higa 1963, 14).

Among the various points of dispute between USCAR and the local legislative and executive bodies, by far the most important (1954-1958) was the burning question of compensation (1955) for the approximately 40,000 land-owners whose 40,000 acres, of which 44% was farmland, were taken from them for military purposes (Higa 1963, 40-56). The occupied soil constituted 13% of the total area.

What with the provisional character of the present status of the Ryukyus the legal status of the Japanese language could hardly become problematic to a limited degree; since the islands are only loosely and temporarily "attached" to the United States, a lingual assimilation of the population can hardly be desired or attempted. English and Japanese were both official languages, not side by side but rather above and below with clearly separated spheres of application. English was the only official language of USCAR, Japanese the only official language of the native islands government (GRI).

In all schools (not considering those for the approximately 50,000 Americans) Japanese was the only language of instruction. This applies also to the university in Naha, which was founded in May 1950, and which had approximately 2,200 students in 1959. Prior to the war the islands had no university.

Since 1957 the instruction of English has been intensified with the aid of experts from the University of Michigan so that English might later serve as second language of instruction (see *Civil Affairs Activities in the Ryukyuan Islands* V, 1: 92-93 and passim).

Especially remarkable is the fact that English was missing even as a subject in the elementary schools, and was taught only from the junior high schools (seventh to ninth grades) on up. The status of English in the educational system was therefore substantially more modest than in Puerto Rico (see Section 7-4), indeed even more modest than the status of Spanish in several parts of the United States mainland (see Sections 2-2, 4-4, 5-2).

The School Education Act (Act 3, 1958) last in force in the Ryukyu Islands does not contain statutory provisions requiring elementary schools to conduct classes in Japanese; however, this act required schools to use textbooks in all subjects and at all levels approved by the Central Board of Education. All such approved books were in Japanese except those used in the classes where English was taught as a second language.

As late as 1961 public opinion opposed a proposal to introduce English as subject matter in the elementary schools. A single pilot class with volunteer participants was established. Not until January 1964—on the basis of an agreement with the Department of Education in Naha—was English instruction begun in several places on several islands from the fourth grade on (Ney 1964, 1-2).

In view of these conditions it is obvious that the indigenous cultural life was also fully developed in the private sphere. There were two large Japanese dailies in Naha (the *Okinawa Times*, circulation 60,000, and the *Ryukyu Shimpo*, circulation 50,000) plus 15 other newspapers with a total circulation of 22,000. There were numerous magazines for all possible subjects ranging from banking to education which competed against those imported from Japan (approximately 250,000 copies per month). Two of these magazines were started by Americans: the *Konnichi-no-Ryukyu* (*Ryukyu Today*), founded in 1957, circulation 15,000, and the *Shurei-no-Hikari* (*Light of Courtesy*), founded in 1959, circulation 110,000.

There were 92 movie theaters of which in 1959, 23 showed also English films with Japanese subtitles, while the others showed only Japanese films. There were two purely Japanese television stations, started in 1959 and 1960. The three purely Japanese radio stations had the largest exposure of all "mass media," reaching 80% of all the inhabitants. There were also several English-language newspapers, magazines, and three radio stations.

Many readers may consider as regrettable results of an imperialist American policy the fact that the Japanese inhabitants of the Ryukyus for the time being had to live under American rule. To present the facts in their proper perspective, it seems advisable to compare them with the fate of the Japanese in those territories which were annexed by the Soviet Union. On Southern Sakhalin, which had become Japanese in 1905, there was a population of 3,000 in 1905, 106,000 in 1920, 327,000 in 1937, and in 1945 over 400,000 persons, 97% of whom were of Japanese descent. The Soviet government expelled the entire Japanese population and settled the area with Russians. The same procedure was adopted with respect to the Japanese inhabitants of the Kurile Islands, who numbered, however, only 15,000.

The Ainus, however, were kept in both areas (1,500 in Southern Sakhalin, several hundred in the Kurile Islands) and even became the target of extensive wooing (Kolarz 1956, 104-105). Walter Kolarz, who reports these events, remarks quite accurately (1956, 67-68): "The revolutionary nationality policy of the Soviets during the Twenties would have had a simple solution to the problem; the transformation of Karafuto (Southern Sakhalin) into a Japanese Socialist Soviet Republic." But it is the Americans in the Ryukyus and not the Soviets on Sakhalin who have created an autonomous self-governing corporate body of the Japanese under their control.

The authoritative work in a Western language on the Japanese pioneer work on Sakhalin is Martin Schwind (1942).

On November 21, 1969, President Nixon and Prime Minister Sato issued in Washington a joint statement announcing that a commission would be set up to prepare reversion to take place in 1972. But one wonders whether some Ryukyuans would not like to see their islands retain a higher degree of self-government than that usually accorded to a Japanese prefecture. After all, the pre-1945 Ryukyuans considered themselves a subnationality of the Japanese. "Thus they were Japanese in about the same way the Scots are British" (Newman and Eng 1948, 384), and don't we see today a strong movement for home rule in Scotland?

8-5   BONIN ISLANDS

See Section 8-4 for the former legal position of the Bonin Islands—in English, Bonin Islands, in Japanese, Ogasawara Gunto (until the eighteenth century, Bunin-To). The 27 islands are located 800 miles east of the Ryukyus and have an area of 40 square miles with 175 inhabitants, not counting members of the American armed forces and their dependents about whom no figures are available.

White persons coming from Hawaii settled the uninhabited islands in 1830 and were later joined by other whites and natives from the South Seas. Americans and Englishmen attempted several times to annex the islands but they had no clear success, even though Commodore M. C. Perry attempted in 1853 to establish some kind of self-administration among the inhabitants (Schneyder 1941, 164-165).

The first Japanese attempt at settling and occupation from 1861 to 1863 ended when the settlers were recalled, but in 1875 the islands were formally incorporated into the Japanese Empire (Japanese Foreign Office 1947; League of Bonin Evacuees 1958). Its inhabitants from pre-Japanese times were naturalized by 1882. The number of inhabitants increased steadily: from 500 in 1886 to 4,200 in 1896, 5,800 in 1921, and 7,400 in 1940. Of these, 4,200 lived on the island of Chichi Jima, where the pre-Japanese colonists formed the little settlement of Yankeetown, 2,000 on Haha Jima, and 1,200 on the southern islands of Iwo Jima and Kita Iwo Jima which from a strictly geographical point of view form by themselves a tiny archipelago, the Volcano Islands (Sampson 1968, 128-144).

In July 1944 most of the inhabitants were evacuated to Japan; the approximately seven hundred young men who were permitted to stay on were deported by the Americans immediately following occupation. Inhabitants of American or European descent and their spouses (in all about 135 souls) were permitted to return in 1946. They settled down on Chichi Jima, while Haha Jima, Iwo Jima, and Kita Jima remained completely empty.

The islands were administered by the Department of the Navy of the United States. The department's budget also contained that of the islands. The administration with its seat in Agana on Guam was in the hands of the "Commander Naval Forces Marianas," who is under the command of the Commander Pacific Fleet. The inhabitants elected a five-member Bonin Islands Council which exercised not only advisory but also decision-making functions (taxes, fines, local laws, and appointment of a native Chief of Police).

Most inhabitants had English as their mother tongue; some still had a command of Japanese. English was used in the administration and in the only public school.

In July 1947 the evacuated Bonin islanders in Japan founded the League of Bonin Evacuees for Hastening Repatriation. The league subsequently submitted numerous petitions (by 1953 there were already about 150) to American authorities for permission to return to the islands. Several personal negotiations were also conducted. For example, a delegation of these evacuees visited Washington in 1955; and in June 1955, Prime Minister Kishi discussed this question during his stay in the United States (League of Bonin Evacuees 1958). The American ambassador in Tokyo, R. Murphy, supported these efforts as early as 1952. Among reasons cited for the American refusal were the fact that the food supply of the island was insufficient and the present white inhabitants were opposed to coming under the domination of a Japanese majority again.

Japan tried to press for the right of the islanders to return until in 1958 Dulles assured Foreign Minister A. Fujiyama that this was out of the question, thereby reversing what he had told Prime Minister N. Kishi the year before. Thereupon Japan started negotiations concerning compensation for the expellees, which led to an American-Japanese exchange of notes on July 8, 1961, in which America promised to pay $6,000,000. Japan, which originally had demanded $12,500,000, accepted this sum with the reservation that this did not mean that Japan, representing the Bonin evacuees, gave up their property claims and the claims to return to those islands; the sum is not considered compensation for the property itself but merely compensation for the present impossibility of using this property. It is of particular interest to listen to the arguments advanced for or against this settlement by members of Congress. The subcommittee concerned held hearings in 1959 where the chairman, Representative Zablocki, criticized the government proposal.

Here are some of Zablocki's arguments (Z) and their refutations by Parsons (P), Assistant Secretary of State, or by Representative Judd (J) (Committee on Foreign Affairs 1960):

1. Z: The United States did not evacuate these peoples; the Japanese did; their government owes them compensation.
   P: This holds for the time prior to the peace treaty. But they could have gone back at no expense to us if we had been willing to let them go back.
2. Z: The ordinary rules of compensation for private property are not applicable, because "we took the islands as a prize of war."
   J: But we . . . have been at peace with Japan since 1951. . . . We ought to reimburse them in the proper amount for the very reason that we believe in private property. If we do not, let us become Communists.
3. Z: This sets a dangerous precedent. (To this, no specific answer was given.)

Actually this was a most praiseworthy precedent which should be heeded wherever people have been expelled from their ancestral homes, whether in Oceania, Asia, or Europe. It should be noted that the United States paid this compensation in spite of the fact that the Japan of World War II was still being considered an aggressor. Parsons even went so far as to declare that in view of the heartache caused to the Bonin Islanders by the loss of the ancestral land any purely financial settlement could be but a second-best solution. The methods applied to calculate the damages caused to the expellees would be deserving of a special study.

Japan, however, accepted the sum "with the understanding that the acceptance did not mean the transfer to the United States of the above-mentioned property rights or interests, or prejudice in any way the claims of the Japanese nationals concerned for return to those islands." And on April 5, 1968, the United States and Japan signed an agreement for the return of the Bonin and the Volcano Islands (called Nanpo Shoto in this document) to Japan. In Article V (1) "Japan waives all claims of Japan and its nationals against the United States of America and its nationals, and against the local authorities of Nanpo Shoto and other islands, arising from the presence, operations, or actions of forces or authorities of the United States of America in these islands, or from the presence, operations, or actions of forces or authorities of the United States of America having had any effect upon these islands, prior to the date of entry into force of this Agreement." But in Article V (3) "it is confirmed that during the period of United States administration of Nanpo Shoto and other islands, the United States or local authorities have not taken any official action to transfer title to the property rights and ownership interests in these islands belonging to Japan and its nationals who during that period have been unable to enjoy the use, benefit, or exercise of such property rights or interests due to measures taken by the United States of America." This meant that the property rights of the expellees have been considered valid and inviolable over a span of twenty-three years.

The problems of the Bonin Islands are particularly interesting since the right to return to one's home country was involved. Apart from the temporary evacuation of Japanese living on the American mainland during World War II and the expulsion from Micronesia of the very recent Japanese immigrants (cf. Section 8-6), this seems to be the only case where in the nationality policy of the United States this right to one's home country of members of a separate ethnic group, the "Heimatrecht," was questioned.

8-6   TRUST TERRITORY OF THE PACIFIC ISLANDS

The Trust Territory of the Pacific Islands extends over three large island groups: the Marianas (without Guam), the Carolines, and the Marshall Islands, for a total of 96 islands with 90,900 inhabitants in 1970 and an area of 840 square miles (Trumbull 1958; Cammack 1962; Saudelmann 1953). Geographically speaking the Trust Territory is identical with Micronesia without Gram, Nauru, and the Gilbert Islands. The term Trust Territory of the Pacific Islands is therefore not very precise.

Spain had ruled over the Marianas since the eighteenth century and expanded her rule during the second half of the nineteenth century to the Caroline Islands. Both island groups were sold to Germany in 1899, which in 1885 had already annexed the Marshall Islands. After World War I all three archipelagos became Japanese-mandated territory with the administrative seat on the island of Koror (West Carolines). Japanese settlers, among them many Ruykyuans, were brought into the mandated territory. In 1932, they numbered 32,000 (as compared to 48,000 natives); of this number 25,000 alone were in the Saipan district (Clyde 1935, 152-154). In 1938, there were 70,000 Japanese (as compared to 50,000 natives) with 55,000 in the Saipan district (Report to League of Nations 1939), and in 1940 there were 132,000 Japanese.

In 1938 the Japanese settlers constituted in the Saipan district nine-tenths of the population (with only 4,200 Micronesians), on Palau over two-thirds, but in the Ponape district only one-half, in each of the Yap and Truk districts, one-half, and in the Jaluit district (including the Marshall Islands) only one-twenty-first of the inhabitants. The Japanese established separate twelve-grade primary schools for the Japanese and five-grade public schools for the Micronesian children. In all the schools Japanese was the language of instruction. From 1928 on separate textbooks for the public schools were issued. The social spheres of the Japanese and Micronesians remained separated. For example, Garapan on Saipan, the center of the sugar industry (in which no Micronesian workers were employed) was an entirely Japanese town with 12,000 inhabitants at last count. All the Japanese were expelled by the Americans.

Today jungle covers the former site of Garapan. In 1944 the islands were conquered by the United States, which has administered them since 1947 on behalf of the United Nations (*U.N. Treaty Series* 1947, 190ff.).

They were organized as a trust territory or, to be more precise, as a strategic trust territory—a move designed to quiet those people in the United States who had demanded outright annexation because of the strategic location of the islands.

Organizing the islands as a strategic trust territory meant, according to Article 83 (1-3) and Article 24 (2) of the United Nations Charter, that this trust territory was under the control of the United Nations Security Council rather than the United Nations Assembly. The former makes practically the same use of the Trusteeship Council as the latter, the only difference being that it is mandatory for the Assembly to act through the Trusteeship Council while the Security Council is "only" permitted to act through it (Chowduri 1955, 41-43, 119-125, 167-168; Toussaint 1956, 31, 150-151). In the treaty arranging for the trusteeship—up to now the only United Nations treaty for a "strategic" trust territory—it is clearly stated that the provisions for supervision, as specified in Article 87 of the United Nations Charter, shall apply.

The administrative seat for the Trust Territory was in Honolulu until 1954 and from 1954 to 1962 in Agana on Guam, i.e., still outside of the Trust Territory, a fact which was repeatedly objected to by the United Nations Trusteeship Council. Since 1962 it has been on Saipan.

From 1947 to 1951 the administration was in the hands of the Department of the Navy, and, since June 1951, the Department of the Interior had administered the territory. But in November 1952 the islands of Saipan and Tinian and in July 1953 the remaining North Marianas (with the exception of Rota) were again put under the control of the Department of the Navy, this time as the Saipan District (Executive Orders 1951, 1952, 1953). The Department of the Interior administered the Trust Territory through a High Commissioner, who headed six District Commissioners for the various island groups; the Department of the Navy administered through a Naval Administrator in Agana, whose rank was equal to that of the District Commissioners and who was directly responsible to the Commander of the Pacific Fleet. The Commander of the Pacific Fleet and the High Commissioner coordinated the policy of their administration without outside interference.

The inhabitants of the Saipan District were, like the inhabitants of the Caroline and Marshall Islands, citizens of the Trust Territory. These two factors (continuing mutual coordination and uniform citizenship) made it possible to treat the Saipan District and the rest of the Trust Territory as one political entity and not as two (as, for example, the Ryukyu and Bonin Islands). The American annual reports to the United Nations about the Trust Territory included the Saipan District, but the district had its own budget which was contained in that of the Navy Department.

This dual structure, which came close to a partition of the Trust Territory, was frequently criticized in the United Nations (Jacobson 1960, 56-66m esp. 62). A lasting subordination of trust territories under a military administration was considered a violation of the spirit of the trusteeship provisions. It was furthermore feared that the separation might become permanent, particularly since corporate bodies of the Saipan District asked in 1950 for incorporation into the United States, either as a possession or as a territory (Document T 10/5 of 6/121 1950, 2; Report of the Visiting Mission 1950). In 1960 the Congress of the

Saipan District was even more precise and asked for incorporation into the Territory of Guam. This action was immediately favorably received by the legislature of Guam (Jacobson 1960, 62). A resolution of the legislature of Guam to appoint a legislative commission which would "bring to the attention of the people of Guam the possibility of a reunification of the Marianas" was not carried out. As far as I know no new steps have been taken. The Saipan District was, incidentally, the only district which as yet showed elementary forms of political parties. The administration of the Trust Territory proceeded then to inform the inhabitants of the Saipan District that the United Nations would not approve a partial cessation of the trusteeship relation which would apply only to the Saipan District. This was expressly approved by the United Nations Security Council (Report on Trust Territory 1960/61, 141), but I was informed by the American delegation at the United Nations in April 1960 that the Security Council never took up the matter. According to the Yearbook of the U. N. (1960, 485), the Trusteeship Council of the United Nations received a petition of the Congress of Saipan without acting upon it. In 1959 a Visiting Mission sent by the United Nations into the Trust Territory expressed, without disputing the close relation-ship between the Chamorro of Guam and the Saipan District, the desire that the "unity and identity" of the Trust Territory be preserved (*Yearbook of the U.N.* 1959, 590). In 1962 the pattern of dual control came to an end by Executive Order No. 11021 of May 7, transferring the Saipan District back to the Secretary of the Interior (Report on Trust Territory 1965, 8).

Since, according to Article 73 (b) of the United Nations Charter, it is the function of the administration of the Trust Territory to bring about "self-government or independence" and since "incorporation" into Guam would in orthodox interpretation represent a third solution, a contradiction seems, at first glance, to exist between Article 73 (b) and the principle of self-determination (Toussaint 1956, 59). In my opinion, however, this contradiction would only be fictitious. To evaluate this question, consult the provisions for the conditions under which the obligation to report to the United Nations about a previously dependent territory would end, adopted by the United Nations on November 27, 1953, and December 21, 1960 (Doc. A/2630 Suppl. 17; Doc. A/RES/1541 (XV) 21-23). The 1953-1962 question was complicated by the United States in a manner difficult to understand by the special treatment given to the island of Rota, a Mariana Island, which remained part of the Trust Territory proper and which in 1955 became a separate (Seventh) district. The Chamorro were therefore divided into three parts: Guam, Rota, and the remainder of the Marianas. The problem was accentuated by the fact that the Chamorro, as a result of their century-long cultural contact with the West, consider themselves superior to the other natives in the Trust Territory. (Incidentally, one fourth of the inhabitants of Saipan consist of descendants of immigrants from the Caroline Islands who retained their Caroline dialects.)

The natives of the Trust Territory are neither citizens nor nationals of the United States. As citizens of the Trust Territory they enjoy a partly more favorable legal position than do American citizens; the latter are not permitted to acquire real estate or start private enterprises which could pose a threat to those established by the natives.

The administration worked very quickly toward the introduction of local and district self-administration in the Trust Territory. The lack of experience of the natives, their lingual division, and the distances between the islands made the immediate establishment of a general representative body seem unsuitable. But gradually district councils and legislatures came into existence for the individual island groups. The first was, in 1947, a council for the Palau District which was transformed several years later into a decision-making body (the Palau Congress), while other districts for the time being possessed only councils. After 1956 there was an Inter-district Advisory Committee for the entire Trust Territory whose members were initially appointed; later they were delegated by the corporate bodies of the districts.

In 1965 the Advisory Committee, by Order No. 2882 as of September 28, 1964, of the Secretary of the Interior, was replaced by a full-fledged legislature, the bicameral Congress of Micronesia. According to section 17 (f) "All legislative proceedings shall be conducted in the English language: Provided, that knowledge of the English language shall not be qualification for membership in the Congress. Nothing herein shall limit the right of a member to use his native language if he lacks fluency in English, and the Congress shall provide for interpretation into English in such cases." The journals of both Houses appear only in English (High Commissioner of . . . Pacific Islands 1965, 13-14, 17-18). All of the territorial and most of the district congress members are elected by popular vote; only the district legislatures of the Marshall Islands and of Palau have certain members who acquire membership because of their hereditary status; in the Palau Congress they do not have the right of voting.

Many high-ranking government officials were Micronesians: in 1973, all District Administrators and three out of eight heads of major program departments in the Executive Branch.

In 1967 President Johnson proposed to Congress that a special commission on Micronesia establish political alternatives for the Trust Territory. Under the President's proposal, a plebiscite conducted by the United States would be held before June 30, 1972. This proposal was passed by the United States Senate on May 30, 1968 (Senate Joint Resolution 106). However, no action on the measure was taken in the House of Representatives beyond hearings held by the Committee on Interior and Insular Affairs. Similar proposals to establish a political status commission were introduced in the 91st Congress (1969), but these did not specify a plebiscite date.

In May 1969, Secretary of the Interior Hickel during a visit to the Trust Territory invited the Congress of Micronesia to send representatives to Washington to help develop legislation for submission to the United States Congress which would end the United Nations trusteeship and build a lasting political partnership with the United States.

On July 21, 1969, following two years of wide-ranging study, a six-member territorial commission on the future political status of the Trust Territory reported back to its parent body, the Congress of Micronesia. It recommended a redefined but continuing partnership with the United States. Thereupon, the Congress of Micronesia passed a joint resolution urgently requesting the President and the Congress of the United States to "give serious consideration to the future political status of Micronesia and the ways in which this Status should be finally resolved." Since the fall of 1969 negotiations for the future political status of the Marshalls and Carolines (which presently comprise five districts of the Trust Territory) have been continuing between the United States and the Congress of Micronesia. The Marianas Islands District and the United States have completed two years of political status negotiations and on June 17, 1975, the people of the Marianas voted in a United Nations observed plebiscite to approve a "Convenant to Establish a Commonwealth of the Northern Marianas Islands in Political Union with the United States of America," the approval margin being 78.8%. This points to a future break-up of the Trust Territory along ethnic lines—Chamorro vs. non-Chamorro—a solution which would run counter to a stubborn U.N. majority policy which insists on the perpetuation of that most artificial and unnatural of colonial innovations, namely, colonial boundary lines.

The earlier resettlement of the inhabitants of Bikini (1946), Eniwetok (1947), Rongelap, and Utirik to other parts of the Trust Territory in connection with the American A-bomb tests constitutes a delicate problem (Trumbull 1952, 43-49).

The 75,800 inhabitants in 1960 were subdivided into nine language groups of which one, with 700 persons, belongs to the Polynesian, two (Chamorro and Palauan) with 18,400 persons to the Indonesian, and six with 56,700 persons to the Melanesian language family. Most of these nine languages in turn are themselves subdivided into dialects. There are 9,100 people on the predominantly Chamorro-speaking islands (the northern Marianas) and 9,300 people on the Palauan-speaking islands. Polynesian is spoken on the Nukuoro and Kapinga-marangi Atolls in the eastern Caroline Islands. The six Melanesian languages are those of the Caroline Islands (Yap, Ulithi and Woleai, Truk, Ponape, and Kusaie) and that of the Marshall Islands (with 14,900 inhabitants). The dialect of the islands of Sonsoral and Tobi, which we considered as a form of Palauan, is considered a separate language by some linguists. On Saipan (one of the Marianas) one-fourth of the population is made up of the descendants of nineteenth-century immigrants from the Carolines who have retained their language. A certain emigration from the Trust Territory takes place on Palau and is primarily directed toward Guam.

The introduction of one general language was necessary in a region characterized by such a diversity of languages, and it would have surprised nobody had the United States practically ignored the native languages of the Trust Territory. To be sure, a knowledge of English could not be presupposed among the adults even after fifteen years of United States administration; but it was nevertheless not inevitable (a Romance nation would act differently), but only practical, that around 1960 the district congresses and councils not only conducted their deliberations but also kept their records in the native languages (Report on ... the Trust Territory 1961, 21) and that, "In the district and community courts, proceedings are ordinarily in the principal indigenous language, and records are kept either in that language or in English" (ibid., p. 36). In the High Court, proceedings and reports are ordinarily in English, but pleadings in indigenous languages are frequently accepted. Proceedings in the Trial Division are normally translated orally in open court into the principal indigenous language of the area where the proceedings are being held. Further translation is also provided for any defendant who understands neither English nor such principal indigenous language.

It is surprising that even the public elementary schools gave instruction entirely in the native language. Also the intermediate schools—usually located in the district capitals—were bilingual, even though the major emphasis was on English. Only the high school in Ponape was conducted entirely in English. A directive of the High Commissioner of 1959 read as follows (*13th Annual Report ... on the Trust Territory* 1961, 145):

> "Teachers and students should be encouraged to use and esteem their island languages. ... What the students know at the beginning of their language training, is their mother tongue. Therefore, it should generally be the mother tongue of the students in which instruction is given at the level of the elementary schools. Teaching aids, textbooks, and other reading material should be made available in all island languages. In the intermediate schools, English should be emphasized more clearly but not at the expense of the native languages."

Even as a subject, English for a long time was taught only in isolated instances in elementary schools because only a few teachers had sufficient command of the language. The use of visiting teachers was not practical because of the tremendous distances. (But a Romance state would have hired only Romance teachers.) In cooperation with the Literature Production Center of the South Pacific Commission at Honiara, Guadalcanal (Solomon Islands), instruction material in the mother tongues was prepared for and by the schools (*13th Annual Report 1961*, 124; *14th Annual Report* 1962, 113). In addition, simple mimeographed news-sheets were compiled either by some of the intermediate schools or by the district governments, for example, *The Truk Review*, a bilingual mimeographed monthly (English and Truk languages).

The administration of the Trust Territory also had certain documents of basic importance translated into the most important island languages, for example, the United Nations resolution of December 14, 1960, about the termination of imperialism and a brochure on the character and functions of the administration of the Trust Territory. And, what is most important, the Trust Territory code has been translated into the major district languages.

In the missionary schools, which have fewer students than the public schools at the elementary level but considerably more at the intermediate and high school level, the language problem was solved in a similar fashion.

In 1962 a complete change of policy took place; from that time on, all teaching was to be done in the English language with the indigenous languages being relegated to the status of auxiliary tongues. The High Commissioner's Report for 1965 states that English is now the language of instruction "in conformance with the desire of the Micronesians." But in 1968 a new change took place with the launching of a five-year territory-wide program for Teaching English as a Second Language (TESL). The basic goals of the TESL program are: (1) to develop English language skills so that Micronesians can best participate in ongoing educational programs and so that English may truly become the general language of communication and instruction; and (2) to teach literacy in the Micronesians' own language. The Tate Oral English syllabus, a system of instruction which has proved effective in other Pacific island areas, forms the basis of the English program. Elementary pupils receive a minimum of one hour of English language instruction daily, while secondary students receive from one to four hours daily. No attempt to teach English reading is made until pupils have had one year of oral English instruction and have learned to read in their own language.

In May 1967, the English Language Supervisors from each district of the Trust Territory met at Headquarters with the English Language Supervisor and others of the Education Department Staff to restate the TESL Program policies for the schools of the Trust Territory. The basic objective, as now stated is: "English shall become the general language for communication and instruction in the Trust Territory." In addition, the following basic principles were established as policy:

1. "Elementary school children, starting in grade one, shall be taught to read in their local language.

2. "English shall be taught as a second language. The TESL Program includes two major areas: (a) oral English and (b) literacy in English.

3. "English shall become the medium of instruction in the schools as soon as the students indicate sufficient evidence of their ability to comprehend other subjects in English."

It is important to note that as a result of the progressive language policy of the administration of the Trust Territory the language of the Chamorro enjoyed substantially more rights there than on Guam. It is furthermore worth noting that twice there have been American enthusiasts at work to strengthen the cause of the vernaculars: in the early years of American administration (1945 to about 1956) a small number of trained linguists; since 1966 nearly 600 Peace Corps volunteers, who are required to learn the local language and for whom new lesson materials in these languages were developed.

The generous policy pursued by the Americans of using the native languages along with English in Micronesia gives rise to an interesting question of a more basic nature. At the moment it no doubt serves not only the presumable wishes of the inhabitants but also their objective interests; there is no possible aspect under which this policy could be criticized. But quite another question is whether it is in the interest of the inhabitants that their languages be preserved in perpetuity or whether it would not facilitate their entry into the modern world if they were gradually to adopt the exclusive use of English. If this point of view were to become prominent among them, it would presumably become evident that this change of languages would have been made not more difficult but, on the contrary, much easier as a result of the present generous language policy of the Americans. Even the integration of the North American Indians into the English language, judging from all experiences of anthropological psychology, would have been facilitated and expedited rather than impeded or delayed if the Anglo-Saxons had at first enabled the Indians to learn how to read and to write in their own languages and in this manner to acquire that minimum degree of modern attitudes which constitutes the best basis for a gradual adoption of the English language.

8-7   THE AMERICAN VIRGIN ISLANDS

The "Virgin Islands of the United States," an island group in the Caribbean, was occupied during the seventeenth century first by the Netherlands and in 1672 by Denmark. When, soon after the Civil War, Denmark considered ceding the islands to the United States there was a plebiscite. It was held in January 1868, the first of its kind in the Western Hemisphere (cf. Wambaugh 1920, pp. 149-155, 945-976): Negroes were entitled to vote. A majority voted for joining the United States; Congress, however, never ratified the Copenhaguen treaty (Oct. 24, 1866) underlying the plebiscite, and the islands remained Danish until 1917, when Denmark sold them to the United States. The capital is Charlotte Amalie. The population amounted to 32,100 in 1960 and rose rapidly to 62,500 in 1970. The inhabitants generally spoke English at the time of the purchase so that no language or nationality problem existed for the entire island group. But there exists a race problem, since more than four-fifths of the inhabitants are Negroes. One event in the legal history of the Virgin Islands is also directly important for the development of nationality law. In 1936 the islands became a territory of the fourth category with an elected representative body consisting of members of both local chambers. But in 1954 Congress deemed it necessary to reduce the degree of self-government by a new Organic Act (Butler 1954), perhaps the only case of such a retrograde development in United States history, comparable perhaps to the reduction in status imposed on Newfoundland by England in 1934. Article 17 of the Revised Organic Act provides for a federal "government comptroller" who shall be appointed by the Secretary of the Interior and who shall supervise the finances of the island government. In 1970 for the first time the governor was elected by popular vote on the basis of P.L. 90-496 (Aug. 26, 1968) which also revised the 1954 Organic Act by giving greater autonomy to the territory. Yet resentment concerning the status of the Islands remained strong. Said a Virgin Island senator at a 1967 Washington hearing: "The British West

Indies Islands all around us were once many light years behind us in home rule. Yet beginning February 27, Antigua will become an associated state comparable to the Commonwealth of Puerto Rico." A female colleague added: "Will it be said that the United States Virgin Islands are at the bottom of the Caribbean ladder with regard to self-government?" (Hearings before the Territories and Insular Affairs Subcommittee 1967, 43, 50). It would seem that she had never heard about the French Antilles. As of 1975 no change in political status seemed imminent, although the nonvoting Virgin Islands Delegate to the U. S. House of Representatives, Ron de Lago, introduced legislation endorsing the calling of a constitutional convention for the territory.

The islands are characterized by a number of ethno-lingual conditions: In earlier times, the so-called Negro-Dutch (a Creole derivation of the Dutch language and practically extinct today) was used as an everyday and church language (Kloss 1952, 154-155, with bibliography).

In 1850 French-speaking fishermen from the island of St. Barthelemy came to St. Thomas, where their descendants (called Cha-Cha on the Island) formed two groups, one living in a quarter of Charolotte Amalie, the other living in scattered settlements. Under Danish rule these Frenchmen had at least one private French school and a branch of the Alliance française. Both closed after 1917 but were reopened in the mid thirties.

In recent decades Puerto Ricans have immigrated to the island of St. Croix (Wells 1953, 86-92, 146, 179-180; Butler 1954). They were unpopular because of their Spanish language, their Catholic religion, their diligence, and their preference for farm work, which has been held in low esteem among the Negroes since the days of slavery. In 1960 the Puerto Ricans constituted approximately one-third of the inhabitants of St. Croix, in 1969, 42%. But under the Organic Act of 1936 they were unable to assert themselves, despite the fact that after 1917 they had become American citizens, the right to vote having been made dependent upon a literacy test in English; but Congress, against the opposition of the local Negroes, dropped this language clause in the Organic Act of 1954 (section 4) at the request of the Puerto Ricans. An association of Virgin Islanders living in New York declared in connection with the request for the deletion of the language clause: "It gives latitude for the passage of Spanish legislation over the heads of American people" (Butler 1954, 62-63). Thus the 3,000 Puerto Ricans succeeded where 800,000 of their countrymen failed in New York (see Section 3-1). About 1968, the lower grades (K to grade 2) of a school in Kingshill on St. Croix became bilingual (Andersson and Boyer II, 1970, 254). And a law of April 19, 1972, made bilingual instruction obligatory for all schools with at least 10 pupils knowing no or very little English. Bilingual education was being encouraged in the schools.

8-8 CANAL ZONE

The Canal Zone is a strip of land of 655 square miles, which stretches along both sides of the Panama Canal. In 1903 the newly established Republic of Panama ceded to the United States the right to exercise sovereignty in perpetuity without, however, terminating the Panamanian claim to sovereignty (see Section 8-1). At that time, the Zone was almost uninhabited. The treaty of annexation (Article VI) does mention the protection of land titles (*Canal Zone Code* 1934, 841), but not the protection of possible inhabitants. Thus there was no established Spanish-speaking minority. Since private ownership of land is not permitted in the Zone, such an ethnic group, settling permanently in the area and gradually establishing itself, can hardly be formed.

In 1960, of the 40,100 inhabitants of the Canal Zone, only 10,400 were born in the Zone itself, 19,600 in the United States proper, 1,100 in United States possessions, 7,200 in the Republic of Panama, and 1,200 in the British West Indies.

The administration is headed by a governor, who by virtue of his office is at the same time President of the Panama Canal Company (founded in 1951). The Governor is directly responsible to the President of the United States; the Secretary of Defense supervises his activities. The capital is Balboa Heights. The only official language is English. But Spanish translations of documents are published if necessary; the annual reports of the Governor, however, are published only in English (Letter from Canal Zone Government, Sept. 12, 1961).

For decades there existed in the Canal Zone not so much a problem of the Latin American language group but more a racial problem concerning the Negroes. When in 1906 the first public school was opened, 90% of its students were black, and in 1939 there were still 3,300 black as compared to 3,249 white students. The former attended separate public schools. In 1934 even a separate teachers' college was established to serve these "black" schools (Cook 1939). From the very beginning, most of the blacks were foreigners with English as their mother tongue, i.e., West Indians. For example, in 1920 of the 27,700 inhabitants (excluding the military), 10,900 foreign-born Negroes had English as their mother tongue while only 3,800 had Spanish. There were only 1,100 whites of English (600) or Spanish (500) tongue. Since there was only a relatively small Spanish-speaking minority, English became by necessity the only official language of the Canal Zone.

Since then, blacks born in the British West Indies have almost disappeared in the Canal Zone (in 1950 only 4,500; 1960 only 1,200). Even though of the 42,100 inhabitants in 1960 there are still 13,900 blacks, 5,900 of them have been born in the Zone itself and 5,100 in the Republic of Panama; 220 whites also list the Republic of Panama as their country of birth. Negroes born in the Canal Zone as well as in the Republic of Panama are predominantly descendants of immigrants from the British West Indies. In 1954 the segregated schools for Negroes were abolished in the zone.

Schools in the Canal Zone are operated primarily for the children of employees of the Panama Canal Company and Canal Zone Government resident in the Zone. The schools are divided into two segments, Spanish-language schools for Panamanian citizens and English-language schools for United States citizens—from kindergarten through grade twelve.

The curriculum in the Spanish-language schools approximates that pre-scribed by the Ministry of Education for the schools in the Republic of Panama.

The curriculum in the English-language schools follows the educational pattern in the United States. Teachers in the Spanish-language schools are Panamanian citizens and are recruited locally in the Republic of Panama, while teachers in the English-language schools (except for foreign language teachers) are United States citizens.

Dependents of private United States citizens resident in Panama are accepted into the English-language schools on a tuition basis. Dependents of United States citizens who are employees of other United States Government agencies are accepted into the English-language schools with costs for their education reimbursed to the Panama Canal Company by the other agencies. Students who are not American citizens may be accepted into the English-language schools on a tuition basis to the extent that there is space available and after passing a test in English-language proficiency. There is not always sufficient space to accept all such applicants.

Spanish is taught as a foreign language to all pupils in the English-language elementary schools in grades one through six. It is an elective course for pupils in the English-language secondary schools, grades seven through twelve.

In the Spanish-language schools English is taught as a foreign language to all pupils in grades three through twelve. According to an administrative agreement with the Republic of Panama, the program of instruction in the schools for Panamanian children, i.e., the Latin-American schools, shall parallel that provided by the Ministry of Education in Panama. That implies the use of Spanish as the main teaching tool; in the high schools, however, English is used as a language of instruction in science and mathematics. Instruction in grades thirteen and fourteen at Canal Zone College is conducted in English. Though established for the children of employees who are United States citizens, admission is open to all residents of the Canal Zone on the basis of examinations. Students are also admitted from Panama on a space-available basis. There is a reduced tuition for all residents of the Zone regardless of citizenship.

In 1970 there were about 11,000 students in the English-language elementary and secondary schools, 2,500 in the Spanish-language schools, and 1,300 (mostly part-time) at Canal Zone College.

8-9 SMALLER ISLANDS WITH NO EVIDENT NATIONALITY PROBLEM

For the sake of completeness, several minute overseas possessions of the United States may be mentioned which have no evident nationality problem. None of these possessions has more than 2,500 inhabitants, and in all cases these inhabitants do not constitute an established population that was present before Anglo-Saxon arrival but are made up of recent and mostly fluctuating arrivals (Table 8-3).

Canton Island is claimed by both the United States and Great Britain and in 1939 came provisionally under a joint administration of both powers. It became uninhabited when long-range jet aircraft rendered its airport superfluous. Of its former (1960) 320 inhabitants, 131 (41%) stemmed from the Fiji and Gilbert and Ellice Islands, while 172 were American and 17 were white British citizens.

Table 8-3   Population of Small Overseas
                 Possessions of the U. S.

Island	1970	1960	1950	1940
Midway	2,220	2,356	416	437
Wake	1,647	1,097	349	
Johnston	1,007	156	46	69
Canton		320	272	44

Great Corn Island, leased from Nicaragua, does not belong to the American sphere of sovereignty. The island, which was settled under British rule by English-speaking Negroes, has belonged to Nicaragua since 1887. It was formed into a district (distrito) in 1890, and leased to the United States for ninety-nine years in 1914. In 1950 the island had 1,304 inhabitants of whom 1,241 were citizens of Nicaragua, 1,100 of them Negroes or Zambos (Indian-Negroes). Of the inhabitants, 1,258 were of English, 33 of Spanish, and 13 of Indian mother tongue. Corn Island is the only inhabited overseas possession of the United States which is under the administration of the State Department. Under the silent approval of the State Department and not affected by the American lease of the island, Nicaragua continues to handle the practical administration. Therefore, Spanish is presumably the official and the school language. The administrative seat is Bluefields, the capital of the Department of Zelaya. Information from the State Department (signed G. E. Pearcey) in Washington and the Ministerio de Relaciones Exteriores in Managua tells us that in 1962 there were an estimated 1,632 inhabitants. The census held in 1963 did not include a question concerning the mother tongue.

Finally, there are the numerous uninhabited islands and atolls which are considered part of the American sphere of sovereignty. Several are at the same time claimed by Great Britain (as, for example, Enderbury), others by New Zealand. Little Corn Island, leased, like Great Corn Island, from Nicaragua, is also uninhabited.

CHAPTER NINE

The Summing Up

9-1 REVIEW

Contrary to the opinion generally held outside the United States, which is also rather prominent within the United States, the American nationality laws were extraordinarily varied and well developed. Almost without exception the lingual assimilation which the non-English groups on the mainland underwent has been considered to have been the result of a purposeful assimilation policy on the part of the state. Considering the numerous non-English groups of immigrants, so it is stated, the Americans could not help but insist upon the sole use of English in all elementary schools—and the result would consequently have been the almost general Anglicization of the descendants of the immigrants.

As our study shows, on the other hand, the non-English ethnic groups in the United States were Anglicized not *because of* nationality laws which were *unfavorable* toward their languages but *in spite of* nationality laws relatively *favorable* to them. Not by legal provisions and measures of the authorities, not by governmental coercion did the nationalities become assimilated, but rather by the absorbing power of the highly developed American society. The nationalities might be given innumerable possiblities for systematic language maintenance; the manifold opportunities for personal advancement and individual achievements which this society offered were so attractive that the descendants of the "aliens" sooner or later voluntarily integrated themselves into this society.

Nor can it be denied that, individually and as a group, or as a subset of a group, the members of the dominant majority did much to discourage language retention. This holds for civil servants, including teachers, quite as much as for the rest of Anglo-American society. Derision was, and still is, in store for those who master English imperfectly, and they will find it difficult to climb the economic ladder. Even a marked foreign accent may become a hallmark of social inferiority. Thus not only achievements of American society are responsible for the shrinkage of communities of non-English speech, but also societal attitudes displayed toward (and sometimes against) members of linguistic minorities.

Do, after all, the facts presented in this book justify our speaking of an American bilingual tradition? For various reasons, I am convinced that they do.

I. The one outstanding phenomenon is the almost unlimited freedom to cultivate non-English languages among and for adults. There have been the traditional tools serving the cultivation and retention of a language, such as churches, clubs and other associations, the press, the stage, private libraries, and publishing houses. To these have been added in recent times the movies, television, and, most of all, radio broadcasts. That the latter have become of paramount importance becomes evident from the fact that in 1960 only 3 of the 50 states (Kentucky, North Carolina, Tennessee) had no regular non-English radio broadcasts. In the other states the number of stations broadcasting foreign language programs ranged from 1 (Delaware, South Carolina) to 80 in New York, 81 in Pennsylvania, 106 in Texas, and 116 in California (Fishman 1962, 44-77, esp. 72).

This liberal tradition has been almost uninterrupted since 1776, the one major exception being the rigorous clamping down on the use of German during and immediately after World War I.

II. Even more telling and convincing is the fact that throughout large periods of American history, including our times, there have been polities under the American flag which were officially and completely bilingual. The four most outstanding examples are:

1. The official bilinguality of Louisiana in the period between the attainment of statehood and the Civil War, a development culminating in the language clauses of the 1845 and 1852 constitutions and the 1847 school law.

2. The official bilinguality of New Mexico since the attainment of territorial status in 1852, a bilinguality which only gradually and slowly faded away in our century.

3. The official bilinguality of Puerto Rico since 1900, which gradually has evolved in such a way that today Spanish is what the French would call *la langue prioritaire* with English clearly relegated to a position of lesser importance.

4. The continuing bilinguality of American Samoa, which is restricted merely by certain limitations inherent to the Samoan language; that is, the small number of its speakers and its still rather underdeveloped state.

III. In the United States there have been these two phenomena: general tolerance for the cultivation of all non-English languages among adults and promotion of certain non-English languages up to (and in Puerto Rico even beyond) complete equality with the national language. Between these two poles, there are numberless other instances bearing witness to American liberality, of which the three following may be singled out as particularly striking:

1. The high degree of promotion-oriented rights accorded to all sizable groups that came to North America in colonial times: the Germans in Pennsylvania and their offspring in early Ohio, later reinforced by newcomers from Germany; early Hispanos in California, Texas, Colorado.

2. Regard for immigrant languages in many, probably a majority, of the public libraries.

3. Almost complete freedom to cultivate ethnic tongues in nonpublic schools down to World War I, only partially restored in and since 1923. The 1967 Bilingual Education Act is the first major measure adopted at the federal level in order to promote bilingualism. It may be said to be much more in keeping with widespread though little-known American traditions than some of those who fought for its adoption may have been aware of.

The conclusion that it is justified to speak of an American bilingual tradition must not be understood to imply that it was the prevailing, let alone the, American tradition with regard to language policy. There always has been and still is a powerful tradition upholding the merits and desirability of "one country, one language," a tradition which has been so much in the foreground that the rival tradition has been well-nigh forgotten, especially during its partial eclipse in the years after World War I.

Admittedly, large-scale assimilation was facilitated by the fact that many immigrants, when entering the country, were prepared to see their children give up the inherited tongue, an attitude which differs widely from that prevalent among minorities in Europe. This readiness to yield to the impact of a new culture might soon have disappeared, however, had they come to look at the culture of the New World as inferior to that of their old country.

There were only isolated instances of an oppressive state policy aiming at the elimination of non-English languages. There were, however, a great many instances in which individuals (including public school teachers) and groups exerted unofficial moral pressure upon members of the minority groups, especially children, so as to make them feel that to stick to a "foreign" tongue meant being backward or even un-American.

Legal provisions and legal practices and contents and the application of the legal norms certainly did not always or everywhere coincide. But where they differed from each other, legal practices were often even more favorable than the written law was. In Ohio, for example, German in Cincinnati had become a tool of instruction of the public elementary school in 1840. A school law of 1870 reduced German to the position of a subject. German nevertheless retained its position as a tool of instruction until World War I. In contrast, where the written law was more favorable than the legal practice, this situation was often the result of the fact that the Americans retained a legal provision in favor of a minority language, even though the minority had long since become uninterested in this provision and no longer made use of it. In Louisiana the French ethnic group had from 1890 on become almost completely indifferent and had in a certain sense ceased to voice a desire for language provisions in such fields as the schools or the promulgation of laws. Only the constitution of 1921 and a law of 1922, for example, took final notice of this changed condition of the French ethnic group as far as the school system was concerned. In Pennsylvania, German editions of the Governors' messages were rarely requested after 1850 and not requested at all after 1880 by the old established population. Nevertheless the German editions were frequently authorized until the 1890s. The German press of eastern Pennsylvania survived after 1890 because of the official notices to which it had a legal claim because of older laws. Even though the editors of English-language newspapers complained, these laws were not abolished until the newspapers had died from internal exhaustion, in spite of this artificial nourishment.

In two areas above all we have met two really great achievements of the American nationality policy: on one hand, the creative application of the right of self-determination and on the other hand, in the area of language policy, the careful, but purely pragmatic and never theoretical, development of a system of laws for old established settlers and a system of laws for later immigrants.

Speaking at first about the right of self-determination, the unorthodox way in which it was solved in Puerto Rico deserves to be particularly emphasized. It is a cardinal mistake to see the exercise of the right of self-determination as meaning a change of the existing political affiliation. As the decision of the Ticino in 1798 in favor of Switzerland and that of the Puerto Ricans in favor of the United States have demonstrated, the right of self-determination can be exercised also in the sense that an ethnic group decides to remain in the same state under more honorable and more liberal terms than before.

This contribution of the Americans to the practice of the right of self-determination has already shown its results in several United Nations documents. On November 27, 1953, the General Assembly of the United Nations recognized that the Commonwealth status for Puerto Rico freed the United States from any further obligation to include the island in the annual reports on United States dependencies. On the same day, the General Assembly recognized also the principle of association as one of the possibilities of realizing the right of self-determination. The distinction between the terms "association" and "integration," which was still unclear at that time, was substantially improved in 1960 (Document A/2630; Document A/RES/1541; Kloss 1962, 75-78, 93-94; Fahrni 1967). The result is that since then the United Nations recognizes three possibilities of doing justice to the principle of self-determination: independence, integration (which would have meant statehood in the case of Puerto Rico), and association. In this connection it must be noticed that two concepts of association have developed since then which are interrelated but, nevertheless, quite different from each other. The one concept, put into practice in the case of Puerto Rico and referred to in the United Nations resolution of 1960, interprets association as the legal relationship between two partners in which one of the partners retains a clearly superior position with respect to the other so that association remains here

an alternative to independence (or integration). Similar relations exist (van Heldingen 1957, 1960; van Panhuys 1958, 1; Sady 1957, 97) between

>The Cook Islands and New Zealand
>The Faroe Islands and Denmark
>Six island states in the Caribbean and Great Britain
>"Dutch America" (Surinam, Netherlands Antilles) and the Netherlands

Furthermore:

de jure but not *de facto* relations between Kashmir and India.
de facto but not *de jure* between West Berlin and the Federal Republic.

Friedrich (1959, 16-17) has pointed out a certain analogy between West Berlin
and Puerto Rico. According to Friedrich, West Berlin occupies *de jure* the position
of a state but *de facto* that of an internally associated entity.

In contrast to this concept, Greece's association with the European
Economic Community, for example, and de Gaulle's former plans for an
association of Algeria with France are based on the assumption that both partners
are independent states and as such are subjects of international law.

These two forms of association may be distinguished as internal association
(of the United States-Puerto Rico type) and external association (the EEC-Greece
type). Both forms of association have as a common characteristic that two
political entities conclude a treaty, on the basis of voluntary agreement, in which
one partner joins the other, who is given increased responsibility and power of
decision in the areas which form the contents of the treaty.

We may, for example, also consider as cases of external association the
relationship between New Zealand and West Samoa as it was established by the
Friendship Treaty of August 1, 1962 (New Zealand Treaty Series 1962), and the
relationships between Tonga and Great Britain and between Liechtenstein and
Switzerland. It is, incidentally, hard to understand why Puerto Rico with its
present status would be unable to join some branch organizations of the United
Nations as an associated member, for example, UNESCO where today several
territories are already represented even though they are not independent. In 1961,
e.g., some associated members of UNESCO were Mauritius, Ruanda-Urundi,
Singapore, Tanganyika, the West Indies Union, all areas which were not yet
sovereign at that time. In March 1963, we find Katar, Mauritius, and Singapore.
With the Food and Agriculture Organization (FAO) of the United Nations were
associated in March 1963: British Guiana, Jamaica, Mauritius, Rhodesia, and
Nyassaland.

But America's contribution to the right of self-determination in the case of
Puerto Rico must not blind us to the not less important contribution that the
United States made in freeing the Philippines. This provided the first case where
an area was decolonized which had previously been a regular colony and not a
mandated territory (like Iraq) or a protectorate (like Egypt). Just as the War of
Independence of the United States attained for the first time the right of

self-determination of a white nation living in colonial dependence, the independence of the Philippines means a decisive break-through on the road to the decolonization of the nonwhite nations.

The American achievement is equally impressive in the field of language laws. In the United States the language laws are primarily a function of the degree to which an ethnic group has become established in its area of settlement. All other factors, such as numerical strength or the percentage of the total population, the compactness of the settlement, the similarity or dissimilarity with the racial or religious composition of the dominant ethnic group, the greater or lesser lingual distance, the pattern of settlement (language islands), all prove to be of secondary importance.

This becomes evident if we compare the legal status in Hawaii of the Hawaiian language to that of the far more widely spoken Japanese language, or if we compare the language laws of the approximately 200,000 old established Spanish-speaking inhabitants in New Mexico with those of the 2,000,000 more recent Mexican immigrants in California and Texas or those for the 800,000 Puerto Rican newcomers in New York. The generosity with which the languages of minute Pacific language groups in Micronesia and Samoa are being promoted is also characteristic.

Many more detailed gradations than those between old established settlers and recent immigrants could be established in several instances.

The tolerance-oriented nationality laws benefited all lingual minorities alike, including even the cosettlers. The same goes for certain branches of the promotion-oriented nationality laws, especially the use of non-English languages in the public libraries and in official notices.

Other forms of promotion were reserved for the "sole later immigrants," i.e., those German groups which came into existence as a result of the immigration during the years 1830-1850 or those minorities which, as far as the United States was concerned, were mere immigrants (i.e., coimmigrants), but as seen from their respective states were original settlers, as the Scandinavians of the Midwest and the Czechs in Texas. In this category belong the cultivation of the nationality languages in the public schools and the publication of certain official documents in the languages of the minorities which were intended for a wider public as, for example, governors' messages and new state constitutions; all this has been documented not only for German, but also for Czech, Scandinavian, French, and Dutch. It is a rare exception to this rule when, shortly before 1914, languages of recent immigrant groups, like Polish and Italian, were admitted in the public schools of Milwaukee (see Section 4-4).

The state goes even further in the promotion of such groups as belong to the old established settlers but which are not "sole old-established settlers" but co-original settlers who came into the country together with the Anglo-Saxons. Such groups as the Germans in Pennsylvania and Ohio attained the right to a non-English or bilingual public school as well as a right to have specialized

government documents printed in their language, for example, the session records
and, in both states, the annual reports of the various departments. Finally the sole
old-established settlers, the Spaniards in New Mexico and the French in Louisiana,
who had settled in their areas before the Anglo-Saxons, attain in important areas
even full equality, especially with respect to the legislature, but also in part for
administration and the courts; see, for example, for New Mexico the test of the
1889 law given in Section 5-2. This holds true to an even higher degree for those
sole old-established settlers who live in outlying areas without a substantial
Anglo-Saxon immigration. In Puerto Rico the nominal equality of Spanish, the
language of the old-established settlers, and of English led in practice to a
predominance of the former; the Anglo-Saxons in Puerto Rico play the role of a
minority whose language does not enjoy full equality. The absolute dominance of
Japanese in the Ryukyus was almost unrestricted.

Nevertheless the basic differentiation between old-established settlers and
recent immigrants remains decisive; it forms the real legal juxtaposition whereby
the coimmigrants and the sole old-established settlers represent the most extreme
possibility in each case. The nationality laws of the states follow the different
degrees to which ethnic groups have established themselves, so that it is quite
possible to compile a kind of organic or natural system of language laws for all
immigrant groups on the basis of the development of these language laws. The
proposition that all immigrant groups have a just claim to a very high degree of
toleration for their languages in the private sphere is basic for an organically
structured system of ethnic law. Such tolerance-oriented nationality rights have to
be granted wherever an ethnic group desires to cultivate its language and traditions
and is ready to make sacrifices for the necessary private institutions. This rule,
disregarding certain interruptions, has always been observed in the United States.

But the proposition cannot be set up that all ethnic groups are entitled to
the enjoyment of promotion-oriented nationality laws. First of all, there will
always be, especially in immigrant countries (and the history of the United States
has proved this), large ethnic groups who do not even wish the preservation of
their language. It would be sheer nonsense if the state should attempt to preserve
these languages against the will of their native speakers.

On the other hand, wherever a minority may desire to cultivate its language,
the state is by no means obligated to promote this language. It is understandable
that recently immigrated groups often resist the imminent loss of their native
language. Is this only a rather spontaneous but fickle and short-lived sentiment on
the part of the immigrants themselves, or is it a deep-rooted urge for
self-preservation which is shared by the children and grandchildren of the
immigrants? Only when the immigrant generation has succeeded in giving its
native languages firm roots among the grandchildren, only when the immigrant
generation has made the sacrifices for a private cultivation of the language, only
when they have taken root in the new country while retaining their native
language, can they demand that the state come to their aid and promote their

language. Such claim to promotion can be considered a natural right only beginning with about the third generation, i.e., only for "natives of native parentage."

The comprehensive toleration of the immigrant languages was in the best interests of America. More important than the quickest possible lingual assimilation of the immigrants is their spiritual and intellectual integration. If the state completely ignores the immigrant languages, this integration may suffer. As far as new immigrants are concerned, it has to be expected that for many years they have no knowledge of English, or that their knowledge is insufficient. This may not affect the operations of the highest level of government, but the work of the local administrative machinery may suffer when immigrants cannot understand local ordinances and announcements and take no notice of their contents. It is, therefore, in the interest of the state itself to accommodate the first-generation immigrants of a new foreign-language minority with respect to the language of official notices.

For the second generation, the children of the immigrants, it can usually be expected in the cities that the language of the dominant group is well understood. The state, therefore, is generally no longer interested in publishing official notices in their native languages. On the other hand, the state has an interest in seeing that the children of immigrants have a reasonable knowledge of the language of their parents in addition to that of the dominant group. If this is not the case and, for example, a monolingual Italian generation is immediately followed by a monolingual English generation, a break in continuity and tradition occurs. The parents are no longer respected by their children and are therefore unable to exert any influence. They are unable to teach them certain moral standards for their future life and the children grow up, like orphans, without the benefit of personal formative influences. This alienated condition of the children is very dangerous for society; it has even become, in many of the largest North American cities, one of the major causes of gangsterism. For example, a 1927 study in Chicago showed that there existed, in addition to 45 entirely Anglo-American and 88 Negro or racially mixed gangs, 396 gangs whose members belonged predominantly or exclusively to one single immigrant nationality, and 351 gangs in which certain immigrant nationalities intermingled. In these last named 747 gangs, members of the second generation (i.e., the first native-born) were by far the most numerous; only a few foreign-born were members of these gangs (Thrasher 1927).

It is one of the most urgent tasks for students of nationality laws to compile a catalog of basic rights for immigrant groups with respect to their languages (*Europa Ethnica* 1961, 51, 54). For this task that faces the experts in international law, the United States has made an outstanding contribution.

We should like to point out some more specific achievements which are partial manifestations of that comprehensive generosity in the areas of the right of self-determination and language laws.

It is especially important that often areas with non-English population and voters' majorities were granted territorial status with an elected legislature:

Louisiana in 1804, New Mexico in 1850, Hawaii and Puerto Rico in 1900, the Philippines in 1907. This achievement is often not recognized even in the United States itself, because the degree of self-government found in a territory is measured here in terms of the much higher degree of self-government that is found in a state, and logically this often leads to criticism because the latter degree, statehood, was granted to New Mexico and Hawaii only after they had developed a majority of English-speaking voters. Measured in terms of unitary states, however, regardless of whether they have a decentralized administrative structure like Great Britain or a highly centralized one like France or Italy, even this territorial phase offered an unusual safeguard. What would it mean for Catalonia, Brittany, or even Wales to have an administrative setup such as existed in Louisiana from 1804 to 1812, in New Mexico from 1850 to 1912, and in Puerto Rico from 1917 to 1952, i.e., prior to statehood!

The extensive promotion of all larger old-established ethnic groups in the field of language laws is closely related to this recognition of the right of old-established nationalities to self-government. This promotion found its clearest expression in the equal status the non-English languages enjoyed in the legislatures of New Mexico and Louisiana, the publication, for decades, of German session records of the Pennsylvania legislature, and, above all, of course, in the establishment of non-English or bilingual public elementary schools in these three states and in Ohio. These facts have remained largely unknown in Europe, and almost in the United States as well!

Other notable features of the American nationality laws which deserve mention are found in the fields of libraries and radio. The extensive consideration given to non-English languages in the public libraries is an especially laudable achievement of the United States. This is, incidentally, an area where the recent immigrant groups were perhaps treated with even greater consideration than were the old-established settlers. The extensive development of radio programs for various nationalities makes it possible for even the smallest group to enjoy some radio hours in its own language. This foreign-language radio has found a central advisory office in the American Council for Nationalities Service (formerly Common Council). The growth of non-English radio broadcasts is, however, a by-product of the liberal private structure of the American radio in general and in this respect is only indirectly part of the official nationality policy.

Many Americans are not aware of the high quality of the American nationality laws. At a meeting of UNESCO in June 1960, when experts dealt with discrimination in education, J. Simsarian, the representative of the United States, opposed far-reaching language laws. During the following debate, the representative of the Soviet Union pointed to the generous language policy in the various republics of the Soviet Union such as in the Ukraine and Uzbekistan. Simsarian answered that America had no intention of criticizing this language policy, but would reserve the right to treat its own numerous immigrant minorities differently. This juxtaposition had no logical basis. The counterpart to the immigrant minorities of North America is the millions of Ukrainians (Mytziuk

1943, 70-102) and other members of the European nationalities of the Soviet Union who migrated to Soviet Asia; and it seems that, as far as language rights are concerned, they are in an inferior position to the immigrant ethnic groups in North America. A comparison between official Soviet and Ukrainian exile language maps makes evident that the Ukrainians, for example, claim large areas north of Vladivostok and around Slavgorod as being populated by their ethnic group, while the Soviet Union treats these areas as almost entirely Russian (Kulyuckyj 1953; *Karta Narodov SSSR* 1962). It must also be considered that a private sphere for independent activities of the ethnic groups hardly exists in the Soviet Union. Consequently all possibilities for such activities in press, radio, associations, literature, and private schools like those which exist in America within the framework of the tolerance-oriented nationality laws disappear as soon as the language of an ethnic group ceases to be promoted by the government.

A large measure of genuine toleration is, by the very nature of things, possible only in a nontotalitarian society. In rightist totalitarian states a private sphere can exist only indirectly. Under governments like those of former Italian Fascism or that of German National Socialism, this private sphere, even though it still exists on the statute books, is in fact completely under state control and at any time subject to restrictions or abolition. In leftist totalitarian countries, almost all societal activities are quite officially regarded only as tools to implement the political will of the state. The publication of a newspaper, the opening of a movie theater, the founding of a club in which the language of a nationality is to be cultivated, form parts of a uniform cultural policy which is directed by the state and the party. An at least nominally free sphere in which the language of a nationality can be cultivated without the express authorization of the state is found at most in the family circle and in the church, which is not exactly being encouraged by the state.

On the other hand, we have the situation in a constitutional state like the Prussian Kingdom, which was not friendly to minority groups and was not even democratic and which did not consider promoting its minorities. Here, the Poles, up until 1914, were able to build up a kind of private self-government of high quality, thanks to the constitutional respect for the private sphere.

The counterpart to the Soviet nationality policy toward the Ukraine or Uzbekistan is the American nationality policy toward Puerto Rico. In respect to language rights, the United States here is at least as generous as is the Soviet Union. In respect to political rights, it is more generous, because twice it gave the Puerto Ricans a genuine chance to exercise their right of self-determination in free plebiscites.

I am far from romantically idealizing the Americans and their nationality law, which shows significant shortcomings, especially where it intersects racial law, as is the case in the treatment of immigrant Mexicans (Section 3-1). The persecution of Germans during the period from 1917 to 1923 remains a phenomenon which is difficult to explain and to pardon. (During World War II such an enmity would have been more understandable, but it did not occur.) In the spirit of a perfect toleration-oriented law, one would further wish that after 1918 many individual states, following the example of Rhode Island, had been more generous in permitting bilingual instruction in the private elementary schools. Even the status of Puerto Rico, which in principle is exemplary, would bear important improvements (Section 7-4).

I should also not like in any way to imply that an egoistic desire to see their own language spread among the "allophones," the non-English, was completely alien to the members of the English-language group in the United States. Every healthy language group has the desire to preserve and, where conditions are favorable, to expand the realm of its own language, a desire which could perhaps be compared to the urge to acquire, keep, and increase one's personal property which exists in every normal individual person. It is not objectionable that the individual has this urge to acquire property, but that he follow it without inhibitions. It is therefore quite justified that the members of a speech community have the desire to integrate other people into their group—doubly justified in the case of a nation internally and externally yet unfinished and not yet completely certain of its spiritual unity, as was the case in America in the nineteenth century. It would have been objectionable only if the language group had resorted to measures which violated the tolerance-oriented nationality law instead of, as it happened, restraining its natural instincts by reason and a sense of justice.

In this process the Americans made an important experiment of general validity; that is, that urban immigrant ethnic groups which do not have their own compact area of settlement are, as a rule, unable to preserve their own language for any lasting period of time even under favorable nationality laws. The proof: yesterday and the day before yesterday the decline of the German language in the big cities; yesterday and today that of Polish; today and tomorrow that of French (in New England). This disposes of a much disputed legal question as only an imaginary problem, that is, the question as to whether urban immigrant ethnic groups in industrialized areas have the right to retain their language forever or not. It is an imaginary problem because, objectively speaking, the possibility for such a permanent retention exists only to an insignificant degree. This disregards, of course, cases where immigrants differ from the native population so markedly as a result of their religion, color of skin, level of education, etc., that mixed marriages, for example, remain an exception. If we view the legal question from our sociological knowledge, the question therefore has to be rephrased as follows: Have urban immigrant ethnic groups the right to delay to the best of their ability the decline of their language?

Other sociological problems, which are related to the nationality problem, have found their answers in America. The problems of bilingualism and of a bilingual educational system have been clarified theoretically and approached practically in and for Puerto Rico from the twofold aspect of how to retain one's own mother tongue and how, since it was considered absolutely necessary, to learn English at the same time. As a theoretical contribution, we must mention especially the important report which Columbia University presented in 1926 about bilingualism in the educational system of Puerto Rico (International Institute of Teachers College 1926). The preceding year the same university had published a similar report for the Philippines (International Institute of Teachers College 1925). As a practical contribution, we mention the systematic use of findings of structural linguistics in the teaching of English in the elementary schools of Puerto Rico. The authors of the Columbia Report declare proudly that this represents the first time that a problem of bilingual instruction had been systematically and thoroughly studied anywhere. And it is true that in Europe only the 1927 Congress on bilingual education in Luxemburg covered this research area without confining itself to some specific geographic region (*Le Bilinguisme et l'Education* 1928). In contrast to this, most of the valuable studies on the problems of bilingualism on the North American mainland serve to explore not so much the behavior of the nationalities as groups but rather that of their members. Finally, the literature about special questions of the linguistic assimilation process is truly immense (Francis 1957, 517-548; 1958, 233-247, 401-417).

However, we must mention this literature only in passing, since it treats the subject without exception from the position that an accelerated disappearance of the non-English languages is desirable and only very seldom accepts the premise that two language groups or language cultures should coexist in the same country for a longer period of time or even permanently. The European reader should moreover be warned against misunderstandings which are caused by the fact that American scholars during recent decades often expressed the opinion that it is desirable that the descendants of the immigrants retain the "culture" of their ancestors. What is meant here by culture is frequently not firmly bound up with language, and the authors envision not the coexistence of various nationalities but an attractive intermingling and colorful enrichment of the Anglo-American culture. However, the American nationality policy not only provides sociological insights but introduces us also to a whole series of substantial innovations and perspectives bearing directly on linguistic and nationality laws.

The fundamental achievements of America's policy in this field are: in the area of language laws, the coexistence of carefully elaborated laws for old-established settlers and a generously nonpublic sphere giving latitude to all recent immigrants; in the area of self-determination, the early readiness to set colonial populations free and the establishment of a middle road toward "association" which runs between integration and outright independence.

After I have given a detailed description of the strong features of American nationality laws, I would like once more to point out some of its limitations and weaknesses:

1. The high-water mark of tolerance-oriented nationality laws occurred before 1914 or, more exactly, about 1890, when the non-English private school in which English was only a subject was permitted in the larger part of the country. Justifiably since then—with the exception of some overseas areas, especially Puerto Rico and the Ryukyus—such a weak position of English in the curriculum

was no longer permitted, but it is regrettable that in most parts of the country (Rhode Island was the one shining exception) the bilingual private school in which all subjects were taught in both languages was, until recently, also prohibited.

2. The treatment of non-English languages in the courts was in many parts of the country not so generous as would have been desirable; for example, the exclusion of the German language in the nineteenth century from the courts in Pennsylvania caused considerable hardship.

3. The highest degree of nationality rights, namely, the elevation of a nationality to a public corporation, was reached only once, and even here only in a very incomplete manner; in the establishment of the "People of Portorico" as a public body corporate (1900 until 1952). For three reasons this attempt cannot be rated so highly: The "People of Portorico" included also the resident Anglo-Americans and other non-Iberians. The number of these non-Iberians was so small, on the other hand, that territorial and personal autonomy almost coincided. Finally, this body corporate and the creation of a separate Puerto Rican citizenship, which flowed from it, were not created to grant something to the Puerto Ricans but to deny them something valuable, namely, American citizenship (see Section 7-4; see Section 2-1 for an attempt at recognition of the corporation of an ethnic group in the civil domain).

Other single phenomena which have to be evaluated negatively either occurred during only a few years (such as the cruel treatment of the Germans during World War I and of the Japanese during World War II; cf. Section 3-1) or else they belong to the sphere of racial relations, especially the widespread social discrimination against the immigrant Mexicans, which is caused not by their language but by the color of their skin.

9-2   NATIONALITY POLICY OF THE UNITED STATES AND ATTITUDE OF THE UNITED STATES TOWARD PROTECTION OF MINORITIES IN INTERNATIONAL LAW

The remarkable achievements of the United States in the field of nationality rights may lead easily to the assumption that its representatives have also in the international sphere regularly stood up for the protection of ethnic minorities and the expansion of nationality laws in the field of international law. This is not the case. I said before (Section 9-1) that the American ethnic law represents a triumph of justice over natural egotism and the will toward expansion which is inherent to a larger or lesser degree in every speech community. Many Americans are so unaware of this that internationally they have often sided with the rather barbaric instinct rather than with instinct-conquering, law-revering reason. It often happens that states which internally pursue a harsh and unjust policy loudly proclaim in international bodies their adherence to the ideals of tolerance and justice. The United States offers the rare example of the opposite attitude: while generally treating the nationalities in its own sphere of sovereignty with enlightened, tolerant, and progressive methods, the United States in the international arena has often proclaimed its adherence to the principles of reactionary, intolerant, and unjust nationality policy. A parallel case is the way in which the multinational state of India practices a generous nationality policy internally but in international bodies has often recommended a rather narrow-minded nationality policy. Furthermore we can find an inversion of the methods followed by the United States in its nationality policy when we consider the racial policy of the United States, which advocates a radical policy of equality in the international field but has been rather slow in abolishing remainders of domestic inequality.

In the United Nations a strong group of nations existed from the very beginning which endorsed the right of a state to assimilate its citizens who speak other languages, even if, as immigrant countries, they were of the opinion that the immigrant by leaving his home country had voluntarily opted in favor of the language of his new host country; even if they suspected in the toleration or even establishment of separate institutions for certain ethnic groups an open or hidden policy of discrimination; even if they considered that the attempt to preserve an inherited language constituted a weakening of the national power and sovereignty which is based on unity; or even if they considered the cultivation of language ties which tied ethnic groups to foreign countries a threat to their external security. The advocates of assimilation succeeded in establishing an early U.N.O. policy regarding minorities which according to Inis L. Claude (1955, 176), was "the policy of subsuming the minority question under the problem of universal respect for human rights, while giving implicit endorsement to the right of states to follow a policy of assimilation." (See also Ermacora 1964.)

Claude (1955, 166) points out also that, whenever this problem presented itself within the framework of the United Nations, the United States led the advocates of assimilation: "Whenever the issue must be squarely faced, the United States takes the lead ... in opposing the concept of special minority rights." Individual examples of this attitude are plentiful. The United States led that group of states which succeeded in deleting the provision about "cultural genocide," that is, the forceful elimination of a language from the draft of a genocide convention (ibid., p. 164). When in 1952 the Convention of Human Rights of the United Nations discussed the problem of self-determination, it was the United States, represented by Eleanor Roosevelt and followed by the Afro-Asian states, which demanded that the provisions in favor of self-determination should not include similar provisions for the protection of minorities, while the states of the Eastern bloc and some West European countries, notably Belgium, advocated a coupling the right of self-determination and nationality laws (Claude 1955, 173-175; Documents E/CN4/SR256, E/CN4/SR737). Parallels may be drawn between the statements by Mrs. Eleanor Roosevelt and the writings of H. von Treitschke in which he used the same arguments to justify Germany's right to assimilate her minorities. When at the end of 1960 the question of South Tyrol was debated, the American representative, Miss Willis, emphatically and unqualifiedly endorsed the Italian position.

There is similar evidence for instances outside of the United Nations. In 1938 the United States voted in favor of a resolution (XXVII) at the

Pan-American conference in Lima, which declared that the international provisions for the protection of minorities as they existed in Europe under the
sponsorship of the League of Nations were not applicable in the Western
hemisphere. "The system of protection of ethnical, linguistic, or religious
minorities cannot have any applications whatsoever in America, where the
conditions characterizing the groups known as minorities do not exist" (*American
Journal of International Law* 1940; Dahm I, 402). This may have caused some
headshaking in Puerto Rico. Ethnic groups like the three groups of Quechua-
speaking Indians of Peru, Ecuador, and Bolivia, which together total approximately 7 million people, can be denied the character of nondominant groups at
best if they and their language are considered for racial reasons as not capable of
development and adjustment to modern civilization.

Since 1942 the United States in the annual conferences of the foreign
ministers of the two Americas has supported the position that minority protection
need not go beyond the protection of human rights (Demichel 1960, 27-28).

At the Paris Peace Conference of 1946 the American representative, Bedell
Smith, declared that his country could not understand why one would attempt to
retain a minority instead of absorbing it: "If the provisions protecting a minority
are applied in one state, then they have also to apply in all other states"
(Schechtmann 1951, 1-11, esp. 9). When in June and December 1960 a
convention was prepared within the framework of UNESCO in Paris against
discrimination in education, the American representative, Simsarian, contributed
to keeping rather vague the provisions of Articles 2 and 5 affecting national
minorities.

American delegates have repeatedly declared on such occasions that the
United States could not be expected to endorse an international protection for
minorities since the United States played host to a vast number of immigrant
minorities whose continued existence could well endanger the national unity of
the United States.

This attitude of so many spokesmen has various reasons. Among the most
important we can include—in addition to an inadequate knowledge of their own
tradition—the confusing effect which is generated by the complex issues of human
rights and racial relations. In both these areas equality is as a rule—but not
always!—assured by the abolition of separate institutions for certain parts of the
population, for example, by permitting members of all races to attend the same
schools and colleges. These problems have remained so much in the foreground of
world politics since the end of World War II that judgment about the questions of
nationality laws was thereby imperceptibly determined. The demand that separate
institutions be abolished or reduced, a demand which is generally justified in the
field of racial relations, was carried over into the field of nationality laws, where
this demand amounts to approval of injustice and unfairness. The effect of this
misunderstanding can be observed when in 1956 Robert F. Kennedy, within an
otherwise well-founded criticism, charged the Soviets with practicing racial
discrimination in Central Asia and proved these charges by pointing out that the

Soviets maintained separate schools for Russians and native children in Uzbekistan: "The communists practice rigorous segregation in this area, with separate school systems for the European Russian children and for the local children" (R. F. Kennedy 1956). This one-sided insistence on human rights and racial nondiscrimination is motivated also by the desire on the part of the United States to secure the support of the Latin American states, which as a rule are rather cool toward linguistic minorities, and by a lack of clarity concerning the essential difference between laws for recent immigrants and for groups of old-established settlers.

The reluctance of the United States to accept the principles of international agreements about nationality laws may also have been increased by the fact that, according to Article VI (2) of the United States Constitution, all treaties which the federal government, with the consent of the Senate, enters into have the same force as federal laws, a state of affairs which has come under increasing criticism since about 1953 (*Missouri* v. *Holland*; Guradze 1956, 26-29; Schwelb 1959, 48-49).

The one-sided overall picture which we have painted here about the behavior of the United States in questions of international nationality laws becomes even darker if we consider that the United States has repeatedly found it necessary to give economic and military assistance to nations which pursued a distinctly hostile course toward their linguistic minorities, as for example, Turkey against the Kurds. The prestige of the United States has suffered by this involuntary "nationality policy of the left hand." It is certainly debatable whether the United States would have been able to change the nationality policy of the nations it assisted to any significant degree even if it had intended to do so, but it seems hardly debatable that the United States has hardly become conscious of the problem. During international conferences of Kurdish students in 1960 and 1961 the author had the opportunity to observe the effects of the American alliance and assistance policy on the attitude of this people.

The picture which we must paint here seems irreconcilable with the panorama that we had to draw of domestic United States nationality rights. Fortunately it is incomplete, for it ignores an earlier major tendency as well as a recent side effect of American foreign policy in matters of protection for nationalities.

One earlier main tendency: Temporarily the United States under Wilson became the major advocate of an international protection for minorities. That the Paris treaties contained such provisions has to be credited primarily to Wilson and his advisers, especially the lawyer David Hunter Miller and the historian Archibald Coolidge (Viefhaus 1960). By 1917 Wilson had already started that group of experts called "Inquiry" on questions of the European nationality problems. The chairman of this group was S. E. Mezes; among the members were D. H. Miller and Walter Lippmann. The program of this group differed from Wilson's later program in that, among other things, it put less emphasis on independence and included also African problems.

Even Wilson himself did not initially endorse the dissolution of Austria-Hungary, but a far-going autonomy of the nationalities, which was viewed as "self-determination." In a letter of June 26, 1918, to Lansing, Wilson first expressed his opposition to the preservation of Austria-Hungary (Mamatey 1957, 269). Lansing, in a letter to Wilson of May 21, 1918, with reference to the Czechs, spoke of a "hope of independence or at least self-determination" (ibid., 255), which meant presumably that self-determination was viewed, in the sense of Karl Renner, as an alternative to independence. It is also possible that he distinguished between independence granted without any previous conditions (and called this independence) and the holding of a plebiscite about the question (what he called self-determination). When the ideas of independence won precedence with the breakup of the Dual Monarchy, it was the Americans who insisted that there should be a concomitant commitment to nationality rights. Wilson intended to include even a passage in the Charter of the League of Nations which would have bound all future new states, and according to a later version (January 20, 1919) even all future members of the League, to minimum standards of minority protection (Viefhaus 1960, 109, 113). On the other hand, it was Wilson who, on May 3, 1919, changed the protective provisions of Article 93 of the draft treaty so as to make them refer to private instead of group rights, by having "communities" replaced by "inhabitants" (Viefhaus 1960, 158-159). On this issue he put himself in opposition to his major adviser, David Hunter Miller, and also to Louis Marshall, the representative of the American Jews at the peace conference (Viefhaus 1960, 82, 145, 151). It was later maintained by National Socialist scholars, such as Hans J. Beyer, that it was particularly the representatives of the American Jewry who insisted on a merely individual regulation, a claim which puts the facts upside down. Beyer (1937, 10) wrote: "It was intended to force old-established groups of an old people to live according to the laws of a liberal assimilated Jewry or the Eastern Galuth (Diaspora)," and he called this attempt "a tricky, because hardly recognizable in its purpose, tool for the destruction of the German people." At any rate there were Americans who were quite willing to go further than Wilson was willing to go.

What at that time was a major tendency of American foreign policy became repeatedly evident within the United Nations as a side tendency. In 1949 the American delegate to the U. N., Jonathan Daniels, pushed a resolution demanding that the General Assembly make every effort to assure that the national minorities be permitted to preserve their cultural heritage through the Subcommission against Discrimination and Minority Protection. This resolution was, however, boycotted by the Human Rights Commission to which the Subcommission was subordinate (Claude 1955, 162; Document E/CN4/351, 13-14). On October 8, 1951, Daniels and the British representative, Miss Elizabeth Monroe, presented a comprehensive draft resolution for minority protection (Document E/CN4/sub. 2/L4). The draft demanded, as minimum rights for those ethnic minorities which desired to retain their language, the right to have court procedures conducted in their mother tongue and the right to cultivate their mother tongue in the state-financed schools. This draft further suggested varied activities of the United Nations in this field: the drafting of special model provisions; permanent reporting about minority rights in the *Yearbook of Human Rights*; establishment of a board of complaint so that the minorities would not be forced to resort to appeals to a foreign government and thus endanger the peace; and finally the establishment of a panel of experts who should be at the disposal as members in ad hoc committees as well as advisers of individual governments. The realization of this latter suggestion would, for example, have been of considerable benefit for the Tyrol problem.

At the beginning of 1956 a preliminary draft of the report by Charles Ammoun about discrimination in education was discussed in the same subcommittee, and a sentence which was omitted in the published final version of this classical document was discussed on January 11. This sentence denied immigrant ethnic groups the right to call themselves "minorities" (Ammoun 1957). This report formed a basis for the Anti-Discrimination Convention which was adopted by UNESCO in 1960. The preliminary draft discussed in 1956 constitutes United Nations Document E/CN4/Sub.2/L92). In this connection the American representative, Professor Philip Halpern, a jurist, declared, according to the record: Immigrant groups "are entitled like all minority groups to preserve their language and culture at their own expense." It would in fact be a violation of fundamental human rights for the host government to prevent them from doing so. On the other hand, they are not entitled to special protection or financial aid from the government. His land (the United States) has room for different cultures and ethnic groups; indeed their existence enriches its national culture and strengthens it as a nation. He believed that true democracy is built on a mosaic of variegated cultures. This formulation, with its clear juxtaposition of merely acquiescent tolerance-oriented nationality laws for recent immigrants as against promotion-oriented nationality laws for the old-established groups, corresponded exactly to domestic American practice.

This study of the bilingual tradition in the United States shows that it is only the view represented by Jonathan Daniels and Philip Halpern that does justice to America's honorable past in this field. And it is based more on deeds than on verbal tradition.

In 1956 the UNO-sponsored Ljubljana "Seminar on the Multinational Society" came to the conclusion (Seminar 1965, pp. 17-18, cf. also ibid. pp. 21 and 29) that "While immigrant groups had the right to use their own language in everyday life, and to preserve their cultural identity if they wished to do so, the majority was under no obligations to subsidize the language of a minority immigrant group." Thus, it would seem that a world-wide consensus regarding this principle is not entirely beyond reach, and in an article I wrote in 1971 in the "International Migration Review" (Kloss 1971) I have tried to elaborate on this principle.

In the question of international protection for minorities, we find, consequently, two opposing American views. Since Willis and Simsarian acted directly as representatives of the United States, while Daniels and Halpern were only experts speaking as individuals, only the former, it is claimed, expressed the opinion of the government, while the latter spoke at most for an academic opposition. However, the borderline between government representatives and its experts is quite unclear. Most members of so-called United Nations and UNESCO expert panels are in reality government representatives. This was clearly stated by Claude (1951, 300-312), among others, for the members of the United Nations Subcommittee against Discrimination and for Minority Protection. Typically Simsarian, for example, was the spokesman of the United States on the question of discrimination at the so-called conference of experts which UNESCO held in Paris in June 1960. It must also be considered that the opinion of opposition experts may, under certain circumstances, have a higher degree of moral and logical persuasion in their own country than has the official government opinion and that the opposing view of today may well be the government view of tomorrow. Since the enactment, in 1967, of the "Bilingual Education Act" the American bilingual tradition represented by such men as Daniels and Halpern has grown better and stronger. In all, between 1965 and 1975, a drastic change occurred in the attitude of American authorities, educators, and scholars toward the problem of language maintenance. No longer is it generally held to be an indisputable moral duty of a progressive nation to make all minority tongues disappear as fast as possible. There is even an incipient realization that language shift may be slowed down by a rigorous assimilation program, while the "bridge approach" permits schoolchildren to use and study their mother tongue, at least in the lower primary grades. There is a growing awareness of the complexities of language-related educational problems, and a growing willingness and even desire to arrive at a unified and yet flexible language policy which takes into account the needs of the most diverse non-English groups. For the first time in American history a language policy was shaping up sympathetic to the problems of the nonwhite groups (Amerindians, Eskimos, Samoans, etc.) as well as to those of the white non-English groups of long standing in such places as Louisiana and New Mexico, and to the later immigrant groups, down to such recent arrivals as the postwar emigrants from Cuba.

Unfortunately this policy was marred by restricting its favors chiefly to economically underprivileged groups, instead of stressing the overall merits and desirability of temporary ("bridge approach") or permanent language mainten-ance per se. Yet the situation in the mid 1970s constitutes no mean achievement. We have only to look at the strengthened position of French in Louisiana, Chamorro in Guam, Spanish in a number of states and in the Virgin Islands, and most impressively, the ascent of a number of Amerindian languages, especially Navajo, which was beginning to spread even at the secondary school level and may even become some day the second official language of some newly emerging polity in the Southwest.

Nor is this growing strength of the minority or other hitherto nondominant tongues in the United States an isolated phenomenon restricted to the United

States. For as has been said in the introduction to this book, the shift on the domestic stage is only part of a groundswell beginning to transform the whole picture of language policy in the two Americas. Quasi-Pan-American developments in the field of language policy are not isolated phenomena; they must be viewed in the broader context of emancipation. The recent history of mankind is governed by the rise of five huge emancipatory movements striving to bring about equality and freedom of unfoldment for all segments of society:

1. The middle and more recently the "proletarian" strata of society.

2. Religious bodies and other world-view-based groups, including atheists (which previously had to go underground).

3. The nonwhite races.

4. Women.

5. Linguistic groups from major but formerly subdued nations and tribal groups speaking preliterary tongues.

While emancipation is the denominator, these five movements have in common an upsurge which was neither simultaneous nor coordinated. Religious tolerance, once far ahead of (for example) racial emancipation, underwent a sharp decline in the twentieth century, which silently witnessed such reactionary actions as the total suppression of religious services in Albania (since about 1967). The interests of linguistic and racial minorities are frequently in conflict, because the former wanted first of all separate educational and other cultural institutions while most racial minorities insist on a policy of wholesale integration which would make white, black, and brown children sit on the same benches. In the United States the revolt of racial groups has long overshadowed the needs of linguistic groups. In what has been called the "Revolt of the Minorities" in the United States (Mackey and Verdoodt 1975, 335-353) it was racial rather than linguistic discrimination which was resented and fought. But once the Black minority had been joined by the Hispano-Americans and the American Indians whose complaints had sometimes to do with their respective mother tongues almost as much as with the color of their skin, the linguistic aspect became co-focal.

Another unforeseeable windfall had helped the cause of the linguistic minorities. The Spanish-speaking element, once an army with far too few trained officers, was greatly strengthened by the inflow, after 1959, of a mass immigration from Cuba comprising numerous intellectuals and other middle-class people. The Spanish language is now what German was until 1917: by far the most important minority tongue spoken in the United States.

That the United States has done justice to this emancipatory movement, continuous since 1776, and is doing so now in a much more outspoken fashion constitutes a well-deserved claim to fame, one which we have attempted to outline in this book as an unassuming, but quite distinct, American Bilingual Tradition.

APPENDIX I

Mother Tongue by States, 1970

	Total	Native of Native Parentage			Total	Native of Native Parentage
Alabama			5 Japanese	159,500	34,100	
(Non-English 6%)			6 Yiddish	145,000	16,600	
1 German	16,000	5,900	7 Chinese	144,000	14,200	
2 Spanish	7,400	4,500	8 Portuguese	110,000	21,400	
Alaska			*Colorado*			
(Non-English: 24.5%)			(Non-English: 21.7%)			
1 German	6,400	3,100	1 Spanish	194,700	165,000	
2 Spanish	3,600	2,300	2 German	93,400	36,400	
Arizona			*Connecticut*			
(Non-English: 30.5%)			(Non-English: 32.7%)			
1 Spanish	259,100	139,600	1 Italian	222,400	29,000	
2 German	40,100	16,500	2 French	142,100	59,200	
Arkansas			3 Polish	114,200	22,400	
(Non-English: 6.9%)			*Delaware*			
1 German	13,900	3,900	(Non-English: 14.7%)			
California			1 Italian	11,700	1,900	
(Non-English: 28.5%)			2 Polish	9,800	3,500	
1 Spanish	2,150,000	799,400	*District of Columbia*			
2 German	563,200	171,300	(Non-English: 17.1%)			
3 Italian	346,300	58,300	1 German	55,900	18,900	
4 French	200,800	81,100	2 Spanish	49,700	15,100	

	Total	Native of Native Parentage		Total	Native of Native Parentage
Florida (Non-English: 19.9%)			*Maine* (Non-English: 20.8%)		
1 Spanish	381,200	68,100	1 French	141,500	71,800
2 German	159,700	44,500	2 Italian	5,500	1,200
Georgia (Non-English: 7.1%)			*Maryland* (Non-English: 14.6%)		
1 German	27,200	9,500	1 German	80,900	29,600
2 Spanish	18,600	9,900	2 Italian	50,100	9,800
Hawaii (Non-English: 42.2%)			*Massachusetts* (Non-English: 28.7%)		
1 Japanese	125,600	29,500	1 French	367,200	153,900
2 Chinese	24,400	6,500	2 Italian	288,300	39,100
			3 Polish	134,000	30,700
Idaho (Non-English: 11.7%)			4 Portuguese	122,800	19,300
1 German	17,300	6,700	*Michigan* (Non-English: 18.8%)		
2 Spanish	13,200	6,800	1 Polish	280,500	85,600
Illinois (Non-English: 24.6%)			2 German	261,200	94,100
1 German	498,300	190,800	3 Italian	113,100	14,200
2 Polish	346,100	85,200	*Minnesota* (Non-English: 25.3%)		
3 Spanish	295,100	135,700	1 German	316,000	183,000
4 Italian	222,000	31,700	2 Norwegian	156,000	67,800
Indiana (Non-English: 11.2%)			3 Swedish	105,300	24,900
1 German	154,000	99,500	*Mississippi* (Non-English: 6.4%)		
2 Spanish	49,400	25,800	1 French	7,900	6,700
Iowa (Non-English: 14.6%)			2 German	5,900	2,300
1 German	168,000	86,215	*Missouri* (Non-English: 12.2%)		
2 Norwegian	27,700	13,100	1 German	178,400	106,200
Kansas (Non-English: 12.5%)			2 Italian	31,000	6,100
1 German	106,000	56,000	*Nebraska* (Non-English: 18.5%)		
2 Spanish	31,000	16,000	1 German	107,000	47,900
Kentucky (Non-English: 7.2%)			2 Czech	33,800	16,000
1 German	32,800	15,400	*Nevada* (Non-English: 22.1%)		
2 Spanish	6,800	4,100	1 Spanish	16,800	8,100
Louisiana (Non-English: 24.5%)			2 German	10,500	3,900
1 French	572,000 (84,700 nonwhite)	559,400	*New Hampshire* (Non-English: 26.2%)		
			1 French	112,600	48,400
2 Spanish	42,600	16,100	2 Polish	7,900	1,800

	Total	Native of Native Parentage
New Jersey (Non-English: 30.3%)		
1 Italian	503,700	71,000
2 German	269,500	52,800
3 Spanish	258,100	136,000
4 Polish	214,700	46,700
5 Yiddish	118,400	14,100
New York (Non-English: 34.8%)		
1 Italian	1,277,400	159,600
2 Spanish	1,266,700	895,900 (only 144,300 declaring as nonwhite)
3 Yiddish	697,700	62,000
4 German	609,900	102,900
5 Polish	390,700	95,400
6 French	208,800	60,800
North Carolina (Non-English: 6.4%)		
1 German	21,900	7,800
2 Spanish	13,800	8,700
North Dakota (Non-English: 32.4%)		
1 German	94,000	41,700
2 Norwegian	51,200	18,900
Ohio (Non-English: 15.7%)		
1 German	359,800	165,000
2 Italian	162,400	24,600
3 Polish	132,000	36,300
Oklahoma (Non-English: 9.3%)		
1 German	37,400	16,800
2 Spanish	21,800	13,700
Pennsylvania (Non-English: 32.4%)		
1 German	454,300	248,000
2 Italian	433,600	60,800
3 Polish	273,100	67,000
4 Slovak	164,000	29,900
5 Yiddish	121,600	14,800

	Total	Native of Native Parentage
Rhode Island (Non-English: 35.7%)		
1 French	101,300	47,900
2 Italian	76,400	13,000
South Carolina (Non-English: 6.8%)		
1 German	10,900	3,600
2 Spanish	7,100	4,400
South Dakota (Non-English: 24.0%)		
1 German	68,900	33,600
2 Norwegian	19,900	6,500
Tennessee (Non-English: 7.1%)		
1 German	16,900	7,000
2 Spanish	8,400	5,200
Texas (Non-English: 25.7%)		
1 Spanish	1,793,500	1,050,300
2 German	237,600	142,000
Vermont (Non-English: 18.4%)		
1 French	42,200	15,900
2 Italian	5,200	1,200
Virginia (Non-English: 8.8%)		
1 German	47,700	18,700
2 Spanish	31,500	14,000
Washington (Non-English: 16.9%)		
1 German	124,000	43,100
2 Norwegian	50,400	11,100
West Virginia (Non-English: 7.6%)		
1 Italian	16,000	2,300
2 German	8,700	3,200
Wisconsin (Non-English: 25.5%)		
1 German	512,800	279,500
2 Polish	118,600	50,300
Wyoming (Non-English: 15.7%)		
1 Spanish	13,300	10,400
2 German	10,500	4,000

Bilingual Education: Languages Other Than Spanish
(and English) Used in BEA-Funded
Projects, 1974-1975

1. Only One Non-English Language Used

1.1 Post-Columbian Languages

Language–Polity	No. of School Systems (Projects)	Estimated No. of Pupils
Chinese		
California	1	Unknown
French		
Louisiana	5	3,506
Maine	2	1,136
New Hampshire	1	170
Vermont	2	373 **4,885**
Ilocano (Philippines)		
California	1	Unknown
Hawaii	1	664 **(664)**
Italian		
Louisiana	1	440
New York	2	887 **1,327**
Korean		
California	1	Unknown
Portuguese		
Massachusetts	1	880
Rhode Island	1	120 **1,000**

Language–Polity	No. of School Systems (Projects)	Estimated No. of Pupils
Tagalog-Pilipino		
California	2	1,039
	1	Unknown **(1,039)**

1.2 Pre-Columbian Languages

Language–Polity	No. of School Systems (Projects)	Estimated No. of Pupils
Aleut s.		
Yupik		
Apache s.		
Mescalero		
Athabaskan s.		
Yupik		
Bannoch-Shoshoni		
Idaho	1	**98**
Chamorro		
Guam	1	641
Trust Territory	2	375 **1,016**
Cherokee		
Oklahoma	1	**1,470**

1.2 Pre-Columbian Languages (continued)

Cheyenne				Navajo		
Northern Mon-				Arizona	6	2,840
tana	1	446		New Mexico	4	639
Choctaw				Utah	1	449	3,928
Mississippi	1	374		Palauan s.		
Oklahoma	1	885	1,259	Ponopean		
Cree				Papago		
Montana	1	248		Arizona	1	46
Crow				Passamaquoddy		
Montana	2	366		Maine	1	80
Eelaponke				Ponopean and		
Florida	1	85		Palauan		
Hulapai				Trust Territory	1	166
Arizona	1	149		Samoan		
Inupiat s,				California	1	Unknown
Yupik				American Samoa	1	919	(919)
Keresan				Seminole,		
New Mexico	1	135		Shoshoni-Bannock		
Kusaien				Florida	1	41
Trust Territory	1	61		Tewa		
Lakota				New Mexico	1	55
South Dakota	3	577		Trukese		
Marshallese				Trust Territory	1	100
Trust Territory	1	60		Yapese		
Menominee				Trust Territory	1	110
Wisconsin	1	70		Yupik		
Mescalero, Apache				Alaska	3	592
New Mexico	1	117		Yupik, Unupiat,		
				Aleut, Athabaskan		
				Alaska	1	2,636

2. Language(s) Used Alongside Spanish (and English)

State–Languages	No. of School Systems (Projects)	Estimated No. of Pupils
California		
Chinese-Cantonese + Tagalog-Pilipino,	3	3,124
Portuguese	6	2,632
Japanese	1	500
Chinese-Cantonese	2	1,183
Chinese-Cantonese + Japanese	1	357
Pomo	1	159
Chinese, Japanese + Tagalog-Pilipino	1	331
Colorado		
Ute, Navajo	1	845
Connecticut		
Italian-Portuguese	1	450
Illinois		
Chinese-Korean	1	480
Massachusetts		
Chinese-Cantonese + Mandarin	1	510
French-Greek	1	160

Language–Polity	No. of School Systems (Projects)	Estimated No. of Pupils
New Mexico		
Keresan + Acoma + Navajo	1	986
New York		
French, Greek, Italian	1	840
Chinese-Cantonese + Mandarin	1	1,080
French-Haitian	4	1,626
Italian	7	3,625
Yiddish	1	1,054
Greek, Italian	1	500
Italian, Portuguese	1	1,217
Oregon		
Russian	1	524
Pennsylvania		
Arabic	1	137
Portuguese	1	260
Italian, Portuguese	2	755
Washington		
Chinese-Cantonese	1	165
Tagalog, Pilipino	1	305

It will be noticed that no bilingual program is listed for German, the ancestral tongue of one of the oldest and largest ethnic groups in the United States. A sample survey conducted in November 1969 by the United States Bureau of the Census yielded the following figures as to ethnic descent (f. Ethnic Origin 1971):

Ethnic Origin (in thousands)

German	19,961	Italian	7,239
English	19,060	Polish	4,021
Irish	13,282	Russian	2,152
Spanish	9,230	Others	105,633 (among whom some 22,000 Negroes)

Not reported   17,635

The gap between the leading position of German among the ancestral mother tongues and its zero position in present-day bilingual education is remarkable. At first sight it certainly seems to contradict our thesis that Americans have been quite generous in handling the problems of non-English minorities. It must be remembered, however, (1) that actually the German language over several decades was firmly entrenched in the public life of the nation, and that it (2) became the target of suspicion and even disdain as the language of America's most powerful external enemy. Besides, German also suffered from the fact that nearly all persons of German descent are at least moderately well-to-do and therefore cannot easily profit from the 1961/68 BEA legislation which, as we have seen, was designed chiefly to assist the children from economically backward minorities. It would mean a new step forward if Americans realized that discrimination against those minorities who never requested or even needed governmental aid is not fully compatible with the American Dream.

SOURCES

Ackerlund, G. C. (1950), *Federal Attitudes towards Public Support of Sectarian Education,* Dissertation, Ann Arbor, Mich.

Adam, B. (1959), *Hawaii, the Aloha State,* New York.

Adler of Reading, Pa., Mar. 5 and 11, 1833.

Administration in Hawaii, Hearing before the Committees on Territory and Insular Affairs, U. S. Senate, Jan. 16, 1933 (1933), Washington, D.C.

Alip, Eufronio M. (1958), *Philippine History,* 7th ed., Manila.

Allison (1907), *The Government of Illinois,* 1790-1799.

Alvord, C. W. (1922), *The Illinois Country,* 1673-1818 (Centennial History of Illinois, I), Chicago, Ill.

American Committee for the Protection of the Foreign Born. See Petition of the American Committee for the Protection of the Foreign Born.

American Council of Learned Societies (1932), *Report of the Committee on Linguistic and National Stocks in the Population of the United States,* Washington. Reprinted from the *Annual Report of the American Historical Association for 1931,* Washington, 1932.

American Journal of International Law (1940), vol. 34, suppl. 198.

American Notes and Queries (1943), vol. 3, 173.

Americanization Conference (1919), *Proceedings of the Americanization Conference,* held under the auspices of the Americanization Division, Bureau of Education, Department of the Interior, Washington, May 12-15, 1919, Washington.

Amerikanische Schultzeitung (1870-1871, 1874), 1:39, 71-72, 352, 439; 4:7, Lousiville, Ky.

Ammoun, Charles (1957), *A Study on Discrimination in Education,* New York.

Andersson, Theodore (1969), *Foreign Languages in Elementary Schools. A Struggle against Mediocrity,* University of Texas Press, Austin, Tex., and London.

Andersson, Theodore, and Boyer, Mildred (1970), *Bilingual Schooling in the United States,* Government Printing Office, Washington, 2 vols.

Annual Report of the Governor to the Secretary of the Interior (1955, 1956, 1960, 1967), Washington, D.C.

Arizona governor's office (Jan. 12, 1961), Phoenix, Ariz.

Arizona Revised Statutes, Sec. 15-202.

Arndt and Olson (1961), *Deutsch-Amerikanische Zeitungen*, German-American *Newspapers and Periodicals* 1732-1955, Heidelberg (Deutsche Pressforschung, vol. 3).

Aspinwall, D. B. (1960), *Languages in Hawaii*, PMLA75(4) (September 1960), 7-8.

Austin, Mary (1921), in R. E. Park and H. A. Miller, *Old World Traits Transplanted*. . . New York and London.

Ayer, H. W. (1880), *Directory of Newspapers and Periodicals*.

Babcock, K. C., *Scandinavian Element in the United States*, Urbana, Ill.

Bagster-Collins, E. W. (1930), *The History of Modern Language Teaching in the United States*, New York.

Ballantine, J. W. (1953), The Future of the Ryukyus, *Foreign Affairs*, 33:663-674.

Balzac v. People of Puerto Rico, 258 U.S. 298 (1922).

Bancroft, H. H. (1888), *History of the Pacific States of North America*, vol. 12, San Francisco, Calif.

Barry, J. M. (1933), *The French-Canadian Pioneers of Willamette-Valley*, Portland, Ore. This volume was not available to me.

Bartels v. Iowa, 191 Iowa 1060, 181, NW 508.

Beaglehole, E. (1937), *Some Modern Hawaiians*, Honolulu, Hawaii, University of Hawaii Res. Publication 19.

Beard, Charles (1924); *American Government and Politics*, 4th ed., New York.

Bek, William G. (1907), *The German Settlement Society of Philadelphia*, Philadelphia, Pa.

Benjamin, Gilbert G. (1908-09), *Germans in Texas, German-American Annals*, new series, vol. 6 (1908) -7 (1909); the quotation is from vol. 7 p. 237). In 1911, Benjamin 1908-09 was reprinted as *Americana Germanica Monograph* Ser. no. 11.

Benson, Adolph B. (1952), *American Scandinavian Studies*, New York.

Beyer, Hans J. (1937), *Auslanddeutsche Volksforschung*, 1:10.

Bezou, letter signed by, from the Athénée Louisianais to Kloss. The treatment in Lauvrière (1939) is ambiguous.

Le Bilinguisme et l'Education (1929), Travaux de la conférence internationale tenue a Luxembourg (1928), Geneva, Bureaux international d'éducation.

Bland, see Le Blanc.

Blegan, T. C. (1940), *Norwegian Migration to America*, Northfield, Minn.

Bloom, L., and Donnelly, T. C. (1933), *New Mexico History and Civics*, Albuquerque, N.M.

Bloom, L., and Riener, R. (1949), *Removal and Return*, Berkeley, Calif.

Blue Book of Puerto Rico (1923).

Blue Book of Wisconsin (1909).

Board of Education v. Allen, 392 U.S. 236.

Board of School Commissioners v. State ex rel. *Sander*, 129 Ind. 14.

Bofardus, E. S. (1930-1931), The Mexican Immigration and Segregation, *American Journal of Sociology*, 36:74-88.

––– (1934), *The Mexican in the United States*, Los Angeles, Calif.

––– (1940-1941), Current Problems of Mexican Immigrants, *Sociology and Social Research*, 25:166-174.

Bohning v. Ohio and *Pohl v. Ohio*, 102 Ohio State 474, 132 NE 20.

Bou, Ismael R. (1966), Significant Factors in the Development of Education in Puerto Rico, in *Selected Background Studies Prepared for the United States–Puerto Rico Commission on the Status of Puerto Rico*, Washington, D.C.

Boudreau, Elia (1940), writing on Oakdale in the *Modern Languages Journal*, 24:427-430.

Bradford-Prince, Le Baron (1910), *New Mexico's Struggle for Statehood*, Santa Fe, N.M.

Braibanti, Ralph (1954), The Ryukyu Islands, Pawn of the Pacific, *Am. Pol. Sci. Rev.*, 48:472-498.

Brauns, E. (1828), *Mitteilungen aus Nordamerika, die höheren Lehranstalten und die Englisierung der dortigen Deutschen*, Braunschweig.

Breunig, M. (1961), *Foreign Languages in the Elementary Schools of the United States*, 1959-1960, New York.

Broom, L., and Kitsuse, J. I. (1956), *The Managed Casualty: The Japanese-American Family in World War II*, Berkeley, Calif., and Los Angeles, Calif.

Broussard, J. (1942), *Louisiana Créole Dialect*. Baton Rouge, La.

Brown, E. S. (1920), *Constitutional History of the Louisiana Purchase*, Berkeley, Calif.

Brown, F. J., and Roucek, J. S. (1937), *Our Racial and National Minorities*, New York.

Brown, S. W. (1912), *The Secularization of American Education*, New York.

Buffington, A. F., and Barba, P. A. (1954), *A Pennsylvania German Grammar*. Allentown, Pa.

Butler, Hugh (1954), *Virgin Islands Report*, Washington, 83d Congress, 2d Session, Committee Print.

Cabreram F. Manrique (1956), *Historia de la literatura puertoriqueria*, New York.

Caldwell, Genelle (1967), The Teaching of Social Studies in a Foreign Language at the High School Level, in Christian 1967 (ed.), *Reports of Bilingual Education Research and Teaching*.

California 1967: Sec. 71 Ed. Code, 3d Paragraph.

California Education Code, Sec. 6601-6603, Amendment to Sec. 71 (1967).

California Labor Code, Ch. 1918, Sec. 1695.

California Statutes (1933), Ch. 988. Text in Kloss (1940), 418.

California Vehicle Code (1968), Ch. 955, Sec. 1656b.

California Welfare and Institutions Code, Ch. 1784, Sec. 1060; Ch. 1667, Sec. 5325.

Cammack, F. M. (1953), *Pacific Islands Bibliography*. This work has not been available to me.

Canal Zone Code (1934), Washington.

Canal Zone v. *Christian, Canal Zone Superior Court Reports* III.

Canal Zone Superior Court Reports I, III, quoted in Woolsey (1925).

Carano, Paul, and Pedro C. Sanchez (1964), *A Complete History of Guam*, Rutland, Vt., and Tokyo.

Cardona v. *Power*, 384 U.S. 679 (preliminary edition). The dissenting opinions of Judges Douglas and Fortas, 384 U.S. 675.

Carter, C. E. (1956), *The Territorial Papers of the United States*, vol. 12.

Catholic Encyclopedia (1913), Article on Schools in vol. 13, New York.

Caulfield, R. Van Allen (1929), *The French Literature of Louisiana*, New York.

Cebollero, Pedro (1945), *A School Language Policy for Puerto Rico*, San Juan, Puerto Rico.

Chávez, Angélico (1954), The Penitentes of New Mexico, in *New Mexican Historial Review*, 29:97-123.

Chicago and Cook County, A Union List of Their Publications (around 1930), Documentary Section, University of Chicago Libraries, Chicago, Ill.

Chicago v. *McCoy*, 11LRA413.

Chowduri, R. H. (1955), *International Mandates and Trusteeship Systems*, The Hague.

Christian, C. (1967), editor II: Teaching Content in a Foreign Language, in *Reports of Bilingual Education Research and Teaching*, Nov. 10-11, 1967, Hilton Inn, El Paso, Tex.

Ciencias Politicus y Sociales (1959), 5:275-305, Mexico.

Cincinnati v. *Bickett*, 260, 49 (1875).

Cincinnati Soap Co. v. *U.S.*, 301 U.S. 308.

Cist, Carl (1795), *Akten, welche in der General Assembly der Republik Virginia paszirt worden sind*, Philadelphia, Pa.

Civil Administration of the Ryukyu Islands (July 1, 1963, to June 30, 1964).

Civil Affairs Activities in the Ryukyuan Islands, II, 3:76; V, 1:92-93 et passim; VIII, 2:S.X.

Claghorn, K. H. (1923), *The Immigrant's Day in Court*, New York.

Clarke, R. C. (1927), *History of the Willamette Valley, Oregon*, vol. I, Chicago, Ill.

Claude, Inis L. (1951), *International Organization* (May), pp. 300-312.

――― (1955), *National Minorities, An International Problem*, Cambridge, Mass.

Clyde, Paul H. (1935), *Japan's Pacific Mandate,* New York.

Cochran v. *Louisiana State Board of Education,* 281 U.S. 370 (1930).

Cohen, Andrew (1974), The Culver City Spanish Immersion Program: The First Two Years, *Modern Language Journal,* 58, no. 3, pp. 95-103.

––– (1975), Successful Immersion in North America, *Working Papers on Bilingualism,* Toronto, no. 5, pp. 39-46.

Commager, Henry Steele (1958), *Documents of American History,* vols. I and II, New York.

Commissioner of Education, see *Report of the United States Commissioner of Education.*

Committee on Foreign Affairs (1960), Hearings before the Subcommittee on the Far East and the Pacific; House of Representatives, 86th Congress, first session on S. 2130: A Bill to Authorize a Payment to the Government of Japan, Washington.

Common Council on American Unity, Letters from, dated Feb. 3, 1961, and Apr. 12, 1961.

Comptes Rendus de l'Athénée Louisianais. See also Dimez (1877), Mercier (1889), and Athénée Louisianais.

Congressional Globe, First Session, 28th Congress, 18, 42-44.

–––, Second Session, 28th Congress, 7.

–––, First Session, 29th Congress, 23.

–––, Second Session, 29th Congress, 11-12.

–––, First Session, 30th Congress, 12.

–––, Second Session, 37th Congress, col. 1820-1822, 1842.

Conseil de la S. D. N., 67e Sess., Journal Off., July 1932.

Cook, K. M. (1939), *Public Education in the Panama Canal Zone,* U.S. Department of the Interior, Office of Education Bulletin 1939, no. 8.

Cooley, T. M. (1905), *Michigan,* Boston, Mass.

Correll, Ernst (1946), The Congressional Debates on the Mennonite Immigration from Russia, 1873-1874, *Mennonite Quarterly Review,* 20:178-222.

Cosenza, M. E. (1933-1934), President, Italian Teachers Association, *Thirteenth Annual Report.*

––– (1934-1935), President, Italian Teachers Association, *Fourteenth Annual Report.*

Coudert, F. R. (1926), Evolution of the Doctrine of Territorial Incorporation, *American Law Review,* 60:801-864.

Coulter, C. W. (1919), *The Poles in Cleveland,* Cleveland.

Coulter, J. W. (1957), *The Pacific Dependencies of the U.S.,* New York.

Coyle v. *Smith,* 221 U.S. 559 (1911).

Cubberly (1934), *Public Education in the United States,* Boston.

Cumberland, Charles C. (1960), The U.S. Mexican Border, A Selective Guide to the Literature of the Region, *Rural Sociology,* 25 (2), 236 pp., June 1960.

Cunz, Dieter (1948), *The Maryland Germans,* Princeton, N.J.

Cutler, James E. (1905), *Lynch-Law,* New York.

Dahm, Georg (1959-1961), *Völkerrecht,* I-III, Stuttgart.

Daniels, John (1920), *America via the Neighborhood,* New York and London.

Dartmouth College v. *Woodward,* 17 U.S. 518. Text also in Kloss (1942), 946; Commager I (1958), 220.

Davie, M. R. (1936), *World Immigration with Special Reference to the United States,* New York.

Day, A. G. (1960), Hawaii, New York.

Debates and Proceedings of the Minnesota Constitutional Convention (1857), St. Paul, Minn.

Debates and Proceedings of the United States, Fifth Congress (1851), Washington, col. 1337-1380.

A Decade of American Foreign Policy, Basic Documents, 1941-1949 (1950), Washington.

Deiler, H. (1909), *The Settlement of the German Coast and the Creoles of German Descent,* New Orleans.

Delgado et al. v. *Bastrop Independent School District.*

De Lima v. *Bidwell,* 182, U.S. 540.

Del Norte Thérist, M. See Thérist.

Demichel, A. (1960), L'Evolution de la protection des minorités depuis 1945, in *Revue Générale de Droit Int. Publications,* 64: 27-28.

Department of Northern Affairs and National Resources, Ottawa, Letter, Oct. 3, 1961.

Desdunes, R. (1911), *Nos hommes et notre histoire,* Montreal.

Deutsch-Amerikanisches Conversations-Lexikon, VII (1872), New York.

Deutsche Vierteljahresschrift, Tugingen (1839), 1:69.

Deutschen Pionier-Vereins. See *Mitteilungen des deutschen Pionier-Vereins.*

Deutscher Pionier, Cincinnati (1817), 3:37, 167, 214, 233, 301.

——— (1886), 18:50ff.

Dexter, E. G. (1922), *A History of Education in the United States,* New York.

Dieckhoff, John S. (1965), *NDEA and Modern Foreign Languages,* New York.

Dietz, Paul T. (1949), The Transition from German to English in the Missouri Synod, *Concordia Historical Institute Quarterly,* 22 (3):97-121.

Digest Pennsylvania State Law (1921), Sec. 10.562.

Digneo, Ellen H. (1968), *Teaching Spanish to the Spanish-Speaking Child,* Santa Fe, N.M.

Diocese of Worcester. See *The Holy Ghost French Series.*

Ditchy, J. K. (1932), *Les Acadiens Louisianais et leur parler,* Paris.

Dixon Case. See *Zellers* v. *Nuff.*

Dixon v. *Goethals, Canal Zone Superior Court Reports,* III.

Document (United Nations) A2630, Suppl. 1017, 21-23 A/RES/1541/(XV) for Dec. 21, 1960.

——— E/CN4/351, 13-14.

——— E/CN4/sjb 2/L4

——— E/CN4/Sub. 2/L92.

——— E/CN4/SR256 (statement of Apr. 17, 1952).

——— E/CN4/SR737

——— T (1950), /:et 10/5, June 12, 1950, p. 2. Compare Report of the Visiting Mission (1950).

Documents on the Constitutional History of Puerto Rico (1964), vol. 2, Washington, D.C.

Dooley v. *U.S.,* 182 U.S. 222.

Dooley v. *U.S.,* 183 U.S. 151.

Dorr v. *U.S.,* 195 U.S. 138 (1904) 148.

Dorrance, W. A. (1935), *The Survival of French in the Old District of Genevieve,* University of Missouri Studies, vol. 10, no. 2, Columbia, Mo.

Downs v. *Bidwell,* 182 U.S. 244, 292.

Dubroca v. *Favrot,* 3 La. Ann, 272, Text in Kloss (1940), 195.

Dumez, E. (1877), in Comptes Rendus de l'Athénée Louisianais, July 1, 1877.

Dunlop (1835), in *Proceedings and Debates of the Pennsylvania Constitutional Assembly,* vol. 5.

Dunton v. *Montoya,* Colorado 99, 100.

East, W. E. (1928), in E. T. Hiller, ed., *Rural Community Types,* University of Illinois Studies in the Social Sciences, vol. 16, Urbana, Ill.

Education. U.S. Commissioner of; see also *Report of the United States Commissioner of Education.*

Educational Conditions in Arizona (1917), Bulletin of the United States Department of Education, no. 4.

Edwin, B., and Merrick, T. (1925), *The Revised Civil Code of the State of Louisiana,* 3d ed., New Orleans, La.

Eibert, S. H., and Keala, S. A. (1961), *Conversational Hawaiian,* Honolulu, Hawaii.

Eibock, J. (1900), *Die Deutschen von Iowa*, Des Moines, Iowa.

Eikel, F. (1954), *The New Braunfels German Dialect*, Baltimore, Md.

Elkin, A. P. (1957), in *Enquête sur l'Anticolonialisme*, Lisbon, Portugal.

Ellis, Frances H. (1954), Historical Account of German Instruction in the Public Schools of Indianapolis, 1869-1919, *Indiana Magazine of History*, 50:119-138, 251-276, 357-380.

Encyclopedia of the Philippines, Z. M. Galang, ed., Manila.

Engel v. Vitale, 82S.Ct.126 (1962).

Engerrand, George C. (March 1934), "The So-Called Wends of Germany and Their Colonies in Texas and in Australia," *University of Texas Bulletin*, Austin, Tex.

Epstein, M., ed. (1956), *All about Hawaii*, Honolulu, Hawaii.

Ermacora, Felix (1963), *Handbuch der Grundfreiheiten und Menschenrechte*, Vienna.

――― (1964), *Die Minderheiten in der Arbeit der Vereinigten Nationen*, vol. 2 of Ethnos, Vienna.

Erziehungs-Blätter für Schule und Haus (1892), 23:9. Milwaukee, Wis.

Escanaba v. Chicago, 107 U.S. 678 (1882).

Eshleman, C. H. (1938), *Pennsylfawnisch-Deitsch Eck*, Feb. 26, 1938.

Espinosa, Aurelio M. (1911), *The Spanish Language in New Mexico and Southern Colorado*, Sante Fe, N.M.

――― (1930), *Estudios sobre el Español de Nuevo Méjico*, Buenos Aires, Republica Argentina. This is a translation of an article which appeared 1911-1914 in English in the *Revue de dialectologie romane*.

Espinosa, J. E. (1960), *Saints in the Valleys*, Albuquerque, N.M.

Ethnic Groups, United States Department of Commerce, Bureau of the Census: (Characteristics of the Population by Ethnic Origin), November 1969, Series P-20, no. 221, Apr. 30, 1971.

Europe Ethnica (1961), 18 (2):51, 54, Vienna.

Evans, L. H. (1945), *The Virgin Islands*, Ann Arbor, Mich.

Evening Bulletin of Philadelphia, Pa., Nov. 28, 1969.

Everson v. Board of Education of Ewing, 330 U.S. 1 (1947).

Ewert, J. G. (1919), *Die Hutterischen Mennoniten im Militargefangnis*. Hillsboro, Kans.

Executive Orders 9066, Feb. 19, 1942. 9102, Mar. 18, 1942.

――― 10965 of June 29, 1951; 10408 of Nov. 10, 1952; 10470 of July 17, 1953.

Ex Parte Endo, 323 U.S. 283.

Fahrni, Peter (1967), *Die Assoziation von Staaten mit anderen Staaten*, Zurich.

Farrand, M. (1896), *The Legislation of Congress for the Organized Territories of the U.S.*, 1789-1895, Newark, N.J.

――― (1900), Territory and District, *American Historical Review*, 5:676-681.

Farrington v. Tokushige, 273 U.S. 284.

Fay, E. W. (1898), *History of Education in Louisiana*, Washington, D.C.

Fergusson, Erna (1952), *New Mexico, A Pageant of Three Peoples*, New York.

Fernos-Isern, Resident Commissioner, letter of Apr. 13, 1961.

Ficatier, M. E. (1957), Les Louisianais Français, *Revue de Psychologie des Peuples*, 12:261-293, Le Havre.

55th Annual Report of the State Commissioner of Common Schools (1909).

Fischer, Georges (1954), Le Commonwealth de Porto-Rico et les Etats-Unis, *Rev. Juridique et Politique de l'Union Française*, 8: 169-199.

――― (1960), Un cas de Dicolonisation, *Les Etats-Unis et les Philippines*, Paris.

Fishman, Joshua A. (1962), How Have Franco-Americans Fared in Preserving the French Language in the United States? *Les Conferences de l'Institute Franco-Americain de Bowdoin*, 2d ed., vol. 2, Brunswick, Me.

――― (1966), ed., *Language Loyalty in the United States*, The Hague, the Netherlands.

――― (1974), *A Sociology of Bilingual Education*, New York, unpublished preprint completed under USOF Contract AFCO/73/580.

Fick, H. H. (1935), letter to Kloss.

Flanagan, Hallie. See McDermott, D. (1965).

Florida State Library Board, letter to Kloss.

Foerster, R. F. (1919), *The Italian Emigration of Our Times,* Cambridge, Mass.

Forbes, W. C. (1928), *The Philippine Islands,* Boston, Mass.

Fortier, A. (1891), The Acadians of Louisiana, *Publications of the Modern Language Association.*

Fosdieck, Lucien J. (1906), *The French Blood in America,* New York.

France in New York (1950), a directory, New York.

Francis, E. K. (1956-1958), Minderheitenforschung in Amerika, *Kolner Zeitschrift für Sociologie und Sozialpsychologie,* 9:517-548; 10:233-247; 401-417.

Frangulis, M. A. F. (1957), *Dictionaire Diplomatique,* Paris.

Freund, Ernst (1904), *The Police Power,* Chicago.

Friedrich, Carl J. (1959), *Puerto Rico, Middle Road to Freedom,* New York.

Fritz, George (1904), publisher, *Chamorro-Wörterbuch,* Berlin.

— — — (1963), Chamorro Grammar, *Mitteilungen Seminar für Orientalische Sprachen.*

Fuji v. *State of California,* 217 Pac. (2nd) 481 (1940), Federal District Court of California.

Gaarder, Bruce (1967), Organization of the Bilingual School, *Journal of Social Issues,* 23:110-120.

— — — The Challenge of Bilingualism, *Foreign Language Teaching—Challenges to the Profession,* Reports of the Working Committees, Northeast Conference on Foreign Language Teaching, Modern Language Association.

— — — Two Patterns of Bilingual Education in Dade County, Florida, Northeast Conference on Foreign Language Teaching.

Gad, Dinn (1957), *Den groelande skole . . . Arende Som Berora Samerna.* Helsinki, Finland.

— — — (1960), Greenland Schools and Their Relation to the Problems of Cultural Contact, *The Lapps Today in Finland, Norway and Sweden,* Paris, France. (Bibliotheque Arctique, I).

Galang, Z. M. (1957), ed., *Encyclopedia of the Philippines,* Manila.

Galbraith (1925), *History of Ohio,* vol. 2.

Gamio, M. (1930), *Mexican Immigration to the United States,* Chicago, Ill.

Gammel (1898), *The Laws of Texas,* vols. 1 and 2.

Gerhard, E. S. (1943), The History of Schwenkfelder Schools, *Schwenkfeldiana,* 1(3):5-21.1 (3):5-21.

Gerhard, H. (1915), *Das Deutschtum in der amerikanischen. Politik* Leipzig.

Gerhard's Banknoten-Reporter (1856-1865), see Reading, *Adler,* Nov. 16 and Dec. 21, 1858, June 21, 1859, and Arndt and Olson (1961).

German Gymnastics Association of Louisville v. *City of Louisville,* 117 Kentucky 958; 80SW201, 65LRA 120.

Gisler, Anton (1912), *Der Modernismus,* Einsiedein, Switzerland, and Waldshut, Germany.

Gonzalez, Nancie L. (1967), *The Spanish Americans of New Mexico, a Distinctive Heritage,* Mexican American Study Project, Advance Report no. 9, Los Angeles.

Gordon, L. K. (1953), *Journal of Politics,* 15:42ff.

Government v. *Diaz, Canal Zone Superior Court Reports III.*

Grammar v. *Standard Dredging Co.,* 224 U.S. 362 (1912).

Greiner, M. (1841), *The Louisiana Digest,* New Orleans.

Grey, J. A. C. (1960), *American Samoa. A History of American Samoa, Its U.S. Naval Administration,* Annapolis, Md.

Griebach, M. (1912), *German-American Annals,* 10:250.

Gross, Herbert (1935), *The Lutheran School Journal,* 71 (2).

Greuning, Ernest (1954), *The State of Alaska,* New York.

Guradze, Heinz (1956), *Der Stand der Menschenrechte in Völkerrecht,* Töttingen.

Haenich, W. (1937), *Die auswärtige Politik Ryukyus seit dem Anfang des 19. Jahrhunderts,* Erlangen.

Hagwood (1940), *The Tragedy of German America,* New York, London.

Hammerich, L. C. (1954), The Russian Stratum in Alaskan Eskimo, *Word,* 10:401-428 (esp. 426).

Hancock, R. (1960), *Puerto Rico,* Princeton.

Handschin, Charles H. (1913), *The Teaching of Modern Languages in the United States,* U.S. Bureau of Education, Bulletin 3, Washington, D.C.

––– (1913), *History of Modern Language Teaching in the United States,* New York.

Handwörterbuch des Grenz- und Auslanddeutschtums, III (1938), New York, Breslau.

Harris, W. T. (1903), on the meeting of the National Deutschamerik Lehrerbunde in Cincinnati; see Viereck (1903), 240.

Harrisburg v. Dauphin Deposit Bank, 6 Dauphin 4 (1963).

Hart, R. W. (1928), *The Philippines Today,* New York.

Hartzler, J. S. (1922), *Mennonites in the World War,* Scottsdale, Pa.

Hattori, Shiro (1948), The Relationship of Japanese to the Ryukyu, Korean, and Altaic Languages, *Transactions Asiatic Society of Japan,* 3d Session, vol. I.

Hattstaedt, O. F. (around 1928), *Gesch. d. Sud-Wisconsin-Districts der ... Synode von Missouri,* St. Louis, Mo.

Haugen, E. (1953), *The Norwegian Language in America,* I, Philadelphia.

Hawaii v. Mankichi, 190 U.S. 197.

Hawes, H. B. (1932), *Philippine Uncertainty,* New York, London.

Hayden, J. R. (1928), *Foreign Affairs,* 6:633-644.

––– (1942), *The Philippines,* New York.

Hearings before the Territories and Insular Subcommittee (1967), *Guam-Virgin Islands Elective Governors,* 90th Congress, 1st Session, Washington.

Heim, A. (1915), *Monatshefte,* 16:182.

Helfield, D. M. (1952), *Revista Juridica de la Univ. de Puerto Rico,* 21:225ff.

Henderson, Alice C. (1937), *Brothers of Light: The Penitentes of the Southwest,* New York.

Henkel (1812), *Leutenant Gouverneurs Brief an die Gesetzgebung, Rathstube, den 2ten Dezember 1811,* New Market; see Wust (1953).

Hense-Jensen, W., and Bruncken, E. (1902), *Wisconsins Deutsch-Amerikaner b.z. Schluss des 19 Johrhunderts,* II, Milwaukee.

Hentschel, W. R. (1930), in 60th anniversary edition of the *Colorado Herald* (Denver), Oct. 19, 1930.

Higa, Mikio (1963), *Politics and Parties in Postwar Okinawa,* Vancouver.

High Commissioner of ... Pacific Islands (1965), *Report of the High Commissioner of the Trust Territory of the Pacific Islands to the Secretary of the Interior,* New York.

High, Stanley (1937), *The Saturday Evening Post,* 210 (21):34.

Hirabayashi v. U.S., 320 U.S. 81.

Hodgson, James G. (1930), Introduction, *Chicago and Cook County. A Union List ... ,* which see.

Hoffman, J. L. (1911), *Mitteilungen des deutschen Pionier-Vereins von Philadelphia,* 20:18.

The Holy Ghost French Series (1954ff.), The Diocese of Worcester, Mass., published at Putnam, Conn.

Hoover v. Evatt, 324 U.S. 652.

Horne (1873), *The Pennsylvania Dutchman,* 1 (3), Lancaster, Pa. Text in Kloss (1940), 229-280.

Houck, Louis (1908), *A History of Missouri,* vol. II, Chicago, Ill.

House of Representatives Committee on Interior and Insular Affairs (1961), 87th Congress, 1st Session, Committee Print no. 1.

Howard, P. H. (1957), *Political Tendencies in London 1812-1952,* Baton Rouge, La.

Howe, Albert H. (1901), *The Insular Cases* (56th Congress, 2nd Session, H.R. Doc. 509), Washington, D.C.

Hubbe, Ines (1959), *Learn Chamarro Quickly,* Agana, Guam.

Hudson, Leslie (1934), *Czech Pioneers of the Southwest,* Dallas, Tex.

Huérta, C. L. (Sept. 25, 1961), Assistant Attorney General of Arizona, letter to Kloss.

Hugelmann, K. G. (1934), ed., *Das Nationalitatenrecht des Alten Österreich,* Vienna.

Humphrey, N. D. (1943-1944), The Detroit Mexican and Naturalization, *Social Forces,* 22:322-355.

Hunt, C. L. (December 1953), *Pacific Affairs,* 331-349.

Hunt, Thomas, *Historical Sketch of the Town of Clermont* (Clermont).

Hunter, Robert J. (1959), *Puerto Rico: A Survey* . . . Washington, D.C. (86th Cong., 1st Sess., Comm. Print no. 10).

Indiana Historical Magazine (1918), 14:124.

Indiana Magazine of History (1916), 12:340.

Indiana School Laws, 1824, Sec. 12.

Indiana State Library (Oct. 4, 1961), letter to Kloss concerning Governor Wright's message of Dec. 6, 1849.

International Institute of Teachers College (1925), *A Survey of the Educational System of the Philippine Islands,* Manilla.

——— (1926), *A Survey of the Public Educational System of Porto Rico,* Made under the Direction of the International Institute of Teachers College, Columbia University. Authorized by the University of Porto Rico, New York.

Jacobson, H. K. (1960), Our "Colonial" Problem, *Foreign Affairs,* 39:56-66, esp. 62.

Japanese Foreign Office (1947), *Minor Islands Adjacent to Japan Proper, III: The Bonin Island Group: The Volcano Island Group,* Tokio.

Jockelson, W. (1933), *History, Ethnology and Anthropology of the Aleut,* Carnegie Publ. no. 432, Washington, D.C.

Jockers, E. (1926), *Deutschamerikanischer Musenalmanach,* Milwaukee, Wis.

Johnson, Amandus (1911), *The Swedish Settlements on the Delaware,* New York.

Journals of the Continental Congress, 1774-1789. Edited from the Original Records, vol. 1, 1904, through vol. 34, 1937, Washington, D.C.

Kalaw, Teodoro M. (1948), *Documentos Constituciales sobre Filipinas,* 1915-1916.

——— *Philippine Government,* Manila.

Kane, H. T. (1943), *The Bayous of Louisiana,* New York.

Karta Narodov SSSR (1962), Official Soviet publication.

Kashevaroff, A. P., Alaska Historical Library and Museum, Juneau, Alaska, Letters of 1931 and 1936 to Kloss.

Kattenbach v. *Morgan,* 384 U.S. 651 (preliminary edition), The dissenting opinion of Judge Harlan is found 384 U.S. 659-671.

Kaufman, W. (1911), *Die Deutschen im amerikanischen,* Munich and Berlin.

Kellog, L. P. (1918-1919), *Wisconsin Magazine of History,* 2:3.25.

Kennedy, Robert F. (1956), Letter to the editor of *The New York Times,* Jan. 25, 1956.

Kennedy's *Banknoten-Reporter,* German edition (1853-1858) See *Reading Adler,* Nov. 16 and Dec. 21, 1858, June 21, 1859, and Arndt and Olson (1961).

Kepner v. *U.S.,* 195 U.S. 100 (1904).

Kernitz v. *Long Island City,* 3 N.Y. Suppl. 144.

Kerr, George H. (1953), *Ryukyu: Kingdom and Province before 1945,* Washington.

——— (1954), *The Ryukyu Islands: A Reference List of Books and Articles in English, French and German,* Stanford University, mimeo.

Kibbe, Pauline R. (1946), *Latin Americans in Texas,* Albuquerque.

Kilpatrick, William H. (1912), *The Dutch Schools of New Netherlands and Colonial New York,* Washington, D.C.

Kindred, L. W. (1938), *Public Funds for Private and Parochial Schools,* Dissertation, Ann Arbor, Mich.

King, Grace, and Ficklen, John R. (1893), *A History of Louisiana,* New Orleans.

Kirchenblatt (1935), 27:7, Columbus, Ohio.

Kirk, Grayson L. (1936), *Philippine Independence,* New York.

Kirkconnell, Thomas W. (1961), letter to Kloss concerning early years of Vincennes University.

Kjolseth, Rolf (1972), Bilingual Programs in the United States: for Assimilation or Pluralism, in B. Spolsky (ed.), *The Language Education of Minority Children, Studies in Bilingual Education,* pp. 94-121, Newbury House, Rowley, Mass.

Klees, Frederic (1950), *The Pennsylvania Dutch,* New York.

Klein, S. L. (1940), *Social Interaction of Creoles and Anglo-Americans in New Orleans,* New Orleans, La.

Kloss, Heinz (1931), *Die pennsylvaniadeutsche Literatur, Mitteilungen der deutschen Akademie.*

——— (1937), *Um die Einigung des Deutschamerikanertums. Die Geschichte einer unvollendeten Volksgruppe,* Berlin.

——— (1938), Art. Louisiana, *Hwb. des Grenz und Auslandsdeutschtums,* 3:402-405.

——— (May 7, 1938, and Oct. 2, 1954), in *Pennsylfawnisch-Deitsch-Eck,* Allentown, Pa.

——— (1940), *Volksgruppenrecht in den Vereinigten Staaten,* vol. I, Essen.

——— (1942), *Das Volksgruppenrecht in den Vereinigten Staaten,* vol. II, Essen.

——— (1950), The Legal Nature of the School District in the United States (Das juristische Gepräge der Schulgemeinden in den Vereinigten Staaten), *Bildung und Erziehung,* 3:676-683.

——— (1952a), *Die Entwicklung germanischer Kultursprachen,* Munich.

——— (1952b), Assimilationsfragen des Pennsylvania, *Pfalzer Heimat,* 3:83-87.

——— (1953), Die Muttersprachenzählung von 1940 und die Zukunft der nichtenglischen Sprachen in den USA, *Erakunde (Bonn),* 7:220-225.

——— (1954), *Mitteilungen des Institus für Auslandbeziehungen,* 4(3/4):118, Stuttgart.

——— (1960), ed., *Grunderziehung, Hilfe für Entwicklungsländer,* Stuttgart, Germany.

——— (1961a), Die Nationalitätpolitik der Vereinigten Staaten, *Osterreichische Zeitschrift für Aussenpolitik,* 1 (6), 357-375.

——— (1961b), Typen der Selbstverwaltung, *Schmollers Jahrbuch,* 81:61-93.

——— (1962), *Vereinte Nationen,* 3.

——— (1967), *Zum Problem des Fremdsprachenunterrichts an den Grundschulen Amerikas und Europas,* Godesberg.

——— (1967), Abstand Languages and Ausbau Languages, *Anthropological Linguistics,* 9(7):29-41.

——— (1969), *Grundfragen der Ethnopolitik,* Vienna: Braumller, and Bad Godesberg: Wissenchaftliches Archiv.

Kolarz, Walter (1956), *Russland und seine asiatischen Völker,* Frankfurt, Germany.

Komer, G. (1884), *Das deutsche Element in den Vereinigten Staaten,* 2d ed., New York.

——— (1909), *Memoirs I,* Cedar Rapids, Iowa.

Kopel v. Bingham, 211 U.S. 468, cited in *Documents on the Constitutional History of Puerto Rico,* p. 290.

Korematsu v. U.S., 214.

Kuder (1945), *Far Eastern Review,* 119-126.

Kulyuckyj, Mikota (1953), *Ethnographical Map of the Soviet Union,* Edinburgh.

Kuykendall, R. S., and Day, A. G. (1949), *Hawaii: A History,* 2d ed., New York.

Lafon v. Smith, 3 La. 473 (1832). See also Kloss (1940), 196.

Laing, F. S., in *Kansas State Historical Collections,* vol. II.

Lamott, John H. (1921), *History of the Archdiocese of Cincinnati,* 1821-1921. New York and Cincinnati.

Lane (1934), comment on Read's *Louisiana French,* 10:323-333.

Language Development in Action (1960), University of Massachusetts, Amherst, Mass., 178 pages hectographed.

Lassiter v. *Northhampton Election Board,* 360 U.S. 45.

Lauvrière (1939), *Histoire de la Louisiane,* Paris.

Law of Oct. 14, 1940, Art. 303 (a5) (U.S.C.903 a 5).

Law of Mar. 21, 1942, 56 Stat, 172C.191, 18 USCA, section 97a; text also in 323 U.S. 227.

Law of Aug. 1, 1950, Art. 4b (64 Stat. 385).

Laws (1864), Section 68, 1H 402.

Lawton, R. J. (1919), ed., *Franco-Americans of the State of Maine,* Lewiston, Maine.

League of Bonin Evacuees (1958), *History of the Problem of the Bonin Islands,* Tokio.

Learned, Marion D. (1901), in *Monatshefte,* 3:88.

Le Blanc v. *Dubroca,* 6 La. Ann, 360; concerning the question of court orders, see also *Lafon* v. *Smith.* See also Kloss (1940), 196.

Leibowitz, Arnold H. (1969), English Literacy; Legal Sanction for Discrimination, in *Notre Dame Lawyer,* 45 (1):7-67.

——— (1971), Educational Policy and Political Acceptance: *The Imposition of English as a Second Language of Instruction in American Schools.* Washington: ERIC.

Lemaire, H. B. (1962), *French in New England, A Socio-Historical Portrait,* Language Resources Project, New York, mimeographed.

Lemoine, A. (1921), *L'Evolution de la race française en Amerique,* Montreal.

Lemon v. *Kurtzman,* 403 U.S. 602 (1971); *Levitt* v. *Committee,* 413 U.S. 825 (1973).

Lenker, J. N. (around 1915), a pamphlet, *Settlement Language, Its Place of Honor after English in Public Schools, With Special References to Scandinavian.*

Le Sage Tisch, J. See Tisch.

Liao, S. C. (April 1958), *Fil.-Sin. Journal,* 5:10.

Library of Congress, Washington, D.C., letter to Kloss; the Library of Congress at his request checked the Collection of Early State Records (Alc Rec. Is 1-2) including the *Pensacola Gazette,* 1823-1830.

Lind, A. (1939), *American Journal of Sociology,* 45:207.

Linebarger, G. C. (1958), in R. Strausz-Hupe and H. W. Hazard, eds., *The Idea of Colonialism,* New York.

Littler, Robert M. C. (1929), *The Governance of Hawaii,* Stanford, Calif.

Lohr, O. (1931), *Mitteilungen der deutschen Akademie,* Munich, 1931:283-290.

——— (1938), in *Deutschtum im Ausland,* 24:161-165.

Loon, L. G. van. See van Loon (1938).

Louisiana (1950), Ex: Sess. No. 282. See also Wolff (1920).

Louisiana Board of Education (1938), *Suggestions for the Teaching of French in the Elementary Schools of Louisiana,* mimeographed.

Louisiana Foreign Languages (1955-1956), a hectographed pamphlet entitled *Foreign Languages in the Elementary Grades in Louisiana during 1955-1956.*

Louisiana Law (1936), no. 286.

Louisiana Statutes. See Phillips (1856).

Lowrie, S. H. (1932), *Culture Conflict in Texas 1821-1835,* New York.

Lucas, H. S. (1955), *Netherlands in America,* Ann Arbor, Mich.

Luckenback v. *U.S.,* 280 U.S. 173.

Lyles v. *State,* 41 Texas 172.

Mackey, W. F., and Verdoodt, A. (1975), eds., *The Multinational Society,* Newbury House, Rowley, Mass.

Malaret, Augusto (1937), *Vocabulario de Puerto Rico.* San Juan, Puerto Rico.

Mallot, Jean (1934), *Les Amitiés Catholiques françaises,* Paris, Dec. 15, 1934, 15.

Malory, W. M. (1910), *Treaties, Conventions ... between the U.S.A. and Other Powers,* Washington, D.C. The text of the Peace Treaty of 1783 is to found here and in Miller (1934), not in Thorpe.

Mamatey, V. S. (1957), *The U.S. and East Central Europe,* 1914-1918, Princeton, N.J.

Marden, C. F. (1952), *Minorities in American Society,* New York.

Margolin, M. Z. (1961), *Qualifications for Voting. Summaries of State Laws . . .* , Library of Congress Legislative Ref. Service, JK 1876 A.

Marsh, William R. (1967), ed., *North to the Future, The Alaska Department of Education in Alaska*, 1785-1967, Juneau, Alaska.

McCollum v. *Board of Education*, 333 U.S. 203; also in Commager, II (1958), pp. 726-728, with literature.

McDermott, D. (1965), in *German Quarterly*, 38:325-334. The author refers to Hallie Flanagan, Arena, New York, 1940.

McDonough, E. C., and Richards, E. S. (1953), *Ethnic Minorities in the United States*, New York.

McGee, Clare M. (1955), *The Causes and Effects of the Dixon Case*, Washington, D.C.

McGrath, Commissioner of Education (1953), text of speech appears in *Modern Language Journal*, 37:115-119.

McIntosh, William (1955), Constitutional Government in Puerto Rico, *Revista Juridica de la Univ. de Puerto Rico*, 24:205.

McMurtrie, Douglas (1931), *Early Printing in Michigan*, Chicago, Ill.

Medina, E. (1955), *Spanish for Boys and Girls. A Handbook . . .* , State of New Mexico, Department of Education, Curriculum Guide for the Elementary Schools, Bulletin 25, vol. 1.

Meixner, E. C. (1941), *The Teaching of the Scandinavian Languages and Literatures in the United States*, Philadelphia.

Mencken, H. L. (1923-1936, 1948), *The American Language*, 1923 is 3d ed.; for 4th ed. (1936); see p. 621; cf. J. Dyneley Prince.

Mendez Case: Rep. 9th U.S. Circ. Ct. of Appeals, no. 11, 310, Apr. 14, 1947.

Mercier, A. (1889), in *Comptes Rendus de l'Athénée Louisianais*, no. 6.

Meyer v. *Nebraska*, 262 U.S. 390 (1929); see also *Yu Cong Eng* v. *Trinidad*.

Meynen, Emil (1937), *Bibliography on German Settlements in Colonial North America . . . 1683-1933*, Leipzig.

——— (1939), Das pennsylvaniendeutsche Bauernland, *Deutsches Archiv für Landes- und Volksforschung*, 3:253-293.

Mighican State Historical Society (1935), letter to Kloss.

Mildenberger, K. M. (1955), in *Modern Language Journal*, Status in 1955, pp. 13-14.

——— (1961), in *Internationale Zeitschrift für Erziehungswissenschaft*, 7:402-409.

Miller, Henry H. (1934), *Treaties and Other International Acts of the United States*, vol. 4, Washington, D.C.

Minnesota (1959 Laws, Art. 7 (7)); with only immaterial changes of the wording, Sec. 126.07 Minn. Stat. An.

Missouri v. *Holland*, 252 U.S. 416 (1920).

Mitteilungen des Deutsch-Amerikanischen Nationalbundes (1911), Philadelphia. Feb. 1911, no. 2, May 1911, no. 5.

Mitteilungen des Deutschen Pionier-Vereins von Philadelphia, 9:27 (1908).

Monatshefte (1901-1902), 3:284 (1907), 8:157.

——— (1909), 10:276-277.

——— (1911), 12:246.

——— (1912), 13:85.

——— (1913), 13:383; (1913), 14:273.

——— (1913), 14:377; (1914), 15:135.

——— (1914), 15:357; (1915), 16157.

Monatshefte für deutschen Unterricht (1914), 15:259.

Moreno Rios v. *U.S.* (1938).

Mormon Church v. *U.S.*, 136 U.S. 1,42.

Morrison, J. C. (1958), *The Puerto Rican Study*, 1953-1958, New York.

Musgang. See Pempeit (1932).

Mytziuk, Alexander (1943), Die Ukrainer in Sowjetasien, *Volksforschung,* 6:79-102.

Namba v. *McCourt,* 204 Pac. (2nd) 569 (1949), Supreme Court of Oregon.

Nebraska v. *Taylor.* See *State* v. *Taylor.*

Nebraska District v. *McKeivie,* 104 Nebr. 93, 175NW 531,7 ALR 1688.

Newman, M. T., and E. L. Eng (1948), *Annual Report Smithsonian Institution,* Washington.

New Mexico ex parte de Vore, 18 N.M. 246 (1913).

New Mexico S.A. Sec. 77, 1-2.

New Mexico *Statutes* (1953), 16-1-6, the law already contained in the 1884 code, and 36-5-8, the law of 1889. Other statutes as cited in the text. For 10-2-11, this is an amendment of 4648 of the Code of 1915. Compare Courtright (1929), 113-104 (p. 1440). Courtright erroneously reads publication instead of population.

New Mexico Territory v. *Thomasson,* 13 Pac. 223.

Newton, L. W. (1933), Creoles and Anglo-Americans in Social Conflict–A Study in Cultural Conflicts, *Southwest Soc. Quarterly,* June 1933-March 1934.

New York Bar Association (1919), Memos 158-159 of the Chamber.

New York Letter dated Oct. 2, 1969, from the New York City office of the Migration Division of the Ministry of Labor at San Juan, Puerto Rico.

New Zealand Treaty Series (1962), no. 5, Department of External Affairs, Publication no. 256, Wellington.

Ney, James W. (1964), *Linguistic Reporter,* 6:1-2.

Nichols, Jeannette P. (1924), *Alaska, A History of Its Administration,* Cleveland, Ohio.

Nonpublic Assembly of the Commonwealth of Pennsylvania, June 19, 1968.

Non-Self-Governing Territories . . . Information Transmitted . . . during 1950 (1951), New York. (ST/TRI/Ser.A/5, reprint of Doc. A/915/Add. 1).

Norlie, O. M. (1925), *History of the Norwegian People in America,* Minneapolis.

North Dakota (1960), Cent. Code 46-06-2.

Norval Act. Text in Kloss (1942), 772.

Notes and Comments on the Constitution of the Commonwealth of Puerto Rico (1952), Washington, D.C.

O'Gorman, Thomas (1894), *A History of the Roman Catholic Church in the United States,* American Church Historical Series IX, New York.

Ohio General Code (1910), sec. 11,684; sec. 5704; text in Kloss (1940), 483.

Ohio Legislative Reference Bureau (1961), in a letter to Kloss signed by W. P. Lewis.

Ohio *Revised Statutes* (1879), I sec. 329, text in Kloss (1940), 443-444.

Ohio State Commissioner of Common Schools; see *55th Annual Report. . . .*

Ohio *Statutes* (1869), Chapter 88 (12), Session Laws, 12 sec. XII.

Oldendow, Knud (1939), Groenlaendere og Danske, *Det Groenlandske Selskabs Aarskrift* (German title, *Die Kulturpolitik der Dänen unter den Eskimos auf Grönland,* Stuttgart, 1942).

Olmstedt, F. L. (1860), *A Journey through Texas,* New York.

Opinions of the Attorney General of Ohio (1912), I, 216; (1916), I, 840; (1916), II, 1,939; (1916), II, 1,774; (1918), II, I, 614.

Ornstein, Jacob (1958), Foreign Language Training in the Soviet Union–a Qualitative View, *Modern Language Journal,* 42:382-392.

Österreichische Zeitschrift für Aussenpolitik; see Kloss (1961a).

Osuna, J. J. (1949), *A History of Education in Puerto Rico,* Rio Piedras.

Oyama v. *State of California,* 332 U.S. 633 (1948), Supreme Court of the United States.

Paddleford, N. J. (1940), American Right in the Panama Canal, *Am. J. Int. Law,* 34:416-442.

Padgog. Monatshefte (1899-1901), 1:47, Milwaukee.

Padin, J. (1916), *The Problem of Teaching English to the People of Porto Rico,* San Juan, Puerto Rico.

Panhuys; see van Panhuys.

Park, R. E. (1922), *The Immigrant Press and Its Control,* New York and London.

Patterson, B. F., and Monroe, T. B. (1920), Leyes de Texas, civiles y criminales traducidas al español, anotadas hasta esta fecha, Liga instructive mexicana, San Antonio, Tex.

Pempeit, Mrs., née Musgang (1932), Cultural Interests of the Germans of St. Paul 1855-1870, unpublished Ph.D. dissertation, St. Paul, Minn.

Pennsylvania (1949): Sec. 1511 (P.L. 30, 1949) as amended in 1968.

People v. Day, 277 III, 543 (1917).

People of Puerto Rico v. Muratti, 245 U.S. 639 (1918).

People of Puerto Rico v. Shell, 302 U.S. 253, 1937.

People of Puerto Rico v. Tapia, 245 U.S. 639 (1918).

Pepke v. U.S., 183 U.S. 151.

Perales, Alonso S. (1948), Are We Good Neighbors? San Antonio, Tex.

Perkins v. Board of County Commissioners of Cook County, 217, III.449, III NE580 (1916).

Pernthaler, Peter (1962), Der Schutz der Gemeinschaften durch individuelle Rechte, Europa Ethnica, 19 (2/3):50-89.

Petition of the American Committee for the Protection of the Foreign Born (1959), in English as the Brochure, "Our Badge of Infamy. A Petition . . ." Spanish version in Ciencias Politicas y Sociales, 5:275-305, 1959, Mexico.

Phillips (1856), Revised Statutes. The Text of the then longer version is in Kloss (1940), 214. The present version of the Louisiana Revised Statutes (1951), according to a letter from the Supreme Court of Louisiana.

Philipps, H. F. (1936), Etude du parler de la paroisse Evangéline, Paris.

Pierce, Taylor, and King (1852), Civil Code, Article 4, p. 147.

Pierce v. Sisters (1925). See Yu Cong Eng v. Trinidad.

Pisani, L. F. (1957), The Italian in America, New York.

Pitt, Leonard (1966), The Decline of the Californios, A Social History of Spanish-Speaking Californians 1846-90, University of California Press, Berkeley and Los Angeles, Calif.

Pochmann and Schultz (1953), Bibliography of German Culture in America, Madison, Wis.

Pohl v. Ohio and Bohning v. Ohio, 102 Ohio State, 474:132NE20.

Pomeroy, E. S. (1944), The American Colonial Office, Mississippi Valley Historical Review, 30:521-532.

Pomeroy, J. N. (1888), Introduction to the Constitutional Law of the U.S., Boston, 10th ed.

Ponce v. Roman Catholic Apostolic Church, 210 U.S. 296 (1908).

Post, A. C. (1933), Some Aspects of Arizona Spanish, Hispania, 16:35-42.

Powell v. Board of Education, 97III:375:37 Am. Rep. 123.

Pratt, J. W. (1950), America's Colonial Experiment, New York.

Preliminary Inventory of the Records of the Bureau of Insular Affairs, Rec. Gr. 350 (1960), Washington, D.C.

Pressing, Edward Ritter von (1918), Dictionary and Grammar of the Chamorro Language, Government Printing Office, Washington, D.C.

Prince, J. Dyneley, The Jersey Dutch Dialect, Dialect Notes, 3:459ff.

Proceedings of the Americanization Conference. . . . See Americanization Conference.

Proceedings of the Constitutional Convention of Hawaii (1960), vol. I, Honolulu, Hawaii.

——— (1962), vol. II, Honolulu, Hawaii.

Publication L.85-864 of Sept. 2, 1958, 85th Congress, H.R. 13.247,72 Statute 1583.

Publication L.87-864, Oct. 3, 1961, 75 Statute 759.

Puerto Rico v. Rosaly y Castillo, 227 U.S. 274 (1913).

Puerto Rico v. Shell Co., 302 U.S. 253 (1937).

Quiason, Sersfin D. (1958), The Japanese Colony in Davao, 1940-41, Phil. Soc. Sc. Rev., 23:215-230.

Quinoñes, F. M. (1957), Apuntes para la Historia de Puerto Rico, Rio Piedras.

Rabl, K. (1958-61), ed., Das Recht auf die Heimat, vols. I-IV, Munich.

Rasmussen v. U.S., 197 U.S. 516.

Raschhofer, H. (1931), Hauptprobleme des Nationalitätenrechts, Tübingen.

Ratterman, H. A. (1879), *Deutscher Pionier*, 11:217-218.

––– (1911), *Gesammelte Ausgewählte Werke*, vol. 12.

Read, W. A. (1931), *Louisiana French*, Louisiana State University Study no. 5, Baton Rouge, La. See also comment by Lane in *Language*, 10:232-333.

Redslob, Robert (1914), *Abhängige Länder, Eine Analyse des Begriffs der ursprünglichen Herrschergewalt*, Leipzig.

Reichard, H. H. (1918), Pennsylvania German Dialect Writings and Their Writers, *Proceedings of the Pennsylvania German Society*, vol. 26.

Reichmann, Felix (1950), German Printing in Maryland, *Reports of the Social History of the Germans in Maryland*, 27:15.

––– (1961), letter to Kloss dated Feb. 23, 1961.

Reinecke, S. E., and Tokimasa, A. (1934), *American Speech*, 9:48-58.

Report of the Department of Education (1961), signed M. J. Senter, Pago, Pago, Dec. 8, 1961.

Report of the League of Nations (1939), *On the Administration of the South Sea Islands under Japanese Mandate for the year 1938*, Tokyo.

Report of the Philippine Commission, 1900, vol. I.

Report of the Population and Resources of Alaska at the 11th Census 1890 (1893), Miscellaneous Doc. 340, part 7, Washington, D.C.

Report on Trust Territory (1960/1961), *14th Annual Report to the United Nations on the Administration of the Trust Territory of the Pacific Islands*, Department of State Publication 7362.

Report on ... the Trust Territory (1961), *13th Annual Report to the United Nations on the Administration of the Trust Territory of the Pacific Islands*, Department of State Publication 7183, Washington, D.C.

Report on the Trust Territory (1965), *17th Annual Report to the United Nations on the Administration of the Trust Territory of the Pacific Islands*, Washington, D.C.

Report of the United States Commissioner of Education for the Year Ending 1872; 1878; 1887-1888; June 30, 1891; 1894-1895.

Report of the Visiting Mission (1950), *Report of the Visiting Mission of the United Nations*, Document T/789, Aug. 15, 1950.

Reynolds, Annie (1933), *The Education of Spanish Speaking Children in Five Southwestern States*, Washington, D.C., U.S. Office of Education Bulletin No. 11, Government Printing Office.

––– (1933a), in *Bulletin of the United States Bureau of Education*, no. II.

Rice, George P. (1941), The Dutch Language in New York State, *Journal of Speech*, 27:271-274.

Richter v. *Cordes*, 100 Mich. 278:58NW110 (1894).

Rivera, Carlos (1954), in *Modern Language*, 37:493-496.

Robacker, E. F. (1943), *Pennsylvania German Literature, Changing Trends from 1683 to 1942*, Philadelphia, University of Pennsylvania Press.

Rostow, E. V. (1945), Our Worst Wartime Mistake, *Harper's*, 191:193-200, September 1945.

Rowell, George P. (1869-1908), *Directory*.

Rumilly, Robert (1958), *Histoire des Franco-Americains*, Montreal, Canada.

Russell, John C. (1937-1938), State Regionalism, New Mexico, *Social Forces*, 6:268-271.

Ryukyu Islands Facts Book (November 1961), San Francisco, mimeo.

Sady, Emil V. (1957), *The United Nations and Dependent Peoples*, 2d ed., New York.

Sakamaki, Shunzo (1963), *A Bibliographical Guide to Okinawa Studies*, Honolulu.

––– (1963), *Ruykyu, A Bibliographical Guide to Okinawan Studies, Surveying Important Primary Sources and Writings in Ryukyuan, Japanese, Chinese, and Korean*, Honolulu.

Sallet, R. (1931), in *Jahrbuch der Deutsch-Amerikanischen Gesellschaft von Illinois*, 31:66.

Sampson, Paul (1968), The Bonins and Iwo Jima Go Back to Japan, *National Geographic Magazine*, 134 (1):128-144.

Sargent, Kate (1925), Catholicism in Massachusetts Schools, *Forum*, 74:740-742.

Saudelmann, John (1953), *Some Observations on the Problem of Self-Government in the Trust Territory*. This work was not available to me.

Schafer, J. (1927), *Four Wisconsin Counties*, Madison.

——— (1926-1927), in *Wisconsin Magazine of History*, 10:455-461.

Schechtmann, J. B. (1951), Decline of the International Protection of Minority Rights, in *Western Political Quarterly*.

Schlager, E. (1874), *Die sociale und politische Stellung der Deutschen in den Vereinigten Staaten*, Berlin.

Schmitt, Alfred (1951), *Die Alaska-Schrift*, Marburg, West Germany.

Schneyder, Alfred K. H. (1941), Die Bonin-Inseln im Wechsel der Weltpolitik, *Kieler Blätter*, 3 (4):165-165.

Schulze, F. (1926), Erziehungstätigkeit ... in den Vereinigten Staaten, *Theolog-prakt. Quartalsschr.*, 79:457-472.

Schwelb, Egon (1959), *Arch. des Völkerrechts*, 8 (1):48-49.

Schwind, Martin (1942), *Die Gestaltung Karafutos zum japanischen Raum*, Gotha. This is the authoritative work on the Japanese pioneer work on Sakhalin in a Western language, *Peterm. Geogr. Mitt.*, supplementary volume, 239.

Sealsfield, Charles (1846), *Lebensbilder aus der westlichen Hamisphäre*, 3 vols., Stuttgart.

Seidenstiker, O. (1878), *Deutscher Pionier*, 10:309-316.

——— (1893), *The First Century of German Printing in America*, Philadelphia.

Sellin, Thorston (1935-1936), Racial Prejudice in Justice, *American Journal of Sociology*, 41:212-217.

Senate Documents, 56th Congress, 1st Session, no. 208, part I.

Serrs v. Mortiga, 204 U.S. 470.

Sibayan, Bonifacio P. (1970), The Philippines, pp. 196-200, in *Current Trends in Linguistics*, The Hague.

Sixteenth Census of the U.S.: 1940, Series P-15, no. 10, *Mother Tongues of the White Population*, 1943.

Sloan v. Lemon, 413 U.S. 825 (1973).

Smith, Stewart, and Kyger (1964), report of a pertinent petition sent to the House of Delegates in 1792.

Smith, T. Lynn, and Hitt, H. L. (1952), *The People of Louisiana*, Baton Rouge, La.

Smith, E. L. (1958), *The Amish People*, New York.

Smith, H. C. (1927), *The Coming of the Russian Mennonites*, Berne, Ind.

Society of Sisters v. Pierce, 268 U.S. 525.

Sorauf, F. O. (1959), *American Political Science Review*, 53:777-791.

Souffront, Luiz Muniz (1950), *El problema del idioma en Puerto Rico*, San Juan, Puerto Rico.

Speranza, Gino (1923), *Race or Nation?* Indianapolis.

Springer v. Philippine Islands, 227 U.S. 189.

Stainback v. M. O. Hook 336 U.S. 968-368 (1949).

State v. Cincinnati, 8 C.C. 523, 527 (1894).

State v. Taylor, 122 Neb. 454; 240NW 573.

State of New Jersey v. Mayor, etc., of Orange, 14LRA62.

Statehood for Hawaii (Hearings before the Subcommittee ... 186th Congress, 1st Session (1950), Washington, D.C.

The Status of the Foreign Language Program in Hawaii's Public Schools (1965), Research Report 18, Honolulu, Hawaii.

Status. See Laws.

Stephenson, G. M. (1926), *A History of American Immigration, 1820-1924*, Boston, Mass.

Steuernagel, B. (1936), *The Belleville Public Library*, Belleville, Ill.

Stierlin, L. (1873), *Der Staat Kentucky ... mit besonderer Berücksichtgung des deutschen Elements*, Louisville, Ky.

Stimson, F. J. (1923), *The American Constitution as It Protects Private Rights.*
Stonequist, E. V. (1937), *The Marginal Man,* New York.
Story, J. (1873), *Commentaries on the Constitution of the U.S.,* 4th ed., vol. 2, Boston, Mass.
Stoudt, J. J. (1955), *Pennsylvania German Poetry, 1685-1830,* The Pennsylvania German Folklore Society, vol. 20, Allentown, Pa.
Stuart v. School District of Kalamazoo, 30 Mich. 69.
A Survey of the Public Educational System of Porto Rico, Made under the direction of the International Institute of Teachers College, Columbia University, authorized by the University of Porto Rico (1926), New York.
Takao Ozawa v. U.S., 260 U.S. 178.
Taylor, P. S. (1930), *Mexican Labor in the United States, Dimmit County,* Berkeley, Calif.
Texas Code of Civil Procedure (1877), sec. 405.
Texas Laws (1905), sec. 102, Revised Civil Statutes, Article 2,782.
Texas State Library (1961), letter to Kloss dated July 18, 1961, Austin, Tex.
––– (1961), letter dated Sept. 6, 1961, and signed by Miss Connerly.
Theobald, R. (1961), letter dated Sept. 29, 1961, from the Wisconsin Legislative Reference Library and signed by Theobald.
Thérist, M. Del Norte (1940), French in the Elementary Schools in Louisiana, *French Review,* 13:344-346.
Thomas, D. S., and Nishimoto, R. S. (1946), *The Spoilage,* Berkeley, Calif.
Thomas and Znaniecki (1927), *The Polish Peasant in Europe and America,* II, New York.
Thompson, Laura (1947), *Guam and Its People,* Princeton.
Thompson, R. F. V. (1920), *Schooling of the Immigrant,* New York and London.
Thorpe, F. N. (1909), *The Federal and State Constitutions, Colonial Charters, and Other Organic Laws of the States, Territories and Colonies Now or Heretofore Forming the United States of America,* Washington, vols. 1-7 (House of Representatives 59th Congress, 2d Session, Document 357).
Thrasher (1927), *The Gang,* Chicago, quoted by Brown and Roucek (1937) p. 704.
Thwaites, R. G. (1908), *Wisconsin,* Boston and New York.
Tinker, E. L. (1932), *Les Ecrits de langue Française en Louisiane au XIXe siècle,* Paris.
––– (1933), *Bibliography of the French Newspapers and Periodicals of Louisiana,* Worcester, Mass.
Tireman, Lloyd S. (1948), A community school in a Spanish-speaking village (Nambé), Albuquerque, University of New Mexico Press.
––– (1951), Teaching Spanish-speaking chilren, Albuquerque, University of New Mexico Press.
Tisch, J. Le Sage (1959), *French in Louisiana,* New Orleans.
Toussaint, Ch. E. (1956), The Trusteeship System of the United Nations, London.
Tracy, Floy (1919), Public Education of White Children in Alaska (Education in the Territories and Dependencies, Washington, Bull. 12 (1919)).
Treaties and Other International Acts Ser. 4853 (1961), Washington, D.C.
Trepte, H. (1932), in *Deutsch-Amerikanische Geschichtsblatter,* 32:327.
Trifonovitch, Gregory J. (1970), Trust Territory of the Pacific Islands, *Current Trends in Linguistics,* pp. 204-224, The Hague.
Trinidad v. Simpson, 5 Colorado, 65, 70.
Trumbull, Robert (1958), *Paradise in Trust: A Report on Americans in Micronesia, 1946-1958,* New York.
Trustees of Dartmouth College v. Woodward, 17 U.S. 518 (1819); text in Kloss (1942, 946-947) and Commager (1, 1958, 220-223).
Tuck, Ruth (1946), *Not with the Fist: Mexican Americans in a Southwestern City,* New York.
Tydings-McDuffie Act (1934), C 84, 48 Stat. at L.455, 48USCA, Sec. 1231.
Tyler v. Bowen, I Pittsburgh 225.

Underwood, John J. (1913), *Alaska,* New York.

UNESCO (1953), *The Use of Vernacular Languages in Education,* Paris, France.

United Nations Documents. See under Documents.

United Nations Treaty Series (1947), vol. 8, pp. 190ff. gives the test of the trusteeship treaty of July 18, 1947.

United States Census (1960) of Population, Final Report PC (1)-53A.

United States Commissioner of Education; see Report of the U.S. Commissioner.

University of Chicago Libraries, Documentary Section; see *Chicago and Cook County . . . Upper Hanover Road,* 44 Pennsylvania 277.

The Use of the Vernacular Languages in Education (1953), Monographs on a Fundamental Education VIII, Paris.

van Heldingen, M. W. H. (1957), *Het Statuut vor het Koninkrift der Nederlander,* The Hague.

——— (1960), *De rechsorde in het Koninkrift der Nederlanden,* 2d ed., The Hague (Schakels S32; I.A. S31NA26).

van Loon, L. G. (1938), *The Dutch Dialect of Old New York,* quoted by Rice (1941).

van Panhuys, H. F. (1958), The International Aspects of the Reconstruction of the Kingdom of the Netherlands in 1954, *Nederlands Tijdschrift voor Int. Recht,* 5:1.

Vernon (1933), *Texas Penal Code.*

——— (1959), *Annotated Civil Statutes of Texas.*

Verrichtungen der 6, Spezial-Conferenz der Evangelisch-Lutherischen Prediger im Staate Ohio un dem westlichen Teil von Pennsylvanien, held in New Lancaster, Fairfield County, Ohio, Aug. 31, Sept. 1, 2, 3, 4, 1916. Lancaster, Ohio.

Viefhaus, Erwin (1960), *Die Minderheitenfrage und die Entstehung der Mindertenschutzverträge auf der Pariser Friedenskonferenz 1919,* Würzburg.

Viereck, Louis (1903), *Zwei Jahrhunderte deutschen Unterrichts in den Vereinigten Staaten,* Braunschweig, English version, *German Instruction in American Schools,* Washington, 1902.

Vogelin, C. F. (1941), North American Indian Languages Still Spoken, *Language, Culture and Personality, Essays in Memory of E. Spair,* Menosha, Wis.

Walker, Helen W. (1928-1929), Mexican Immigrants and American Citizenship, *Sociology and Social Research,* 13:465-467.

Wambaugh, Sarah (1920), *A Monograph on New York.*

Warne, F. J. (1904), *The Slav Invasion and the Mine Workers,* Philadelphia and London.

The Washington Post, Oct. 22, 1961.

Wayland, John W. (1907), *The German Element of the Shenandoah Valley of Virginia,* Charlottesville, Va.

Weaver, S. P. (1959), *Hawaii, U.S.A.,* New York.

Webb, N., and Webb, J. F. (1959), *The Hawaiian Islands,* New York.

Weightman, G. H. (1954), *Phil. Soc. Sc. Rev.,* 19:25-39.

Wells, Henry (1953), in *Development towards Self-Government in the Caribbean, A Symposium,* The Hague and Bandung.

——— (1959), *Enquête sur l'anticolonialisme,* Lisbon, Portugal.

Werkmeister, W. H. (1931), in *Tägliche Omaha Tribune,* The Golden Anniversary Edition, May 23, 1931.

Wertenbaker, J. (1938), *The Founding of American Civilization, The Middle Colonies,* New York and London; the portion on p. 116 is based on Thomas Hunt's volume, which see.

Wessel, B. B. (1931), *Ethnic Survey of Woonsocket, Rhode Island,* Chicago.

Westminster School District of Orange County v. *Mendez et al.,* 161 F 2d 774 (no. 11,310).

Whyte, William F. (1926-1927), *Wisconsin Magazine of History,* 10:363-390.

Williams, Michael (1932), *The Shadow of the Pope,* New York.

Willoughby, W. F. (1905), *Territories and Dependencies of the U.S.,* Washington, D.C.

Wilson v. *Shaw,* 204 U.S. 24.

Wisconsin. See also *Blue Book of Wisconsin.*

Wisconsin Legislative Reference Library. See Theobald, R. (1961).

Wisconsin Stat. Ann. 59.09 (4) and 324.20.

Wisconsin Supervisor of Education (1905), *Laws of Wisconsin relating to Common Schools.*

Wittke, Carl (1936), *German-Americans and the World War with Special Emphasis on Ohio's German-Language Press,* Columbus, Ohio.

––– (1957), *The German Language Press in America,* Lexington.

Wolff, S. (1920), *Constitution and Statutes of Louisiana,* vol. 2. sec. 1558.

Wolfradt, K. D. (1886), in *Deutscher Pionier,* 18:50-55, Cincinnati.

Wood, Ralph C. (1943), ed., *The Pennsylvania Germans,* Princeton, N.J.

––– (1945), Pennsylvania High German, *Germanic Review,* 20:299-314.

––– (1952), in W. Stammler, ed., *Deutsche Philologie im Aufriss,* vol. 1.

––– (1968), The Four Gospels Translated into Pennsylvania German Dialect, *Publications of the (2nd) Pennsylvania German Society,* 1:7-; 84.

Woolsey (1925), *Am. J. Int. Law,* 20:117.

Worcester, C., and Hayden, R. (1930), *The Philippines,* New York.

Worcester, Diocese of. See *The Holy Ghost French Series.*

Wust, Klaus G., ed., *Washington Journal,* personal communication.

––– (1953), *German Language Publications in Virginia,* Bridgewater, Va.

––– (1959), *German Historical Society of Maryland,* 30th report.

––– (1967), *The Virginia Germans,* Charlottesville, Va.

Wyman, R. E. (1968), Wisconsin Ethnic Groups and the Election of 1890, *Wisconsin Magazine of History,* 51 (4):269-293.

Yearbook of the United Nations (1954, 1959, 1960), New York.

Young, D. R. (1932), *American Minority Peoples,* New York.

Yu Cong Eng v. Trinidad, 271 U.S. 500. In the explanation, reference is made among others to *Meyer v. Nebraska* (1923) and *Pierce v. Sisters* (1925).

Zeleny, Carolyn (1944), *Relations between the Spanish Americans and Anglo-Americans in New Mexico: A Study of Conflict and Accommodation,* Ph.D. thesis, Yale University, New Haven, Conn.

Zellers v. Nuff, 55 N.M. 501 (1951).

Zeydel, E. H. (1961), *The Teaching of German in the United States,* reprinted from Reports and Studies . . . Modern Language Association, New York.

Zorach v. Clauson, 343 U.S. 306 (1952).

Zucker, A. E. (1943), Bibliographical Notes on the German Theater in the United States, *Monatshefte,* 35:255-264.

Zwerlein, F. J. (1926), *The Life and Letters of Bishop McQuaid,* vols. II, III, Rome and Louvain.

INDEX

Spanish Americans (cont.)
126, 132, 180, 182, 185ff
Spanish language, 14ff, 18ff, 37, 47ff, 50,
56ff, 59, 77, 82, 84, 95ff, 101ff, 126,
128ff, 151, 172, 179ff, 185ff, 194,
197, 211, 221, 243, 279ff, 301ff, 311
in California, 181ff, 288
in Louisiana, 107, 117, 120ff, 123
in New Mexico, 125ff, 232, 288
in Philippines, 236, 242ff, 247ff
in Puerto Rico, 213, 229ff, 284,
289
in Texas, 172, 174ff, 288
in United States schools, 24, 35ff,
38ff, 42, 56, 78, 80, 96ff, 99ff,
106, 120, 123, 134ff, 177ff,
183, 186
Spanish people, 17, 37, 39, 42, 67, 82,
107, 126, 137, 171, 175, 179ff, 185,
194, 244
as minorities, 171ff
in Florida, 105, 186ff
in Guam, 250ff, 253
in Louisiana, 107, 112, 120
in New Mexico, 11, 16, 18, 48ff,
125ff, 129, 186, 286
in Philippines, 235ff, 242, 245,
247
in Puerto Rico, 18, 212ff, 236
Spanish-S program, 187
Speranza, Gino, refs., 117, 131
Springer v. *Philippine Islands,* 237
St. Louis, Missouri, 70, 79, 86, 91ff, 101,
103, 163
St. Paul, Minnesota, 66, 70, 79, 91
Stainback v. *M. O. Hook,* 211
State of New Jersey v. *Mayor, etc., of
Orange,* 85
State v. *Cincinnati,* 156
State v. *Taylor,* 64
States With Small, Long-established Dutch
and German Minorities (Sec. 6-3), 188ff
States With Small, Long-established French
Minorities (Sec. 6-1), 163ff
States With Small, Long-established Span-
ish Minorities (Sec. 6-2), 171ff
Stephenson, G. M., refs., 70, 184
Stuart v. *School District of Kalamazoo,*
7, 88
Sulu Islands, 245ff
Supreme Court (*see* United States Supreme
Court)
Surinam, 197, 217, 221, 287

Swain's Island, 255ff
Sweden, 13, 142
people of, 17, 77, 79, 93, 140
Swedish language, 14ff, 18, 56, 82, 84,
102ff, 142
in United States schools, 24, 36, 94
Switzerland, 221, 234, 287
people of, 45
Syrian language, 33, 59, 106

T
TESL Program (Teaching English as a
Second Language), 100, 277
Tagalog language, 212, 235, 239, 242ff,
247, 251, 308, 310
Takao Ozawa v. *United States,* 21, 205
Teaching English as a Second Language
(*see* TESL)
Tennessee, 32, 90, 98, 163, 284, 305
Territories (*see specific place*). 10, 11
Texas, 8, 12, 16ff, 36ff, 40, 49, 52, 57, 84,
96, 100, 108, 125, 127, 179, 205,
284ff
background of, 171ff
Czech language in, 94ff, 101, 173,
288
German language in, 69, 92, 101,
176ff, 305
Germans in, 18, 172ff
language policy of, 175ff, 288
laws of, 176ff
schools of, 62, 64, 66, 96ff, 99,
176ff
Spanish in, 82, 171, 175
Spanish language in, 96ff, 174ff,
288, 305
Thayer Bill, 61
Thomas and Znaniechi, refs., 58, 75
Thompson, Laura, refs., 251ff
Thompson, R. F. V., refs., 52, 71
Thorpe, F. N., refs., 9, 11
Tisch, J. LeSage, refs., 107, 121, 123
Title I, Elementary and Secondary Act of
1965 (ESEA), 39
Title III, Elementary and Secondary Act
of 1965 (ESEA), 39
Title VII, Elementary and Secondary
Amendments of 1967 (ESEA), 37ff
Tlingit language, 56, 198ff, 201
Toleration of Promotion From Abroad
(Sec. 2-6), 42ff
Toussaint, Ch. E., refs., 272ff

Treaties (and Other International Acts), 129, 170, 197, 214, 246, 259, 261, 298
Treaty of Guadelupe Hidalgo, 21, 125, 127, 129, 179
Treaty of Paris,
  of 1783, 164
  of December 10, 1898, 235
Trinidad v. *Simpson,* 180
Truk, 271
  language of, 275ff, 309
Trumbull, Robert, refs., 271, 275
Trust Territories, 38, 251, 271, 273, 276
Trust Territory of the Pacific Islands (Sec. 8-6), 271ff. *Also* 5ff, 38, 251, 271ff, 308ff
Trustees of Dartmouth College v. *Woodward,* 55
Tydings-McDuffie Act, 239, 242, 246
Tyler v. *Bowen and Upper Hanover Rd.,* 146

U

UNESCO (United Nations Educational, Scientific, and Cultural Organization), 139, 242, 287, 291, 297, 300ff
UNNRA (United Nations Relief Association), 240
USCAR (United States Civil Administration of the Ryukyu Islands), 261, 264ff
Ukrainians, 64, 79, 221, 291ff
  language of, 14ff, 18, 56ff, 78, 80, 103
Unionists (Federalists), 215ff
United Nations, 5, 48, 51, 194, 196, 198, 240, 250, 272ff, 286ff, 296, 299ff
  and minorities, 296, 299, 301
  and Puerto Rico, 220ff, 223, 225
  and Ryukyu Islands, 259, 261, 264, 266
  and Trust Territory of the Pacific Islands, 271ff
  charter of, 50, 225ff, 272ff
United Nations Educational, Scientific, and Cultural Organization (*see* UNESCO)
United Nations Relief Association (*see* UNNRA)
United States (*see also* America *and specific item*), 1, 5ff, 11ff, 20ff, 27, 29ff, 42ff, 47ff, 54, 56, 60, 70, 101ff, 111, 125, 164, 172, 179ff, 185, 187,

United States (cont.)
  189, 202, 206, 283ff, 290
  and Alaska, 198ff
  and Louisiana, 107, 109ff, 127
  and minorities, 5ff
  and nationality laws, 19ff, 283ff
  and nationality policy, 295ff
  and nationality rights for immigrants, 81ff
  and New Mexico, 127, 133, 139
  and overseas possessions, 249ff
  and Philippine Islands, 235ff, 248
  and Puerto Rico, 214ff, 219ff, 223, 225ff, 234, 286, 292
  and territories, 7ff
  bilingual programs in, 37ff, 99, 171
  immigrant languages in, 19, 288, 290
  judicial system of, 116ff
  language of, 3, 15, 24ff, 69, 71, 99
  non-English languages in, 20, 33ff, 52ff, 71, 173, 291
  outlying areas of, 193ff
  schools of, 61ff, 71ff, 85ff, 123, 161, 178, 184, 199
United States Civil Administration of the Ryukyu Islands (*see* USCAR)
United States Commissioner of Education, 36, 40, 63, 68, 75ff, 159, 187, 200
United States Office of Education, 34ff
United States Senate, 6, 8, 11, 37, 110ff, 166, 239
United States Supreme Court, 3, 6, 8ff, 21, 42, 46, 50, 53, 55, 129, 205, 210
  and outlying areas, 195ff, 205, 210ff, 215, 217, 223, 225, 229, 236, 240, 247, 249
  and schools, 63ff, 68, 73ff, 161
United States v. *Figueros Rios,* 224
United States v. *Wong Kim Ark,* 21
University of Hawaii, 100, 205, 209, 211
University of Pennsylvania, 34, 100, 148
Utah, 8, 37, 63, 98, 127, 309
Ute language, 56, 310

V

Vermont, 71, 98, 305, 308
Vernon, refs., 177ff
Viefhaus, Erwin, refs., 298ff
Viereck, Louis, refs., 75ff, 90, 100
Virgin Islands, 5ff, 65, 128, 194, 196, 223, 234, 249ff, 252, 254, 278ff, 301
  bilingualism in, 38, 99, 194